Knowing the Past

KNOWING THE PAST

Victorian Literature and Culture

Edited by SUZY ANGER

Cornell University Press

ITHACA AND LONDON

First published 2001 by Cornell University Press
First printing, Cornell Paperbacks, 2001

Printed in the United States of America

Library of Congress Cataloging-in-Publication Data

Knowing the Past: Victorian Literature and Culture / edited by Suzy Anger.
   p. cm.
  Includes bibliographical references and index.
  ISBN 0-8014-3884-5 (cloth : alk. paper) — ISBN 0-8014-8765-X (pbk. : alk. paper)
  1. English literature—19th century—History and criticism. 2. Knowledge, Theory of—History—19th century. 3. Hermeneutics—History—19th century. 4. Knowledge, Theory of, in literature. I. Anger, Suzy.
  PR468.K56 K58 2001
  820.99008—dc21
2001002877

Cornell University Press strives to use environmentally responsible suppliers and materials to the fullest extent possible in the publishing of its books. Such materials include vegetable-based, low-VOC inks and acid-free papers that are recycled, totally chlorine-free, or partly composed of nonwood fibers. Books that bear the logo of the FSC (Forest Stewardship Council) use paper taken from forests that have been inspected and certified as meeting the highest standards for environmental and social responsibility. For further information, visit our website at www.cornellpress.cornell.edu.

Cloth printing   10 9 8 7 6 5 4 3 2 1
Paperback printing   10 9 8 7 6 5 4 3 2 1

For my mother, Elizabeth

Contents

Preface

In 1996 I organized a panel on Victorian knowing for the annual meeting of the Modern Language Association. The motivation for such a panel was my sense that current literary criticism did not, on the whole, take Victorian views on hermeneutics and knowledge seriously. Rather, Victorians were often read as either precursors of postmodern views or as unsophisticated realists on interpretation. I believed that the Victorians should be read on their own terms. Is it possible to do that, however?

Thus, one of this book's central questions is, can we know others or the past? My own answer is that we can understand both to a greater extent than most recent literary theory has allowed. Equally important, it is worth looking closely at what the Victorians had to say about knowledge and interpretation because their sophisticated deliberations can help us rethink currently dominant positions on these issues. As a whole, however, the book does not take any one position, and other contributors offer different answers to the question. But together the essays revise and advance current debates on knowing the past and the Victorians.

I am grateful to the University of Maryland, Baltimore County, for a summer grant that helped with the editing of this collection, and I thank the English Department of the University for a grant that helped make it possible to reproduce the painting on the cover of the paperback edition.

I would also like to thank my friends and colleagues for their contributions to this book. In particular, I acknowledge with gratitude George Levine and Carolyn Williams for their generous suggestions, advice, and support on this project. I also thank Gary Handwerk for his intellectual guidance throughout a dissertation project closely related to the topic of this collection. Finally, I am especially indebted to Tom Bittner for discussing every aspect of this book with me and for his day-to-day support and encouragement.

S.A.

Knowing the Past

Introduction

Knowing the Victorians

Suzy Anger

"The history of the Victorian Age will never be written," wrote Lytton Strachey in 1918. "We know too much about it."[1] Today the obstacle to such an account would seem to be not that we have too much knowledge, but rather that "epistemology shows that we can never really know the past."[2] In recent decades, debates over the status of knowledge and our ability to know anything—others, the meaning of texts, past history, reality—have dominated theoretical debate in a wide range of academic disciplines. Epistemological skepticism has been pervasive, and the conception of truth that allows for the possibility of objective knowledge has come to be regarded as naïve and suspect. Debates on knowledge have taken on moral and political urgency, and skepticism and subjectivism are often assumed to be connected with radical leftist political positions. Contemporary approaches to literature and culture are on the whole committed both to respect for the "other" and to a view that all descriptions of that "other" are constructions, shaped by the interests and perspectives of the investigators. These perhaps inconsistent positions give rise to a number of questions, both theoretical and practical, which this book seeks to explore.

Without attempting to address their full contemporary range, this volume treats these epistemological issues within the space of a specific historical period: the Victorian era. Such a focus, providing a set of particular examples, anchors the abstract philosophical problems in a way that demands a reconsideration of the terms of the debate. The Victorians also provide an important locus for investigating epistemological questions because they were

---

[1] *Eminent Victorians: Cardinal Manning—Florence Nightingale—Dr. Arnold—General Gordon* (New York: G. P. Putnam's Sons, 1918), vi.
[2] Keith Jenkins, *Re-Thinking History* (London: Routledge, 1991), 9.

already engaging them with considerable sophistication. Theirs was the moment of the fullest expansion of empire, the richest development of hermeneutics, and the emergence of modern historiography and anthropology; and with them questions of knowledge of others and the past became pressing both intellectually and politically.

Addressing problems of knowledge through the Victorians offers the additional advantage that they have been the subject of a great deal of theoretical treatment from contemporary critics. Yet these critics, surprisingly, have sometimes failed to recognize that our own vexed theoretical questions concerning subjectivity/objectivity, self/other, and absolutism/relativism were central to Victorian speculation as well. The Victorian answers to these questions have more than historical significance, for they often throw light on what contemporary approaches have overlooked. So, to borrow a line from Carlyle's *Past and Present,* one of this book's aims is to "strive to penetrate a little...into a somewhat remote century; and to look face to face on it, in hope of perhaps illustrating our own poor century thereby."[3]

The tendency of contemporary critics toward relativist and subjectivist positions on historical and ethnographic knowledge is represented by several essays in the volume. In exploring the alternatives, we would be oversimplifying if we were to deny the difficulties—both theoretical and practical—that face any attempt to come to terms with the otherness of different cultures and past history. But this book also presents a number of arguments offering more optimistic accounts of the possibility of knowledge and understanding than those currently dominant; some seek to recuperate the discredited concepts of objectivity and intentionality.

The essays, diverse in perspective and orientation, do not propose anything like a single theoretical viewpoint on the questions the book raises. Yet collectively they indicate that literary theory and cultural criticism are in the process of rethinking the dominant epistemological positions of recent decades. The rethinking is difficult and is informed by the important insights that skepticism, relativism, and social construction have foregrounded, but it also suggests that other models may help us in reconceptualizing our relationships to language, to texts, to others, and to the past.

I

It is not surprising that the Victorians should exhibit a deep interest in the questions that are at the center of current literary theory, given that it was in their period that many aspects of current intellectual culture first appeared. New disciplines (the very disciplines to whom these questions are of the great-

---

[3] Thomas Carlyle, *Works,* Centenary Edition, ed. H.D. Traill, 30 vols. (London: Chapman and Hall, 1896–1899). Henceforth cited in the text as *Works,* with volume and page number.

est import today) emerged in the Victorian universities—modern history and literature, for example, and anthropology—and the first British historical and philosophical journals were published, journals that fostered the kind of intense debate we now engage in. While recent theory has seen itself as largely indebted to developments in German thought, it has overlooked the ways in which the Victorians—often working within the British empirical tradition, though often themselves influenced by German thought—have contributed to and shaped the current discussion.

Questions of historical knowledge were central to Victorian intellectual debate, as was the Victorians' sense of themselves as historical beings (which Mill famously called "the dominant idea" of the age[4]). Roland Barthes has charged that nineteenth-century historiography promoted a naïve objectivity and blindness to the workings of representation.[5] There were, of course, those newly professional Victorian historians whose aim was a positivistic treatment of history and who took the objectivist school of history, commonly associated with Ranke, as their model. Indeed, the *English Historical Review* inaugurated its first issue in 1886 with an introductory preface that explained that "the object of history is to discover and set forth facts."[6] Still the characterization of the Victorians as simply proponents of a naïvely positivist historiography, emulating the objective methods of science and believing in the ability of language to represent transparently what really happened in the past, is disproved by their diverse speculations on history and interpretation.

One has only to look to Carlyle around the beginning of Victoria's reign to see that the Victorians were well aware of the difficulties of knowing the past. In his historical texts, Carlyle continually reminds his readers of the inaccessibility of the past, through his use of fictive techniques, his self-reflexivity about his project, and his reiterated assertion of the inadequacy of narrative to history: "Narrative is *linear,* Action is *solid*" (*Works,* 27:89). His writings on history already manifest much of what is often regarded as contemporary: awareness of the effects of representation, the textuality of historical knowledge, and the impossibility of a fully objective account of the past: "Nay, even with regard to those occurrences which do stand recorded, which at their origin have seemed worthy of record, and the summary of which we now call History, is not our understanding of them altogether incomplete; is it even possible to represent them as they were?" (*Works,* 27:87). But it was not just literary writers who called into question the truth of representations of the past. J. A. Froude, who became Regius Professor of Modern History at Oxford in 1892, wrote: "It is not questioned that if we

[4] John Stuart Mill, "Spirit of the Age" (1831), in *Collected Works,* ed. Ann P. Robson and John M. Robson, vol. 22 (Austin: University of Texas Press, 1986).

[5] Roland Barthes, "The Reality Effect," in *The Rustle of Language,* trans. Richard Howard (New York: Hill and Wang, 1986), 140.

[6] "Prefatory Note," *English Historical Review* 1, no. 1 (1886): 4.

could arrive at a full daguerreotyped objective account of things, such an account would be of profit to us. But judging from universal experience no such account is possible."[7] And F. H. Bradley, in his first philosophical work, *The Presuppositions of Critical History* (1874), asserted that "in every case that which is called a fact is in reality a theory."[8] Already, then, Victorians were alert to problems of knowledge and representation in historiography, and were even satirized in W. H. Mallock's very funny send-up of Victorian intellectuals, *The New Republic,* which underscores the difficulties of knowing the past by linking each of its central characters to a distinctive view on history.[9]

The Victorians likewise grappled with questions of textual interpretation, with broad social and cultural consequences. Textual meaning was most significantly called into question in the fierce debates on biblical exegesis, as seen in the controversies over the Higher Criticism's new modes of interpretation, the heated responses to *Essays and Reviews* (1860), and the theological reactions to evolutionary theory. Benjamin Jowett and others worried about the problems of reading meaning across history and cultures and argued that a text must be read in its historical context and understood from the viewpoint of the original writer. The meaning of the biblical narratives was to be discovered through an understanding of the historically conditioned consciousnesses of the writers.[10] But the Victorians offered a much wider range of ideas than those influenced by David Strauss and other Higher Critics.

Needing to account for and defend historical variations in the Catholic church's understanding of Scripture, John Henry Newman imagines an alternative response to historical change: a method of interpretation based on development, the theory that revelation unfolds progressively in time. In the *Development of Christian Doctrine* (1845), exploring views that were to become important to the work of Gadamer and Jauss, Newman argues that tradition always plays a role in understanding, that readings will inevitably change over time.[11] The reactions to the new methods often have a familiar ring to those who have followed current debates, drawing attention to the clear continuities between scriptural exegesis and contemporary literary criticism. For Jowett, it "becomes almost a political question how far we can venture to disturb" the readings of the Church, while an opponent of the

[7] J. A. Froude, "History: Its Use and Meaning," *Westminster Review* 62 (1854): 423.

[8] F. H. Bradley, *The Presuppositions of Critical History* (Don Mills, Ontario: J. M. Dent, 1968).

[9] W. H. Mallock, *The New Republic* (Gainesville: University of Florida Press, 1950).

[10] Benjamin Jowett, "On the Interpretation of Scripture," *Essays and Reviews,* 144, in John Drury, *Critics of the Bible, 1724–1873* (Cambridge: Cambridge University Press, 1989), 139–151.

[11] John Henry Cardinal Newman, *An Essay on the Development of Christian Doctrine,* in *Conscience, Consensus, and the Development of Doctrine,* ed. James Gaffney (New York: Doubleday, 1992), 395.

new modes of interpretation argues that they are "to be condemned because they do violence to Scripture, foster a style of interpretation by which the text is forced to say whatever the interpreters desire."[12]

Victorian discussions of interpretation, however, are frequently attentive to and emphasize different aspects of the problems of intention, truth, and morality than do ours. As the sophisticated exegetical debates extended outward into secular hermeneutics, the issue of how authority was to be established for an interpretation became increasingly significant. F. J. Furnivall, for instance, demanded a rigorous scientific and statistical approach to meaning, one that would make criticism "independent of mere subjective feeling," while Oscar Wilde was soon to propound interpretive relativism, claiming that the best "modes of art" "by their imaginative beauty make all interpretations true, and no interpretation final."[13] Yet, it is often overlooked that in the same dialogue in which Wilde's Gilbert puts forth these subjectivist views, he also proposes other possibilities of textual interpretation. He contends at one point that in order to "truly understand" a literary work, an interpreter must reconstruct the general character of the period in which it was written, read widely in contemporary texts, and possess extensive knowledge of literary history and philology. Unlike most recent theorists, Wilde presents interpretive relativism as a choice, based on aesthetic and political reasons, and not as an inevitable consequence of the nature of language.

The increasingly important field of philology was crucial to textual and historical interpretation, for the study of language was regarded as giving access to the past. John Herschel, for example, wrote: "Words are to the anthropologist what rolled pebbles are to the Geologist—Battered relics of past ages often containing within them indelible records capable of intelligible interpretation."[14] Philological inquiry took up questions of language's relation to reality as well, the sorts of questions we now associate with Saussure's linguistics. F. Max Muller, the Oxford philologist, insisted that there is no important connection between word and concept—in other words, that the signifier is arbitrary. Nor did he believe that language merely named things that existed prior to it, nor that words are merely a tool for expressing thought. "Language and thought," he argued, "are inseparable."[15] "There never was an independent array of determinate conceptions waiting to be matched with

[12] Marcus Dods, *The Book of Genesis,* 1, quoted in Nigel M. de S. Cameron, *Biblical Higher Criticism and the Defense of Infallibilism in 19th Century Britain* (Lewiston, N.Y.: Edwin Mellen Press, 1987), 303.

[13] F. R. Furnivall, *New Shakspere Society Transactions* (London, 1874), 19; Oscar Wilde, "The Critic as Artist," in *Complete Works of Oscar Wilde* (New York: Harper and Row, 1989), 1031.

[14] W. F. Cannon, "The Impact of Uniformitarianism: Two Letters from John Herschel to Charles Lyell, 1836–1837," *Proceedings of the American Philosophical Society* 105 (1961): 308.

[15] F. Max Muller, *Lectures on the Science of Language,* vol. 1 (London: Longman's, Green, 1899), 527.

an independent array of articulate sounds."[16] If this is not the linguistics of Saussure, still it is anything but a naïve realism that takes language as a transparent medium.

Questions of cross-cultural understanding also became pressing for the Victorians, and knowledge of other cultures increased as the developing discipline of anthropology paralleled Britain's imperial supremacy. Though Victorian anthropology is typically condemned as hierarchical, race oriented, and supremacist, some of our best commentators on the subject have assessed the Victorians' contributions more sympathetically. George Stocking, to take a prominent example, asserts that the Victorians did not recognize cultural relativity as anthropology does today. But he also points out that Victorian ethnography was crucial to the recognition of and the attempt to know different cultures.[17] Similarly, Christopher Herbert argues that "nominally, 'savage' society is pronounced worthless, an evolutionary failure, by evolutionary theory. But this negative judgment is belied overwhelmingly by the ethnographic investigation which each of these texts carries out."[18]

We need not ignore the worst of the Victorian anthropologists' views to notice as well that they were strongly aware of the difficulties of knowing others. E. B. Tylor writes in his *Mind* review of Spencer's *Principles of Sociology:* "It may here be remarked that the besetting sin of us all who study primitive ideas is to treat the savage mind according to the needs of our argument." He goes on to accuse Spencer of being "prone to a tightness of interpretation" "in dealing with the phrases by which rude races convey their thoughts" and notes that this "may give wrong notions of what actually passes in their minds."[19] No doubt, the rhetoric of superiority is there, but there is also the recognition of otherness, rather than an easy appropriation of it.

The Victorians, then, were already engaging questions of knowledge in ways as sophisticated as ours. Considering how they approached these problems is not only an exercise in intellectual history; it should also throw light on a range of possibilities, among which are epistemological and hermeneutic models that diverge from those that are currently dominant in literary theory.

---

[16] F. Max Muller, *Lectures on the Science of Language,* vol. 2 (London: Longman's, Green, 1899), 70.

[17] "To argue that culture actually existed among all men, in however 'crude' or 'primitive' a form, may be viewed as a major step toward the anthropological concept, especially as it focused anthropological attention on manifestations of culture which on account of their 'crudity' were below the level of conscious cultivation where 'civilized' culture was to be found." George W. Stocking Jr., "Arnold, Tylor, and the Uses of Invention," in *Race, Culture, and Evolution* (New York: Free Press, 1968), 69–90.

[18] Christopher Herbert, "Epilogue: Ethnography and Evolution," *Victorian Studies* 41, no. 3 (1998): 489. Cf. Gillian Beer, "Speaking for the Others: Relativism and Authority in Victorian Anthropological Writing," in *Open Fields: Science in Cultural Encounter* (Oxford: Oxford University Press, 1996).

[19] Edward B. Tylor, "Mr. Spencer's 'Principles of Sociology,'" *Mind* 2, no. 6 (1877): 144.

II

This volume is designed to present a series of alternative responses to the questions about knowledge and interpretation that have proven so important and so contentious in recent scholarly debate; but it does so within the frame of an argument for a less skeptical epistemological position. This introduction, then, in addition to providing the customary overview of the contributors' essays, sets out my own position as an additional point of entry for the debate, although many of the contributors might not entirely agree with my view. I begin by outlining some of the main intellectual currents to which the essays are responding. Here I give only a broad sketch of what I regard as widely accepted positions in contemporary literary theory. The views I describe are of necessity rather rough versions of arguments advanced by writers central to recent theory and must leave out many of the subtleties of the original accounts. But I take these rough views to be reasonable representations of the form in which these ideas often have been broadly disseminated in contemporary critical thought.

Concerning the issue of the possibility of knowledge of the past (or of other minds, cultures, or a text's meaning), the two extreme poles are objectivism and constructivism. Objectivism contends that it is possible to acquire certain knowledge of the past, while constructivism proposes that we can only know our own subjective constructions of the past (the other, meaning, or reality).

Very few literary critics have aligned themselves with any version of objectivity in recent cultural and literary theory. Most are skeptical about our ability to gain real or objective knowledge of others or of the past. Objectivism in much recent theory has been linked to various kinds of biases, in matters of gender, race, or national identity. Many contemporary scholars argue that it has been used to promote what are really ideologically charged positions (in the interests of social and cultural power) in order to give them a veneer of legitimation as certain and absolute. That is to say, the concept of objectivity is taken to be ideologically motivated. There is a widespread belief, following from the work of Michel Foucault, that knowledge is always inextricable from power, that it is not discovered, but instead discursively constructed. Under such views, there is no reality independent of observers and their ways of conceiving reality; the world they seek to describe objectively is constituted by their own beliefs, practices, and institutions, and there are no transcultural or context-independent standards for them to appeal to in making judgments about this world. Knowledge is relative, contextual, and local. Facts are not out there, independent of our judgments. They are instead interested products of our representations of the world. As Steve Woolgar expresses this view: "There is no object beyond discourse.... The organization of discourse *is* the object. Facts and objects in the world are inescapably textual constructions."[20]

[20] Steve Woolgar, *Science: The Very Idea* (London: Tavistock, 1988), 73.

Normally accompanying such constructivist positions is the view that language, rather than corresponding with reality, is self-referential. Insofar as this relates to the interpretation of texts, antirealism tends to discredit the notions of fixed meaning and intention, and on some accounts interpretation is seen as largely unconstrained (a view that Derrida influentially characterized as "the affirmation of a world of signs without fault, without truth, and without origin which is offered to an active interpretation"[21]). A text does not convey a speaker's meaning, but instead always signals the lack of presence, difference, a sliding chain of signifiers that cannot reach back to original grounding signifieds.

Similarly, in historiography the distinction between history and fiction has been questioned.[22] The meaning of history is created by our narratives, which can never reach out to describe the way things really were. Thus our historical representations cannot be taken to be referential, and so "historiography which looks at past reality as a substance to be epistemologically revealed has to be given up."[23] Hayden White has been among the most influential historians in arguing against the epistemological authority of historiography: "When it comes to apprehending the historical record, there are no grounds to be found in the historical record itself for preferring one way of construing its meaning over another."[24] It follows that texts from the past cannot be understood by an appeal to their historical contexts, because context is itself text, constructed from other texts, thus giving rise to the same problems of interpretation that any text, fictional or nonfictional, will inevitably provoke. Further, in recent theory developing from Foucault's thought and deconstruction, discontinuity, fragmentation, and rupture have replaced the concepts of continuity, coherence, and progress.

An outcome of this perspective has often been the belief that to claim understanding of others, another culture, or the past amounts to a sort of imperialism. Our efforts to understand those from another culture are inevitably impeded by the constraints of our own culture, historical moment, and personal biases, and contemporary theorists often regard such endeavors as attempts to efface difference or to impose our perspectives on others.[25]

---

[21] Jacques Derrida, "Structure, Sign, and Play," in *The Structuralist Controversy,* ed. Richard Macksey and Eugenio Donato (Baltimore: Johns Hopkins University Press, 1972).

[22] See Peter Novick, *That Noble Dream* (Cambridge: Cambridge University Press, 1988), for a history of the idea of objectivity in professional historical scholarship.

[23] Robert Braun, "The Holocaust and Problems of Representation," *History and Theory* 33, no. 2 (1994): 196.

[24] Hayden White, *The Content of the Form* (Baltimore: Johns Hopkins University Press, 1987), 75. See also the postmodernist historiography of F.R. Ankersmit, *History and Tropology* (Berkeley: University of California Press, 1994). Extensive debates on postmodernism and objectivity in historiography have been carried on in the pages of the journal *History and Theory*.

[25] But see Donald Davidson, "The Very Idea of a Conceptual Scheme," in *Inquiries into Truth and Interpretation* (Oxford: Clarendon Press, 1984). Davidson argues that presupposed in our considering something to be a culture is the claim that we can interpret it and understand it. If it really were unintelligible to us, we would not regard it as another culture.

Representation, on one such account, "aims at 'understanding' and, through 'meaning,' at hiding the alterity of this foreigner." Consequently, "understanding" has been reread by many postcolonial critics as mastery and assimilation of difference, and the ideal of sympathetic knowledge based upon an attempt to enter into another's position, to see from his or her point of view (the hermeneutics advocated by nineteenth-century German Romanticism) has been reinterpreted as appropriation.[26] Ethnography, as Michel de Certeau describes it, is an instrument of domination: "In the West, the group (or the individual) is legitimized by what it excludes (this is the creation of its own space), and it discovers its faith in the confession that it extracts from a dominated being (thus is established the *knowledge* based upon, or of, the other: human sciences)."[27]

The overall effect of this direction of argument is to claim important moral and political value for the rejection of the possibility of knowledge (as traditionally understood). Current theory insists upon the impossibility of knowing another culture or the past, because the refusal of understanding is viewed as a way of shielding others from the power that is inevitable in all acts of knowing. As Gayatri Spivak has expressed it, Derridean thought is "less dangerous" "than the first-world intellectual masquerading as the absent nonrepresenter who lets the oppressed speak for themselves."[28] There is then a strong ethical and political urgency behind contemporary skeptical epistemology as, its theorists might claim, there is behind all epistemologies.

But this widespread view among cultural critics and postcolonial theorists raises at least as many questions as it resolves. Arguably, it misperceives the relationship between epistemology and politics and exaggerates the consequences of the impossibility of obtaining absolute knowledge.[29] While it would be a mistake to minimize our epistemic difficulties, nevertheless this extreme skepticism with its rejection of knowledge as a goal must be rethought. I suggest that we can have more knowledge of the past and of others than most recent theory has been willing to allow; that in many cases current skeptical and relativist views are not thought through in rigorous ways

[26] "By leading the interpreter to transform himself, so to speak, into the author, the divinatory method seeks to gain an immediate comprehension of the author as an individual." Friedrich D. E. Schleiermacher, *Hermeneutics: The Handwritten Manuscripts*, ed. Heinz Kimmerle, trans. James Duke and Jack Forstman (Missoula, Mont.: Scholars Press, 1977), 150.

[27] Michel de Certeau, *The Writing of History* (New York: Columbia University Press, 1988), 3, 5.

[28] *Spivak Reader: Selected Works of Gayatri Spivak*, ed. Donna Landry and Gerald Maclean (New York: Routledge, 1996), 292.

[29] Both Gerald Graff and E. D. Hirsch claim that no political position necessarily follows from any epistemological position. Graff dismisses the view that "if certain theories of the determinacy of textual meaning are maintained or overthrown, such and such political effects will ensue" in "The Pseudo-Politics of Interpretation" (145). Similarly, Hirsch writes, "I want to claim that *neither* epistemological idealism nor epistemological realism has any direct practical bearing on the politics of interpretation" in "The Politics of Theories" (328). Both essays in *The Politics of Interpretation* (Chicago: University of Chicago Press, 1982). See also Michael Brint, William G. Weaver, and Meredith Garwich, "What Difference Does Anti-Foundationalism Make to Political Theory?" *New Literary History* 26, no. 2 (1995): 225–37.

and often oversimplify the philosophical issues; and that although attaining knowledge is obviously difficult, knowledge of others might well be put to the very moral and political work that skeptical theorists advocate—and perhaps more effectively.[30] In arguing this, I am not denying the validity of claims about selectivity, the effects of systems of representation, or the history of the organization of knowledge. One might grant all of that without accepting that it must necessarily lead to the sort of radical skepticism that much current theory attempts to sustain.

Certainly there are important problems—epistemological and political—with naïve realism or pure objectivity, and it would be a misjudgment to undervalue the contributions to the debate about knowledge made by contemporary theorists. Recent theory has given us important insights into the often discreditable ways in which appeals to objectivity have operated. It is essential that we interrogate the reality of so-called natural categories and confront the contingency of what we might take as inevitable. I am not, then, suggesting that objectivity and realism are entirely divorced from ideological implications; rather, I am suggesting that there are strong moral reasons for moving toward an epistemology that is less skeptical and relativist than that embraced by much current theory.[31] Much recent theory has claimed for antirealist epistemology the *exclusive* position of virtue. Yet it is also worth thinking about what ethical and political values an affirmation of objective knowledge might provide (both as methodological presuppositions and in a set of assumptions about the way the world is). I also want to question whether some of the desirable consequences attributed to radical skepticism are really there to be had.

In recent theory, there has been a tendency to slide from the recognition of the lack of absolute certainty into extreme relativism and skepticism. Many of these arguments depend on characterizing opposing views in overly simplistic ways. In general, the version of realist epistemology that is taken as a target by skeptics is a crude positivist view on which representation can achieve exact mimesis of external reality. It is important to emphasize that there are different and more complex philosophical models of knowledge

---

[30] Arguments about the self-refuting nature of relativism are well known. Many claim that rejecting truth leaves no ground from which to oppose dangerously distorting accounts. In history, debates on relativism have focused most extensively on recent revisionist accounts denying the reality of the Holocaust. See Saul Friedlander, ed., *Probing the Limits of Representation: Nazism and the "Final Solution"* (Cambridge: Harvard University Press, 1992).

[31] Satya P. Mohanty defends such a view in his excellent *Literary Theory and the Claims of History* (Ithaca: Cornell University Press, 1997), wherein he describes "a postpositivist realism," which he maintains "would be attentive to the postmodernist's cautions about the social and historical entanglements of knowledge and would enable us to explain the distortions of ideology and political power. At the same time, however, it can provide us with a sophisticated and usable notion of objectivity as an ideal of inquiry" (xii).

See also Alasdair MacIntyre, "Relativism, Power, and Philosophy," in *Relativism: Interpretation and Confrontation,* ed. Michael Krausz (Notre Dame, Ind.: University of Notre Dame Press, 1989), 182–204.

and objectivity than those usually invoked in the discrediting of these ideas. In philosophical thought, positivist theories have been replaced by various fallibilistic models of knowledge, whether foundationalist or coherentist, that avoid many of the most serious objections raised against their predecessors.

As a number of commentators have pointed out, there is a strange either/or logic to many poststructuralist arguments on knowledge. [32] Either language transparently represents reality or it is opaque and self-referential. Either history is a perfectly mimetic account of the past or it is fiction. Either representations exactly correspond with reality or they are arbitrary. Either concepts capture a mind-independent reality or what they refer to are constructions. Not knowing everything becomes not knowing anything. Such arguments set up false dilemmas by failing to acknowledge that there are a variety of other options that have not been taken into account. There is no denying that knowledge is partially a social construction. It is indeed true that there is a great deal we cannot know, that all knowledge is situated, that there is no—in Karl Popper's famous phrase—"knowledge without a knower," that interests and biases are always at work.[33] But absolute certainty is not required in order to maintain that some understandings are nearer to correct than others, that some conceptual schemes better represent the world than others.[34] Agreeing that absolutely objective knowledge is unattainable—acknowledging that belief is conditioned, that observations are always theory-laden, that there are limitations on what we can know—does not require us to slip into a radical skepticism and a fundamental distrust of efforts to come up with better conceptual schemes, more accurate representations of the way things are. It should, rather, drive us to greater awareness of the ways in which the search for knowledge might go wrong.

As philosophical issues, these questions most likely cannot be resolved. How much objectivity we can achieve and how subject we are to the effects of interests, power, and perspective probably cannot be determined. It is not, however, necessary to come up with a definitive response to longstanding philosophical controversies to recognize that there are versions of objectivism and realism at least as plausible as the views now dominant in cultural discourse.[35] Without offering a single philosophical alternative, then,

---

[32] For a well-developed argument along these lines see Noel Carroll, "Interpretation, History, and Narrative," *The Monist* 73 (1990): 134–67.

[33] K. R. Popper, *Objective Knowledge* (Oxford: Clarendon, 1972), 109.

[34] See Ian Hacking, *The Social Construction of What?* (Cambridge: Harvard University Press, 1999); John Searle, *The Construction of Social Reality* (New York: Free Press, 1995); and Frank B. Farrell, *Subjectivity, Realism, and Postmodernism: The Recovery of the World in Recent Philosophy* (Cambridge: Cambridge University Press, 1996).

[35] Objectivity is a contested term, used to refer both to methods of proceeding (those most likely to lead to truth) and to a metaphysical view about the way the world is (realism). Some strong philosophical arguments for versions of objectivity or realism include Alvin Goldman, *Knowledge in a Social World* (Oxford: Clarendon, 1999); Thomas Nagel, *The View from Nowhere* (New York: Oxford University Press, 1986); and *The Last Word* (Oxford: Oxford University Press, 1997), which offers a convincing case that reason provides a minimal objectivity

I want to ask a more answerable question: what is at stake in the epistemological positions we adopt? What do we get from denying the possibility of knowing in general, and particularly of knowing others? My primary concern is with our disposition toward the possibility of understanding: I would like to measure the benefits of achieving understanding against those of a skepticism that would connect all knowledge with power, all understanding with domination.

More positive accounts of knowledge carry their own compelling ethical and political justifications. If we cannot know another culture, another mind, or the past in any real way, then we threaten to cut off one very important way of revising our own world views. Charles Taylor puts it this way in his "Understanding and Ethnocentricity": "We are always in danger of seeing our ways of acting and thinking as the only conceivable ones. That is exactly what ethnocentricity consists in. Understanding other societies ought to wrench us out of this; it ought to alter our self-understanding."[36] Of course, it is just such a view—in the name of greater openness to the other—that has been rejected in current thought.

These questions of meaning and understanding are the core issues of hermeneutics, which in its traditional forms sought to explain how we could come to have adequate knowledge of the past, of a text, or of the intentions of others. Nor was this a naïve enterprise among the hermeneuticists, who recognized the complexities of their project and the improbability of complete success. Here, the nineteenth century clearly anticipated our contemporary debates. As Schleiermacher writes: "The task of hermeneutics is endless."[37] Yet, in the face of these difficulties, the aim remained the understanding of others, the correct interpretation of an utterance, or reliable knowledge of the past.

Such hermeneutic theories provide models that recognize the difficulties of these endeavors yet continue to stress the importance of understanding and shared knowledge. Hans-Georg Gadamer's contemporary hermeneutics develops from a critique of certainty, absolute knowledge, and pure objectivity.

---

that allows for universality; and Nicholas Rescher, *Objectivity and the Obligations of Impersonal Reason* (Notre Dame, Ind.: University of Notre Dame Press, 1997).

In historiography, see Roger Chartier, *On the Edge of the Cliff*, trans. Lydia G. Cochrane (Baltimore: Johns Hopkins University Press, 1997); Carlo Ginzburg, *History, Rhetoric, and Proof* (Hanover, N.H.: University Press of New England, 1999); Thomas Haskell, *Objectivity Is Not Neutrality* (Baltimore: Johns Hopkins University Press, 1998); and Richard J. Evans, *In Defense of History* (New York: W. W. Norton, 1999) for defenses of objective historical knowledge.

Useful works in the philosophy of history that accept that we can attain real knowledge of the past include R. F. Atkinson, *Knowledge and Explanation in History* (Ithaca: Cornell University Press, 1978); Louis Mink, *Historical Understanding* (Ithaca: Cornell University Press, 1987); and Alex Callinicos, *Theories and Narratives* (Durham, N.C.: Duke University Press, 1995).

[36] Charles Taylor, *Philosophy and the Human Sciences: Philosophical Papers,* Vol. 2 (Cambridge: Cambridge University Press, 1985), 129.

[37] Schleiermacher, *Hermeneutics: The Handwritten Manuscripts,* 95.

History, he argues, always conditions understanding. Yet he does not therefore reject the possibility of understanding. Rather, he conceives of it on the model of a dialogue, and he cautions that "it is constantly necessary to inhibit the over hasty assimilation of the past to our own expectations of meaning. Only then will we be able to listen to the past in a way that enables it to make its own meaning heard."[38] Gadamer urges the interpreter to adopt an attitude he believes best furthers understanding: one must have the "good will" to understand.

In connection with Gadamer's view, let me return to the ideas I posited at the start as characteristic of contemporary theory's skeptical position on understanding others. These involved two claims, the first a practical or ethical one involving respect for (refraining from oppression of) others, and the second a theoretical one that denies the possibility of objective knowledge of others. There is a valuable insight in this conjunction, in that it underscores that interpretation is unavoidably linked to ethical questions. Yet there is an inconsistency between the moral injunction and the theoretical skepticism. If one cannot know others, how does one respect them? What would count as respecting them, if we cannot begin to consider their beliefs, desires, and intentions? Satya Mohanty incisively articulates some further problems with this view:

> Whether or not relativism is underwritten by the epistemological view Lyotard and other postmodernists hold, cultural relativism of any kind is unlikely to be of help in engaging another culture in a non-colonizing dialogue. If "we" decide that "they" are so different from "us" that we and they have no common "criteria" (Lyotard's term) by which to evaluate (and, necessarily, even to interpret) each other, we may avoid making ethnocentric errors, but we have also, by the same logic, precluded the possibility that they will ever have anything to teach us. Moreover, we may gain only an overly general and abstract kind of tolerance, divorced from an understanding of the other culture.... We are equal but irredeemably separate.[39]

Mohanty's critique seems right in its recognition of the costs of giving up on understanding. I believe the view that we cannot understand others' meanings threatens unacceptable consequences, and so I propose a shift in the ethical valences, a reconceiving of the pursuit of understanding and adequate knowledge as itself moral—a move that might be seen as Victorian.[40]

At this point, I want to return to the Victorians, who are the primary focus of the essays in this book. They addressed precisely the questions I have been

[38] Hans-Georg Gadamer, *Truth and Method*, 2d ed., trans. Joel Weinsheimer and Donald G. Marshall (New York: Crossroad, 1989).
[39] Mohanty, *Literary Theory and the Claims of History*, 144.
[40] See Lorraine Daston and Peter Galison, "The Image of Objectivity," *Representations* 40 (1992): 81–128. They argue that in the Victorian period there is a moralization of objectivity (and a concomitant emphasis on self-restraint) in scientific representation.

discussing, and they provided epistemological models that, despite acknowledging the obstacles, remained more optimistic about acquiring knowledge and more convinced of the value of that endeavor than much current thought. Their views, then, can help us in reconsidering our own. Moreover, looking closely at the Victorians is itself an act of historical recuperation of the sort I want to claim is both possible and important.

III

In an 1882 article in *Mind,* the first British philosophical journal, Francis Abbot writes:

> As the case now stands, philosophy has two great schools, equally founded on a reasoned subjectivism which *denies the possibility of knowing,* in any degree, an objectively existent cosmos as it really is: while science rests immovably on the fact that she *actually knows* such a cosmos, and proves by *verification* the reality of that knowledge which philosophy loudly and emphatically denies.[41]

Current idealist tendencies, he believes, lead ineluctably to "solipsism," and the consequences trouble him. "So far," he writes, "as the social and moral interests of mankind are concerned, the present philosophical situation has become simply intolerable" (466). His "theory of objective knowledge" instead "teaches that knowledge is a dynamic correlation of object and subject...that experience has both an objective and a subjective side...that the objective side of experience depends on the real existence of a known universe, and its subjective side on the real existence of a knowing mind...that 'things in themselves' are partly known and partly unknown" (484–85).

Such epistemological issues were at the center of Victorian intellectual speculation, and Abbot's terms of debate are easily recognizable from current controversies. Radical empiricism was fully explored in the period, as was the positivism against which so much current thought sets itself, and which was challenged later in the century by a wave of idealist epistemologies. As I have already argued, hermeneutic debate in various forms was carried on in the work of newly professionalized historians, biblical exegetes, literary critics, ethnographers, philologists, and even among literary writers.[42] The Victorians, then, were far from unaware of these questions.

If on the one hand Victorians have been characterized as positivist, imperialistic proponents of bourgeois individualism, naïvely (or determinedly)

---

[41] Francis Ellingwood Abbot, "Scientific Philosophy: A Theory of Human Knowledge," *Mind* 7, no. 28 (1882): 483.

[42] See W. David Shaw, *The Lucid Veil* (Madison: University of Wisconsin Press, 1987) for a fine study of hermeneutic strands in Victorian thought. In much of his writing J. Hillis Miller has importantly called attention to the Victorian concern with interpretation.

maintaining a belief in purely objective knowledge and absolute truth, on the other they have been taken by some recent critics as occupying the other extreme. Because of their pervasive concern with epistemology and interpretation, Victorians have often been read as slightly flawed precursors of poststructuralists, partially aware of the problems of meaning and truth, but backing off from the full consequences of that awareness. While the former picture—despite having generated notable new understandings of the period—has often functioned as a straw man, the latter view seems to minimize the important differences between the Victorians and us and to serve too easily as evidence that we can read only from our current perspectives. Both interpretations tend to obscure the complexities of the Victorians' own views and to prevent us from seeing the way in which their own formulations and traditions have shaped our approaches to the issues.

Views such as Abbot's that grant that "nothing can be known except as it is known by the knowing faculties," and yet remain confident that truth can be achieved, are common in Victorian thought. To the extent that one might locate a single prominent disposition of a time, the Victorians might be characterized as theorists who were likely to acknowledge the epistemic difficulties, yet who persisted in developing accounts on which knowledge was attainable despite the limitations. James Sully, founder of *Mind*, discussing "the question of certitude of knowledge which agitated some of the earliest thinkers," notes that ancient philosophers such as Parmenides, Heraclitus, and Anaxagoras were in many respects pessimistic about knowledge. "At the same time," Sully continues, "they did not lapse into absolute skepticism, but held that in some way, by a difficult process, truth was attainable."[43] However persuasive Sully's interpretation of Greek thought, his reading clearly identifies the Victorian stance I have been describing.[44] Such Victorian views counterbalance the tendency of recent criticism to emphasize only the skeptical side.

George Eliot, for example, who was well grounded in philosophy, explores with great sophistication a complex theory of interpretation in her novels and nonfiction (a theory that is often read in recent criticism as essentially poststructuralist). As early as *Adam Bede*, in the famous remarks of chapter 17, she comments on her attempt "to give a faithful account of men and things as they have mirrored themselves in my mind."[45] Although she has at times been charged with holding to a naïve realism at this stage in her thought, she is in fact already aware of the difficulties in the way of knowing: "The mirror is doubtless defective; the outlines will sometimes be disturbed, the reflection faint or confused" (174). Throughout her writings, Eliot

---

[43] James Sully, *Pessimism: A History and a Criticism* (London: Henry S. King, 1877), 40.

[44] Thomas Nagel's assertion that "it is necessary to combine the recognition of our contingency, our finitude, and our containment in the world with an ambition of transcendence, however limited may be our success in achieving it," might have been written to characterize this attitude. Nagel, *View from Nowhere*, 9.

[45] George Eliot, *Adam Bede* (New York: Signet, 1961), 174.

attempts to formulate a theory of interpretation in which, though she is deeply aware of subjective viewpoint, she also holds on to a form of objectivity as a regulative ideal. (In their essays in this volume, George Levine and Jonathan Loesberg discuss Eliot's views on knowledge in ways that depart from some of the tendencies of many current interpretations.)

Similarly, Walter Pater, often seen as a strong subjectivist, identifies his own epistemological position as reconciling subjectivist and objectivist thought. Despite his fascination with it, he rejects Plato's aim to arrive at "a kind of absolute and independent knowledge (independent, that is, of time and position, the accidents and peculiar point of view of the receiver)." In a discussion of epistemological views, Pater makes clear that he also dismisses the opposite extreme of nominalism. He explains that his own position locates him on a middle ground: "Taking our own stand as to this matter somewhere between the realist and the conceptualist." Conceptualists, as Pater describes them, take abstractions or universals to be "mere subjective thought" rather than "things in themselves" as they are for the realist.[46] (Carolyn Williams's essay on Pater, in which she argues that he should not be regarded as promoting solipsism, is alert to the contexts and nuances of his philosophical thought.)

This is not to say that no Victorians were skeptical about knowledge. Frederick Harrison, in a passage evoking contemporary constructivism, writes: "The truly relative conception of knowledge should make us habitually feel that our physical science, our laws and discoveries in Nature, are all imaginative creations—poems in fact."[47] (In his contribution, Christopher Herbert explores Victorian skepticism—what one late nineteenth-century philosopher describes as the "view commonly held in our day, that knowledge is subjective and reality unknowable."[48]) Even Carlyle, often seen as the most authoritarian and absolutist of Victorians, writes that "for the present, I will confess it, I scarce see how we can reason with *absolute* certainty on the nature of fate or *any*thing; for it seems to me we only see our own perceptions and their relations; that is to say, our soul sees only its own partial *reflex* and manner of existing and conceiving."[49] Yet as a sophisticated thinker who had already recognized the epistemological difficulties that we

---

[46] Walter Pater, *Plato and Platonism* (New York: Macmillan, 1907), 151. Abbot identifies conceptualism as the view "that universals have no substantive existence at all, but yet are more than mere names signifying nothing; and that they exist really, though only subjectively, as concepts in the mind," and he quotes the 8th edition of the *Encyclopaedia Britannica,* which asserts that conceptualism is "the doctrine of ideas generally believed in at the present day" ("Scientific Philosophy," 475).

[47] Frederick Harrison, "The Subjectivist Synthesis," in *The Philosophy of Common Sense* (New York: Macmillan, 1907), 33.

[48] Henry Jones, *Browning as a Philosophical and Religious Teacher* (New York: Macmillan, 1891), 247.

[49] Thomas Carlyle, *Two Notebooks of Thomas Carlyle,* ed. Charles Eliot Norton (New York: Grolier Club, 1898), 97.

worry about, Carlyle ultimately responded to them differently: for Carlyle, perspectivism does not completely undercut traditional notions of truth and meaning. Although Victorians recognized the problems that have played such crucial roles in recent theory, seldom does this recognition carry with it the devastating consequences for knowledge that it has in current thought.

Another case in point is James Sully's fascinating 1888 study, *Illusions*. The book examines the many ways in which our search for knowledge goes astray. He describes in detail various errors of perception and forms of misinterpretation that result from personal biases, faulty memory, and desire (in ways that are strikingly similar to George Eliot's). "The conditions of an accurate reading of others' minds are rarely realized" due to our "disposition to ascribe a certain kind of feeling to others in accordance with our wishes and fears."[50] One of his intentions in providing a taxonomy of "illusions," however, is to suggest ways in which they can be worked against and corrected.

Science, as Abbott indicates, figured for many Victorians as a way of resisting skepticism. Harrison and others may insist on the relativity of knowledge. (Though for the Victorians, deeply influenced by Kantian thought, "relativity" of knowledge usually means only that our knowledge is conditioned and of the phenomenal world. Hence George Henry Lewes could write: "It is clearly open to us to attain absolute certainty of relative knowledge."[51]) Yet Harrison goes on to insist that the "poems" of scientific discovery do "strictly correspond within the limited range of phenomena we have before us" ("Subjectivist Synthesis," 33). He emphasizes that his "doctrine of the relativity of knowledge" must be distinguished from skepticism: "Philosophical Scepticism is the Despair of Philosophy. It undertakes to prove that nothing can be in the truest sense known" (25). His philosophy, on the other hand, insists "as fully as any others on the discoverability of philosophical truth. Only we say that philosophical truth is relative" (25). This is the familiar move of Victorian positivism, the circumscribing of a limited sphere in which valid knowledge is possible. Using a different strategy, the philosopher of science William Whewell, although convinced that knowledge is always inseparably both subjective and objective and that there are "no special attributes of Theory and Fact which distinguish the one from another," nevertheless defended science as a source of objective truth. "Man is the interpreter of Nature, Science is the right interpretation."[52] Whewell's theories focused on accumulating evidence and arguments for justification.

---

[50] James Sully, *Illusions: A Psychological Study* (New York: Da Capo Press, 1982), 229, 226.

[51] George Henry Lewes, *Problems of Life and Mind: The Foundation of a Creed*, first series (Boston: Houghton, Osgood, 1875–1880), 72.

Cf. "We arrive then at the conclusion that we can never know but *relative* truth, our only medium of knowledge being the senses, and this medium, with regard *to all without us*, being forever a false one; but being *true to us*, we may put confidence in its relativity." G.H. Lewes, "Hints towards an Essay on the Sufferings of Truth," *Monthly Repository* 2 (1837): 314.

[52] William Whewell, *The Philosophy of the Inductive Sciences, Founded upon Their History*, 2 vols. (London, 1840), vol. 1, xvii.

In recent thought, of course, scientific rationality has been seen by many as no more than intersubjective community standards. On such a view, science remains deeply subjectivist, deeply inside of culture. Whewell believed, in contrast, that subjectivism was a legitimate route to an independent reality.

We might, in Nietzschean fashion, take these gestures as signs of fear, desperate attempts to resist the consequences of the recognition that objectivity of knowledge is impossible. But that would be to fail to attempt to take these views on their own terms, and so to miss what we might learn from them. Victorian thought provides us with theories that both deeply appreciate the problems of access to knowledge, meaning, and the past *and* maintain an ideal of objective knowledge. If we straightaway move to discount a part of their thought, then we will inevitably find simply a confirmation of present views. It may be that many Victorians' valuing of objectivity was just that: they believed that the goal of reaching out to a reality outside the self carried with it social and ethical benefits worth holding on to. But if epistemological skepticism is also largely motivated by political and moral arguments, then it is useful to examine what those Victorians took to be the value of a less skeptical epistemological position.

IV

The essays in this volume explore the epistemological problems described above via a series of arguments—some clearly resisting the directions of my own arguments—about the Victorians' representations of themselves and of these issues in their writing. Half of the essays provide readings of the Victorians as a means of reflecting on what it is to try to understand the historical past; the other half examine the Victorians' own contributions to these debates. In all cases, the theoretical arguments are grounded in close (literary) attention to the particularities of the Victorian texts they analyze.

The varied theoretical views represented by the essays offer a range of possible responses to the questions the book as a whole is examining. While some of the contributors argue that we can attain real knowledge of the past, others are more skeptical about the possibility of knowing. Others want to sidestep the direct epistemological question—can we know the past?—and replace it with different questions that they believe offer more productive ways of approaching the problems. Most accept the inevitability that the present directs our understanding to some degree. Yet, none settles for the idea that the only options are a naïve realism or a radical antirealism. They instead offer complicated accounts that refuse a simple "yes, we can know the past" or "no, we cannot."

The essays in Part I, "Theorizing the Victorians," directly take up the epistemological questions, asking to what extent we can know the Victorians (or to what extent it makes sense even to ask such a question). At the same time, the essays examine what Victorians had to say on these questions. The section begins with Gerhard Joseph's brief provocation, "Text vs. Hypertext: Seeing the Victorian Object as in Itself It Really Is," which presents the extreme formulations of the epistemological positions (the radical opacity or the radical transparency of the past) and suggests that we can locate those formulations in the Victorians themselves. To these admittedly simplified alternatives he brings the concept of hypertext. While Joseph's model, which allows for a constant simultaneous movement between theoretical positions, might be taken to be largely metaphorical, it anticipates the ways in which most of the contributors will recast the alternatives—and thus suggestively provides a framework for the arguments that come after his.

In the essays that follow, Joseph's binary oppositions are played out through studies of the Victorians' negotiations of these issues. Christopher Herbert offers a primarily skeptical (or at least agnostic) account and George Levine finds a model for more objective knowledge. Herbert sees in late Victorian ethnography a pervasive skepticism about knowledge that anticipates and parallels current views. Tabling the epistemological question, Herbert shifts the ground to its genealogy. He argues that it was the Victorians who firmly established the belief that the situated perspective of the investigator makes objective understanding of the thing studied impossible. Finally, he suggests that we might usefully turn our attention from the question of what we can know, to ask instead why we have resisted questioning the construction of the Victorians as thoroughly alien to us. Admittedly, Herbert does offer a reading of the past that would indicate that he can know it, but, as he contends, this is largely for practical rather than epistemic reasons: Victorian studies would vanish without such interpretations.

George Levine, in contrast, examining through George Eliot the Victorian engagement with epistemological questions, argues that there is no inevitability to our contemporary conjunction of relativism and particular political positioning. While Levine concedes the dangers of universalism, he believes that giving up on objectivity can lead only to solipsism or to the kind of prejudice that in *Daniel Deronda* manifests itself as anti-Semitism. Eliot, he argues, in her final novel presents an epistemology that affirms the centrality of the human in the project of knowing and yet recognizes that there is a reality outside the self that resists human desire. Levine concurs with the novel's assertion that the "present significance of knowledge...need not be an act of domination or a disqualification of the knowledge."

Part II, "Victorians Theorizing," focuses on the way particular Victorians engaged with the theoretical issues with which this book is concerned and demonstrates how their arguments have consequences for current thought. Carolyn Williams, in contrast to the Pater that Joseph's essay sketches, reads Pater as offering a theory of knowledge that affirms, in complicated ways, that we can know "under conditions." On Pater's account, the historical object is constituted in and contingent upon the interpreting subject and thus is necessarily known from the vantage point of the present. A subsequent "process of objectification" is required for knowledge. Pater should not, Williams insists, be seen as a radical subjectivist; his views are formulated as a reaction to Victorian skepticism, and he offers an account of knowledge on which any historical object is "an epistemological and aesthetic construction—but no less 'real' for all that."

In a rereading of Arnold, Herbert Tucker, while affirming the critique of the ideals of disinterestedness and objectivity currently associated with Arnoldian interpretation ("disinterestedness is interpretation by other means"), shows how Arnold's project is central to what criticism does today. But the centrality Tucker discusses is not the usual conservative one, which associates Arnold with a debunked objectivist criticism. In subordinating poetry to criticism, Arnold validated critical theory and its aims in ways crucial to current approaches such as the new historicism and cultural studies, and, most importantly, gave us "the idea of a canon."

Jonathan Loesberg, in a reading of George Eliot on epistemology and ethics, claims that contradictions critics have found in Eliot's work can be better understood if her realism is considered in the context of the German idealism that she knew well. Loesberg concludes his essay by suggesting that the "formal contradictoriness" that he believes is essential to Eliot's ethics is also crucial to current ideological models of interpretation that seek to understand the past in ways in which the past could not know itself. Loesberg appeals to Arthur Danto's philosophy of history in support of his contention that attaining knowledge of the past cannot mean knowing it as the Victorians did. In describing the period, we use post facto conceptions that were not and could not have been available in the past; hence the meanings we ascribe to past events will inevitably be different from past meanings.

Part III, "Continuities," contains three readings of the Victorians that respond in various ways to the epistemological questions. All of the essays, however, agree that knowledge of the past is necessarily mediated by subsequent history and texts. Our understanding of the Victorians depends upon resources available to us now. But the essays also maintain that there are important continuities between past and present, the Victorians and us, and that there is value in recognizing this.

Mary Poovey reads the Victorians in light of a theoretical account of anxiety that was developed after the Victorians. Arguing that the use of abstractions in the emerging field of social science in the nineteenth century is associated with the rise of an epistemology relying upon abstract representation rather than on the empirical observation of particulars, she links the use of such abstractions to multiple anxieties. Freud's later theorizing of anxiety allows us to identify the structural role anxiety plays in social science and Victorian narrative, a role that would not have been identifiable by Victorians since such an account had not yet been constructed. We understand retrospectively, reading the past through current knowledge. Poovey nevertheless regards her methodology as a "moderate objectivity" that aims to respect the meanings of the past and to take these as constraints in her interpretations.

Bruce Robbins approaches the issues by reading *Great Expectations* as a narrative of the emerging social welfare state, at the moment at which Victorian society begins to break from the ideology of the bourgeois family. His essay adds a new twist to the argument by denying the value of the epistemological question insofar as it remains at the level of philosophical abstraction. We engage the past as a consequence of engagement with social questions raised by the present. Yet there is a practical need, he argues, not to give up on the project of knowing and the recognition of continuities. He interrogates the emphasis on absolute otherness in contemporary theory, regarding it as a form of essentialism that seems out of keeping with most aspects of contemporary thought. "Anti-essentialism," he writes, "aligns us against the notion that others are radically unknowable."

Judith Stoddart negotiates a position between extremes, both acknowledging our situatedness as interpreters and accepting that we can attain some knowledge of the past. Like Herbert, she suggests that we ought to put aside the epistemological question, to cease asking whether we can or cannot know the Victorians, and instead to examine the ways in which some of our conceptions are inherited from the Victorians. Demonstrating that the Victorian construction of sentimental art has been unreflectively naturalized in recent criticism, she argues that critics have failed to see it as the complex, historically situated phenomenon that it is and have consequently overlooked revealing continuities between Victorian ways of seeing and our own.

Part IV, "Victorian Meanings," contains three essays that read against some of the tendencies of contemporary theory by assuming that we can, to a good extent (although all admit the limitations on the project), recover historically situated meaning and that there are strong motivations for doing so. For each of these writers, careful attention to the particularities of language affords access to a text's meaning.

In her essay on Dickens, Rosemarie Bodenheimer focuses on the ways in which current criticism has adopted a model according to which the present has greater knowledge and understanding of the past than the past did of itself. She contends that what critics have regarded as "repressions" in *David Copperfield* (the narrative's refusal to see, for instance, class oppression or the instabilities of the construction of bourgeois identity—aspects of the story that we can see from our current critical standpoint) are, in fact, "known" by the novel itself. These critics are not discovering gaps that reveal what Victorian ideology attempts to exclude, but instead finding what the text puts there to be seen. Bodenheimer, then, affirming the importance of present concerns about class and subjectivity, argues that we should not fault the past for not knowing these things, since Dickens did know and write about them.

Margery Sabin also questions some tendencies in contemporary readings of the Victorians, arguing that recent readings of the autobiography of the working-class reformer William Lovett have effectively silenced his voice, thus ironically replicating Victorian views (of Carlyle or Gaskell, for instance) regarding the inability of the lower classes to articulate their own meanings. The commitment to indeterminacy and skepticism misfires, working to make critics unable to hear what Lovett has to say. In effect, Sabin sees contemporary readings that deny our ability to understand another's meaning as themselves repressive. Accepting the possibility of knowing is to be equated not with domination, but with hearing the voice of the dominated.

Finally, Gillian Beer dramatizes, as she argues for, the possibility of knowing the past by attempting to know Edith Simcox. While recognizing that this knowing is unusual in that it is one-way—Beer knows Simcox but Simcox cannot know Beer—Beer believes nonetheless that she knows Simcox "intimately" and can show that she does. If some form of presentism is inevitable, she does not doubt that Simcox's texts convey her intentions and give access to her mind.

The contributors do not hold the same views on all of these complex issues. None of the essays, of course, wants to assert the possibility of purely objective knowledge about the past, others, or a text, but neither does any of them want to reject completely our ability to acquire knowledge of the past. Instead the essays present sophisticated accounts of the ways we can know the past and others that offer new knowledge of the Victorians and make us reassess some of our claims about knowledge. In reexamining the currently dominant epistemological positions, each essay seems to be impelled by the assumption that there is a lot at stake in knowing; together they suggest that contemporary criticism is moving toward revised views on these questions.

P A R T   I

THEORIZING THE VICTORIANS

1. Text vs. Hypertext

Seeing the Victorian Object As in Itself It Really Is

GERHARD JOSEPH

For was, and is, and will be, are but is;
And all creation is one act at once,
The birth of light: but we that are not all,
As parts, can see but parts, now this, now that,
And live, perforce, from thought to thought, and make
One act a phantom of succession.

Alfred Tennyson, The Princess

There is no space or time out here, or in here, or wherever [Sister Edgar] is.
There are only connections. Everything is connected. All human knowledge
gathered and linked, hyperlinked, this site leading to that, this fact referenced
to that, a keystroke, a mouse-click, a password—world without end, amen.

Don DeLillo, Underworld

The Victorian object and the modern subject, the past and the present moment, they and we: with whatever originality such binaries have been examined within contemporary hermeneutics, such an exploration may also be seen as the pouring of old wine into new bottles, as the latest version of an old interpretive chestnut. In what Terry Eagleton has called the modern "drama" of the subject and object—"the fraught narrative of their couplings and splittings, their matchings and misalliances"—can the individual/collective subject make, or can it not make, pretty immediate contact with the individual/collective object that was/is "the past"?[1] With all the necessary qualifications that take alternative strategies and intermediate possibilities into account, can we surmount the perspectivism that marks our

---

[1] Terry Eagleton, *The Ideology of the Aesthetic* (Oxford: Basil Blackwell, 1990), 70.

immediate horizon of expectations to approximate an earlier point of view? Can we, that is, see the Victorian historical "other" or "object" with Victorian eyes, or are we necessarily limited to the vantage point to which our immediate consciousness or interpretive community commits us?

My answer is that the advent of an apparently antisequential electronic hypertext as an alternative to the sequentiality of the printed text presents us with a new way to interrogate the hermeneutic purchase of the modern subject upon the Victorian object. In support of that argument, I'd like to present three sequential mini-texts for the price of one seamless text—or, alternatively, three *lexias*, George Landow's term (appropriated from Roland Barthes's *S/Z*) for the discrete blocks of texts that make up a nonsequential electronic hypertext—since, as my diagram toward the end of this essay suggests, I conceive of this argument and want my audience to conceive of it simultaneously, as it were, in textual and hypertextual forms.[2] The reasons for this will, I trust, become clear at my close.

The first mini-text is my thumbnail sketch of what a paper on three specific Victorians, Matthew Arnold, Walter Pater, and Oscar Wilde, "as in themselves they really were" from a Victorian perspective, might look like were I indeed to believe (as I don't) in the radical transparency implied by Arnold's famous dictum to the effect that "to see the object as in itself it really is" constitutes "the function of criticism at the present time" (the title of the essay formulating that thesis). The second one, even at the risk of sounding merely fashionable, supplements the first in the service of a radical opacity—in the service, that is, of the belief that we cannot transcend and are deluding ourselves in asserting that we can so transcend the biases of our personal and our age's historical constructions. And because I find neither of these extreme positions viable, my third mini-text attempts a collapse, via the Derridean "always already" formula, of the either/or, transparency/opacity opposition of the first two mini-texts—which presents its own hermeneutic difficulties that hypertext helps to alleviate, or so I would argue.

So here's mini-text or *lexia* number one (actually a compressed version of the introduction to an earlier Wilde essay of mine).[3] An off-hand list of the figures who count these days in the undermining of a classical view of representation—say, Saussure, Heidegger, Gadamer, Lacan, Derrida, and Foucault—suggests the extent to which Anglo-American criticism has been swamped by a Continental tradition, one in turn inspired by such nineteenth-century Continental giants as Hegel, Marx, Nietzsche, and Freud. But if such be the mainstream of contemporary theory, this does not deny the existence of a native English tributary that has had its influence. That nineteenth-

---

[2] Roland Barthes, *S/Z*, trans. Richard Howard (New York: Hill and Wang, 1974); George Landow, *Hypertext: The Convergence of Contemporary Critical Theory and Technology* (Baltimore: Johns Hopkins University Press, 1992).

[3] Gerhard Joseph, "Framing Wilde," in *Critical Essays on Oscar Wilde*, ed. Regenia Gagnier (New York: G. K. Hall, 1991), 179–85.

century English line, to simplify, goes from Arnold to Pater to Wilde. "To see the object as in itself it really is," Arnold tells us is the function of criticism at mid-century,[4] as if the Kantian "thing in itself," what Arnold's contemporary Henry James called the Real Thing, were more or less readily accessible to clear-sighted perception and reference. And it is of course but a short and well-known-enough step to Pater's qualification in *The Renaissance* that the function of criticism is to know one's *impression* of the object as it really is (since the "thick world of personality" will cut off an unoccluded view of the object)[5]—and an even shorter distance to a full reversal of Arnold in Wilde's affirmation in "The Critic As Artist" to the effect that "the highest Criticism... is more creative than creation, and the primary aim of the critic is to see the object as in itself it really is not."[6] The full context for each of these statements is of course complex and variegated, but when we line the three sentences up sequentially as I have done we hear a pretty tight temporal, historical reverberation, one that feels transparently and immediately "Victorian" in a way that would seem to affirm the possibility of getting back to the Victorians as they saw themselves, as getting back to strict Victorian intentions. As Pater had intentionally framed Arnold's key sentence, so Wilde had intentionally stepped back to frame the sentences of both his predecessors, but especially that of Arnold, and I in June 2000 from the vantage of *my* frame think I've got the matter pretty well right with respect to *my* three historical objects, if only because of the lockstep semantic repetition of the "seeing the object" phrase in Arnold, and then Pater, and then Wilde. It's the reiteration of the phrase within three echoing syntactical contexts that makes me think I'm describing something outside of my isolated consciousness and beyond my narrow cultural expectations.

And yet—and here comes mini-text or *lexia* number two—and yet there's that notion of "reiteration." Reiteration! The very word is like a bell to toll me back to my sole self. Adieu, the fancy of historical objectivity cannot cheat so well as she is famed to do, deceiving elf. For whereas I have argued in text number one that a threefold iteration makes for a Tinkers-to-Evers-to-Chance elegance, for a sense of smooth filiation within the same epistemic ballpark, I would argue in mini-text number two that such iteration makes rather for difference both *within* my three Victorian objects and among them. Take Arnold's foundational Victorian dictum about seeing the object, which may indeed serve as a *locus classicus* for the truism that the Victorian period was the heyday of a belief in, if not exactly "disinterestedness" and "objectivity," at least the sort of asymptoptic approximation of such perceptual

---

[4] Matthew Arnold, "The Function of Criticism at the Present Time," in *Poetry and Criticism of Matthew Arnold*, ed. A. Dwight Culler (Boston: Houghton Mifflin, 1961).

[5] Walter Pater, *The Renaissance* (London: Macmillan, 1910).

[6] Oscar Wilde, "The Critic As Artist," in *The Artist As Critic: Critical Writings of Oscar Wilde*, ed. Richard Ellmann (Chicago: University of Chicago Press, 1969), 369. While "The Critic As Artist" is a dialogue between Gilbert and Ernest, Gilbert, from whose mouth the dictum emerges, is usually taken as more significantly capturing Wilde's critical position.

ideals. If Arnold's dictum seems to affirm the possibility of "seeing the object" clearly, it may also be said to imply doubt about such a possibility through the reiteration and redundancy of "in *itself*" and "as it *really* is." That is, after Derrida we—or at any rate I—can no longer accept "iteration"[7] as an affirmation of presence and sameness as we may heretofore have been wont to do; we must see it as precisely the production of those "folds" that constitute difference (not to mention *différance*) not only between texts but also within them—as Arnold's "in itself" and "as it really is," I would suggest, illustrates to perfection. This iterative procedure generates the undecidables that radically destabilize meaning. One can thus see that Arnold's very protesting-too-much assertiveness is almost (but of course not quite) the equivalent of Wilde's denial—just as certain inconsistencies in Wilde's denial, in ways I spelled out in my earlier Wilde essay, are a covert return to Arnold's ambivalently "folded" affirmation.

In brief, Wilde was outraged, during one of his trials, that a purloined letter (in Lacan's sense) of his to Alfred Douglas had been circulating in public and that its meaning had been seriously distorted by hostile readers. Such outrage undermines Wilde's principle that the aim of criticism is "to see the object as in itself it really is not," at least when it's a matter of one's own ox that's being gored, of one's own object whose intention is being misprisioned. The punning title of my essay, "Framing Wilde," while it referred early on to Wilde's framing of Arnold and Pater in the manner outlined above thus ended with the implication of Wilde's being framed (as in a criminal "frame up") by unsympathetic readers who saw him as they—not he—insisted that he in himself really was. Arnold, I suggested in my closing sentence, thus "has the latest frame after all." Within the context of the present argument, I would amend that hierarchical judgment by suggesting that Arnold's "seeing the object as in itself it really is" and Wilde's "as it is not" inhabit each other, constitute each other's supplement.

And then there's Pater's frame, which is a lot more complicated than the simple sentence I've attributed to him in the service of mini-text number one's argument for transparency. For one thing, he tells us in the introduction to *The Renaissance* that "knowing one's own impression as it really is" is merely "the first step towards seeing the object as it really is"—presumably there are additional steps toward the achievement of transparent vision, though he never tells us what they are.

But at least Pater's introduction to *The Renaissance* is consistent with Arnold and Wilde in the acceptance, in threefold turn, of a Cartesian subject/object dualism, however the writers may differ in their beliefs as to the subject's ability to bridge the gap between the two. Whatever their dis-

---

[7] For a discussion of whether iterability does or does not undermine original authorial intention, see the debate between John Searle and Jacques Derrida in the latter's *Limited Inc.* (Evanston: Northwestern University Press, 1988).

agreements, Arnold and Pater and Wilde seem to believe in the existence of an aesthetic object that has a certain shaped "thingness," what Stephen Dedalus calls its Aristotelian/Thomistic *quidditas,* a certain iconic mass and depth (i.e., "as *in* itself" it can be) and a boundary that can be specified—in short, what M.H. Abrams in *The Mirror and the Lamp* called a heterocosm.[8] Or do they? For, if that is indeed the case for Pater within the introduction to *The Renaissance,* the conclusion presents us with a counter-notion: there the solid-seeming object dissipates into what he calls a "tremulous wisp": the clear, perpetual outline of face and limb and external object become "but an image of ours under which we group them—a design in a web, the actual threads of which pass out beyond it." The bounded "object" of the introduction to *The Renaissance* becomes, in other words, the unbounded and woven "text" of the conclusion, as we remember that the etymology of "text" is the Latin *texere,* to weave. One might thus say that in what happens between the introduction and the conclusion of *The Renaissance* we move from a Victorian to a modern and even postmodern notion of the aesthetic object; we move, that is, "from work to text," as Roland Barthes has put it in the important essay so titled.[9] If Pater may thus be said to embrace the textual web of mysterious origin in the conclusion to *The Renaissance,* that conclusion and his work more generally may be seen "as in itself it really is" as the specifically English—as opposed to Continental—pan-textu(r)al prison house of language—especially since so many contemporary theorists from Heidegger through Barthes, Derrida, and Foucault consciously pick up on the etymological implications of the aesthetic and epistemic artifact as woven text without definable origin.[10]

Well! (as Arnold and Pater would say), in drawing such a connection between the Victorian "work" or "object" and the structuralist/poststructuralist "text," we have surely moved from seeing the Victorians as they saw themselves to something rather different—to a sense of how the Victorian object is difficult to "see" except as an anticipation of our contemporary interpretive habits, since *The Renaissance,* at the very least, is inevitably inhabited by our postmodernist reading of it. We can't help, that is, but see the Victorians as they *are* to our perspective—and cannot at all surmount that present tense *as* perspective except by deluding ourselves that we're doing so. From one perspective, the past is more or less recoverable; from another, an interpretation of the past is always in some measure a back formation of the present, a function of the present reader's horizon of expectations, a

---

[8] M.H. Abrams, *The Mirror and the Lamp: Romantic Theory and the Critical Tradition* (New York: Oxford University Press, 1953).

[9] "From Work to Text," in *Image-Music-Text: Roland Barthes,* trans. Stephen Heath (New York: Hill and Wang, 1976).

[10] For a survey of recent allusions to the text-as-woven-cloth metaphor, see "Interweave My Lady('s) Shuttle: The Alienation of Work into Text," in Gerhard Joseph, *Tennyson and the Text: The Weaver's Shuttle* (Cambridge: Cambridge University Press, 1992), 113–23.

"screen memory" writ large of something irrecoverable except in highly distorted and tendentious fashion. (One is tempted, in light of such bifurcated temporal moves, to throw up one's hands and repeat to oneself Tennyson's words to Emily Sellwod: "Annihilate within yourself these two dreams of Space and time," a sentiment echoed in Princess Ida's visionary proclamation, which appears as the first epigraph for this essay.[11])

Still, this side of such mystical flights, how can we, in mini-text or *lexia* number three, reconcile the two very different hermeneutic perspectives, in one of which we can and in the other of which we can't break through to the Victorian past and its aesthetic objects? The answer I would suggest (and "suggest" is indeed the deeply contingent operative word) is through adoption of the Derridean "always already" formula and its grammatical companion, the present perfect tense, both of which follow hard upon his theory of iterative folds referred to above. That is, in asserting that we "see the Victorian object—Arnold, Pater, and Wilde, say—as they in themselves really always already have been," we arguably deny neither putative authorial intentions in the past nor the fact that those intentions now look a certain way. Rather we merely say that we are unsure of where one left/leaves off and the other began/begins. And it is this fact of uncertainty, of undecidability, of indeterminacy as to the border of past and present, where I would like to end.

But not quite: For how "undecidable" is my undecidability as to the relation of present and past? Caught within the present theoretical moment and my own temperamental inclination in the matter, I may cite a poststructuralist undecidability that is as mother's milk to me, although a reader might well see in the pattern of my three mini-texts the rather hoary ghost of a nineteenth-century dialectical mode of thought: my "always already has been" formula, that is, might well be read as a neat (and rigid) enough Hegelian *Aufhebung* (or sublation) arising out of the thesis that is the past tense and the antithesis that is the present. And that is why in closing (itself a tell-tale gesture of linearity) I offer in figure 1.1 a nonlinear (or better, multilinear), hypertext version of my argument as a suggested alternative to the linear thrust of this essay, with its sequential, temporally divided sections and its sublated poststructuralist third term.

Four *lexias,* with six possible links—not a very intricate hypertext, to be sure. We are here hardly in the league of Michael Joyce's hypertext narrative *Afternoon,* with its 539 *lexias* accessed by way of 950 links, or Stuart Moultrop's *Victory Garden,* with its 991 places read by way of 2,800 links.[12] But the diagram of my primitive hypertext does at least suggest an undermining of the hierarchizing impulse that even the most deconstructive of

---

[11] Hallam Tennyson, *Alfred Tennyson: A Memoir by His Son,* 2 vols. (London: Macmillan, 1897), I.171.

[12] For an analysis of Joyce and Moultrop's hypertextual fiction, see J. Yellowlees Douglas, "'How Do I Stop This Thing?' Closure and Indeterminacy in Interactive Narratives," in *Hyper/Text/Theory,* ed. George Landow (Baltimore: Johns Hopkins University Press, 1994).

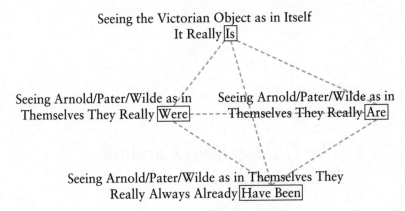

Figure 1.1. Seeing the Victorian object as in itself it really is, was, or always already has been

printed texts cannot avoid. For within hypertext the writer/reader and reader/writer may start in the same place—the *lexia, for instance,* that constitutes my essay title (a title that I would now revise into "Seeing the Victorian Object As in Itself It Really Was, Is, or Always Already Has Been")—but the reader and I can stop at whatever *lexia* makes the most epistemological sense, my own preference being to continue circling about cyberspace to keep the hermeneutic possibilities alive. The classical "hermeneutic circle" of German nineteenth-century interpretation theory was the reciprocal constitutive force—what we in a cybernetic age would call the feedback loop—of part and whole,[13] to which E. D. Hirsch has added the loop of genre and trait.[14] The new electronic technology foregrounds yet a third, a grammatical circularity. With its concentration upon the verbal nodes through which its linkage moves electronically, a hypertext version of an argument (or at any rate of the present one) highlights more directly than its textual alternative the shape-shifting epistemology behind its verbal grammar: the fact that grammar—and specifically the network of tenses in our given language—is the hermeneutics by other means through which we may circle, if we so desire, world without end, amen.

[13] For the centrality of the feedback loop to the first, homeostatic "wave" of cybernetic thought at the Macy Conferences (1943–54), see Katherine N. Hayles, *How We Became Posthuman: Virtual Bodies in Cybernetics, Literature, and Informatics* (Chicago: University of Chicago Press, 1999).

[14] E. D. Hirsch, Jr., *Validity in Interpretation* (New Haven: Yale University Press, 1967), 68–77.

2. *The Golden Bough* and the Unknowable

CHRISTOPHER HERBERT

Is it possible, at this late date, to attain so clear an insight into the mental world of the Victorian age as to enable us to see the world as the Victorians themselves did, to understand what they consciously or unconsciously *meant* in the words and images which they have passed down to us and in their various social practices, to know them, in effect, as they knew themselves?

The question may strike scholars in the contemporary dispensation as an idle conundrum (or perhaps as a hopeless predicament) rather than as an issue for serious debate. Victorianists can hardly afford to abandon the ideal of historicized interpretation of nineteenth-century cultural and psychological phenomena; without such an ideal, the field of Victorian studies as a coherent scholarly discipline essentially dissolves. Yet the question posed as the theme of this volume takes on an air of nonsense the moment we subject it to critical analysis. How could the category of an authentically "Victorian" view of the world be so defined as to possess even a minimally scientific character? René Wellek surely had this dilemma in mind when he issued a definitive pronouncement on the question at hand in the pre-postmodern year of 1960. In forming scholarly judgments of literature, he says, some argue that modern readers need to "adopt the criteria of the past: that we must reconstruct and apply the values of the period we are studying." A vain project, Wellek asserts. The truth is "that these standards cannot be reconstructed with certainty, that we are confronted with insurmountable difficulties if we want to be sure what Shakespeare intended by his plays and how he conceived them or what the Elizabethan audience understood by them." No such potential knowledge lies within the scope of our research, he declares: as far as rigorous scholarship is concerned, there is *no such thing* as "historically authentic interpretation."[1] It would be hard nowadays to muster compelling arguments against this verdict.

Still, there the persistent question is, and despite Wellek's reference to Shakespeare, it carries a peculiar charge of scholarly pathos in connection with Victorian studies; in fact, it can be seen as the organizing theme of this field. This is because, in the historical script we have written for them, the Victorians are made to play a uniquely equivocal role vis-à-vis scholarship of the late twentieth century. They may initially strike us with an appearance of great likeness to ourselves, of transparency and easy legibility. Much of their popular fiction is as accessible to ordinary readers today as it was then, for example. But on more extended acquaintance, the Victorians (those imaginary beings conjured out of nineteenth-century documents to enact twentieth-century imperatives) come to tantalize us with signs of an insuperable remoteness, and to seem like strangers after all, speaking to us from the other side of a great historical divide. This in effect is their raison d'être: by provoking a special pang of estrangement, they signify the modern intuition that the known and familiar may prove to be incurably foreign after all, cut off from us by "insurmountable difficulties"—which is why texts like "The Lady of Shalott" or "Isolation—To Marguerite" seem so keenly expressive of the Victorian ethos.

This distinctive alienation effect gains its leverage from a longstanding cultural mythology (one which is never disinterested). As we know, the late-Victorian and Edwardian years are full of testimonies to a supposed transformation of consciousness sharply separating the Victorian age from the one that comes after—a change evoked as poignant loss, traumatic upheaval, or emancipation, depending on the witness's point of view. All these registers coexist, for instance, in Edmund Gosse's *Father and Son* (1907). Gosse narrates his life as a parable of a passage between "two epochs," which is to say, a movement to a new phase of consciousness in relation to which the previous phase seems strange and incomprehensible, requiring already, in 1907, a great effort of retrieval and of historical imagination to recapture.[2] A seismic reorganization of sensibility has taken place in the space of his own lifetime: this is Gosse's theme. When Virginia Woolf declares from the vantage point of 1924 that "in or about December, 1910, human character changed," producing necessarily a shift in "all human relations" and thus in "religion, conduct, politics, and literature," she offers another version of the same insistent myth of a radical discontinuity between the Victorians and us folk of the twentieth century.[3] "We are sharply cut off from our predecessors,"

---

[1] René Wellek, "Literary Theory, Criticism, and History," in *Twentieth-Century Literary Criticism: A Reader,* ed. David Lodge (London: Longman, 1972), 552–53.

[2] Edmund Gosse, *Father and Son: A Study of Two Temperaments* (1907; New York: Norton, 1963), 9.

[3] Virginia Woolf, *Collected Essays,* 4 vols. (London: Hogarth, 1966), 1:320, 321. Samuel Hynes identifies Woolf's declaration with the opening of the first British exhibition of the post-

she says elsewhere.[4] Writing in 1909, William James gives a more evolutionary aspect to the same proposition. In his lifetime, he says, he has witnessed "one of those gradual mutations of intellectual climate...that make the thought of a past generation seem as foreign to its successor as if it were the expression of a different race of men."[5] Such examples go to show that the category of "the Victorians" was inscribed from the moment of its invention with this primary, defining characteristic of radical estrangement from ourselves, and that in addition to the other functions which they have been assigned to perform in our cultural cosmos (chiefly that of ensuring for subsequent generations, by negative contrast, the role of bearers of enlightenment and sophistication), the Victorians were established as a historical institution in order to mark precisely the point at which our capacity for intuitive cross-cultural understanding fails.[6]

These prefatory remarks will suggest that my aim in this essay is not to seek to unriddle the question with which I began (can we learn to see the world through Victorian eyes?), as to which a devout agnosticism may be the soundest policy. Rather, I wish to present this question as *a momentous historical construction in its own right*—one at which Victorian intellectuals, in particular, labored, sensing its epochal significance and little suspecting that they themselves would before long figure among its specially designated objects. Nonsensical as it may finally be, it is of course only the historian's variant of the dilemma or pseudodilemma that has ramified throughout humanities and social science research, notably in such fields as cultural anthropology (is it possible for a "participant observer" to achieve understanding of a tribal society from that vantage of presumptive authenticity which Malinowski called "the native's point of view"?[7]), philosophy of science (is translatability of terms possible across the boundary lines separating opposed "paradigms"?), and literary criticism (is authorial intention determinable in principle, and if so, does it govern the interpretation of a literary text?). All these cognate questions express the distinctively modern

---

impressionists on November 8, 1910; he then affirms the historical reality of a sharp shift in British thinking around 1910 though he experiences no apparent anxiety about the possibility of reconstructing that thinking through the medium of historical documents. *The Edwardian Turn of Mind* (Princeton: Princeton University Press, 1968), 325–26, 346.

[4] Woolf, *Collected Essays*, 2:157–58.

[5] William James, *A Pluralistic Universe* (1909; New York: Longmans, 1916), 29.

[6] In *The Victorian Frame of Mind*, Walter E. Houghton proposed a revision of this well-established outlook, arguing "that continuity rather than contrast is the conclusion to be drawn from comparing the Victorians with ourselves." *The Victorian Frame of Mind, 1830–1870* (New Haven: Yale University Press, 1957), 13. In making such a claim, he reinforces the point that the defining motive of Victorian studies is to calibrate the degree of proximity between the Victorians and us, and that the point of departure for scholarship is the theory of a sharp discontinuity.

[7] Bronislaw Malinowski, *Argonauts of the Western Pacific: An Account of Native Enterprise and Adventure in the Archipelagoes of Melanesian New Guinea* (1922; London: Routledge; New York: Dutton, 1932), 25.

sense that one's point of view may make it forever impossible to know or understand key elements of one's domain of study.

In order to trace one strand of the emergence of this trend of thought, I will focus in what follows on the field of nineteenth-century evolutionary or "comparative" anthropology, as represented in particular by Frazer's Golden Bough, setting this text in relation to a theme of scholarly discourse which emerges with the effect of an intellectual revolution in the second half of the nineteenth century: the theme of what Herbert Spencer, who called it his chief philosophical category, designated "the Unknowable."

❧

One writer who sharply highlights the themes which I wish to trace is the turn-of-the-century French anthropologist Lucien Lévy-Bruhl. Standing as he does just at the cusp of the supposed transition from the Victorian to the disillusioned modern mentality, Lévy-Bruhl is wont to criticize Frazer and the other proponents of the British school of anthropology for their assumption that Western modes of logical thought may be generalized to other societies, particularly to "primitive" societies, and confidently invoked in explanation of their cultural development.[8] In such works as *Ethics and Moral Science* (1903) and *How Natives Think* (1910), Lévy-Bruhl postulates that profound, unbridgeable differences of mentality may in fact divide us from peoples we seek to study, making understanding of them in their own terms next to impossible. "No matter what effort we make we become almost incapable of reconstructing the ordinary mental states of men who have not the same linguistic and logical habits," he declares; primitive societies in particular operate in terms of "a logic, a symbolism, a whole mental life which we cannot read as an open book merely by bringing it into relation with ours."[9] The very fact of employing scientific method in anthropological investigation precludes us, in effect, from attaining scientific understanding: this is Lévy-Bruhl's paradoxical theme. Just as T. S. Kuhn proposes long afterward that in the aftermath of a paradigm shift in science, "we may want to say that...scientists are responding to a different world" and that "the scientist with a new paradigm sees differently from the way he had seen before,"[10] so Lévy-Bruhl insists that "primitives see with eyes like ours, but they do not perceive with the same minds," and thus that "the external world they perceive differs from that which we apprehend" (*HNT*, 44, 43). This differential effect testifies, he argues, to the overwhelming influence of cultural systems in the mental construction of reality. Lévy-Bruhl does claim to

---

[8] Lucien Lévy-Bruhl, *How Natives Think,* trans. Lilian A. Clare (1910; Princeton: Princeton University Press, 1985), 18, 23. All further references cited in the text as *HNT*.

[9] Lucien Lévy-Bruhl, *Ethics and Moral Science,* trans. Elizabeth Lee (1903; London: Constable, 1905), 63, 167–68. All further references cited in the text as *Ethics*.

[10] Thomas S. Kuhn, *The Structure of Scientific Revolutions,* 2d ed. (Chicago: University of Chicago Press, 1970), 111, 115.

be able to describe in general terms the governing mechanisms of primitive thought, but his stress falls continuously on the law of the radical relativity of knowledge and of value, and consequently on the virtual impossibility of gaining access to a mentality anchored in a cultural milieu other than our own. He quotes approvingly in this connection a 1904 essay by the Polynesianist Elsdon Best. "We hear of many singular theories about Maori beliefs and Maori thought, but the truth is that we do not understand either, and, what is more, we never shall," says Best categorically, in a formula which Wellek seems to adapt long afterward to the field of literary criticism. "We shall never know the inwardness of the native mind," he concludes (*HNT*, 70).

Lévy-Bruhl presents this relativistic and epistemologically pessimistic schema, as I said, in the guise of a critique of an allegedly credulous Victorian tradition, as embodied in Sir James Frazer in particular. A fuller account of this tradition may help open the way to a view of Frazer less in thrall to the hostile special pleading of his successors (from Lévy-Bruhl and Durkheim to Ruth Benedict to Clifford Geertz and Mary Douglas). As a first step in this direction, we can approach *The Golden Bough* by way of Herbert Spencer, one of Frazer's chief co-practitioners of Victorian "comparative" anthropology.

In Spencer's 1862 manifesto *First Principles,* he predicates modern scientific inquiry on the doctrine that the reality of nature is radically, permanently inaccessible to the human intellect and will forever remain as opaque to knowledge as the Maori mind seemed to Elsdon Best. Spencer did not originate this theory; it has roots in Humean and Kantian philosophy, and more immediately it comes to Spencer, as he emphasizes, by way of two early-Victorian theological philosophers, Sir William Hamilton and H. L. Mansel.[11] But it was Spencer more decisively than any other theorist of his day who identified himself with the doctrine that *the unknowability of the real world was its fundamental characteristic,* and that sophisticated modern science in all its branches needed first and foremost, as the prime condition of intellectual integrity, to incorporate this axiom. He laid down for modern thought, we may say, the paradoxical principle not that knowledge was beyond our grasp—he expressly disavowed any version of philosophical nihilism[12]—but that knowledge and "the Unknowable" were inextricably part and parcel of one another, and that unknown factors condition every

[11] William Hamilton, "Philosophy of the Unconditioned," in *Discussions on Philosophy and Literature, Education and University Reform,* by Sir William Hamilton (New York: Harper, 1855), 9–44; Henry Longueville Mansel, *The Limits of Religious Thought Examined* (1858; Boston: Gould and Lincoln, 1859).

[12] The whole exposition of *First Principles* is designed, he says, to preserve readers "from that error of entire and contemptuous negation, fallen into by most who take up an attitude of independent criticism." Herbert Spencer, *First Principles,* 6th ed. (London: Williams and Norgate, 1908), 8. All further references cited in the text as *FP*.

particle of our knowledge in ways that we have no means of detecting, measuring, taking into account. The implication running through his work, as we will see in a moment, is that any pretense to disentangling these two inseparable categories, the known and the unknowable, can only be fraudulent, demagogic, and dangerous.

In his *Principles of Psychology* (1855), Spencer had previously formulated a detailed account of his theory of the gulf by which the external world was cut off from human understanding. According to this account, which would soon become commonplace among radical thinkers like Ernst Mach, Karl Pearson, and others, all that we are able to know of the world are the sensations or "feelings" which it somehow produces in our perceptual apparatus. By no effort of reason is it possible to infer the nature of external objects on the basis of our perceptions, for between the two "there is no likeness," he says, "either in kind or degree."[13] Even the tragic metaphor of the Lady of Shalott falls short of rendering Spencer's theory of the relation between the observer and the world, since he banishes from this relation all principles of correspondence or mimetic reflection: a perception in no way can be said to resemble or reproduce or have anything in common with the agent which provokes it. Furthermore, perceptions are radically relative to the perceiver, and therefore radically variable, he claims: a given external object is differently perceived by members of different species, by different human observers, even by the same observer at different moments. "Very possibly the ratio [between external cause and subjective effect] is never twice the same," declares Spencer (*PP* 1:198). The nature of reality, as a result, is absolutely "unknown and unknowable" (*PP* 1:206). All we can say with confidence, according to Spencer, is that perceptions stand in a symbolic relation to the real world: "All the sensations produced in us by environing things are but symbols of actions out of ourselves, the natures of which we cannot even conceive" (*PP* 1:194).

Spencer's principle of the impermeability of the real world to direct knowledge has potentially wide significance for a spectrum of fields of intellectual endeavor and of politics, but it applies with unusual directness and force to the field of the human sciences, and notably to that area of it which we now term "anthropology." Spencer develops some of these implications in the oft-reprinted *Study of Sociology* (1872–73). Running insistently throughout the book is the theme of the almost-insurmountable difficulty of sociological analysis. For one thing, there is the "incalculable complexity" of social phenomena, where the variety and the multitudinousness of influences upon any social trend makes it almost quixotic to imagine reducing them to intelligible form or doing valid analyses of them.[14] Spencer illustrates this point with

---

[13] Herbert Spencer, *The Principles of Psychology*, 2 vols. (1855; New York: Appleton, 1896), 1:194. All further references cited in the text as *PP*.

[14] Herbert Spencer, *The Study of Sociology*, 22d ed. (1872–1873; London: Kegan Paul, n.d.), 15. All further references cited in the text as *SS*.

recurring exercises designed to illustrate the vast range of different influences that come into play in such social events as a shift in the price of cotton or the production of a printing press (*SS,* 18–19, 126ff).[15] "Phenomena so involved cannot be seen as they truly are, even by the highest intelligence at present existing" (*SS,* 132). The whole enterprise of sociological study has therefore a paradoxical, self-contradicting aspect in Spencer's manifesto: it entails the concentrated study of things which the human mind is incapable of grasping.

The study of human society is also, Spencer explains, uniquely affected by distortions arising from "the unconscious confounding of observation with inference" (*SS,* 92). Nothing is more profoundly anchored in us or harder to transcend, he declares, than the sentiment that the particular social arrangements and values to which we are accustomed are "natural and even necessary" (*SS,* 133). As a result, in our study of societies other than our own or of politically controversial questions in our own society, scientific objectivity is likely to be overwhelmed by the intrusion of prejudices which "conspire to make the media through which the facts are seen, transparent in respect of some and opaque in respect of others" (*SS,* 92). The ambition of establishing a social science worthy of the name seems therefore to be futile. "How shall we count on true representations of social facts, which, being so diffused and so complex, are so difficult to observe, and in respect to which the perceptions are so much perverted by interests, and prepossessions, and party-feelings?" (*SS,* 76). Social science thus presents in Spencer's account an insoluble conceptual dilemma which epitomizes the problematic character of knowledge in general.

The conundrum of social science expresses itself with maximum clarity in the study of "primitive" and "savage" peoples. Very precociously, Spencer lays out the theoretical problematic in anthropology which Lévy-Bruhl rearticulates several decades later. The scientific study of primitive society necessarily takes the form of a process of interpretation, Spencer insists; its goal is to resolve "seeming inconsistencies" (*SS,* 118), "seeming contradictions" (*SS,* 138), "anomalies" (*SS,* 13), "illogicalities and absurdities" (*SS,* 396) which are manifested by a given society. Like a New Critic explicating a difficult poetic text, Spencer presumes that each system of social life possesses its own organic coherence, at least as it is experienced and conceived by the members of the society in question; by the same token, he presumes that it will appear crazily self-contradictory from the point of view of an outside observer. The function of anthropological study thus defined is the relativistic one of rendering an irrational-seeming social order rational-seeming

---

[15] Spencer in such demonstrations echoes Adam Smith's classic analysis of the ramified social systems that are involved in the production of a day-laborer's coat. Adam Smith, *An Inquiry into the Nature and Causes of the Wealth of Nations,* ed. Edwin Cannan (Chicago: University of Chicago Press, 1976), 1:15–16.

to a member of some other order. This we can only do by imposing our own conceptual and experiential categories "automorphically" upon phenomena that may express different categories altogether for the natives of the society in which they occur. We are compelled to proceed in this unsatisfactory fashion, Spencer insists; we cannot escape our own frame of reference, which is forced upon us by virtue of membership in our own society. "The conception which any one frames of another's mind, is inevitably more or less after the pattern of his own mind—is automorphic," says Spencer. "Even if [an ethnographer]...attempts to see things from the savage's point of view, he most likely fails entirely; and if he succeeds at all, it is but partially. Yet only by seeing things as the savage sees them can his ideas be understood" (*SS,* 114, 115).[16] The received history of anthropological theory hardly prepares one to see this whole problematic, with its seemingly insurmountable aporia at the center, stated so clairvoyantly at the early hour of 1872–73.

In a long series of works Spencer thus articulates a new phase of thinking, one in which it is understood to be an inherent aspect of knowledge, and particularly in cross-cultural and historical studies, that it be unable to give a fully coherent account of itself, and in which scientific and scholarly investigation in whatever domain can only claim to be uncompromisingly rigorous once it has come to recognize its own necessarily indeterminate and conditional character. "Human intelligence," as Spencer said, stating his cardinal principle of analysis, "is incapable of absolute knowledge" (*FP,* 50). With more space at my disposal, I would argue that this crucial vector of Spencer's thinking is inseparable from his critique of authoritarian ideological systems, which he abhorred in all their forms, with what he regarded as an ancestral instinct, from boyhood onward.[17] For now, I mean just to highlight the nineteenth-century genesis of that anxiety about the knowability of other cultural worlds which forms, as we saw, the embedded theme of Victorian studies from the inception of the field, and which expresses itself explicitly in the present volume of essays.

≈

In the work of Spencer's contemporary and fellow explorer in the field of evolutionary anthropology, Sir James Frazer, the doctrine of "the Unknowable" is not so much theorized as it is put directly into practice, at very considerable

[16] Plainly, Malinowski's 1922 declaration that the mission of scientific ethnography is to strive "to grasp the native's point of view, his relation to life, to realise *his* vision of *his* world" (*Argonauts,* 25), was not the wholly new paradigm which it is sometimes assumed to have been. His optimism about the realizability of this ideal seems, if anything, naive in the light of Spencer's analysis long before.

[17] In his *Autobiography,* Spencer identifies what he considers his most conspicuous trait of character, his "disregard of authority, political, religious, or social," with his sternly nonconformist family traditions. *An Autobiography,* 2 vols. (New York: Appleton, 1904), 1:13; see also 1:7, 12, 89.

risk, as the basis of scholarly procedures. What can be the form of an intensive scientific investigation aimed at answering a problem *which by its nature is unsolvable?* This head-spinning question could be said to define all
serious inquiry conducted under the modern intellectual regime, and it receives one of its earliest and most exhaustively searching treatments in *The
Golden Bough.*[18]

The theme of the potentially unfathomable problem is not at first posed
in so many words by Frazer, but it underlies the question that he conspicu-
ously fails to raise in his opening pages and afterward: What is the scientific
purpose that justifies so vast a project of research into such a subject as that
of the half-legendary homicidal priesthood at Nemi? The apparent discrepancy between the obscure antiquarian topic and the monumental effort of
analysis and interpretive reconstruction devoted to it in the course of what
became a twelve-volume work becomes increasingly provocative as *The
Golden Bough* proceeds. Frazer emphasizes it by repeatedly drawing attention, as we shall see, to the deep-running instability of his text, in which ram-
pantly multiplying subthemes threaten to cause the structure of the whole to
disintegrate beyond recall. Also, he more than once appeals to his readers to
recognize the value of the project, even if the theory proposed about the
priesthood, identifying it with a pattern of ritual sacrifice of kingly vegeta-
tion gods, should prove to be wholly erroneous—though he somewhat in-
consistently insists in the preface to the second edition (1900) that his great
work is not to be taken as "a general treatise on primitive superstition," but
merely as an explication of the priesthood.[19] Nothing in the text explains
why one should regard this topic as sufficiently significant to warrant long
investigation, apart from Frazer's famous opening sentence: "Who does not
know Turner's picture of the Golden Bough?"

In his preface to the third edition (1910), Frazer does venture a general
formulation of his topic, one that seems to take us back to Spencer and to
his critique of the superstitious worship of authority—or, as he puts it, "the
emotion excited by embodied power."[20] His theme in *The Golden Bough,*
Frazer says here, is that of "men who have masqueraded as gods," and he
claims to have demonstrated, whatever the truth of the specific theses advanced about Nemi, "that human pretenders to divinity have been far com-
moner and their credulous worshipers far more numerous than had been
hitherto suspected" (*Magic Art,* ix). It is hard to square this statement about
the centrality of the motive of unmasking deified rulers with the actual development of Frazer's work, where the focus falls, rather, on the amazing

---

[18] For convenience, I take my references to *The Golden Bough* from the one-volume abridged
edition of 1922, except where specific reference is made to volumes of the twelve-volume edition. James Frazer, *The Golden Bough: A Study in Magic and Religion,* abridged edition (1922;
New York: Collier, 1963). Further references cited in the text as *GB.*

[19] James Frazer, *The Magic Art and the Evolution of Kings,* 2 vols. (1911; London:
Macmillan, 1917), xxi. Further references cited in the text as *Magic Art.*

[20] Spencer, *Study of Sociology,* 173.

variousness of religious and magical practices in human societies, and on the amazing networks of congruencies traceable among these practices as they manifest themselves in the most remote temporal and geographical locations. Yet a convergence of Frazer's underlying themes with Spencer's may still appear if we reconstruct the former's elusive argument in another way.

In declaring emphatically that the data of science are "merely symbols of the actual" (*FP*, 50) and give no access to the real external world, Spencer signifies his participation in a notable trend of nineteenth-century speculation, the leitmotif of which is the eclipsing of directly apprehensible realities by symbolic simulacra. For example, Spencer echoes Ludwig Feuerbach's theory of the inherent craving of the human mind for symbolic imagery; religion, for example, by its deepest nature "sacrifices the thing itself to the image," says Feuerbach.[21] In Spencer, this sacrifice—bloodless, unlike the ones evoked throughout *The Golden Bough*—occurs not as a motivated event but simply as the condition of all human cognition. The doctrine of the symbolic and relativistic nature of reality does not, however, exercise much practical influence on Spencer's expositions of the various scientific fields to which he turns his attention. As he says, he "unreservedly surrender[s]" himself to the materials of science "as relatively true" and proceeds accordingly (*FP*, 184); the principle of the "merely" symbolic nature of reality figures in this context as little more than a reservation of philosophical conscience and entails no crisis of reasoning. In *The Golden Bough*, on the other hand, what Feuerbach called "the sacredness of the image" (*Essence*, 76) takes the form not of metaphysical dogma but of a new conception of the life of human societies. The new conception dictates an array of new investigative methodologies—and marks the research enterprise in this field as proceeding henceforth in a state of unresolvable crisis.

Anthropology in its earlier nineteenth-century forms had focused on the attempted confirmation of theories of racial determinism by means of evidence supposedly derived from craniometry and other sources and on the ethnological project of reconstructing the migrations of prehistoric peoples. Frazer, along with other practitioners of the "comparative method" such as J. F. McLennan, E. B. Tylor, and Spencer, proposed a new conceptual model in which human social life was understood to be above all a fabric of institutionalized symbolic expression. Virtually every element of social life, from domestic practices to large ceremonial and religious systems, appears to Frazer in the guise of a symbolic representation, a figure of something else—and thus as enigmatic by its very nature. The mission of a student of "primitive" or "early" society becomes for him, therefore, that of deciphering the meanings of complexes of symbolism. Social science under the comparatist dispensation became overtly a hermeneutics, a science not of quantification or (except incidentally) of causal explanation but of *interpretation*.

---

[21] Ludwig Feuerbach, *The Essence of Christianity*, trans. George Eliot (1841; New York: Harper, 1957), 182. Further references cited in the text as *Essence*.

It was at this moment that the relativizing project of learning to see the world from the alien point of view of foreign peoples first established itself on the footing of science, along with the key proposition (as expressed, for example, by Spencer and by Elsdon Best) that membership in a given society entailed immersion in a secret network of assumptions and perceptions which an outsider might be able to penetrate only with great difficulty, if at all.

Frazer's conception of social phenomena and his characteristic analytic method may be illustrated by a discussion of May-tree rituals from early in *The Golden Bough*. He begins by asserting that in various European societies the May tree is conceived to embody an indwelling spirit—that the visible tree is in effect the material image of the invisible "tree-spirit." He then dramatizes what turns out to be a recurrent and a crucial moment in his expository narratives of cultural symbolism: that of the detachment of signifier and referent, and thus the opening of the semantic gap which it will be the specific task of comparatist interpretation to bridge. "We have now to show," says Frazer at a key juncture of his argument, "that the tree-spirit is often conceived and represented as detached from the tree and clothed in human form, and even as embodied in living men or women." This migration of the tree-spirit, or rather of the idea of the tree-spirit, from one figurative site to another, making the tree and the human image symbolically and thus magically equivalent, he claims to illustrate by reference to various materials of folklore.

> There is an instructive class of cases in which the tree-spirit is represented simultaneously in vegetable form and in human form, which are set side by side as if for the express purpose of explaining each other. In these cases the human representative of the tree-spirit is sometimes a doll or puppet, sometimes a living person, but whether a puppet or a person, it is placed beside a tree or bough; so that together the person or puppet, and the tree or bough, form a sort of bilingual inscription, the one being, so to speak, a translation of the other. Here, therefore, there is no room left for doubt that the spirit of the tree is actually represented in human form. (*GB*, 144)

What is striking in this passage and in a host of comparable ones is how insistently Frazer portrays these arrays of symbolic imagery as in effect—or, here, quite explicitly—a linguistic system, a network of interdependent signifiers, one in this case actually indexed with built-in keys to correct interpretation, "as if" to signify both the need and also the considerable difficulty of deciphering such sequences of figurative "translations." Frazer's phraseology calls to mind John Tyndall's protest, in an 1870 essay entitled "Scientific Use of the Imagination," against modern scientists' habit of explaining phenomena only in the hypothetical mode, that of declaring that they occur "as if" in accordance with this or that determining influence. "Our sceptical '*as if*'... is one of the parasites of science," says Tyndall, "ever...

ready to plant itself and sprout, if it can, on the weak points of our philosophy."[22] Frazer's explanatory narrative of May-tree ceremonies is indeed rife with potentially weak points. The tree-spirit is represented metonymically by the tree; the bough synecdochically replaces the tree; the doll is a metonymy of the bough; the living person is a personification of the doll: through the reconstruction of this lengthy chain of representations, the person (the King or Queen of the May) is discovered to be symbolically identical, at several removes, with the tree-spirit. Such a system may function as a system of magic causality in accordance with Frazer's broad theory, but first and foremost it is a legible text, a network of symbolic references which seems pointedly to solicit an observer to decipher its occult logic.

With the emergence of a paradigm such as the one exhibited in this passage, the issue of the intelligibility of social forms—the issue of the permeability of these materials to scientific investigation—immediately presents itself in an acute form. Will it ever be possible to retrieve the meanings supposedly lodged in "primitive" cultural symbolism—or perhaps in any cultural symbolism at all? Will interpretation ever furnish conclusive results, ever be more than sheer guesswork fatally handicapped by "automorphic" preconceptions? Is Frazerian science imaginary in Tyndall's sense, hostage forever to the "sceptical 'as if' "? These questions arise ever more plainly and insistently as *The Golden Bough* unfolds.

For one thing, Frazerian analysis is based on an understanding of the dynamics of cultural symbolism which, rather than moving toward the securing of "meanings" by means of the translation of a symbolic image into a real referent, moves in exactly the opposite direction, seeming instead to disperse and proliferate meaning almost uncontrollably along ever-lengthening chains of symbolic imagery. "From the moment that there is meaning there are nothing but signs": Jacques Derrida's formula exactly describes the overriding principle of Frazerian research and predicts the epistemological vertigo which it unfailingly produces.[23] It is true that the cultural symbols explicated by Frazer do in principle have referents in the natural world and in this sense anchor themselves in determinate "meaning." Speaking of the Egyptian divinity Osiris, he declares, for example, that "there are good grounds for classing him in one of his aspects with Adonis and Attis as a personification of the great yearly vicissitudes of nature, especially of the corn" (*GB*, 420). One notes the characteristic parasite of qualification in Frazer's phrase: "there are good grounds" for the identification of Osiris with the corn. There needs inevitably to be such a qualification, since in fact the exegesis deployed by Frazer is *unable to establish a direct link between symbolic construct and natural referent*. On what testimony or authority could

---

[22] John Tyndall, *Fragments of Science*, 6th ed. (1871; New York: Appleton, 1891), 437.
[23] Jacques Derrida, *Of Grammatology*, trans. Gayatri Chakravorty Spivak (Baltimore: Johns Hopkins University Press, 1974), 50. Further references cited in the text as *Grammatology*.

it possibly do so? It can only seek to make interpretive identifications plausible by the persuasiveness with which it moves, by associative leaps, from one analogy to the next, spanning continents and millennia, along many-branching networks of cultural symbolism—along "the chains, and the systems of traces" (*Grammatology*, 65) which Frazer constructs from his immense archive of far-flung ethnographic materials. Frazerian analysis leads the interpreter of symbolic forms only to constellations of further symbolic forms which, however impressive they may be, will always remain in an auxiliary or preliminary position relative to a "meaning."

This definitive effect of *The Golden Bough* can be observed in little in a thousand passages like the one on May tree imagery cited above. It can be observed still more plainly on the level of the large structure of Frazer's text, where the unpacking of the symbolism of the Nemi priesthood leads, by the inescapable logic of "the comparative method," to volume after volume of compilations of analogous or symbolically interconnected folk practices, ceremonials, and myths, among which the thread of the argument often seems to unravel entirely. We may view this unraveling as an intellectual failure on Frazer's part or, alternately, as just the discursive signature of a vast textual experiment with the mode of scientific logic demanded by an uncompromisingly modernist understanding of the relation of mind to reality. In proceeding according to these principles, in any case, Frazer illustrates on an unprecedented scale the interpretive dilemma identified by William Empson, possibly with *The Golden Bough* itself in mind, in *Seven Types of Ambiguity* (1930). To the extent that an interpreter puts into practice the doctrine that statements in poetry are subject to multiple readings and that "very similar devices of sound may correspond effectively to very different meanings" (in other words, that a symbol requires interpretation), it will be almost impossible to avoid what Empson calls "a hedonism tending to kill language by dissipating [the sense of words] under a multiplicity of associations."[24] This dissipation effect (which interpreters commonly seek above all things to expunge from their work) is so overwhelming in *The Golden Bough* that it would probably be impossible for any reader ever to reduce the argument of Frazer's great work, where the unabridged "multiplicity of associations" forms the ruling principle, to coherent statement. In Spencer's terms, Frazer may be said to discover in the Nemi priesthood one of those phenomena of "incalculable complexity" bound always to foil attempts at conclusive analysis, "even by the highest intelligence at present existing."

What Frazer claims to mean by his crucial category of "meaning" is the "original" sense of a certain symbol. But again, there is no way for comparatist analysis to take us back to the hypothetical originary moment when a certain form of symbolism was instituted, or even to suggest what such an

---

[24] William Empson, *Seven Types of Ambiguity*, 3d ed. (1930; London: Chatto and Windus, 1973), 12, 234.

unimaginable moment might have looked like.[25] All it can do, as I have said, is to give itself over to a form of scholarly repetition-compulsion, elaborating strings of alleged thematic resemblances in the cultural materials of one society after another, no matter how remote. Frazer at an early point introduces the notion of a class of myths "which are made up," he says, "to explain the origin of a religious ritual and have no other foundation than the resemblance, real or imaginary, which may be traced between it and some foreign ritual" (*GB*, 6)—a formulation that may or may not give insight into the cultural invention of myths but very precisely describes the logic of his own scholarly research and the foundationless intellectual environment, where reality and the imaginary are so difficult to distinguish, in which it operates. Whether Derrida is right to assert that *"there is no absolute origin"* in the field of meaning I will not venture to say. But this dictum certainly forms the determining principle of Frazerian anthropological investigation, for all its noisy insistence upon origins (*Grammatology, 65*). It is the inescapability of the Derridean rule that causes *The Golden Bough* to grow uncontrollably, as Frazer recognizes ruefully in the preface of the third edition (1910), into "a ponderous treatise, or rather a series of separate dissertations loosely linked together by a slender thread of connexion with my original subject" (*Magic Art,* vii): in compensation for the impossibility of attaining the "original meaning" of a cultural formation, Frazerian analysis builds vast, ever-more-tenuous structures of analogy.

☙

The notion of a foundation of "meaning" underlying cultural symbolism is destabilized in other ways in *The Golden Bough*. Frazer's interpretive system rests ostensibly on the theoretical foundation of the concept of "homeopathic" or imitative magic. Cultural symbolism according to this theory expresses an "original" belief in the magical identity or interconnectedness of things and images which represent them; a primitive magician thus sticks pins in an effigy of someone he seeks to harm. But this thesis, the linchpin of the argument of *The Golden Bough,* is no sooner stated than it is subjected by Frazer to ever-more-radical qualification. For one thing, he stresses that primitive peoples, in constructing their elaborate systems of symbolic homeopathic magic, do not, in fact, possess any conscious idea of the magical mechanics on which their symbolizing practices are supposedly based. With "the

---

[25] The futility of such a proceeding stands out plainly in *Totem and Taboo,* where Freud does try to imagine a specific primordial moment of the institution of cultural symbolism. Sigmund Freud, *Totem and Taboo: Some Points of Agreement between the Mental Lives of Savages and Neurotics,* trans. James Strachey (1913; New York: Norton, n.d.). Freud's theory of the original parricide is definitively refuted by Bronislaw Malinowski in *Sex and Repression in Savage Society* (1927; Chicago: University of Chicago Press, 1985), 148–72.

primitive magician,...as with the vast majority of men," Frazer explains, "logic is implicit, not explicit: he reasons just as he digests his food in complete ignorance of the intellectual and physiological processes which are essential to the one operation and to the other" (*GB,* 13). The laws of magic "are certainly not formulated in so many words nor even conceived in the abstract by the savage" (*GB,* 22). This may be the inaugural formulation of the principle on which cultural anthropology, not to mention psychoanalysis,[26] has depended ever since—the principle that logical systems of thought can be attributed to people who may be wholly oblivious to them or to collectivities which can hardly be said to possess thought processes at all.[27] Frazer is careful to insist, for example, that the worshipers of divine kings have no distinct conception of the all-important magical bond which, according to *The Golden Bough,* obtains between the king's physical welfare and that of the community. "Probably their ideas on the point are vague and fluctuating," he says, "and we should err if we attempted to define the relationship with logical precision" (*GB,* 686). The project of scientific interpretation on Frazerian principles requires one to do exactly this, however. "It is for the philosophic student to trace the train of thought which underlies the magician's practice," Frazer says (*GB,* 13), exposing himself to the charge that the magical symbolic equivalences which he claims to reveal are not native to a system of primitive thought at all but are simply heuristic devices in the mode of "as if," manufactures of scholarly speculation. Such suggestions, so brazenly made by Frazer, as though to introduce a dangerous instability into the heart of scientific rationality itself, risk rendering the notion of meaning a "vague and fluctuating" one indeed.

The ambiguity of the category of "meaning" for Frazer is further emphasized by the central role which he, like E. B. Tylor and other evolutionary anthropologists of this era, attributes to the phenomenon of cultural *forgetting.* In his analysis, mythology—the great vehicle of cultural symbolism in "early" society—arises as a response to the crisis brought about when people forget what they once meant by what they customarily do, and thus need to invent as an alibi, essentially out of thin air, some new meaning for it. Frazer regularly asserts this cardinal doctrine of his: "Men continue to do what their fathers did before them, though the reasons on which their fathers acted have been long forgotten," he declares, for instance. "The history of religion is a

[26] "It would not be difficult to show that Frazer often comes near to developing a psychoanalytic insight into the unconscious and subconscious motives of human behavior." Bronislaw Malinowski, *A Scientific Theory of Culture and Other Essays* (Chapel Hill: University of North Carolina Press, 1944), 189.

[27] It is invoked distinctly by Malinowski in his study of the Kula system in the Trobriand Islands (*Argonauts,* 11, 12, 83), for example, and by Lévi-Strauss in reference to his own study of phenomena like myth. "It is doubtful, to say the least," the latter says, to suppose that primitive peoples, beyond their fascination with mythological stories, "have any understanding of the systems of interrelations to which we reduce them." Claude Lévi-Strauss, *Raw and Cooked: Introduction to a Science of Mythology,* vol. 1, trans. John Weightman and Doreen Weightman (1964; Chicago: University of Chicago Press, 1983), 12.

long attempt to reconcile old custom with new reason, to find a sound theory for an absurd practice" (*GB*, 553).[28]

These derivative and compensatory mythic inventions have a persistent quality of hallucinatory absurdism in their own right. "After an animal has been conceived as a god, or a god as an animal," says Frazer, explicating the mythic complex centered on Demeter, "it sometimes happens...that the god sloughs off his animal form and becomes purely anthropomorphic; and that then the animal, which at first had been slain in the character of the god, comes to be viewed as a victim offered to the god on the ground of its hostility to the deity; in short, the god is sacrificed to himself on the ground that he is his own enemy" (*GB*, 543). As such a text illustrates, Frazerian anthropological investigation becomes a process of organizing masses of cultural symbolism in terms of a set of basic tropes strikingly like those which came to form the vocabulary of Freudian dream analysis: condensation; splitting; what we can call secondary revision (according to which, as we just saw, myth is invented to give an ex post facto appearance of rationality to absurd-seeming customs); and not least, that version of transference in which the analyst of cultural forms becomes, as the analysis proceeds, the half-acknowledged author of the meanings of primitive cultural symbolism. Culture interpreted as a function of these devices has as its chief characteristic its astonishing power of metamorphosis and of free imaginative creation. It is bound to no grid of fixed or natural modes of understanding the world—it is not bound to the world at all. Rather it constructs its own autonomous world in the medium of fantastically exfoliating symbolic imagery, where tree-spirits, shape-shifting goddesses, sacred plants and animals, and priestly kings and queens freely transform themselves into one another. The domain of cultural symbolism described in *The Golden Bough* is, to take a phrase of Frazer's somewhat out of context, an "ever-shifting phantasmagoria of thought" (*GB*, 825).[29] At the same time, it is essential to emphasize, contrary to a long tradition of commentary, that there is never any question in *The Golden Bough* of tracing cultural imagery to the dynamics of individual psychology or to such a factor as an impulse of emotive expression, whether individual or racial or national; the signifying systems studied by Frazer are all understood to be collective and impersonal ones, structures of social institutions.[30] *The Golden Bough* exhibits in an uncompromising

[28] Lévi-Strauss's theory of myth closely duplicates Frazer's. "The purpose of myth," says Lévi-Strauss, "is to provide a logical model capable of overcoming a contradiction." Claude Lévi-Strauss, *Structural Anthropology*, trans. Claire Jacobson and Brooke Grundfest Schoepf (New York: Basic, 1963), 229.

[29] Durkheim could have been thinking of *The Golden Bough* when he observed that "our representation of the external world is undoubtedly a mere fabric of hallucinations." Emile Durkheim, *The Elementary Forms of the Religious Life*, trans. Joseph Ward Swain (1912; New York: Free Press; London: Macmillan, 1965), 259. Freud defines the representational process of dreams as "the transformation of ideas into hallucinations." Sigmund Freud, *The Interpretation of Dreams*, trans. James Strachey (1900; London: Hogarth, 1958), 50.

[30] See Lévi-Strauss, *Structural Anthropology*, 206, who mistakenly chides Frazer, along with Tylor and Durkheim, for basing their anthropology on an "outmoded psychological

fashion that evacuation of sentimental values that Ortega y Gasset, calling it "the dehumanization of art," defined as the distinctive characteristic of modernist writing.[31]

But is it science? Frazerian "armchair anthropology" has long been repudiated in the name of later fashions of fieldwork-based cultural study. It is by no means clear that this shift of methodology ever yielded or could have yielded a more logically coherent or more genuinely scientific definition of culture than Frazer's—but that is not the point here. The point is rather to highlight his insistence on the incurably unstable character of his own methodology and findings, and his intimation that the ideal of a scientific method free of incoherency and grounded in unconditional objectivity may be an unrealistic ideal, even ultimately an unscientific one. In order to claim legitimacy within the modern regime of thought, he suggests ever more pointedly (though never in a complacent way), knowledge must always be deeply marked with unknowing, must always be problematic, paradoxical, inconclusive. He reminds us with almost compulsive insistency that the explanations he offers are bound always to fall short of definitive proof, to remain conjectural and provisional at best. His entire inquiry, he declares at the outset, is an exercise in "inference" where what he calls "demonstration" will never be attained, and where the best that can be hoped for is what he calls "a fairly probable explanation" of such a riddle as the real meaning of the priesthood of Nemi (*GB*, 2–3). In the concluding paragraphs of his final volume he returns to the same theme, expressly identifying his research enterprise with the impediment with which, specifically in reference to Victorian studies, we began: the ultimate unknowability of the experiential world of another culture. "We can never completely replace ourselves at the standpoint of primitive man, see things with his eyes, and feel our hearts beat with the emotions that stirred his," says Frazer here, in language that echoes Spencer and other late-Victorian writers quoted above. "All our theories concerning him and his ways must therefore fall far short of certainty; the utmost we can aspire to in such matters is a reasonable degree of probability" (*GB*, 823).

The prefaces of the successive editions of *The Golden Bough* give increasingly clear expression to Frazer's disavowal of hope of ever being able to solve the riddles which he has posed for himself, given that "the whole fabric of ancient mythology is so foreign to our modern ways of thought, and the evidence concerning it is for the most part so fragmentary, obscure, and conflicting."[32] It is in the preface to the third edition of *Adonis Attis*

---

approach." For similar statements, see Lévy-Bruhl, *HNT*, 23; Malinowski, *Scientific Theory of Culture*, 188.

[31] José Ortega y Gasset, *The Dehumanization of Art and Other Essays on Art, Culture, and Literature* (Princeton: Princeton University Press, 1968).

[32] James Frazer, *Balder the Beautiful: The Fire-Festivals of Europe and the Doctrine of the External Soul*, 2 vols. (1913; London: Macmillan, 1914), xi.

Osiris, in the dire year 1914, that he offers his most tragic formulation of the scholar's predicament:

> The longer I occupy myself with questions of ancient mythology the more diffident I become of success in dealing with them, and I am apt to think that we who spend our years in searching for solutions of these insoluble problems are like Sisyphus perpetually rolling his stone up hill only to see it revolve again into the valley, or like the daughters of Danaus doomed for ever to pour water into broken jars that can hold no water. If we are taxed with wasting life in seeking to know what can never be known, and what, if it could be discovered, would not be worth knowing, what can we plead in our defence? I fear, very little. Such pursuits can hardly be defended on the ground of pure reason.[33]

Just as mythology in Frazer's system is seen as an attempt by the prescientific mind to provide a guise of rationality for the "absurd practice" of customs whose original meanings have been forgotten, so the doomed, self-contradicting enterprise of scientific scholarly interpretation becomes a vehicle for manufacturing knowledge out of "what can never be known," absurd as such a Sisyphean project may appear.

The founding of a science based on the primacy of interpretation entails for Frazer, then, the increasingly explicit recognition of the Spencerian category of "the Unknowable." When J. T. Merz declared in his four-volume *History of European Thought in the Nineteenth Century* (1896–1914) that the theme of the necessary indeterminacy of scientific knowledge had become central to contemporary thinking, he undoubtedly had Frazer's pronouncements to this effect consciously or unconsciously in mind. "If knowledge is limited to that which is defined with exactitude," says Merz, "it appears to be doomed to be hypothetical, provisional, and uncertain."[34] In the immediately post-Frazerian period, such language becomes commonplace in scientific literature, particularly in the high-profile field of physics. In *The Nature of the Physical World* (1928), to mention just one instance, Sir Arthur Eddington states as his primary postulate that "science aims at constructing a world which shall be symbolic of the world of commonplace experience," and declares that as the final consequence of this postulate, modern scientists "must be content to admit [in their conceptions of reality] a mixture of the knowable and unknowable."[35] The premise and the conclusion read like direct quotations from Herbert Spencer or from Frazer. The more rigorous our intellectual method, says Eddington, the more imperative the need to recognize that *knowledge necessarily falls short.*

[33] James Frazer, *Adonis Attis Osiris: Studies in the History of Oriental Religion,* 2 vols. (London: Macmillan, 1914), ix–x.

[34] John Theodore Merz, *A History of European Thought in the Nineteenth Century,* 4 vols. (1896–1914; New York: Dover, 1965), 3:420.

[35] A.S. Eddington, *The Nature of the Physical World* (1928; Cambridge: Cambridge University Press, 1932), xv, 228.

It is a safe guess that one essential reason for the disavowal of Frazerian comparatism as unscientific by spokesmen for subsequent modes of anthropology lies exactly in Frazer's insistence on this element of the unconquerably unknowable in all attempts to penetrate the mental worlds of remote or past social orders—even as these subsequent modes build directly (rarely crediting him as they do so) on his conception of culture as a fabric of institutionalized symbolism. Lévy-Bruhl makes the point overt, criticizing Frazer in Tyndall-like terms for the unscientific "co-efficient of doubt" which everywhere inflects his analyses (*HNT*, 23). Lévy-Bruhl, who called for the full establishment of "the positive science of social phenomena" (*Ethics*, 6), demanded fidelity to an ideal of certain knowledge, as have others for whom Frazer's refusal to pledge allegiance to this ideal can only seem a sort of professional misconduct. One might think, for example, of Clifford Geertz's declaration that the study of culture is "a positive science like any other" and that "the meanings that symbols...embody" are in principle as exactly determinable by empirical study "as the atomic weight of hydrogen or the function of the adrenal glands."[36] Frazer, however, was increasingly unable to attain so confident a conviction about the prospects of his science, which never could be exempted, or so he taught, from the status of an unresolvable predicament. Facts and the process of interpretation are bound up inseparably together, he declared, and consequently, what Spencer called "the Unknowable" can never be disentangled from knowledge. "What we call truth is only the hypothesis which is found to work best," Frazer says at one point (*GB*, 307). Given this conception of his scholarly enterprise, we can perhaps better understand his strange choice of a subject for investigation. Obscure and undocumentable as it is, the Nemi priesthood evidently attracted him not in spite of belonging to the category of "what can never be known, and what, if it could be discovered, would not be worth knowing," but precisely for this reason. The priesthood is Frazer's synecdoche for the large domain of "insoluble problems," which is, as he and his contemporaries saw with ever-greater clarity, the world of scientific inquiry in general.

The increasing salience of the theme of the unknowability of the past, of the "co-efficient of doubt" which affects all historical reconstruction, thus marks *The Golden Bough* as a key text in the emergence of a post-Victorian philosophy of science. The wide ideological implications of this development call for fuller treatment than can be ventured here. For now, I have sought just to stress that the post-Victorian view was in fact of Victorian manufacture, and to highlight the irony of its manifesting itself in the preoccupation of turn-of-the-century observers with the notion that the mental world of the Victorians themselves had become overnight as strange and incomprehensible as that of "a different race of men," as foreign to the enlightened twentieth century as the Maori seemed to Elsdon Best. As I suggested at the out-

---

[36] Clifford Geertz, *The Interpretation of Cultures* (New York: Basic, 1973), 362–363.

set, this tendentious thesis, foundational as it has been to twentieth-century identity, has always tacitly underlain the field of Victorian studies. Yet no early-twenty-first-century historian need accept in doctrinaire or axiomatic fashion the myth of the Victorian Maori, which was conceived by modernist intellectuals for their own strategic purposes. To emphasize the Victorian genealogy of the philosophy of the Unknowable, as I have in this essay, is to trace the continuity of a crucial line of thought running from the nineteenth century through twentieth-century modernism and through the age of Derrida as well. Without wishing for a moment to countenance so mystified a category as that of "historically authentic interpretation," we may at least learn from writers like Spencer and Frazer to be cautious about assuming too readily or too complacently that Victorian paradigms are irretrievably alien to our own. Perhaps it is time to orient the field of Victorian studies toward a skeptical inquiry into the dominating compulsion of post-Victorian generations to disavow their immediate ancestors.

3. Daniel Deronda

A New Epistemology

GEORGE LEVINE

The crisis of Western epistemology is the mind's incapacity to get outside itself. To protect against a debilitating solipsism, philosophers have posited some kind of universal—Descartes's God, Kant's "supersensible"—that somehow makes *common* sense of the mass of particulars and peculiarities of private feeling and perception. But "common sense" is untrustworthy, and contemporary resistance to universals has often led to a sometimes celebratory skepticism in literary and cultural studies. The publication of Malinowski's *A Diary in the Strict Sense of the Term* marked a critical moment of disillusionment with the scientific nature of ethnography that Malinowski himself had been so important in affirming. As James Clifford has put it, "In the wake of the *Diary* cross-cultural comprehension appeared a rhetorical construct, its balanced comprehension traversed by ambivalence and power."[1] There seems now to be an obvious answer to the question, Can we know another culture? "No." Can we know another human being? "No." Can we know the past? "No." Even trying to know has become a suspect activity.

But "no," or at least a simple "no," won't do. Ironically, if gestures of understanding are really only gestures of power—impositions on others of our own assumptions—solipsism is reinforced, as is the radical individualism that critiques of universalism and objectivity have been aimed at demystifying. The old epistemological struggles were not *only* circuitous investments in developing bourgeois ideologies.[2] The transformation of the "bourgeois subject"

---

[1] James Clifford, *The Predicament of Culture: Twentieth-Century Ethnography, Literature, and Art* (Cambridge, Mass: Harvard University Press, 1988), 112.
[2] Terry Eagleton's analysis of Kant's epistemology and aesthetic theory in *The Ideology of the Aesthetic* (Oxford: Blackwells, 1990) makes a strong case for the ideological implications

into a "cogito" reporting things-as-they-are-always-and-everywhere was an effort to resist the corrosive power of individualism. If that particular structure of knowing has done some dirty work, the refusal of detachment and objectivity may do equal damage and be equally incoherent. It takes detachment to locate the secret ideologies disguised by strategies of detachment, and this performance of detachment in the act of denying its possibility is what Stephen Connor calls the "performative self contradictions" of most relativist contemporary theory.[3] The post-Cold War explosion of ethnic violence and genocide may suggest something of the importance of the ideals of detachment and the objectivity of which it is a necessary condition. The extreme condition of radical epistemological skepticism is not the "conversation" enjoined by Richard Rorty, but war. Although I reject the idea that there is an inevitable connection between epistemological theories and political practice, the stakes in the epistemological wars are high.[4]

Disinterest and objectivity are always impossible and always necessary. Amanda Anderson calls "detachment" an "aspiration" rather than an achievement.[5] Dominick La Capra makes a useful distinction between "objectivism" and "objectivity": objectivist epistemology implies the untenable "objectifying status of a transcendental spectator," but one can, he argues, "defend objectivity in a delimited sense that implies the need to counteract

---

of that theory, arguing that Kant struggles both to affirm the bourgeois individual and to contain his dangerous centripetal energies.

[3] This is another form of the perennial argument against relativism that the assertion of the validity of relativism is not relativistic. Barbara Herrnstein Smith in *Contingencies of Value: Alternative Perspectives for Critical Theory* (Cambridge: Harvard University Press, 1988) offers the most thoroughgoing and thoughtful representation of the relativist position extensively criticized by Connor in *Theory and Cultural Value* (Oxford: Blackwell, 1992), see particularly p. 26, and John Guillory, *Cultural Capital: The Problem of Literary Canon Formation* (Chicago: University of Chicago Press, 1993), 283–303. See also Smith's refutation in *Belief and Resistance: Dynamics of Contemporary Intellectual Controversy* (Cambridge: Harvard University Press, 1998), chap. 6.

[4] Richard Rorty's pragmatist rejection of this epistemological dilemma leads him to a total commitment to the "contingent." "We should," he says, "drop the idea of truth as out there waiting to be discovered." This does not entail, he claims, the view that there is no truth. But "'The nature of truth' is an unprofitable topic." As Rorty knows, however, the work of knowing is still largely informed by the Cartesian paradigm. Contingency and entirely humanist understanding of the world have not, historically, been adequate to inspire sustained or politically practical human action and that explains something of why writers like George Eliot, herself an avowed humanist, could not be satisfied without narratives of passionate, quasi-transcendental value. Rorty's important articulation of his pragmatic contingency is most clearly and forcefully made in *Contingency, Irony, and Solidarity* (Cambridge: Cambridge University Press, 1989). See particularly p. 8.

[5] See Amanda Anderson, *The Cultivation of Detachment: Ethics, Aesthetics, and the Victorian Response to Modernity* (Princeton University Press, in press) for a strong representation of the genealogy of detachment and its value in the construction of a creative cosmopolitanism. See also Anderson's first book, *Tainted Souls and Painted Faces: The Rhetoric of Fallenness in Victorian Culture* (Ithaca: Cornell University Press, 1993). There she demonstrates that the "systems-dominated post-structuralist paradigms do not adequately theorize their normative commitments" (233).

projective reprocessing or rewriting of the past and to listen attentively to
the 'voices,' notably when they pose a genuine challenge by resisting one's
desire to make them say what one wants them to say or to have them become vehicles for one's values and political agendas."[6] In this volume, we
have an example of such listening in Gillian Beer's reading of Edith Simcox.
Such listening was a distinctly Victorian project, and it is in large part the
project of this essay.

The Victorians are often accused of a dangerous scientizing of a falsely
"objective" anthropology. But the late-eighteenth- and early-nineteenth-
century literature of "preprofessional modern ethnography," as Christopher
Herbert has shown, rather than "mystifying the moral and epistemological
predicament of the European observer in primitive society...enacts the con-
flictual interplay of prejudice and ethnographic experience...with an anguished frankness."[7] Herbert shows that evangelical ethnographers were
often caught in irreconcilable tensions between a determination to transform
pagan cultures into Christian ones and the need to know those cultures with
something like "objectivity." As, the impetus toward creating true social *sciences* grew in the nineteenth century, the question of how to achieve the sort
of objectivity required to get to know other cultures or even one's own became critical. Social activism, professionalization of science, epistemology,
and ethics ran into each other, and clergy, philosophers, scientists, novelists,
and poets worried the issue.

The practical urgency of the task of knowing others required strenuous intellectual and moral work. Herbert talks of how

> The cultural anthropologist's idea of the necessity of undergoing "an extremely
> personal traumatic kind of experience" as the prerequisite of shedding preju-
> dice and thus attaining ethnographic truth (defined as entering into another con-
> ceptual world) reproduces closely the Evangelical salvation narrative in which
> an influx of awareness of sin is imagined to be the prerequisite of the shedding
> of egoistic selfhood and the spiritual new birth which follows. (174)

This salvation narrative has its counterpart in the whole history of scientific
epistemology, and it had a peculiar efflorescence among the Victorians.[8] A
condition of knowledge within the Western epistemological tradition is "disinterest," self-effacement or, as Carlyle was to put it, *Selbstödung*. From

---

[6] Dominick LaCapra, "The University in Ruins," *Critical Inquiry* 24 (Autumn 1998): 48.
[7] Christopher Herbert, *Culture and Anomie: Ethnographic Imagination in the Nineteenth Century* (Chicago: University of Chicago Press, 1991), 154–55.
[8] For a discussion of this tradition, see my "The Narrative of Scientific Epistemology," *Narrative* 5 (1997): 228–51.

Descartes to Carlyle and beyond, Western epistemology has always had about it something like an evangelical moral urgency.[9]

The most famous of Victorian writers, most of them now indicted for parading the bourgeois subject as universal, were engaged in just the kind of struggle Herbert describes. When they found themselves inevitably skeptical in ways that anticipate our own hermeneutics of suspicion, they could not rest in the condition but were provoked into anguished struggles to get it right. Getting it right was a moral responsibility and a condition for overcoming a splintering and selfish modernity, a modernity given over, Matthew Arnold believed, to "doing as one likes." The moral failures condemned by everyone from Carlyle to George Eliot were the same as the epistemological ones: acquiescence in the obscuring desires of the self. But, of course, it has been strongly argued that the Victorians' moralized resistance to self-assertion was another form of the bourgeois policing of personal identity.[10] At this point, I would only suggest that this very claim, highly moralized itself, is a confident assertion of an intimate knowledge of another culture. This is to say that there is no way to criticize a culture, its explicit or implicit motives, without assuming an epistemological stance that presumes the possibility of knowing that culture—perhaps better than the culture knew itself. Such critique, inevitably driven more or less by explicit moral urgency, may find, as did the Victorians themselves, a deep and necessary contradiction in its work.

The Victorians are for us another culture, though they reside not in a different geography but in a different time. We know a lot about them, and to begin now denying what we know would be to undercut the very enterprise of critique. Moreover, as Herbert has suggested, Victorian culture harbored all the multiplicities and complexities that make talking about a *singular* culture problematic for us now. The Victorians' relation to these issues may be seen as deeply relevant to our own concerns and puzzles. In this essay I will trace George Eliot's handling of the encounter with another culture as both evidence for a reasonable and important affirmation of the possibility of knowing it and as an anticipation of our own contemporary critiques of this possibility.

While the commitment to scientific knowing was very Victorian, so too was the romantic distrust of the potential heartlessness of detachment. Pure

[9] Lorraine Daston and Peter Galison have argued that scientific objectivity was intensely moralized during the nineteenth century. See "The Image of Objectivity," *Representations* 40 (1992): 81–128. In later essays Daston and Galison consider the relation between objectivity and imagination and historicize the concept of objectivity. They demonstrate how facticity was, as Galison puts it, "a time-specific, hard won and contingent category." *Picturing Science Producing Art*, ed. Caroline A. Jones and Peter Galison (New York: Routledge, 1998), 355; and see the other essays included in that volume.

[10] See David Miller's influential *The Novel and the Police* (Berkeley: University of California Press, 1988).

rationality cannot give access to the life of a past culture: after the appropriate Dryasdust saturation in the archives, one needs, as Carlyle insisted, an act of imaginative sympathy. "The journey into history," John Rosenberg claims, "is for Carlyle always a double journey, backward in time and downward into the self."[11] Self obscures but is also a condition for sympathetic knowing. The way to know the other is through some universal uncontingent self, Schiller's "Person," for example, who would shortly become Arnold's "best self." As Carlyle affirms, access to what lies outside the self is at best fragmentary, but through the obstructions of "foolish noises," to perpetually hindered eyesight, "some real human figure is seen moving: very strange; whom we could hail if he would answer—and we look into a pair of eyes deep as our own, *imaging* our own, but all unconscious of us; to whom we, for the time, are become as spirits and invisible!"[12]

George Eliot's work belongs to this Carlylean, romantic extension of the Enlightenment enterprise. While attempting to resist the rationalizing and disenchanting methods of science, Eliot put her faith in a passionate rationalism (Arnold called it "imaginative reason") as a means to true community. But her programmatic realism threatened to disenchant the world, even as it required an obliteration of self. Yet, since her realist aesthetic was built on the project of knowing other consciousnesses, she was committed to the possibility of historical reconstruction (virtually all of her novels, not only *Romola*, are "historical"). For her, the work of knowing was an enterprise of both epistemological and moral importance: the past mattered then as it matters now, not as a Dryasdust antiquarian collection of dead things but as a continuity helping to determine the way we live now.

Daniel Deronda faces the problem directly, within the scope of a world-historical event: Is it possible to know a culture not one's own? Like *Past and Present*, it sees engagement with the other as morally necessary but possible only through acts of radical self-abnegation; yet, also like *Past and Present*, it finds that only through the filter of a modern self, of a self preoccupied in this case with the failures of modernity, can other cultures become accessible or meaningful. It marks a fundamental development in George Eliot's sense of what it means to know, what it means to be moral, and how knowledge and morality connect. Perhaps, through an act of historical sympathy, it will be possible to read George Eliot as a Victorian not ourself who struggles with our issues and, in struggling, throws new light on them.

Daniel Deronda is, as Alexander Welsh has claimed, "a critique of knowledge."[13] Its ethical, national, and cosmopolitan concerns are intimately con-

[11] John Rosenberg, *Carlyle and the Burden of History* (Cambridge: Harvard University Press, 1985), 16. For a discussion of Carlyle's "hermeneutics" and the importance of sympathy in them, see Suzy Anger, "Carlyle: Between Romantic Hermeneutics and Biblical Exegesis," *Texas Studies in Literature and Language* 40, no. 1 (1998): 78–96.

[12] Thomas Carlyle, *Past and Present* (London: Chapman and Hall, 1899), 50.

[13] Alexander Welsh, *George Eliot and Blackmail* (Cambridge: Harvard University Press, 1985), 306. See all of chapter 14.

nected to its working through of an adequate epistemology of otherness. It worries the question of how to imagine a transcendent self in the midst of a contingent world. From its first famous moment—in what might be called a pre-narrative epigraph—it announces the epistemological difficulty: "that men can do nothing without the make-believe of a beginning."[14] Post-Lyellian science is the literal source of this truth that announces its own fictionality. The strongest realist truth is that its narratives are fictions, and nineteenth-century science increasingly moved to a non-Baconian recognition that only through fictions, that is, hypotheses, could access to the real and the true be achieved. The imagination, in a literary reworking of Kant's theory of judgment, is thus understood to make the connection between the realm of the morally necessary and transcendent and the realm of the empirical and practical understanding. The epigraph then links epistemology with necessary revisions of the realist form, but even more directly with "doing."

As I shall be showing in my reading of *Daniel Deronda,* then, realism was for George Eliot a means to "doing" by way of revealing the disenchanted truth. Hitherto, George Eliot had failed to imagine a condition in which the "hard unaccommodating actual," as she was to call it in *Daniel Deronda,* was not debilitating. The price of realism was Maggie Tulliver's death, Felix Holt's political failure, and Dorothea Brooke's deeply compromised life. *Daniel Deronda* spends half its time reaffirming the often deadly cost of realism, but the other half is spent seeking alternatives. Surrender of self for knowledge of the other entails a kind of death, but refusal to attempt to know the other leads to an anomic society. The struggle to know turns novels like *The Mill on the Floss* or *Felix Holt* into narratives of self-annihilation, but by the time of *Daniel Deronda* George Eliot seems to have believed something was amiss with the Carlylean ideal. One may not live adequately with a self-asserting self; but one cannot live at all without it.

Like Carlyle before her, George Eliot had a modernist sensibility to the difficulties of telling the truth.[15] Knowing that the mirror of the mind was defective,[16] she made the question of its defectiveness a continuing motif in *Daniel Deronda.* Even in the most solemn and truthful moments interest might be the real driving force, as when Deronda tries to persuade Hans not

[14] George Eliot, *Daniel Deronda* (Harmondsworth, Middlesex: Penguin Books, 1986), 35. Further references cited in the text as *DD*.

[15] The complexity of her relation to the truth is particularly well elaborated by Rosemarie Bodenheimer, whose analysis of George Eliot's work and letters exposes sympathetically the evasions and disguised interests that mark George Eliot's most solemnly moral writing and the behavior and pronouncements of her protagonists. See *The Real Life of Mary Ann Evans, George Eliot: Her Life and Letters* (Ithaca: Cornell University Press, 1994), 183–88; 257–66.

[16] She had announced in the famous seventeenth chapter of *Adam Bede* that she felt bound to give "a faithful account of men and things as they have mirrored themselves in my mind," and then to tell, "as precisely as I can, what that reflection is, as if I were in the witness-box narrating my experience on oath." George Eliot, *Adam Bede* (Harmondsworth, Middlesex: Penguin Books, 1980), 221.

to exhibit his painting of Mirah in public (see Bodenheimer, 264). In addition, the very enterprise of mirroring, of refusing to impose one's own will and desires on the mirrored world, creates a bleak and demoralizing abstinence.

Even in *Middlemarch,* self-abnegation is imagined as potentially life-giving. Dorothea Brooke's extraordinary dark night of the soul concludes with her awakening to "the largeness of the world and the manifold wakings of men to labour and endurance." She is awarded her prize in Ladislaw because she accepts the self-diminution the vision implies: that "she was part of that involuntary, palpitating life, and could neither look on it from her luxurious shelter as a mere spectator, nor hide her eyes in selfish complaining."[17] But when, in *Daniel Deronda,* a similar moment befalls a less idealized heroine, there is no redemption and no action. As Deronda reveals to her that he will be marrying Mirah, Gwendolen was "for the first time being dislodged from her supremacy in her own world, and getting a sense that her horizon was but a dipping onward of an existence with which her own was revolving" (*DD,* 876). Understanding at last the radical otherness of Deronda and the world he enters, she is perhaps morally redeemed but the very form of the novel confirms her marginalization by turning to the wedding of Daniel with Mirah and the spiritual betrothal of Daniel and Mordecai. The last paragraphs are not about Gwendolen's "incalculably diffusive" good effects, but about world-historical enterprises. Gwendolen's pain is the end of her story.

George Eliot's virtuous protagonists are able to recognize their own marginality and assume the world's hard indifference to their own desires; so the true scientific investigator accepted "self-humiliation," Bacon had said. As John Herschel had put it in 1830, the scientist must strive for "the absolute dismissal and clearing the mind of all prejudice from whatever source arising."[18] Outside of scientific theory, however, knowledge without such dismissal of all things personal, of all desire, resulted simply in disenchantment and debilitation. At best there are Casaubon's pigeonholes; at worst there is the amoral brutality of Grandcourt.

Romola, a pivotal novel in George Eliot's development, repeatedly addresses "the problem [of] where the sacredness of obedience ended and where the sacredness of rebellion began."[19] But is it possible to rebel "sacredly" against the hard unaccommodating actual? That is the crisis of "realism" and of knowledge. Feminists have fairly complained that George Eliot's preoccupation with the dangers of self-assertion produced a series of women who assert themselves only through self-sacrifice. They live out, as Comte puts it, the ideal of true "resignation": "a permanent disposition to endure,

---

[17] George Eliot, *Middlemarch* (Harmondsworth, Middlesex: Penguin Books, 1965), 846. Further references cited in the text as *M.*

[18] John Herschel, *Preliminary Discourse on the Study of Natural Philosophy* (Chicago: University of Chicago Press, 1987), 80.

[19] George Eliot, *Romola* (Oxford: Oxford University Press, 1965), 483.

steadily, and without hope of compensation, all inevitable evils," because they have "a deep sense of the connection of all kinds of natural phenomena with invariable laws"—laws, that is, that cannot be changed by human intervention.[20] Although both Dorothea and Gwendolen learn this Comtist lesson, Gwendolen has virtually nothing to sacrifice herself for. That Gwendolen's is not Daniel Deronda's decisive story suggests that resignation without hope closed out too many possibilities. And the "Jewish part" of the story opens up, at last, those possibilities.

The ideal of self-annihilation supports a realist epistemology and marginalizes Gwendolen. Distrust of self and desire is as old as Plato's *Phaedo,* and in modern skeptical theory it has reemerged, ironically, since that theory is virtually Platonic in its assumption that the insertion of self and desire into the act of knowing turns knowledge into action, reality into a human construction. The test case in *Daniel Deronda* is the transformation of Deronda into a Jew who will abandon Gwendolen. The problem that the novel confronts is whether reality is out there like a hard determinate thing, or partakes of the nature of mind itself. The novel teeters on the brink of constructivism. Its epistemological crisis is not abstract but has to do with nationhood, other cultures, the transformation of knowledge into action, and its various plots replay the central issue: How is it mentally and morally possible to know others without imposing on them the distorting desires of the aspiring self (without which there would have been no particular reason to understand the "other" in the first place)?

The issue of cultural difference is the issue of the "Jewish part," which is no late-career aberration but a continuing concern of George Eliot; facing it directly required a reconsideration of the ideal of selfless objectivity. From George Eliot's point of view, readers' resistance to the "Jewish part"—which she had predicted—enacts the condition the novel self-consciously sets out to correct. In effect, by insisting on the possibility and necessity of knowing another culture *sympathetically,* the novel is committed to teaching its readers how to read it. It dramatizes the urgency of moving to a new epistemology and the conditions necessary for it.

The experiment was a deliberate risk. To Harriet Beecher Stowe, George Eliot explained that she "expected from first to last in writing it, that it would create much stronger resistance and even repulsion than it has actually met with."[21] She notes later in the same letter how the "impious and stupid" attitudes of Christians not only toward Jews but toward "oriental peoples with whom we come into contact" (*Letters,* 6:301) impelled her to write sympathetically of the Jews. Grandcourt in dinner conversation talks of the Jamaican Negro as "a beastly sort of Baptist Caliban," while Deronda "said he had

[20] Gertrude Lenzer, ed., *Auguste Comte and Positivism: The Essential Writings* (Chicago: University of Chicago Press, 1975), 213.

[21] Gordon Haight, ed., *The Letters of George Eliot* (New Haven: Yale University Press, 1955), 6:301. Further references cited in the text as *Letters.*

always felt a little with Caliban, who naturally had his own point of view and could sing a good song" (376). The rendering of this polite table talk, with its epistemological and ethical edge, suggests something of the animus that drives George Eliot's quest for other cultures—an embittered relationship to the England of imperial modernity that sanctioned through custom and ignorance an unselfconscious brutality.

The alternative to Grandcourtian exploitation is not the ideology of the "white man's burden." Deronda's enterprise, and the enterprise of the book, is to discover other cultures in ways that will recognize their intellectual and spiritual equality with our own. But this is only possible if one becomes, as George Eliot did, as learned as the rabbis themselves: "Only learned Rabbis are so profoundly versed in Jewish history and literature as she is" (*Letters,* 6: 196) wrote Lewes.[22] She seemed to share Matthew Arnold's view that the preliminary to right action is knowledge. In *Daniel Deronda,* then, as George Eliot faced the limitations of human knowing, and affirmed the need to move among fictions, she also dramatized that choices among them required the subjective energies of feeling and desire, that informed choices were also moral choices. The problems of the detachment of objectivity are that they leave the knower with no incentive to know or to act. In her preparations for the novel George Eliot enacted the kind of work La Capra describes in trying to know another culture that is also the novel's subject. The enactment was no assertion of power but of resistance to the ignorance and condescension that marked English relations to Jews.

The continuing implication is that knowledge of other cultures *is* possible—not through passive acquiescence in an unmediated given, and not completely, but, like Carlyle's glimpse of those eyes reflecting his own, lit by the moral energy of a desiring self, reflecting the self. Thus *Daniel Deronda* implies a major revision of the ideal of repressive passivity in the epistemological tradition; implying that even interpretive ventures such as this essay can bring new knowledge of a something not ourselves while belonging also to the contentions of our own time. *Daniel Deronda* implies above all, what I myself am trying to argue in this essay: that the present significance of knowledge of others and of the past need not be an act of domination or a disqualification of the knowledge.

The novel focuses in virtually every scene on failures of understanding, obstructions put up by desire, custom, habit, prejudice, and ignorance to the

---

[22] The centrality of the Jewish question to the enterprise of *Daniel Deronda* is carefully laid out in Michael Ragussis, *Figures of Conversion: The "Jewish Question" and English National Identity* (Durham: Duke University Press, 1995). Ragussis sees the novel as belonging to the tradition of conversion fiction and resisting its conventional directions. He quotes another important letter by George Eliot: "A statesman who shall be nameless has said that I opened to him a vision of Italian life, then of Spanish, and now I have kindled in him a quite new understanding of the Jewish people. This is what I wanted to do to widen the English vision a little." (Ragussis, 266; *Letters,* 6, 304).

recognition of the reality of others. Its primary narrative mode, psychological exploration through free indirect discourse, allows for constant juxtaposition of alternating and diverging perceptions, and implies, in the minuteness of the rendering of the characters' minds, that access to others is possible. The manipulations of time in the first fifteen chapters—replaced later in the novel by juxtapositions of the two major narrative lines—slowly give access both to Grandcourt and to Gwendolen and to the significance of the questions of the first pages. The voice of the narrator is learned, authoritative, insightful, but also engaged.[23] It imposes on both characters and readers the responsibility to know the other, not by force and insistence but by meticulous attention to the psychology and texture of their minds.

This "realist" story enacts that responsibility as much as does Daniel's search for Mirah's brother and his own mother, for its climax is the shock Gwendolen feels when she learns that Deronda had a life altogether apart from her, a shock "deeper than personal jealousy" (*DD,* 876). Deronda, though known inwardly by the narrative, is Gwendolen's other and, ultimately, the reader's. Throughout the novel he ranges beyond the limitations of the other selves who have busily interpreted him. Opening all "facts" to interpretation, the narrator never minimizes the difficulty but instead, as Suzy Anger argues, "enacts interpretive conflicts not to demonstrate indeterminacy, but instead to reveal the conditions for correct interpretation."[24] As the book attempts to reimagine those conditions, it also worries and debates them.

The traditional epistemological position is that we can only know an atom, a star, a geological formation, by overcoming the obstacles of self. G. H. Lewes was impressed with the astronomers' use of a formula called "the personal equation," by which the perspectival limitations of any observer of the stars can be overcome by averaging the conclusions of many different observers.[25] As Lorraine Daston and Peter Galison argue, one of the key strategies of nineteenth-century science was to use refined instruments to overcome the personal limitations of scientists,[26] and Theodore Porter describes how statistics, in a positivist tradition in which George Eliot was much implicated, were designed to overcome both the fallibility of human experimenters and the irregularities of experimental data.[27]

---

[23] In *Narrating Reality: Austen, Scott, Eliot* (Ithaca: Cornell University Press, 1999), Harry Shaw argues that the narrator of *Daniel Deronda* is partly historicized; remaining partly inside the "history" she is, from narratorial distance, understanding and analyzing.

[24] Suzy Anger, "George Eliot and Philosophy" in *The Cambridge Companion to George Eliot,* ed. George Levine (Cambridge: Cambridge University Press, 2001).

[25] For an interesting exploration of the phenomenon and its significance for the development of quantification and its relation to cultural history, see Simon Schaffer, "Astronomers Mark Time: Discipline and the Personal Equation," *Science in Context* 2, no. 1 (1988): 115–46.

[26] In addition to the essays mentioned in note 6 see Daston, "The Moral Economy of Science," *Osiris* 10 (1995): 1–7.

[27] Theodore Porter, *Trust in Numbers: The Pursuit of Objectivity in Science and Public Life* (Princeton: Princeton University Press, 1995).

For George Eliot, however, a new epistemology requires the passionate participation of the self,[28] which is both the most formidable epistemological obstacle and a condition of the truest knowledge, the highest morality. To read the novel requires an epistemology like the one implicit in the novel's experiments with narrative. Against the skepticism implicit in her perspectivalism and sense of the infinite possibilities of interpretation,[29] George Eliot's fictional worlds imply the ethical necessity and the real possibility of knowing other cultures. Such knowing is self-consciously distinguished from the assertion of power—imperial knowing is Grandcourt's kind: "If this white-handed man with the perpendicular profile had been sent to govern a difficult colony, he might have won reputation among his contemporaries" (*DD*, 655), reputation because "he had no *imagination* of anything...but what affected the gratification of his own will; but on this point he had the sensibility which seems like divination"(*DD*, 616; emphasis added).

Grandcourt's egocentric intellectual acuity is juxtaposed with Daniel's selflessness. *Daniel Deronda* reverses the realist disenchantment plot, for, as Franco Moretti claims, "The hero is so mature from the very start as to dissociate himself suspiciously from anything connected with youthful restlessness."[30] Although Moretti suggests that the novel is England's last *Bildungsroman,* it may not be a *Bildungsroman* at all. Deronda moves not from country to city by way of disenchantment but maturely through a series of self-abnegating adventures out of the metropolis entirely, to the Near East. Beginning not by imposing his desires on the world, Daniel has no clearly defined desires or selfhood.

His story is for the most part gendered female, down to his loverlike relation to Mordecai, to whom he is more firmly wedded than he is to Mirah: they meet "with as intense a consciousness as if they had been two undeclared lovers" (*DD*, 552). Leslie Fiedler once remarked that Deronda is one of the most impressive heroines in English fiction, and his secondariness is played out everywhere but in the title: Gwendolen is the star of the opening

---

[28] George Eliot's insistence on the relation between imagination and moral sympathy is a leitmotif of her work, spelled out early in her portrait of Mrs. Tulliver, whose failures of imagination are expressed in her incapacity to recognize a metaphor and are almost tragically enacted by her parallel failure to understand how people will respond to her actions. Imagination (and in its best forms "art" and "fiction") are thus conditions of the moral life, ironically, as in the Kantian philosophic tradition, released from the contingencies that constrain mere rationality.

[29] J. Hillis Miller's well-known essay "Optic and Semiotic in *Middlemarch*" in *The Worlds of Victorian Fiction,* ed. J.H. Buckley (Cambridge: Harvard University Press, 1975) deconstructs George Eliot's apparent attempt to render a "totalized" narrative and history. Miller registers George Eliot's deep distrust of totalizing narrative and the tentativeness of her rendering of "reality." But he ignores the energy of *Middlemarch*'s engagement with the epistemological issues and George Eliot's commitment to the rigors the nonverbal world impose on the endless possibilities of language. See also Miller's "Narrative and History," *ELH* 41 (1974): 455-73.

[30] Franco Moretti, *The Way of the World: The* Bildungsroman *in European Culture* (London: Verso, 1987), 8.

chapters, Deronda her secret conscience; Hans is made the star at Cambridge through Deronda's sacrifices for him; Mirah, rescued and protected by Deronda, becomes the singing star of high society London. Ironically, then, like the protagonists of the female *Bildungsroman,* Deronda must learn not to deny but to assert himself. He knows how to know, but he must learn how to desire.

The first epistemological crux comes in the description of Deronda's mind as he floats down the Thames on the day he rescues Mirah. For the most part, the passage is in free indirect discourse, as is much of Gwendolen's experience. But where in the Gwendolen passage that technique allows for juxtapositions and ironies, in the Deronda passages—his mind often rendered inside quotation marks, almost as interior speech—there is a narrative immersion that works like a strong endorsement of the movements of his consciousness. Psychological realism is joined to lyric intensity in a way that has disappointed critics for a hundred years but that is certainly central to the novel's project. In the passage below, the distinction between intellectual and passional work is deliberately blurred:

> It was his habit to indulge himself in that solemn passivity which easily comes
> with the lengthening shadows and mellowing light, when thinking and desiring
> melt together imperceptibly, and what in other hours may have seemed argu-
> ment takes the quality of passionate vision. (*DD,* 229)

(The moment anticipates the scene of Mordecai's virtual evocation of Deronda from the water—a moment blending thought and desire.)

In the sequence that follows, Deronda undergoes that very act of self-obliteration that might be taken as the ideal condition of scientific objectivity. Knowledge becomes possible because the self is decentered:

> He was forgetting everything else in a half-speculative, half-involuntary identi-
> fication of himself with the objects he was looking at, thinking how far it might
> be possible habitually to shift his centre till his own personality would be no less
> outside than the landscape. (*DD,* 229)

Missing from this ideal intellectual prostration, this visionary embodiment of objectivity, is the impetus to act at all.[31] The world of knowledge available to such a mind is limited exactly by the absence of passional energy and thus of the fullest imagination.

[31] It is another version of the crisis described in John Stuart Mill's *Autobiography,* ed. Jack Stillinger (Boston: Houghton Mifflin, 1969): "To know that a feeling would make me happy if I had it, did not give me the feeling. My education, I thought, had failed to create these feelings in sufficient strength to resist the dissolving influence of analysis, while the whole course of my intellectual cultivation had made precocious and premature analysis the inveterate habit of my mind. I was thus, as I said to myself, left stranded at the commencement of my voyage, with a well-equipped ship and a rudder, but no sail" (84). Deronda's selfless floating down the Thames is an embodiment of Mill's metaphor.

Deronda is rescued by the virtues of his selflessness, and by chance. A character without desire depends on chance (that is, the desire of the narrator), and George Eliot rewards her protagonist precisely at the moment of fullest self-annihilation. Mirah is the accident of Deronda's passivity and his reward, providing him with the "sail" that pushes him toward vocation—the true object of Victorian *Bildung*.[32] Decentering the self becomes the preliminary moral *and* intellectual act. Mirah brings with her not only her own life, which would make the typical subject of romance, but her brother's vocation, and both open for Deronda the energies of desire and will. As he tells Gwendolen during their last interview, "what makes life dreary is the want of motive" (*DD*, 839). So in this first exploration of Deronda's epistemological condition the narrative makes clear the importance for meaningful knowledge of a strong selfhood, without which one can only float chancily downstream.

As early as an 1855 essay on Milton, George Eliot had argued against the absolute ideal of impersonality that then reigned, at least theoretically, in the realms of both knowledge and ethics. She claimed that "there is much unreasonable prejudice against this blending of personal interest with a general protest." For, she argued, "if we waited for the impulse of abstract benevolence or justice, we fear that most reforms would be postponed to the Greek Kalends." "Personal interest," she concluded, "may lead to exaggeration... but *in* itself it is assuredly not a ground for silence but for speech, until we have reached that stage in which the work of this world will be all done vicariously, everybody acting for some one else, and nobody for himself."[33]

Deronda's education unfolds within a society whose dessicated culture is attributable in large part to complacently provincial ignorance of its own past and of other cultures on whom it preys and with whom it lives. Like Grandcourt, who becomes its evil representative, Victorian culture is revealed as indifferent to anything but its own phlegmatic will. The narrative implies that British society can only be saved from its decadence by way of a new animation, a reenchantment. Rationalist disenchantment—in effect a form of literary realism—must give way to a new spirit that yet remains faithful to hard unaccommodating reality, differing from the disenchanted past only because it understands that what lies out there to be "discovered" is well beyond what a methodical rationality can perceive. The spirit is finally available only through the culture's understanding of its relations with others and of its own history. Sir Hugo's stables, remodeled from an old chapel, where Deronda takes off his hat and Grandcourt sneers, become a place of reenchantment. In the end Deronda—though with a skepticism that reinforces

---

[32] See Alan Mintz, *George Eliot and the Novel of Vocation* (Cambridge: Harvard University Press, 1978).

[33] "Life and Opinions of Milton," in *Essays of George Eliot*, ed. Thomas Pinney (New York: Columbia University Press, 1963), 156.

George Eliot's commitment to right knowledge and its relation to action—will take the reader back to Biblical origins in order to make a better future. But Gwendolen's disenchanted story, the narrator tells us, is "a small social drama almost as little penetrated by a feeling of wider relations as if it had been a puppet-show" (*DD, 186*).

George Eliot's critique of English culture is most clear in her insistence on the need to fuse knowledge with feeling. As Welsh puts it, "The fusion of knowledge with feeling, something George Eliot has always advised in moral relations, has now become programmatic and an alternative to the commonplace and threatening exchange of information" (*DD, 304*). Klesmer's contempt for the heavy materialist condition of English culture and politics plays out an aspect of George Eliot's view that knowledge only matters when it is informed by feeling; and the stories of Mordecai and his Zionist vision and Deronda and his discovery of his parents provide the ideological and personal energy to make knowledge possible. But the epistemological problem—one which most critics of the novel still insist is not soluble—is to distinguish between the feeling and will that drive an adequate conception of truth and what she calls "the habitual lazy combinations begotten by our wishes" (*DD, 280*).

One of the major difficulties for contemporary readers of the novel is that they regard the specific "truth" Deronda and Mordecai find as disturbing—the commitment to Zionism and what would seem to be nationalism that George Eliot develops as an option to the selfish provincialism of English culture. Here George Eliot seems susceptible to John Mclure's critique of postcolonial literature: The romance quest of Westerners for the redeeming sacred that has been banished from disenchanted post-Weberian modernity reenacts in more subtle ways the strategies of imperial domination and exploitation.[34] Ignoring the particularities of the non-Western cultures, the terrible politics of starvation and repression and exploitation, new postcolonial romancers find spiritual solace in a world they hope is not yet subject to the rationalizing of modernity. What George Eliot seeks in Jewish culture might be seen as just that sort of reenchantment.[35]

Mordecai's romantic nationalism can be dangerously blind to other cultures in just the ways George Eliot's new epistemology would seem designed to avoid. But Deronda's relationship to romantic nationalism is equivocal. The novel explores and values the cosmopolitanism normally associated with the Jew (Catherine affectionately praises Klesmer's "cosmopolitanism" to Mr. Bult, for example): its emphasis on rootlessness is precisely antinationalist and makes it to be just the condition in which we find (the then-still Christian) Deronda at the moment he meets Mirah.

[34] John McClure, *Late Imperial Romance* (London: Verso, 1994).
[35] I have minimized in this analysis any discussion of Zionism, which might be taken as an almost logical outgrowth of the epistemology of the novel and an imperial use of knowledge and history, but which in George Eliot's thought developed in the 1870s provided a means to avoid the imperial moral provincialism the novel partly dramatizes.

I do not mean to deny George Eliot's commitment to a nationalist project, but her nationalism, as it comes through Deronda, is not Mordecai's romantic nationalism. Anderson notes that Deronda becomes a "Zionist" as Mordecai would have him, but as a questioning and not thoroughly converted Jew. He tells Kalonymos, "I will call myself a Jew...But I will not say that I shall profess to believe exactly as my fathers have believed" (*DD*, 792). He insists, rather, on preserving the valued culture of the Christianity he grew up with, and he goes to Palestine not to establish the Jewish state but to inquire into its possibility. His relation to nationalism is "reflective and dialogical"[36] rather than visionary and essentialist. Zionism itself melds with the epistemological project of the novel: when Mordecai asks that his thought be "born again" in Deronda, Daniel replies, "You must not ask me to promise that" (*DD*, 820). Rather, Daniel "must be convinced."[37]

Gillian Beer has argued that rejection of all Victorian anthropologists as racists merely "flatters ourselves." Much to the point of this volume, she adds: "Moreover, such blanket rejection makes it impossible for us to hear a range of available meanings."[38] It is not difficult—consistent with the strategies of much recent cultural study—to discover *Daniel Deronda*'s complicity in the nationalist provincialism it rejects and satirizes; but the novel, like most literature, gets interesting exactly where it resists complicity. As one of her "experiments in life," *Daniel Deronda* explores possibilities George Eliot had earlier rejected and struggles to escape the inevitable containments of culture, self, and society. The novel celebrates attention to detail, in Klesmer's art or in Deronda's sympathetic imagination, and demands of its readers a recognition of the importance of such attention as a requisite for that opening to otherness that is its subject and its moral objective.

Hearing those "available meanings" requires an enormous leap of the moral imagination. That is one of the reasons the Jewish sections open with the crass and banal Cohen family rather than with the messianic Mordecai. The novel assumes a resistant audience, a Bult-like, Arrowpoint-like culture that is vaguely but consistently anti-Semitic. The qualities that lead to the dead individualism of a disenchanted contemporary England are qualities that also close out the potentialities for spiritual revitalization she finds in Judaism. But encountering Judaism requires not a mystified appropriation of a people still unknown and disdained or romanticized but risk-taking efforts at knowledge. When Daniel explains to Gwendolen what he intends to

---

[36] Amanda Anderson, "George Eliot and the Jewish Question," *Yale Journal of Criticism* 10 (1997), 49.

[37] Bernard Semmel, in his *George Eliot and the Politics of National Inheritance* (New York: Oxford University Press, 1994), reads *Daniel Deronda* as the expression of a more rigidly nationalist program than Anderson does but also shows that George Eliot was consistently hostile to imperial ventures and the denigration of other races.

[38] Gillian Beer, *Open Fields: Science in Cultural Encounter* (Oxford: Clarendon Press, 1996), 77.

do, he indicates that it is partly a voyage of discovery, "to become better acquainted with the condition of my race in various countries there" (*DD*, 875). His admiration and affection for Mordecai does not make him a Zionist but makes Zionism a possibility to be pursued only *after* a voyage of discovery: impelled by a Zionist idea, an ideology as Welsh would call it, Deronda pursues knowledge.

George Eliot is aware of the dangers here, and anticipates the kinds of critique that the Victorians and, interestingly, our contemporary readers are ready to level at her. She recognizes the threats of fanaticism, hidden motives and greeds, and the inevitable limitations of particular human consciousnesses, and she tries to distinguish between the practical realities of contemporary Jewish life—threatened by commercial rationalization—and the visionary ideal of Mordecai. (In fact, it is not difficult to detect in the narrator's white-glove consideration of the Cohen family and of Jewish commercial life in the East End her struggles against her own provincialism and prejudice.) Her treatment of Mordecai's intellectual enterprise is the focus of her epistemological experiment. It dramatizes the possibility that it might be invalidated by his passion and provides other characters' skeptical commentary—exactly of the sort to which later critics have subjected it. But his story is a representation of George Eliot's struggle toward a more adequate way of knowing—a way both intellectually rigorous and humanly satisfying.

A valid epistemology, as George Eliot found it argued in the work of Comte and Mill, must cross disciplines and the problem of knowing crosses all its "objects," from inorganic nature, to humans, to culture itself; this continuity is marked in the novel's prose. When Deronda finds Mirah, the narrator notes that "the moment of finding a fellow-creature is often as full of mingled doubt and exultation as the moment of finding an idea" (*DD*, 236). "Who can all at once describe a human being?" (*DD*, 145) asks the narrator, whose business, after all, is to describe human beings.

The book begins problematizing that business. The epigraph is followed by the famous anticipatory questions about Gwendolen (was she beautiful or not, evil or not, what was the "secret form" that "gave the dynamic quality to her glance"). These are also questions about how the observer feels about what he sees, what were the effects upon him of Gwendolen's appearance (*DD*, 35). Such interactions between fact and perception and feeling make the continuing subject of the novel.

One of the reasons deconstructive readings have been good at finding radical indeterminacy in George Eliot's writing is that she was almost preternaturally sensitive to particulars and to the possibility—the inevitability—of multiple interpretations. Deronda knows and the narrator asserts that "there is no guarding against interpretation" (*DD*, 323). So, for example, the relation between Deronda and Gwendolen, as perceived by everyone except Deronda, is interpreted as sexual. Deronda interprets Sir Hugo's silence about

Deronda's paternity and the fact that Sir Hugo imagined him as having a career as a singer as evidence that he is a bastard. The scrutiny of the multiple perspectives and interests that fill her novels makes knowing enormously difficult. Gillian Beer emphasizes George Eliot's attempt in *Daniel Deronda* to dislocate the sorts of sequential and perhaps determinist narrative explanations that mark the earlier novels.[39] But while it is true that the novel points toward an undetermined future and that its manipulation of chronology and juxtaposition of apparently incompatible plots overturn the narrative modes of her earlier novels, these efforts are directed not at a rejection of the possibility of knowing but at a reimagination of epistemology.

It is one of the apparent paradoxes of George Eliot's work that her narrators speak sagely and authoritatively even as they demonstrate that "interpretations are illimitable." Rosemarie Bodenheimer claims that George Eliot's final action after *Daniel Deronda* was an "explicit abandonment of the all-wise narrative voice" (*Real,* 265), because, she claims, in *Daniel Deronda* George Eliot had deconstructed sympathy. In Daniel's mentoring of Gwendolen, the voice is tested, and its limits exposed: Daniel cannot sustain fully sympathetic action, whatever he might say and feel, because he has a life with conflicting commitments and desires. Gwendolen sees him as a potential lover, but Daniel *must* abandon her for another woman and another vocation. The sequence puts to the test the narrator's own authority and all-embracing sympathy by giving Deronda parallel narrative authority with Gwendolen and then dramatizing the impossibility of self-sacrifice unqualified by the compromising conditions of a particular life under particular conditions. Ambivalences and uncertainties emanate from a text so attentive to the ways the desiring self encroaches on wisdom and sympathy.

But such strenuousness and doublings back create the condition for a new epistemology. In another epigraph (to chapter sixteen) George Eliot talks of how "men, like planets, have both a visible and an invisible history. The astronomer threads the darkness with strict deduction, accounting so for every visible arc in the wanderer's orbit," and the "narrator of human actions" would have "to thread the hidden pathways of feeling and thought which lead up to every moment of action" (*DD,* 202). Narrator and scientist, as with Lydgate in *Middlemarch,* who "wanted to pierce the obscurity of those minute processes which prepare human misery and joy" (*M,* 194), must discover and disentangle the multiple threads of connection; a broader and more creative epistemology can grow only from such laborious work at the disturbing contingencies that make the fact difficult to pin down.

George Eliot has no illusions about the possibility of getting it all right. Mere mental energy and systematic thought cannot do it. All of her notebooks and essays and novels insist on limitation and the inadequacy of sys-

---

[39] See Gillian Beer, *Darwin's Plots: Evolutionary Narrative in Darwin, George Eliot, and Nineteenth-Century Fiction* (London: Routledge and Kegan Paul, 1983), 181–209.

tems and formulae: "There is no general doctrine which is not capable of eating out our morality if unchecked by the deep-seated habit of direct fellow-feeling with individual fellow-men" (*M*, 668).

But it is only in *Daniel Deronda* that George Eliot risks challenging the ideal of a rational and detached objectivity with her deep-seated belief that knowledge is always implicated in and sustained by feeling. Objectivity for her is possible not through elimination of the self and feeling but through disciplined intensity of feeling. In a passage titled, "Feeling is a sort of Knowledge," she wrote in her notebooks that

> what seems eminently wanted is a closer comparison between the knowledge which we call rational & the experience which we call emotional. The sequences which are forced upon us by perception, which establish fundamental associations, & are classed as knowledge are accompanied in varying degrees by satisfaction, & denial or suffering, to the organism in proportion as the established sequences are affirmed or disturbed.[40]

That "closer comparison" is the focus of the drama between Mordecai and Daniel, and the epistemological crisis of the book.

That crisis, marked by the validation of Mordecai's wishful enterprise of turning Daniel into a Jew, is dependent on the presence in the novel of George Eliot's old realist and objectivist vision. "The truth is sometimes different from the habitual lazy combinations begotten by our wishes" (*DD*, 286), she notes about the Arrowpoints' assumptions concerning their daughter's marital prospects. And in yet another epistemological epigraph, beginning with the common view that "knowledge is power," George Eliot insists that it is dangerous intellectually, morally, and politically to have what she calls "false conceit of means whereby sequences may be compelled" (*DD*, 268).

The novel does not underplay the way in which Mordecai's mind lives outside the rules of causality, system, sequence, self-restraint, but registers the difference between the moral and intellectual pressure it puts on Gwendolen's story and the passional endorsement it gives to Mordecai. There is an almost defensive care in the narrative's insistence that a commitment to objectivity and disinterest is not incompatible with the vision that ostensibly defies such a commitment.

The aspect of her thought that gets played out most fully in the Mordecai sequences is an idea she had articulated in her essay on the evangelical preacher, Dr. Cumming:

---

[40] George Eliot, *More Leaves from George Eliot's Notebook,* ed. Thomas Pinney, *The Huntington Library Quarterly* 29 (August 1966): 364. Lewes argues at one point that "Ideas are moving forces only in proportion to their emotional values, or, physiologically expressed, to the intensity and extension of the innervation they excite." *Problems of Life and Mind,* 3d series (Boston: Houghton Mifflin, n.d.), 444. The epistemology implicit in the treatment of Mordecai's visionary knowledge is strongly connected to this ostensibly "physiological" theory.

That highest moral habit, the constant preference of truth both theoretically and practically, preeminently demands the cooperation of the intellect with the impulses; as is indicated by the fact that it is only found in anything like completeness in the highest class of minds.

The cooperation of impulses with intellect is a condition of knowing other cultures, and of any true knowing. Mordecai is described as capable of such cooperation. And Deronda, in the face of Mordecai's apparent fanaticism or delusion, is described as having a nature "too large, too ready to conceive regions beyond his own experience, to rest once in the easy explanation, 'madness,' whenever a consciousness showed some fullness and conviction where his own was blank" (*DD,* 551).

The juxtaposition of realist/"intellect" and romantic/"impulse" aspects of the novel develops in the consistent comparison of Mordecai to a scientific investigator. When he sees Deronda rowing toward him, "His exultation was not widely different from that of the experimenter, bending over the first stirrings of change that correspond to what in the fervour of concentrated prevision his thought had foreshadowed" (*DD,* 550). "Visions are creators," Mordecai says, and the novel lets him get away with it because it translates "vision" into "concentrated prevision"—the scientist's passionately attentive imagination of possibility.

But Mordecai is also shown to be practical and sensitive to the particulars of everyday life. He wins the affection of the little Cohen boy, is responsible to the Cohen family, and shrewd and humane in dealing with the father. "He had a mind energetically moving with the larger march of human destinies, but not the less full of conscience and tender heart for the footsteps that tread near and need a leaning place" (*DD,* 605). So the contemptuous judgments of English society, even of the good but morally dense Sir Hugo, who regarded Mordecai as a "consumptive Jew, possessed by...fanaticism" (*DD,* 568), is juxtaposed with the practical realities of Mordecai's life. The narrator anticipates the possibility that Sir Hugo's "common sense" might be right:

> Reduce the grandest type of man hitherto known to an abstract statement of his qualities and efforts, and he appears in dangerous company: say that, like Copernicus and Galileo, he was immovably convinced in the face of hissing incredulity; but so is the contriver of perpetual motion. We cannot fairly try the spirits by this sort of test. If we want to avoid giving the dose of hemlock or the sentence of banishment in the wrong case, nothing will do but a capacity to understand the subject-matter on which the immovable man is convinced, and fellowship with human travail, both near and afar, to hinder us from scanning any deep experience lightly. (*DD,* 569)

Deronda determines to "understand the subject-matter," and thus to entertain the possibility Mordecai's "wish-begotten belief" in his Jewish birth might be a preparation for a real "discovery."

The juxtaposition of the two plots, usually taken, by way of Henry James and F. R. Leavis, as a mistake, is a critical part of the epistemological testing. The movement toward the form of romance (with Gwendolen standing in the wings suffering her realistic anguish) is obviously part of the point. Reshaping the ways in which we know entails reshaping our narratives, and romance is the means by which impulse might be paired with intellect and by which the world might be reenchanted, the strange might become familiar. "The world would be a poor place," says Mrs. Meyrick, "if there were nothing but common sense in it" (*DD*, 629).

At last, through free indirect discourse again, George Eliot approaches the key passage in determining the possibility of taking seriously an epistemology that depends upon wish and desire. Deronda broods on the question of Mordecai's need for him and finds "a more plausible reason for putting discipleship out of the question." The reason:

> The strain of visionary excitement in Mordecai, which turned his wishes into overmastering impressions, and made him read outward facts as fulfillment. Was such a temper of mind likely to accompany that wise estimate of consequences which is the only safeguard from fatal error, even to ennobling motive? But it remained to be seen whether that rare conjunction existed or not in Mordecai: perhaps his might be one of the natures where a wise estimate of consequences is fused in the fires of that passionate belief which determines the consequences it believes in. The inspirations of the world have come in that way too: even strictly-measuring science could hardly have got on without that forecasting ardour which feels the agitations of discovery beforehand, and has a faith in its preconception that surmounts many failures of experiment. And in relation to human motives and actions, passionate belief has a fuller efficacy. (*DD*, 572)

This passage, so often taken as George Eliot's desperate reaching after the ideal, accurately describes many episodes in the history of science in which scientists pursued ideas with "concentrated prevision" beyond their apparent disproof. Darwin, against an extraordinary array of arguments, against failure to find the evidence necessary in the fossil record, against the perhaps decisive fact that species evolution has never been seen, persisted in his theory. Moreover, almost all scientific work is conducted against the evidence until the evidence can be created to affirm the hypothesis. Hypothesis—that is, fiction, often driven by wish—is the motive force of scientific experiment. Michael Ghiselin has argued that Darwin's "entire scientific accomplishment must be attributed not to the collection of facts, but to the development of theory."[41] Scientists do not simply lay themselves open to "vast accumulations of fact," on the Baconian method. They read themselves and their fictions into the facts and try to make their hypotheses true. Darwin did not,

[41] Michael Ghiselin, *The Triumph of the Darwinian Method* (Chicago: University of Chicago Press, 1969), 4.

as he claimed, work on true Baconian principles but, as Jonathan Smith shows, demonstrated that "real science was more interesting, more imaginative, and more difficult than Bacon made it out to be."[42] Deronda's displacement of self into the objects he observed would not have been enough for achieving true knowledge.

In imagining the possibility that Mordecai's "passionate belief determines the consequences it believes in," and aligning that possibility with the real history of science, George Eliot approaches constructivism, which for her is still realism, but with human agency. That is, she is committed to the view that the world is out there to be known, but also to the view that knowing it entails the work and shape of human consciousness. The Kantian skepticism about knowing "the thing in itself" passed into the thought of nineteenth-century positivism, but in their hands, and in George Eliot's, the hard unaccommodating real retained its pragmatic reality and had to be engaged. At the same time she also believed that no system unqualified by the complexities of human feeling and the particularities of each separate instance could ever work.

It is important to note, however, that as "realistic" knowledge requires the obliteration of self, so too, it seems, does the new epistemology, even if it is designed to affirm the value of human life and feeling. The prime knower, Mordecai, like Moses, does not reach complete knowledge. Even as Daniel Deronda moves to an epistemology that breaks from self-humiliation, Mordecai acts out a drama of self-humiliation before the truth he half-creates and half-perceives. *Perhaps* Daniel will enter the promised land, as Moses-Mordecai dies at its borders, but the novel does not say. The ideal of selflessness remains necessary for George Eliot even as her narration attempts to transcend it. The epistemological end of both narratives is oddly the same.

Moreover, while affirmation of the centrality of human well-being to the enterprise of knowing is central to this new epistemology, it brings with it considerable danger, including its capacity to rouse the ire of hard-line scientific realists. The book strategically anticipates the validation of Mordecai's belief about Deronda by way of realistic clues planted from the start so that a careful reading would show that Deronda's Jewishness is not ultimately invented either by George Eliot or by Mordecai but is "realistic." There is reason to be skeptical about this, for it might be taken that George Eliot's manipulations threaten an intellectual and moral authoritarianism that forces the willed transformation of Deronda and gives it the strong moral aura of Mordecai's passionate selflessness.

George Eliot's ideal of self-sacrifice doesn't die easily, and her investment in it may have caused her to miss the way selflessness can become a kind of moral tyranny. Mordecai's romantic mysticism imposes on the weaker Daniel

[42] Jonathan Smith, *Fact and Feeling: Baconian Science and the Nineteenth-Century Literary Imagination* (Madison: University of Wisconsin Press, 1994), 19.

and Mirah, and the epistemology of desire might well encourage that tyranny. Yet with all the negative possibilities and dangers, of the sort that, for example, Victorian empiricists themselves criticized in the thinking of idealists and a priorists, George Eliot's complicated sense of epistemological possibilities, played out in the relations between Mordecai and Deronda, is not merely wishful thinking. It is a difficult conception, the idea that feeling is a condition of knowledge and yet that knowledge must trump desire. When, as in Mordecai's proselytizing of Daniel, the coincidence of desire and knowledge may seem (and does seem) a mere authorial contrivance. But the problem is in the very difficulty of the conception and in the assumptions driving a hermeneutics of suspicion. In the end, it seems to me, that the narrative of *Daniel Deronda,* however awkwardly it stumbles on the way, achieves a valid perspective on epistemology, if a perspective that needs further refinement. George Eliot, I would argue, is right that "objectivity" can never be divorced from feeling; right in the recognition that every case where feeling and objectivity might seem to be in conflict requires the most intense and meticulous scrutiny; right in the recognition that the presence of feeling and desire is *not* disqualifying of the knowledge achieved.

George Eliot never sacrificed her belief in the possibility of knowing, of reaching beyond the limitations of self to facts, and texts, and cultures alien and remote from her own. She insisted on the "the inevitable makeshift of our human thinking" (*DD,* 572), but at the same time recognized and dramatized in *Daniel Deronda* the deadly cost of remaining provincial, of not trying to know. In terms startlingly like those of George Eliot, James Clifford asserts, against the very obstacles he has himself described—of self and cultural difference and disguised ambitions for power—the importance of the ethnological enterprise. "It is more than ever crucial," he claims, "for different peoples to form complex concrete images of one another, as well as the relationships of knowledge and power that connect them; but no sovereign scientific method or ethical stance can guarantee the truth of such images."[43] If the Baconian model of scientific objectivity and receptivity to the facts entailed, finally, a condition of "dying to know," George Eliot sought in her last great novel a way of thinking that could lead at last to the promised land in which instead of dying to know, we live by knowing.

[43] James Clifford, *The Predicament of Culture,* 23.

PART II

VICTORIANS THEORIZING

4. *Walter Pater's Impressionism and the Form of Historical Revival*

CAROLYN WILLIAMS

By 1927 Virginia Woolf could joke—from a point of view focused through the character of Lily Briscoe—about the work of Mr. Ramsay's epistemology:

> Whenever she "thought of his work" she always saw clearly before her a large kitchen table. It was Andrew's doing. She asked him what his father's books were about. "Subject and object and the nature of reality," Andrew had said. And when she said Heavens, she had no notion what that meant. "Think of a kitchen table then," he told her, "when you're not there."

This humorous, offhand advice nevertheless poses a serious challenge. How is it possible to conceive the object in itself? When Lily performs the experiment, she finds herself absurdly blending a mental reconstruction—that is to say, an idea—with present-tense empirical experience, imagining "a phantom kitchen table" suspended "now in the fork of a pear tree, for they had reached the orchard."[1] Could this be the proper way to see a thing-in-itself?

When Woolf herself turns to the same representational challenge in "Time Passes," the central section of *To the Lighthouse,* she takes it up another way, conveying instead the chaos and darkness that reign in the world "when [no one is] there." She pointedly associates this loss of epistemological focus with the Great War and with the death of Mrs. Ramsay. Woolf's bold narrative experiment, then, claims to represent the unrepresentable: the world without an eye to see, an ear to hear, or a mind to know it. Only in the last

---

[1] Virginia Woolf, *To the Lighthouse* (New York: Harcourt Brace & World, 1927), 38.

section of the novel, after "time passes," can the ineffable "nature of reality" at last be retrospectively captured in a static, spatial composition—Lily's abstract, non-representational painting. This closure asserts an aesthetic answer in response to questions that had been posed in other terms. The paradoxes inherent in Woolf's formal experiment here owe a great deal to Pater's epistemological reflections, which formed a significant part of her literary paternity.[2]

A highly informed philosophical thinker, at the apex of a long romantic and Victorian effort to assimilate German idealism to English empiricism, Walter Pater advanced historical aesthetics as the timely realm in which epistemological questions might be answered. I will have more to say later in this essay about Pater's own novelistic narration (and what its form can tell us). For now, it is enough to point out that the epistemological implications of his narrative experiments may easily be seen as a propulsion toward the modernism of Woolf (and others). After all, Pater (and perhaps even more notably, Henry James) carried the experiment of narrating through one intense focalization to its *nth* degree in English. *Marius the Epicurean* (1885) and *What Maisie Knew* (1897) might stand as apt markers, illustrating my point. Their narrative experimentation with the extreme limits of free indirect discourse is often taken to be one primary modality of literary "impressionism." Still, if Woolf dared to evacuate the place of focalization, her epistemological wit draws a great deal of its force from the fact that Pater (and James) before her had so concertedly trained the narrative gaze at one mind in the act of knowing, sensing, feeling, forming ideas, and venturing interpretations.

Aesthetic Objectification

To the question "Can we know 'the object'?" Pater answers in the affirmative, though his affirmation is complex. His answer, of course, involves the familiar modern corollary: the object cannot be known simply, immediately or "in itself," but only mediately and, at first, "in the subject." This is an utterly familiar notion by Pater's time, both in English empiricist philosophy and in English romantic poetry, not to mention in many forms of continental philosophy and literature, which Pater also knew well. In large part because of the very familiarity of these issues within his tradition, it is imprecise—at best banal, at worst misleading—to suppose that Pater could be understood simply as "a subjectivist," much less as a solipsist. Pater shows his familiarity with romantic epistemological dilemmas in their extreme forms, but that is not to say he embraced, believed, espoused, or advocated

---

[2] Though he does not make this particular point, the best study of Pater's influence on Woolf is Perry Meisel, *The Absent Father: Virginia Woolf and Walter Pater* (New Haven: Yale University Press, 1980).

these extreme positions. It is perfectly reasonable to expect a philosophically sophisticated critic like Pater to be fully aware of the difficulties in post-Kantian (or, more proximately, post-Wordsworthian) thought. Pater indicates his own line of (somewhat impatient) self-defense on this issue when he writes of Marius's consideration of "the doctrine . . . of what is termed 'the subjectivity of knowledge' ": "The peculiar strength of Marius was to have apprehended this weakness [in every philosophical account of the universe] on the threshold of human knowledge, in the whole range of its consequences."[3]

Perhaps the error of seeing Pater as a solipsist is largely the effect of seeing him "after" Arnold in a critical tradition that Pater himself did as much as anyone to construct. After Arnold's conviction that we must try to "see the object as in itself it really is," Pater's skepticism perhaps seemed more radical than it really was. But in fact Pater, who was more attuned to the philosophical tradition than Arnold was, did no more—and also no less—than to work out a method of response to the skeptical empiricism that had been familiar since Hobbes, Locke, and Hume. Richard Ellmann made this point most memorably years ago, in the form of a literary-historical legend, when he humorously sketched a line of thinking from Arnold, through Pater, to Wilde on exactly this issue of whether one could "see the object as in itself it really is." Arnold believed one must and could, while Wilde believed one couldn't and anyway shouldn't want to. "Wilde rounded on Arnold by asserting that the aim of criticism is to see the object as it really is not," Ellmann wrote in his much-quoted characterization of the "critic as artist."[4] But Pater's strongly conceived, median stance between the two is what interests us here.

For Pater, the critic was not an artist but an *interpreter,* a word he sometimes printed in quotation marks to emphasize both the etymological finesse of his diction and also his refined conceptual point, for to him interpretation involved the critical activity of intervention.[5] The critic puts himself between the object and other potential viewers, between what is unremarked and what is marked. Ellmann's literary-historical legend, dramatically positioning Pater between a bluff objectivist and a heroic subjectivist, also calls attention to Pater's insistence on the mutual implication of subject and object, his insistence that the primary act of knowing is the critical separation of the object

[3] Walter Pater, *Marius the Epicurean: His Sensations and Ideas* (I, 137–38). Unless otherwise indicated, all quotations from the works of Walter Pater will be taken from the Library Edition in ten volumes (London: Macmillan, 1910; New York: Johnson Reprint, 1973).

[4] Richard Ellmann, introduction to *The Artist As Critic: Critical Writings of Oscar Wilde* (New York: Vintage, 1968), xi–xii. Ellmann's literary-historical legend has been repeated so often as to have become a touchstone in criticism of Arnold, Pater, and Wilde, making it clear, I think, how crucial this epistemological line of thinking is to our construction of the critical tradition.

[5] See, for example, Walter Pater, "Demeter and Persephone," *Greek Studies,* 120.

from the subject—for only when the object has been detached from the subject can the critic offer a precise description of its "virtues."

This is all very clear in the "Preface" to *The Renaissance,* where Pater begins with faux-simplicity by acknowledging the familiar Arnoldian claim (that the "aim of all true criticism whatever" is " 'to see the object as in itself it really is' "). Immediately, however, he narrows the field to "aesthetic criticism" and insists that the "first step" toward the Arnoldian goal is "to know one's own impression as it really is, to discriminate it, to realize it distinctly." All three of those moves are crucial: 1) objects of art will have a special status in his method; 2) impressions will be the original data in a method which imagines knowledge to be the result of a (re)constructive process; and 3) this is only the "first step" in the critical method. After this *"first* step" (italics mine), further steps must be taken "to indicate what the source of [the] impression is, and under what conditions it is experienced." The critic's "end is reached when he has disengaged that virtue, and noted it, as a chemist notes some natural element, for himself and others."[6] We should take seriously the fact that the critical "disengagement" advocated here is not a prior attitude of bland, apathetic indifference in the critic's point of view but is instead precisely the critic's careful practice of *objectification.*[7] There is no knowledge of an object except beginning in a subject, but the "critical" step is the disengagement of the object from that subject and the definition, interpretation, and public articulation of it "for himself and others."

Here in the "Preface," the process of objectification is figured as the process of isolating an element through chemical analysis (when the "conditions," if carefully governed, can be taken into account as part of the scientific experiment). For Pater, in other words, the "conditions" of knowledge were not contextual influences to be ruled out so that the object might finally be seen "in itself," but on the contrary they form a vital part of the representation. The conditions and process of knowing must be represented as a vital part of "the object." Very early in his career, Pater distinguished himself from Coleridge's nostalgic conservatism with the proclamation: "To the modern mind nothing is, or can be rightly known, except relatively, and under conditions."[8] I want to stress the claim, however, that his argument with Coleridge did not mean that he had given up on "rightly knowing." Instead, he formulated a method for knowing "under conditions." The object will be known *in relation* to its contextualizing conditions in the past and in the present (at its moment of origination and at the moment of its being known). Only by taking account of these conditions in representation could Pater hope to make the point that any object ("as in itself it really is")

[6] Walter Pater, "Preface" to *The Renaissance,* ix–x.

[7] This is Pater's response to Arnoldian disinterestedness, and it is much more epistemologically rigorous than has usually been acknowledged. For another view, see David Bromwich, "The Genealogy of Disinterestedness," *Raritan* 1 (1982): 62–92.

[8] Walter Pater, "Coleridge," in *Appreciations,* 66.

is in fact an epistemological and aesthetic construction—but no less "real" for all that.[9]

When the aesthetic process is complete—when the impact of impressions on the subject has been followed by critical detachment—the resulting object is then perceived in the past, and as the past. In other words, the object can be "grasped" or "apprehended" only after the initial impact of its "impression" has been experienced and has passed. Pater turns this romantic irony into a methodological advantage, for it enables him to secure the object as a made thing, projected away from the subject and at a distance in the past. The mutually implicated senses of "distance" or "detachment" here—aesthetic and temporal—are themselves artifactual, to be sure, but we must see that their artifice is itself an epistemological achievement and a powerful theoretical tool. One of Pater's most striking contributions was to have theorized the aesthetic and temporal forms of figurative "distance" as correlatives. (As we shall see, this temporal aspect of critical detachment will be later projected as fully historical.) For Pater, to "know the object as in itself it really is," then, means to know it at a constructed distance from within the subject; and after that distance has been constructed, both the subject's and the object's "sense of objectivity" will have been correlatively (re)constructed.

Thus the object is irreducibly tied to the temporality of its experience in the subject. The object is analogous to—as well as the product of—the act of the mind in knowing it. In Pater's work, the personal figure is of paramount importance in part because it is the stage on which this epistemological drama is enacted. The figure of the art object, too, has a special status in Pater's method because works of art seem to offer a tricky circumvention of the epistemological impasse. They appeal to the senses, to be sure, and therefore they bid fair to leave a strongly delineated, graphic impression on the receptive subject; but moreover, they seem already objectified, predetermined as both aesthetic and historical objects, for they have already been made, at some time in the past. In both respects they "come to you" from the outside, as Pater puts it in the concluding sentence of the "Conclusion."[10] Art objects, then, may be taken on faith as trustworthy epistemological *data* (that is to say, they are "given," already-made). From their place of origination in the past, their artifactuality recalls the activity of the mind (in the present) delineating its objects against the background of (past and present) "conditions."

The object of art therefore stands, in Pater's work, as a figure for the epistemological process itself, in its particular post-romantic situation entangled within "the mighty world / Of eye and ear,—both what they half create, /

---

[9] The banality of one (re)current critical discovery that the object of knowledge is itself always a present "construction" should be happily offset, within Pater studies at least, by his own recognition and promulgation of that claim.

[10] Walter Pater, "Conclusion," to *The Renaissance*, 239.

And what perceive."[11] Positioned within this uncertain distinction between perception and creation—an uncertainty which Pater reinterprets as a vital, logically necessary conjunction—art objects claim their objective status with particular assurance. They are already made, past and separate, but they are also "made" anew through their revival within the aesthetic critic in the present, who trusts them as evidence (of a world outside the self, of a past different from the present), receives their impressions deeply, and then, interpreting, critically projects them away from the subject once more.

Historical Objectification

To the question "Can we know the past?" Pater answers: *only* insofar as an object may be located "in the past" can we begin to "know" it. Epistemology to Pater is irreducibly an aesthetic and historical study; aesthetics and history—and their complex intertwinings—are, quite simply, the realms where objects may be "rightly known." So Pater strategically shifts the epistemological dilemma to an aesthetic and historical register. Objects from the past can be trusted as *data* to be interpreted (for reasons we have seen in the previous section), but only if they are "revived" within and through a present, critical subject. Otherwise, they remain invisible, virtual, lost—until such time as they may be recovered. Needless to say, no work of art could provide a direct representation of the past "as in itself it really was." Pater disdains that aim as "mere antiquarianism," anyway, as we shall see.

In a period noted for its many revival movements, Pater is the greatest theorist of "revival" as an epistemological, aesthetic, and historical project. He first made a name for himself with his 1873 volume, *Studies in the History of the Renaissance,* by elevating that period against the background of Ruskin's famous valorization of the Gothic. But it was not this decisive break with Ruskin that primarily marks his work as "theory." Rather, it is his lifelong meditation on the conditions and principles of "revival" itself. Pater's latter-day English "Renaissance" represents a revival of a revival: an aesthetic recreation of a historical revival, as well as a historicization of an aesthetic revival. In this 1873 volume, Pater's formal techniques of historical periodization created an object, "the Renaissance," according to epistemological strategies we can now recognize. He extended "the Renaissance" almost beyond recognition as a separate, objectified "period" of history. By imagining the Renaissance rising within the Middle Ages and still asserting its influence within his own present age (through Winckelmann's influence on the nineteenth century), Pater extended its boundaries radically. But he

---

[11] William Wordsworth, "Lines Composed a Few Miles Above Tintern Abbey..." lines 105–7, in *William Wordsworth: Selected Poems and Prefaces* (Boston: Houghton Mifflin, 1965), 110.

also represented "the Renaissance" concentrically, with the revival of classical antiquity in fifteenth-century Italy forming the center, and with various spatial and temporal extensions reaching outward from there. Thus he both decisively drew and yet also blurred the outlines of his historical object, creating simultaneously an objectification of historical difference and of identification. In other words, he objectified a specific place and time quite different from his own, yet embedded it within a developmental sequence leading up to his own.

We can perhaps see what Pater was aiming to do in his representation of "the Renaissance" even more clearly if we consider his review, "The Poems of William Morris" (1868), an early essay in large part devoted to the problems and possibilities of aesthetic and historical revival.[12] Morris was particularly concerned with representing not the Renaissance but Greek antiquity and "the middle ages." In his review, Pater praises Morris's ultra-refined medievalism (in *The Defence of Guenevere*) and his re-tellings of Greek legend (in *The Life and Death of Jason*). But Pater especially appreciates Morris—"appreciates" in the double sense of critically adding value, while also marking the way value accrues over time—for his revivals of the two periods of culture together in *The Earthly Paradise*. In this poem a group of Norse mariners have attempted to reach "the earthly paradise." Their long quest having failed, they come finally as old men upon "some western land" whose inhabitants were descended from the ancient Greeks. In conventional epic fashion, both hosts and guests set about telling each other stories from their respective homelands. The form of the poem conveys this historicist, cross-cultural premise by assigning two stories to each calendar "month": one from medieval sources, and one from the myths and legends of ancient Greece. The voice of a lyric poet in the present time of composition gathers all the stories together and conveys them to nineteenth-century readers with a framing "Apology" and "Envoi," as well as a lyric introduction to each month's tales.[13]

In lieu of an actual place, then, this grand revivalist design—the poem itself—becomes "The Earthly Paradise." Its layered narrative temporality—nineteenth-century perspective encompassing a medieval perspective, whose representatives encounter surviving elements of ancient Greek culture—"revives" ancient Greece by making palpable the phases of distance from it. In order to call attention to this distance, Pater singles out for praise the way "charming [medieval] anachronisms" creep into Morris's re-tellings of the Greek legends, for those very anachronisms show that the Greek past can only be revived from a later point of view that also includes the intervening

---

[12] This essay (minus the "Conclusion" to *The Renaissance*, which was taken from it) is now usually called "Aesthetic Poetry," and it is most easily found in *Selected Writings of Walter Pater*, ed. Harold Bloom (New York: Columbia University Press, 1974), 190–98.

[13] Selections from William Morris, *The Earthly Paradise*, in *The Pre-Raphaelites and Their Circle*, ed. Cecil Y. Lang (Chicago: University of Chicago Press, 1968), 279–84.

Christian "middle" age. Pater prizes "this effect, this grace of Hellenism re-
lieved against the sorrow of the Middle Age," and indeed he will practice it
himself many times over, using this strategy of contrastive backgrounding to
isolate the past object more clearly against its "conditions."

Like Pater's construction of "the Renaissance," Morris's structural design
in *The Earthly Paradise* presents a complex figure for the formation of historical knowledge. Interesting for our purposes here is the fact that Pater al-
legorizes the aesthetic history represented in the poem as an epistemological
fable. The Christian Middle Age was "not objective," Pater argues, and it
offered "no real escape to the world without us." (We should note and rel-
ish in passing Pater's diabolical, secularizing gesture of equating solipsism
with historical Christianity!) Within this framework he interprets provençal
courtly love poetry as "a rival *cultus*," continuous with, yet sowing the seeds
of difference from, "the cloister." In this model, in other words, historical
change is described as a process of identification and differentiation, like the
epistemological process of impression and detachment. After the cloistral
(solipsistic) Middle Ages, the world returning in the Renaissance to a life
"open only to the senses" is like the body returning to life itself—like being
reborn, like waking after sleep, like convalescing after sickness, like remembering the formative openness of childhood. This logic expresses aesthetic
and historical revival as an allegory of individual refreshment, renewal, and
recreation. Finally, reinterpreting the historical "period" as an overarching
developmental principle, Pater claims that "renaissance" is "one law of the
life of the human spirit," and "what we call the Renaissance is only a supreme
instance."[14] The moral of this aesthetic-historical fable shows Pater's radical techniques of periodization together with his tacit analogy between individual life and "the human spirit."

So Pater's notion of historical revival depends on the knowing subject in
the present having a dual awareness of the past—identifying with it yet dif-
ferentiating from it. The past itself is internally differentiated, consisting of
contrasting phases that nevertheless form a continuous sequence. Thus, moments of change are almost imperceptible, for they occur through a dialectical reversal of identity into difference, as when the "rival *cultus*" of courtly
love poetry seems at first very much like "the cloister." Thus, the critic in the
present must be able to see the "phases" of the past *both* as mutually implicated and as distinctive:

> In handling a subject of Greek legend, anything in the way of an actual revival
> must always be impossible. Such vain antiquarianism is a waste of the poet's
> power. The composite experience of all the ages is part of each one of us; to
> deduct from that experience, to obliterate any part of it, to come face to face
> with the people of a past age, as if the Middle Age, the Renaissance, the eigh-

[14] Pater, "Aesthetic Poetry," in *Selected Writings,* 195.

teenth century had not been, is as impossible as to become a little child, or enter again into the womb and be born. But though it is not possible to repress a single phase of that humanity, which, because we live and move and have our being in the life of humanity, makes us what we are, it is possible to isolate such a phase, to throw it into relief, to be divided against ourselves in zeal for it, as we may hark back to some choice space of our own individual life. We cannot truly conceive of the age: we can conceive the element it has contributed to our culture; we can treat the subjects of the age bringing that into relief.[15]

First and most obviously, Pater decisively rejects the possibility of any immediate "face to face" representation of a past age. The object cannot be represented "as in itself it really was," and Pater disdains the very attempt at "an actual revival" as "vain antiquarianism." Second, Pater strikingly imagines the historical past internalized within the individual subject: "The composite experience of all the ages is a part of each one of us." (We will return to this difficult notion soon.) This model of internalization bolsters the notion that the aesthetic-historical past can be revived within the present subject, and Pater's description of the process of revival then follows the familiar process of objectification we have been tracing so far, since he claims that a particular phase can be "isolated" against the rest within the subject, and brought "into relief." This figure of "relief" indicates simultaneously both the aesthetic objectification entailed in historical revival and also its refreshing effect on the present subject.

Thus, as Pater puts it, the "aesthetic poetry" of William Morris is not "mere antiquarianism," for Morris "animates his subject by keeping it always close to himself." His poem is *"neither* a mere reproduction of Greek or medieval poetry nor only an idealisation of modern life and sentiment" but something in between, a correlative representation of past and present (italics mine).[16] To Pater, these correlative representations—figures of "relief," in which the past is situated within but differentiated from the present subject, as foreground to background, or in which one historical period is situated within but rising against a prior period in a sequence, as foreground to background—objectify the past as accurately and as vividly as it is possible to do, while also representing the shaping act of representation itself.[17] Thus, Pater's re-creations involve a fierce acknowledgment of at least one problem inherent in representation: that the object must first be lost in order to be known. This loss is itself refigured in the representation as the critical disengagement of historical difference.

---

[15] Ibid., 196.
[16] Ibid., 195.
[17] For a more extended treatment of Pater's metafigural figures of "relief" see "Poetics of Revival" and "Senses of Relief," in Carolyn Williams, *Transfigured World: Walter Pater's Aesthetic Historicism* (Ithaca: Cornell University Press, 1989), 68–77, and 153–67.

Pater's Impressionism (As in Itself It Really Is)

Like Woolf, then, Pater offers an aesthetic response to problems posed in other terms—in purely epistemological terms, but also in terms more grave. As in *To the Lighthouse* Lily's triumphant painting is possible only after the death and subjective evacuation represented in "Time Passes," so in his "Conclusion" to *The Renaissance* Pater begins by meditating on the deadly implications of the modern physical sciences, and only then turns to the implications of modern epistemology. His aestheticism is proposed in direct response to this double threat.

Pater's notion of the impression—and, by extension, his impressionism—is complex and pivotal here. For his aestheticism depends on—and plays between—impressions of sensations that pass and impressions that remain as finished forms, or objects. In this section of my essay, I want to show that Pater deploys antithetical senses of the "impression" in order to transvalue it, specifically to turn its epistemological disadvantages into methodological advantages. He uses these antithetical senses of the impression to construct a model of subject-formation that maps the ratio of surface to depth against the ratio of present to past. This model of interiority allows Pater to imagine historical and aesthetic culture as a part of individual self-culture. Thus Paterian impressionism reaches from the atomism of sensory experience toward a theory of historical knowledge and historical change.

In the second paragraph of the "Conclusion," surely, the term "impression" appears *in malo,* to name the dangerous effects of mental association. When considered in relation to mental experience, impressions rush by on so rapid a "stream" that they can hardly be grasped before they are gone; when considered in relation to any object, impressions "loosen" that object into a mere "group" of attributes, only traces or "relics" of a lost whole. Because impressions are fragmentary and passing so fast, experience itself seems "unstable, flickering, inconsistent." Finally, when taken to its extreme, this line of thinking results both in a vision of the radical subjectivity of solipsism ("each mind keeping as a solitary prisoner its own dream of a world") and, alternatively, in a vision of the incoherent, dispersive, vanishing subject ("that strange, perpetual weaving and unweaving of ourselves").[18] At the extremes of empirical epistemology is this ambivalence: the mind is on the one hand too far from its objects, and on the other hand too close; both objects and subject are on the one hand impermeable, and on the other fragmented, shattered, and dispersed.

But these extreme conclusions are not represented as Pater's own conclusions. The first two paragraphs of the "Conclusion" are brilliant composite representations of the conclusions of others, generated through a synthesizing experiment in which Pater seeks to represent what happens when the

---

[18] "Conclusion," in *The Renaissance,* 235–36.

"tendency" of various strands in "modern thought" are followed out to their extreme limits.[19] He makes this quite explicit. His announced project in the "Conclusion" is to illustrate the notion that "modern thought" tends to "regard all things and principles of things as inconstant modes." In order to demonstrate this premise, he represents the composite conclusions first of one discipline of modern thought and then another. "Let us begin with that which is without," he proposes, and after paragraph one he explicitly turns to consider what we find "if we begin with the inward world of thought and feeling."

Pater is *representing* the "tendency" of whole discourses here—physical science and epistemological philosophy—not "owning," embracing, or advocating their conclusions, except to the precise extent that he acknowledges them, knows about them, has assimilated them, and conveys them to his readers. This is a polemical point in my interpretation of Pater, one I have developed at greater length elsewhere.[20] Pater stages and performs these views here, but turns away from them directly after representing them. His "turn" to aestheticism, after these first two paragraphs of the "Conclusion," represents his own conclusion, a return from the deadly threats of "modern thought." Aestheticism, thus, is a method for "apprehending" or "grasping" objects and correlatively restoring the subject to "life."

Its revivalist strategy depends on Pater's double sense of "impression" and, by extension, on the dialectical structure of his impressionism. If in the "Conclusion" impressions are portrayed in their destructive, dissolving aspect, elsewhere in his work—for example, in the "Preface" (as we have already seen) and in "The Child in the House" (1878), Pater's most succinct theoretical statement of the role of impressions—we find another view altogether. In "The Child in the House," impressions appear *in bono*, most notable for their constructive role in "that process of brainbuilding by which we are, each one of us, what we are."[21] In this little parable of identity-formation, impressions do not race past on the surface of a stream but press themselves into a plastic, malleable interior where they are grasped and permanently held.

This beautiful example of the "imaginary portrait"—Pater's favorite mixed genre: part essay, part story, part character study, part reverie—describes the childhood of "Florian Deleal." To the extent that "The Child in the House" is an essay in empirical psychology, it reflects on the period of early life when

[19] For sources of Pater's composite representations here, see Donald L. Hill, ed., *The Renaissance: Studies in Art and Poetry: The 1893 Text* (Berkeley: University of California Press, 1980), 443–58; and Billie Andrew Inman, "The Intellectual Context of Walter Pater's Conclusion," in *Walter Pater: An Imaginative Sense of Fact*, ed. Philip Dodd (London: Frank Case, 1981).

[20] For a more extended reading of the "Conclusion," including the argument that these are not Pater's "own" conclusions, see Williams, *Transfigured World*, 11–46, especially 11–13 and 37–46.

[21] Walter Pater, "The Child in the House," *Miscellaneous Studies*, 173.

impressions are most sharply experienced and begin to develop into ideas. Thus over time, as "the child" matures, the "house" becomes a "house of thought." Pater's reliance on Hume is discernible *prima facie* in this fundamental distinction. For Hume, "impressions" are "all our more lively perceptions, when we hear, or see, or feel, or love, or hate, or desire, or will." Impressions are simple, direct, and original; ideas are complex, derivative, and distanced from their sources. Impressions are the test of ideas, for ideas, no matter how complex, are built up from or derived from impressions and are "bound" by those impressions.[22] Indeed, concludes Hume, "It is impossible for us to *think* of any thing, which we have not antecedently *felt*."[23] Here, it should be noted, Hume slides quite easily from the perceptual to the affective senses of "feeling." And so does Pater, for this fruitful confusion lies at the heart of his aesthetics as well as the developmental psychology sketched in this imaginary portrait.

The pervasive analogy between the interior of Florian's childhood home and his subjective interiority supports this Humean sense of impressions as *data,* for they come distinctly from "outside" the house. This structural separation makes it possible to imagine the existence of an "outside" world. The walls of the "house," then, are diacritical marks, making a figure across whose border "content" can be imaginatively transferred. Stabilized by this separation, objects take on a vivid, independent life; the subject, in turn, is formed through a process of internalization. This process is figured as an aesthetic—plastic and inscriptive—operation:

> How insignificant, at the moment, seem the influences of the sensible things which are tossed and fall and lie about us, so, or so, in the environment of early childhood. How indelibly, as we afterwards discover, they affect us; with what capricious attractions and associations they figure themselves on the white paper, the smooth wax of our ingenuous souls, as "with lead in the rock forever," giving form and feature, and as it were assigned house-room in our memory, to early experiences of feeling and thought, which abide with us ever afterwards, thus, and not otherwise.[24]

These sensible influences seem scattered at first, seem only to "lie about us," but when they move inside, they are figured so "indelibly" that the traditional Lockean and Aristotelian metaphors seem too weak and must be

---

[22] David Hume, *Enquiries concerning Human Understanding and concerning the Principles of Morals* (reprinted from the posthumous edition of 1777), ed. L. A. Selby-Bigge, 3d edition with text revised and notes by P. H. Nidditch (Oxford: Clarendon Press, 1975), 18–22. Compare the similar treatment of these issues in *A Treatise of Human Nature* (1739–1740), ed. Ernest C. Mossner (Harmondsworth: Penguin, 1969), book 1, part 1, section 1; part 3, sections 5–6; and book 2, part 1, section 4.

[23] Hume, *Enquiries,* 62.

[24] Pater, "The Child in the House," *Miscellaneous Studies,* 177.

trumped by the trenchancy and permanence of the Biblical " 'lead in the rock forever.' "[25] Again and again Pater reiterates his inscriptive and imprinting metaphors for this sense of the profound impressiveness of things: Florian "felt this pressure upon him of the sensible world," whose influence is "impressed how deeply on one!"[26] In this story, impressions do not float quickly past on a stream of consciousness; they float inward from a world outside and mark the difference between outside and inside.

If their formative, permanent imprint on the malleable, plastic interior indicates the aesthetic value of Paterian impressions, their accidental quality indicates their historical value. Pater's stress on accidents, with their adventitious but "indelible" effects, lends a sense of historicity and personal identity to an otherwise abstract portrait of "the child": "Thus, and not otherwise" do the impressions "abide with us ever afterward." Impressions "never afterwards quite detach themselves from this or that accident, or trick, in the mode of their first entrance to us."[27] Impressions, after their opportunistic "entrance," are like found objects, and the subject itself is formed as an aesthetic-historical accretion, made up from its accidentally assembled impressions. Thus, Pater's parable teaches us, we can believe in the coherence of the subject in large part precisely because of the accidental nature of impressions and the utterly individualized "house" they make: "As the house of thought in which we live gets itself together, like some airy bird's-nest of floating thistle-down and chance straws, compact at last, little accidents have their consequences."

We could say, then, that Pater's exemplary subject, Florian Deleal, is insular (Florian *de l'île*) but not solipsistic.[28] Like Woolf's Mrs. Ramsay, Pater envisions an ideal "house" with closed doors and opened windows.[29] Playing on the traditional allegorical figure of the *hortus conclusus,* Pater notes that

the sense of security could hardly have been deeper, the quiet of the child's soul being one with the quiet of its house, a place "inclosed" and "sealed." But upon this assured place, upon the child's assured soul which resembled it, there came

[25] *Selected Writings of Walter Pater,* ed. Bloom, 15, note 8.
[26] Pater, "The Child in the House," in *Miscellaneous Studies,* 189. Locke only infrequently uses the term "impression," but when he does it is in this inscriptive and typographical sense of "imprinting." See John Locke, *An Essay concerning Human Understanding,* ed. Peter H. Nidditch (Oxford: Clarendon Press, 1975), 49–50, where he associates the notion of "impression" with "innate ideas" (against which he is arguing).
[27] Pater, "The Child in the House," *Miscellaneous Studies,* 178.
[28] Thanks to Jacques Khalip for the French pun.
[29] This would be the place to point out the nationalist impulses of this seemingly apolitical story, for Pater's meditation on insularity is conjoined with a paean to the "home counties" of Surrey and Kent as "essentially home-like." Florian's childhood house is also figured as a metonymy for nation, "for Englishmen at least typically home-like." Pater, *Miscellaneous Studies,* 179–80. Woolf's use of the figure after the Great War is, of course, inflected with a sharper sense of the need for national defense of the island home. Both writers, in other words, use the figure to bridge between epistemological and nationalistic senses.

floating in from the larger world without, as at windows left ajar unknowingly, or over the high garden walls, two streams of impressions....[30]

At first Florian's story is little more than an account of "the tyranny of the senses over him,"[31] a mere list of sensory experiences: the sight of a white angora cat, and of a "great red hawthorn in full flower"; the sound of his aunt's cry of grief; the pain of hot sealing wax burning his hand. Soon, however, his impressions take on a more organized, educated character. If we were to ask how "the composite experience of all the ages [can be] part of each one of us," this theoretical fable about internalization would offer us the beginning of Pater's answer. The ambient culture first begins to penetrate as "sensations," only later to be processed as "ideas." When Florian takes in the face and posture of "Queen Marie Antoinette, on her way to execution" (as depicted in David's drawing), Pater implicitly makes the point that self-culture consists of these intertwined aesthetic and historical representations, whose impact is initially felt on a sensory and affective scale.[32]

Finally, the narrator offers a grand retrospective summation: "Thus a constant substitution of the typical for the actual took place in his thoughts."[33] And that, essentially, is the end of the story. For after those mature substitutions "of the typical for the actual" have taken place, Florian leaves his childhood house. But what is the story here? To the extent that it is a "story" at all, it is an abstracted, miniaturized, and truncated *Bildungsroman,* depicting education as the process of building the "house of thought" that will allow Florian—or force him—to leave his epistemological nest and make his way outward into the world. His has been an *aesthetic* education precisely because it has been the result of a process of receiving and then objectifying his impressions. Only after the child has left the house is he detached enough from it that he can see it objectively; only then, only in retrospect, can this story be told.

This is apparent in the form of the narration. Retrospection detaches "the child" from "the man," and a semi-detached narrator (who sometimes, though not often, breaks the objectification to speak in the first person) reports on both. If nothing much happens in "The Child in the House," that fact only makes clear the abstract logic of all developmental narratives, whose tautological form is predetermined by the premise of identity. (For what can an "identity" do but evolve its self-sameness through all its early and later phases of change?) A subjective sense of identity forms, as influences come from without and press within, imprinting the subject with the marks of his environment, whether of "home" or "culture." These permanent, formative

[30] Ibid., 180–81.
[31] Ibid., 186.
[32] Ibid., 182.
[33] Ibid., 194.

marks may be read, re-read (re-marked), and interpreted over the course of time. Even if they are forgotten, they remain; Florian's story makes this clear by opening with a dream, which provokes the story. The fiction of "identity," in other words, stabilizes the flux of subjectivity. Indeed, that is its main purpose: to create a temporal duration which in turn can be read as a pattern of change within the "same" objectified subject.

Thus Pater's impressionism plays between the antithetical values of "impressions"—the fluctuating, atomistic sensations racing past on the surface of present consciousness and the incisive marks pressed into a vulnerable interior—strategically mobilizing them in relation to each other. Thus is the dangerous, associationist sense of "impression" not only answered (in the figure of surface and depth) but also transvalued (as movement, as receptivity, as life itself). Here the dialectical relation between the two sides of Pater's impressionism shows its greatest power and ingenuity; for, functioning in relation to one another, now *both* senses of "impression" can bring a revival of the spirit. The doubled, antithetical structure of Pater's impressionism, in other words, binds surface to depth, temporality to permanence, historical contingency to aesthetic objectification, and present to past—binds them together, but also critically separates them. With this model, temporal flux may be stabilized in a spatialization, a figure within which fleeting experience may be fixed, secured, contained (and thus objectified as "content"), conserved, and comprehended—but only after time passes.

The Form of Historical Revival

Marius the Epicurean (1885), Pater's brilliant generic crossing of *Bildungsroman* with historical novel, complicates the story. In this novel Pater's impressionism becomes a model for historical development. The individual subject still forms the linchpin of the representation, for history is made as Marius is impressed by various features in his environment. Thus (the argument implicitly runs) aesthetic and historical expressions in the culture at large are the results—as well as the causes—of individual impressions. Thus, too, individual and culture exhibit interlocking and homologous developments; for if the individual internalizes impressions of his ambient culture as if they were chiefly personal experiences, so conversely "the life of humanity" develops through the gradual accretion of individual expressions.

Pater's earliest essay, "Diaphaneitè" (1864), is devoted to exploring this dynamic of impression and expression in the history of culture. The title of the essay refers to a particular character type whose way of being in the world allows Pater to imagine "culture" as a macrocosmic version of the receptive individual's self-culture. After a discussion of "types" of character that are recognized by "the world," Pater distinguishes his subject from them, for it is not recognized, not noticed, not seen.[34] Yet this character type is crucial to the world, for its radical "clarity" and "receptivity" permits the transmission "from without of light that is not yet inward." This radical receptivity is an ethical virtue, for it operates like a filter, "unconsciously" choosing what to preserve, revive, and transmit. This type effectively *makes* history by internalizing and then communicating "all that is really lifegiving in the established order of things." The diaphanous character is therefore a "prophecy" of the future; though unseen, he is "revolutionary"; in Pater's view a "majority of such would be the regeneration of the world."

Pater's theory of historical development depends upon the impressionability of just such figures, who afford him a focalization point in the past through which to revive and "animate" the past age, "bringing it into relief" in the present. True to the diaphanous type, Marius avidly but unobtrusively absorbs cultural influences from his early Christian culture, transmitting them to a subtly changed future. Subtitled "His Sensations and Ideas," *Marius the Epicurean* advertises itself as a post-Humean tale. But this novel moves the epistemological fable of "The Child in the House" fully into the realm of aesthetic and cultural history. Marius's process of maturation, then, represents both the particularity of an individual character as well as a representative type of historical development. For crucially—much more than Florian's—Marius's is a distinctly historical consciousness.

Marius not only formulates ideas by generalizing from his sensations; he also "receives" ideas from the philosophy and literature around him. In other words, previously expressed ideas impress him, and he carefully evaluates these received ideas, sifting out what he will retain. To narrativize this activity, the novel's plot places Marius in one historical environment after another: he moves from the pagan countryside to the imperial city of Rome, encountering, interpreting, and selectively internalizing the influences, in turn, of Epicureanism, Stoicism, and finally Christianity. He is strongly influenced by Apuleius, for example, chief for him among the writers of his time. But most important, he becomes the amanuensis to Marcus Aurelius, so that in the logic of the novel he is literally made to be responsible for the transmission of the emperor's words to later history. Totally receptive and "transparent," Marius allows the forces of history—and its aesthetic objects—to pass through him.

The tacit cultural argument of *Marius the Epicurean* is that the protagonist, completely unrecognized by the later historical record, nevertheless was

---

[34] Walter Pater, "Diaphaneitè," in *Miscellaneous Studies,* 247–254. Bloom has translated this title (or type-name) as "the crystal man," and I've used "the transparent hero." Bloom, ed., *Selected Writings of Walter Pater,* vii; Williams, *Transfigured World,* 172–84. Anne Varty argues that a transliteration of this odd Greek or faux-Greek word produces a second-person imperative verb: "[You shall] become transparent!" enforcing the sense of this essay's role as manifesto. Anne Varty, "The Crystal Man: A Study of Diaphaneitè," in *Pater in the 1990s,* ed. Laurel Brake and Ian Small (Greensboro, N.C.: ELT Press, 1991), 205–15.

part of a movement which transformed "the life of humanity." Though he is definitively said to be still essentially "Epicurean" all his life, at the novel's end Marius is "unconsciously" assimilated by Christianity. (Without his request or choice, as he lies dying—and almost literally unconscious—Marius is given the Eucharist. After his death, he is claimed by the early Christians as a martyr to their cause, though he actually died of the plague.) Marius is therefore subsumed within a historical development he does nothing to bring about—nothing, that is, except to *see* it clearly, and to be attracted to the beauty of what he sees. But within Pater's historical and aesthetic impressionism, that is quite a lot. For Pater, those who take in ("comprehend") and transmit "all that is really lifegiving in the established order of things" are the true *makers* of history, the ones who "treat life in the spirit of art." Thus Marius represents all the receptive individuals whose population made Christianity a world-historical force. It is crucial to Pater's argument, however, that Marius remained "the Epicurean" to the end—for the novel is not a pro-Christian argument, but a representation of the evolutionary gradualism of revolutionary historical change.[35]

Marius's ambiguous death figures in another critical way as well. The novel makes much of the fact that burying dead bodies underground is a recently introduced practice of early Christian culture. Thus the plastic, formative receptivity to impression is represented on the cultural level as well as the individual, for with their burial, bodies like Marius's literally make an impression within the ground. Pater's figure here suggests an archaeological conception of preservation deep within the earth. This historical impression will not be "expressed" literally through exhumation—as surely is the case in Pater's moving image of "the buried fire of ancient art" rising "up from under the soil" during the Renaissance.[36] In this case, the historical impression is expressed only through the later cultural recollection of the novel's narrator.

That narrator—like the narrator of "The Child"—is semi-detached, to mark both identification with and difference from the represented past. The narration is closely focused in Marius's consciousness; yet all his "sensations and ideas" are recounted at a distance in the third person, objectified through a mediating, critical perspective. Thus is subjectivity objectified at the same time that the objects of history are subjectified. Pater's intensive pressure on the limits of free indirect discourse is felt every now and then, when the narrator intrudes in *propria persona* with remarks offered quite blatantly from

[35] In fact, if anything the novel is implicitly anti-Christian, or at least powerfully secularizing, in its treatment of Christianity as an aesthetic and historical fact, not as a belief-system. For a recent essay that includes Pater in its treatment of this crucial genre of revival in the nineteenth century, the early Christian novel, see Vincent Lankewish, "Love Among the Ruins: The Catacombs, the Closet, and the Victorian 'Early Christian' Novel," *Victorian Literature and Culture* 28, no. 2 (2000).

[36] Pater, *The Renaissance,* 184.

another time and place. The narrator thus totalizes Marius's *Bildung* retrospectively, while through historical comparisons and contrasts he relates his perspective to Marius's. This narrator—like Pater's critic-interpreter—critically intervenes, putting himself between past and present to mark what survives. In fact the narrator of *Marius the Epicurean* figures to its protagonist as later and earlier phases of a cultural development.[37] Marius's impressions, then, are secured by the narrative point of view in the present time of the novel's writing, a characteristic Paterian reminder that history is made in the past by perfect reception, but it is correlatively (re)made in the present as *revival*. An intensively aesthetic and historicist form, this doubled subjectivity attempts to restore "life" (experience, impressions in their passage, a bygone era) by delicately marking the phases of distance from it. Finally, then, the narrator is, like Marius, "diaphanous": through his figure the past is transmitted into its futures (including our present moment of reading).

Understanding Pater's form of historical revival should afford us a more profound view of literary impressionism, which is usually associated with narrative point of view or stream of consciousness (two techniques for representing experience as if from within a present subject) or with various literary representations of visualization (*seeing* being the quintessential metonymy for empirical experiencing). Like impressionist painting, narrative impressionism records the fragmentation of objects, as light plays and breaks over their surfaces, while romantic "spots of time" and later nineteenth-century "epiphanic" moments out of time (including Pater's) prefigure the disruptions of modernist narration. All these ways of understanding impressionism are relevant to Pater's impressionism, and all of them show, I think, that impressionism marks time while a crisis in representation begins to be registered. Pater's play at the limits of free indirect discourse as it strains toward (yet also resists) "stream of consciousness," for example, shows an attempt to represent mental fluctuation while holding it in place through retrospection. That same purpose is served by the structure I have been describing, the correlation of surface to depth, present to past, "stream" to "house." This structure is unfolded diachronically to generate a model of the mutual relation of impression and expression in aesthetic and historical development.

Pater's version of impressionism is quite literally conservative in the sense that it is concerned with preserving the past as well as restabilizing the pres-

---

[37] For a more extended treatment of this point, see Williams, "Autobiography of the *Zeitgeist*," in *Transfigured World*, 184–93. Jesse Matz has recently argued as well that Pater's impressionism displays a systematic structure involving relative stages of education in time. "Walter Pater's Impressionism," *Modern Language Quarterly* 56, no. 4 (1995). Matz interprets this relation as necessarily homoerotic, reading the two dimensions of the structure as a paiderastic relation between an educated, experienced, active subject and the unreflective object of his desire.

ent subject through retrospection. However—though totalized as "development"—Pater's model of history is gradualistic without being continuous. No phase of the past is ever obliterated, but it may disappear from view, be buried underground, or otherwise forgotten. Pater's recognition that the past is dead and buried, that it can only be revived after a period of loss and forgetting, might be characterized as the more radical, modern side of his historical vision. For Pater, the governing fiction of development must be interrupted for knowledge to be formed; the past can be revived only after a break in continuity or identity has been felt.

The Way We Read Now

Pater's impressionism reflects his particular strategy for reconciling "the proportion of the sensuous and the ideal in human knowledge"; or, to put that same point another way, the object I've delineated as "Pater's impressionism" is meant to serve as a lens through which we can see his particular method of relating empiricism and idealism. These days, Pater's focus on the flux of sensation—its atomism, its accidental fortuity, its fragmentation of objects, subjects, and time, its destabilization of the subject—is apt to seem prescient and bold, whereas his correlative restabilization of subject and object through historical reflection is apt to seem retrograde. Pater's unflinching examination of "what is termed 'the subjectivity of knowledge'...in the full range of its consequences" *is* bold and bracing, a kind of *summa* of the romantic tradition. But today an even greater boldness might be attributed to his repeated insistence that "the doctrine...of what is termed 'the subjectivity of knowledge'" was nothing new but rather has been a transhistorically recurrent problem in philosophy, found not only in romantic "modern thought," but in ancient, classical thought as well. What is historically distinctive is often the proposed circumvention of the epistemological impasse, not the statement of the problem; and in this regard, we can discover the reconstructive side of Heraclitus and Hume as surely as that of Hegel. Nevertheless, though Pater's idealism is historically distinctive, it is precisely his historical idealism that seems objectionable today, as the blatant sign of his undeniably humanist vision.

Foucault puts this line of postmodern critique as well as anyone (though of course he is not referring specifically to Pater here):

> Continuous history is the indispensable correlative of the founding function of the subject: the guarantee that everything that has eluded him may be restored to him; the certainty that time will disperse nothing without restoring it in a reconstituted unity; the promise that one day the subject—in the form of historical consciousness—will once again be able to appropriate, to bring back under

his sway, all those things that have been kept at a distance by difference, and find in them what might be called his abode.[38]

In fact Foucault's argument in this passage characterizes Pater very well, whose developmental history is projected as just such a correlation, expressed as a series of internalizations. The child dwells in his material "house," the adult subject dwells in his "house of thought," and the figure of the developing "human spirit," too, has its ideal abode. Pater's "houses" form a series of stabilizing sublations, posited to contain fluctuations of change within a figure of identity and thus to make those fluctuations knowable as objectified distinctions within an overarching development.[39]

For example: arguing in his essay on romanticism that "oppositions" in aesthetic history (like "classic" and "romantic") should be understood as merely heuristic, critical instruments and not tangibly distinct realities, Pater imagines the identity of his historical culture:

> In that *House Beautiful,* which the creative minds of all generations—the artists and those who have treated life in the spirit of art—are always building together for the refreshment of the human spirit, these oppositions cease; and the *Interpreter* of the *House Beautiful,* the true aesthetic critic, uses these divisions, only so far as they enable him to enter into the peculiarities of the objects with which he has to do.[40]

Like a heavenly museum built for all the objects of past time, this idealization of the critic's hermeneutic function imagines it as a place beyond time, from which that critic, in peaceful recollection, can parse all the particularities of historical difference—objectified as *aesthetic objects.* "Oppositions"—which are the figures used to represent the dialectics of differentiation unfolding in time—are reconciled in this spatial totalization. From this point of view out of time, "oppositions" are diacritical marks merely, used in human thought for the purposes of delineating objects (and "enter[ing]" them as if they too were rooms). However, while time goes on, the *House Beautiful* is still under construction, "always building" (and I think we must hear the pun on *Bildung* here). In the realm of human history—the precincts of culture, not

---

[38] Michel Foucault, *The Archaeology of Knowledge,* trans. A.M. Sheridan Smith (1969; New York: Pantheon, 1972), 14.

[39] Pater's historical objectification works within this idealism. However, it is important to note that Pater was aware of the relative currency of "development" itself. He attributes the idea of development to Hegel and Darwin in his own day, but he points out (making a Hegelian point) that it is itself "a thing of growth, developed in the process of reflection." To demonstrate, he suggested that it had an ancient formulation in Heraclitus. "The entire modern theory of 'development,' in all its various phases,... what is it but old Heracliteanism awake once more in a new world, and grown to full proportions?" "The Doctrine of Motion," in *Plato and Platonism,* 19–20.

[40] Walter Pater, "Postscript," in *Appreciations,* 241. (Pater's emphasis.)

heaven—objects of art express and refresh that familiar anthropomorphism, "the human spirit." That Pater's late-nineteenth century revision of the *House Beautiful* responds to Bunyan's figure from *The Pilgrim's Progress* should alert us to the fact that Pater's impressionism owes a debt not only to the epistemological tradition of skeptical empiricism but also to the long tradition of Christian historicism from Augustine to Hegel. For Pater, like Hegel, history is conceived as History—a developing Spirit that is markedly, but still incompletely, secularized.

Hegel's art history, like Pater's, is also conceived as History. In the *Philosophy of Fine Art* (a work that deeply influenced Pater), it is clear that the history of art, like the individual subject, develops through internalization and expression: "Man's need for art, no less than his need for religion and philosophy, is rooted in his capacity to mirror himself in thought.... Man's spiritual freedom consists in this reduplicating process of human consciousness, whereby all that exists is made explicit *within* him and all that is in him is realized *without*."[41] In examining "Diaphaneitè," "The Child in the House," and especially *Marius the Epicurean,* we have seen how this dynamic of internalization and expression informs Pater's logic of historical development. But it is important to note that this tightly braided relation between individual and historical development is utterly conventional in the late nineteenth century—and may in some representations be seen to derive from Christian strategies of historiography and in others from the biological notion that ontogeny recapitulates phylogeny.[42] The sublationary recourse to phylogeny, in fact, now seems only one more humanist, structural fantasy of "home."

One way to see the object called "Pater" is to assign him a "place" in a critical tradition. Another, representationally quite different, is frankly to position Pater negatively in relation to current critical concerns. *Both* critical strategies work from a position in the present, the first constructing a continuity while the second emphasizes discontinuity. Like Pater, however, we might do well to look both ways. This essay has attempted to work in both modalities—the latter more effaced at the beginning of the essay than it is here at the end—and has suggested at least the following seven lines of thinking about Pater's importance within a critical tradition: (1) Pater's unique version of literary impressionism adds a historicist dimension to our understanding of that early modernist movement. (2) Pater made a lasting contribution by arguing for the role of art and history in the romantic epistemological debates. His correlative theorization of aesthetic and historical

[41] G. W. F. Hegel, *Hegel: On the Arts: Selections from G. W. F. Hegel's Aesthetics (Philosophy of Fine Art),* trans. Henry Paolucci (New York: Frederick Ungar, 1979), 3–4.

[42] For one account of the widespread cultural adaptations of the concepts of ontogeny and phylogeny in the period, see Stephen Jay Gould, *Ontogeny and Phylogeny* (Cambridge: Belknap Press, Harvard University Press, 1977).

"distance" was a novel and powerful response to Arnoldian "disinterested-ness" (as a way of reconstructing objectivity). (3) His phenomenology offers an important prepsychoanalytic model of the shaping power of the mind in the act of perceiving and knowing. (4) Though he secures the subject's fluc-tuations against the background of historical development, Pater's represen-tations of the non-identity and destabilization of the subject still seem radical today. (5) His belief in the continuity of development is accompanied—and often supplanted—by a discontinuous model, in which the past is re-vived against the background of the subject in the present. (6) Though his narrative forms clearly display their debt to Christian historiography, Pater works to detach his thinking from that tradition. He is a powerfully secu-larizing writer. (7) And finally, his romantic view of the critic as "Diaphaneitè" reconciles the aim of hermeneutic intervention with the desire to represent the past objectively. These premises should help to pinpoint Pater's contri-bution.

In closing, however, let me suggest another way of responding to current critique that is not so defensive. For it is precisely due to various forms of current theoretical critique that we can now see "Pater" more clearly, dif-ferentiating ourselves from him, objectifying him anew. One use of theory in our own present moment is to mark a critical difference between what is tacit and what is (re)marked now, as opposed to then. This intellectual pos-ture—reading Pater through the lens of current critique—places him securely in the past. For only after Pater's interpretive model passes out of tacit con-ventionality can we see the form of its implications. To see Pater's impres-sionism "as in itself it really is," therefore, is precisely to see it *as a period piece.*

The hermeneutic effects of this move are profound. Once Pater's writings are imagined as artifacts of the past, secured in their historically different place, their representations will no longer be judged against standards of "ac-curacy," "realism," or theoretical agreement with widely held present views. It is under these conditions that they may be taken not only as passionately beautiful defenses against death and dissolution, but also as assemblages of discourse and figures—in short, as *literary* texts.

In other words, it is partly *because* we can now recognize the conventional elements of his thought that Pater's work may be seen as an aesthetic object in its own right. Thus it is precisely the historicizing perspective that trans-forms "Pater" into an aesthetic object and makes his texts available for a lit-erary reading. This argument exhibits, to be sure, the hermeneutic circle of all literary history, old and new. But on the other hand, it insists that to see from the vantage of the present does not necessarily imply the progressivist assumption of our position at the apex of knowledge. It is wise to remem-ber that we must make a careful discrimination among presentisms. Thus I have been arguing here for what we might call a "strong presentism," the principled assertion that knowledge is formed in the present together with a recommitment to historical knowledge-formation. The most important point here is that "the hermeneutics of suspicion"[43] can give way to the hermeneutics of appreciation without any loss in theoretical finesse—if and only if "appreciation" is understood in Pater's own strong and delicate sense: the critical activity of clearly delineating objects by endowing them with the distinctive values that can only be seen after time passes.

[43] Paul Ricoeur's phrase, in *Freud and Philosophy,* trans. D. Savage (New Haven: Yale University Press, 1970).

5. Arnold and the Authorization of Criticism

HERBERT F. TUCKER

That Matthew Arnold's reputation as a critic overshadows his reputation as a poet is not a matter for dispute; nor, in my judgment, is it a matter for regret. My point here will be that, in the judgment of Arnold himself, it was decidedly not a matter for capricious posterity to settle without plenty of prompting. I hope to show that the supervention of the critical interpreter's office on the creative poet's is an event that Arnold plotted, rehearsed, and performed with great care; and to suggest in passing that this careful critical takeover has exerted on English studies an abiding influence—a culturally authoritative force—which spreads well beyond the current of tastes and beliefs ordinarily specified as Arnoldian. Appreciating the influence means studying the hydraulics of the current that impelled it, and doing that entails returning to its fountainhead early in the poet-critic's career.

I

It tells us much about the balance of emphases in Arnold's reception that the critical preface he affixed to his 1853 *Poems* attracts more respectful attention than does the poem whose suppression furnished the occasion for printing it. The *Norton Anthology,* to look no farther, delivers the preface swaddled in commentary while leaving *Empedocles on Etna* right out. *Empedocles* may not be Arnold's best poem, even by standards more flexible than an anthologist's. But it is generally reckoned his most ambitious poem, and for the argument I shall pursue it is his most revealing—not just in the Nortonian breach but in the observance which *Empedocles* itself enacts, and which uncannily anticipates the poem's repudiation in 1853. In that year, to stern

Doric fanfare, and with the accents of an eminence grise, the thirty-year-old poet drummed out of his third book a work he had regarded well enough only the year before to give it top billing in his second book, *Empedocles on Etna and Other Poems*.[1] The impeccably neo-neoclassicist principles that the preface adduces have drawn and held the notice of historians of poetics, but the principles will concern us less here than the means of attracting attention to them. Arnold could have buried his poem silently, but instead he fed it to his theory and said so through a megaphone. Why take such pains in order to cut a public profile that would be better known for suppressing poetry than for writing it? Arnold must have been betting—shrewdly, to judge from the result—that there was significant wattage, and cultural leverage, to be obtained from the combustion of disposable art. At the head of a still-minor poet's second volume, *Empedocles on Etna* could boast hardly more name recognition in 1853 than in 2003.[2] Now as then, however, as the *Norton* editors know, one need not read the poem in order to appreciate the essentially ritual role scripted for it by the preface. For the preface stages, at maximum visibility, a sacrifice of Arnold's first-born major brainchild to his second thoughts.

Sacrifice involves cashing in something already prized for something reckoned better. What then was at stake in the media event that Arnold constructed around *Empedocles*? Ben Jonson or Alexander Pope might approvingly say that Arnold sacrificed his spontaneous invention to his better judgment. Harold Bloom might disgustedly say that Arnold sacrificed Romantic creative originality to Victorian social conscience. Within a survey of Arnold's whole career, however, what the bloodletting of 1853 most resembles is a sacrifice of poetry on the altar of criticism. For the whole affair—ceremonious publication, ostentatious retraction—openly inaugurated a habit on which Arnold built a career, and on which his reputation has depended ever since. I mean the habit of capitalizing on the critic's power to discriminate and—at the right hand of the judgment seat, or its executive arm—to reject. I mean, as how can I not, the nay-saying Mephistophelean authority that every English Department heir of Arnold claims, the authority to pronounce: That is not it, at all.[3]

---

[1] Also omitted from the 1853 *Poems* were "Stanzas in Memory of the Author of *Obermann*," "A Summer Night," and "The Buried Life"; the first two were soon reinstated in *Poems, Second Series* (1855), while the last stayed underground until 1885.

[2] Its author could boast even less, since the title pages to his volumes of 1849 and 1852 had identified him merely as "A." Only in 1853 was title to the poetry claimed by "Matthew Arnold," in his simultaneous debut as its prose saboteur. About the 1852 *Empedocles* volume J. C. Shairp wrote to A. H. Clough, "I fear Mat's last book has made no impression on the public mind" (quoted in Nicholas Murray, *A Life of Matthew Arnold* [London: Hodder and Stoughton, 1996], 134). According to Ian Hamilton, *A Gift Imprisoned: The Poetic Life of Matthew Arnold* (London: Bloomsbury, 1998), the print run in 1852 was only 500 copies, of which few had been sold before Arnold bought up the remainder himself (154–155).

[3] Lionel Trilling, who should know, gauges the cultural purchasing power of Arnold's sacrifice in *Matthew Arnold* (New York: Norton, 1939), 148: "Arnold's first public critical act is the

This much can be said on the strength of the 1853 preface alone. But there is a further, inward twist. Whoever tracks down *Empedocles on Etna*—as Arnold made easy in 1867 by reinstating it among his collected poems, once its retraction had helped make his name—discovers that the sacrifice of poetry to criticism was performed not *just* on the poem but *in* it, and indeed constituted its climactic plot event. For the sacrifice of poetry to criticism is not a bad description of what happens in the second and final act of this closet drama, which in essence consists of the depressed hero's meditations on the way he has traded the life-giving powers of joy and sympathy and creativity for the different, more austerely intellectual powers of doubt and analysis and judgment. Lest we fail to recognize in this Faustian bargain the swapping of poetic for critical power, the physical action of Act II, such as it is, amounts to Empedocles' stripping off his robes, badges, and laurels and then, in a summary negative criticism of life, jumping into an active volcano. This, the literal action of the piece, is a story soon told; but the closet-drama form extends the action by means of an attenuated dramatic dialogue. The dialogue takes its rise in a sequence of lyrical songs, which the young poet Callicles (a footloose disciple who might have stepped into the drama from Arnold's 1849 *The Strayed Reveller*) devises downslope and offers up as mood-altering therapy for his depressed elder. The dialogue these songs initiate is then clinched by the interpretive sense that the wiser but sadder Empedocles makes of them as they ascend to the summit. In other words, when Arnold gave imaginative form in 1849–52 to what his preface would soon memorably call "the dialogue of the mind with itself," that dialogue took the form of a debate between poetry and interpretation.[4] Callicles in effect beams poetry up the mountainside so that Empedocles may ruminate on it and, treading the crater's edge, produce interpretations. Empedocles keeps up his side of the dialogue by obsessively orbiting a single theme: the losing battle that his imagination is fighting against his reason.[5] He apprehends this battle as part of a larger culture war between mythic and scientific truth—a definitively modern conflict waged, in pre-Socratic camouflage, through the poem's hermeneutic skirmishing between the imaginatively embodied mode of Callicles' songs and the propositionally explicit mode to which Empedocles

---

rejection of his most ambitious single work; few critics have given such earnest of their disinterestedness or acquired a better right to be absolute with their contemporaries." For a biographical understanding of Arnold's sacrifice, see Paull F. Baum, *Ten Studies in the Poetry of Matthew Arnold* (Durham: Duke University Press, 1958), 134; Murray Krieger, *Poetic Presence and Illusion* (Baltimore: Johns Hopkins University Press, 1979), 94.

[4] *The Poems of Matthew Arnold,* 2d ed., ed. Kenneth Allott and Miriam Allott (London: Longman, 1979), 654. All citations of Arnold's verse, and of the 1853 preface, are to this edition. Antony H. Harrison, *Victorian Poets and Romantic Poems: Intertextuality and Ideology* (Charlottesville: University Press of Virginia, 1990), 34, argues for the "dialogical," as opposed to "dialectical," structure of *Empedocles*.

[5] On the contest of mythic lore with intellectual knowledge see A. Dwight Culler, *Imaginative Reason: The Poetry of Matthew Arnold* (New Haven: Yale University Press, 1966), 165–69.

reduces them, and on which Arnold's scenario confers the authority of the last word.[6]

The first of these conferrals takes place after Callicles advances a specimen of poetical geology reminiscent of Shelley's in "Mont Blanc" on the Earthquake Daemon (lines 67–74), or Keats's on the rockbound Titans of *Hyperion* (2.15–28). Callicles' song endows a real volcano, Mount Etna in Sicily, with a supernatural origin: the myth of Typho, a hundred-headed giant whose rearguard insurgency against the upstart god Zeus came to nought. The ordered music of the victors is "lovely" to Olympian ears, Callicles sings,

> Only to Typho it sounds hatefully;
> To Typho only, the rebel o'erthrown,
> Through whose heart Etna drives her roots of stone
> To imbed them in the sea.
> . . . .
> Is thy tortured heart still proud?
> Is thy fire-scathed arm still rash?
> Still alert thy stone-crush'd frame?
>
> (41–51)

Empedocles' instantaneous and utterly characteristic reaction to this myth is to demythologize it: "These rumblings are not Typho's groans, I know" (95). It is not that Empedocles *debunks* the poet's myth; that is neither his way nor the way of Arnold's criticism, which, from this moment on through *God and the Bible* (1875), embraces the primary text on condition that criticism shall retain the upper hand. For what Empedocles does, in token of his superior knowledge, is to *appropriate* the myth Callicles has proposed by recasting it as a concept; by asserting, in other words, the critic's right to declare the old myth's true meaning as an allegory possessing contemporary resonance.

---

[6] True, Callicles' final song (417–468) has the poem's last *words*, Empedocles being no longer alive to gloss it. But the rhythm of verse and gloss is by this point so well established that the reader can take over and does, in many an article and chapter that, even when aligned with Callicles (or Susan Sontag) against interpretation, remains *qua* gloss an Empedoclean act. The best Arnold criticism focuses on this hermeneutic crux itself, bearing out Trilling's insight that Arnold "is ever trying some new subtlety to deny what he has affirmed" (89). See, for instance, Culler's argument that the final song amounts to a repudiation of the drama it follows (176); Sara Suleri's contention that the preemptive obsolescence of the song, "fully conscious of the quaintness of its idiom," enacts a "strategically minor" tactic of survivalist damage control ("Entropy on Etna: Arnold and the Poetry of Reading,"in *Matthew Arnold: Modern Critical Views,* ed. Harold Bloom [New York: Chelsea House, 1987],148–149); James Longenbach's demonstration that the interplay of "reified myth" with "self-conscious fiction" weaves a tradition that "contains its own critique," in "Matthew Arnold and the Modern Apocalypse," *PMLA* 104 (1989): 851.

> He fables, yet speaks truth!
> The brave, impetuous heart yields everywhere
> To the subtle, contriving head.
>
> $(89-91)^7$

This is a remarkable gloss on Callicles' song in a couple of respects. For one thing, it is a highly debatable gloss, since it is far from clear that the poet's Orphic, mythic ode signifies anything, much less the starkly philosophical truth that Empedocles claims to find there.[8] The very arbitrariness of Empedocles' reading suggests that it owes less to properties inherent in the poem than to obsessions brought along by the reader. *He fables, yet speaks truth.* What but this does every hermeneutic act categorically declare? These five words from Arnold's first major work in effect state the premise of the three late books in which he taught disenchanted Victorians how to read their Bible—namely, as literature—by converting the mythic and religious idiom of a collection of archaic fables and chronicles, cultic anthems and memoranda, into the currency of Arnold's own stringently impersonal ethical humanism.[9]

This paradigmatic interpretive maneuver enjoys several reprises during Act II of *Empedocles,* but what is particularly interesting about the instance before us is its profound reflexivity. The passage does the thing it is talking about, and performs what it describes: it is a special instance of the general hermeneutic rule it enunciates. The brave, impetuous poet yields to the subtle, contriving critic everywhere, and that means right here: in what amounts to an allegory of critical allegoresis, these lines describe the process of intellectual capture that brings them into being. That the poetic truth of myths and images cannot hold out against the conceptual truth of propositions is a certainty that Empedocles hates to behold. But, actuated as he is by the occu-

---

[7] "The troubled poet steadily gives way to the prescriptive sage": this actually is a recent critic's comment on the 1853 preface (Hamilton, 157); but its plausibility as a comment on *Empedocles* suggests, again, the recursivity linking preface and poem.

[8] For arguments that Empedocles misunderstands Callicles' songs see Paul Zietlow, "Heard but Unheeded: The Songs of Callicles in Matthew Arnold's *Empedocles on Etna*," *Victorian Poetry* 21 (1983): 241–256; and David G. Riede, *Matthew Arnold and the Betrayal of Language* (Charlottesville: University Press of Virginia, 1988), who also reads in Empedocles' responses a form of "internalized literary criticism" (81 and 93).

[9] Here I hail with thanks J. Hillis Miller's dazzling reading of this crux, in *The Linguistic Moment: From Wordsworth to Stevens* (Princeton: Princeton University Press, 1985). Miller finds his "linguistic moment" epitomized in Empedocles' ungrounded allegoresis (35), and sees moreover that the secondary, figural reinscription of a referentially discredited primary word is a gesture "repeated over and over from one end of Arnold's work to the other" (43), especially in his trilogy on Biblical interpretation. My argument here is an attempt to proceed from Miller's parabolic and elliptical insights and ask what practical torque the linguistic moment packs: What kind of cultural work does this Arnoldian performativity make possible? It is equally unfortunate that Miller leaves the question unasked and that the scholars who do ask it tend to find Arnold's method and meanings so much less "problematic and equivocal" than Miller does—such easy marks, in fact, for blunt detraction.

pational neurosis of the born hermeneut, he would hate even worse not beholding it. For him it is irresistibly the truth, and producing the truth on such terms is his calling.

Being a philosopher with an eye for generality, Empedocles is not slow to enlarge his own plight into one that afflicts an entire society. Neither was Arnold: *Empedocles on Etna* stands to this day as a prime exhibit documenting the radical dilemma that the Victorian era apprehended in religious terms of faith and doubt, and in cultural terms of literature and science.[10] To trace out the implications of this social allegory more fully would entail measuring its Victorian concern for cultural generality against the more personal and subjective Romantic models that Arnold's drama regularly echoes. Inquiry along these lines would highlight, in Act II, Empedocles' evocation of the key Wordsworthian and Coleridgean value "joy" from the "Intimations" and "Dejection" odes; and it would underscore the unmistakable parallel between Arnold's "No, no, ye stars! there is no death with you" (301) and Keats's "Thou wast not born for death, immortal Bird!" in the "Ode to a Nightingale" (line 61)—reading the Victorian poet's responses to Romantic precedent as so many illustrations of the way scientific advance had come, by the mid-nineteenth century, to block poetic appeals to nature if not preempt them.

Such an interpretation might likewise venture back into Act I of the drama to see how a pathology there becomes a philosophy, as the homiletic stanzas Empedocles chants to Pausanias (I.ii.77–426) elevate and amplify a personal malaise into a theory of impersonal resignation. This theory resembles those articulated by Carlyle in *Sartor Resartus* (1834) as demand-reduction (*"lessening your Denominator"*) and by Mill's *Autobiography* (1873) as "the anti-self-consciousness theory."[11] All three Victorian texts disclose a paradoxically self-conscious will to power through self-disregard. I do not mean to pursue this philosophy further here, merely to point out that if I did I would be behaving like Empedocles, imposing on poetry a critical narrative that turned it into a chapter in the history of ideas—like Empedocles, and also like an English professor, a laborer in the field that Arnold helped clear for cultivation.[12] I mean instead, and in the hope of exploring rather than

[10] As Arnold wrote his mother on 5 June 1869, "My poems represent, on the whole, the main movement of mind of the last quarter of a century." *The Letters of Matthew Arnold,* ed. Cecil Y. Lang, vol. 3 (Charlottesville: University Press of Virginia, 1998), 347.

[11] Thomas Carlyle, *Sartor Resartus,* ed. Kerry McSweeney and Peter Sabor (Oxford: Oxford University Press, 1987), 145 (book 2, chap. 9); John Stuart Mill, *Autobiography,* ed. Jack Stillinger (Boston: Houghton Mifflin, 1969), (chap. 5), 85, where Mill expressly credits Carlyle with the theory. On Arnold's undoubted but complicated affiliation with Carlyle see John P. Farrell, *Revolution as Tragedy: The Dilemma of the Moderate from Scott to Arnold* (Ithaca: Cornell University Press, 1980), 254–55.

[12] This is admittedly just half the truth about what an English professor can do with Arnold. Truth's other, better half is treated with great finesse by Timothy Peltason in "The Function of Matthew Arnold at the Present Time," *College English* 56 (1994): 749–765, which defends on literary grounds the imaginative and intellectual virtues of the critical prose, correlating its mod-

just evincing my professional genealogy, to move toward a consideration of Arnold's paradigmatic critical emergence by looking at the final assessment he places in Empedocles' mouth. It is a peroration epitomizing the delicate equilibrium of the critic as such: a figure whose ascendancy exacts the death of the poet, yet who asserts in compensation a definitively Arnoldian kind of dignity, and freedom.

The last dozen lines Empedocles speaks are rhetorically equivalent to a few bounces on the diving board before the suicidal plunge confirms his claim "not to be all enslaved" and to "breathe free" (406–8). What this freedom means has been worked out in the preceding verse paragraph, which may be read as a damaged sonnet in blank verse, legitimate in its proportions if bent sinister on the page:

> Slave of sense
> I have in no wise been;—but slave of thought?...
> And who can say: I have been always free,
> Lived ever in the light of my own soul?—
> I cannot; I have lived in wrath and gloom,
> Fierce, disputatious, ever at war with man,
> Far from my own soul, far from warmth and light.
> But I have not grown easy in these bonds—
> But I have not denied what bonds these were.
> Yea, I take myself to witness,
> That I have loved no darkness,
> Sophisticated no truth,
> Nursed no delusion,
> Allow'd no fear!
>
> (390–403)

It is a driving conviction of Arnold's as of every great critic's work that the truth will make us free. But truth in what form, these lines ask, and free from what bondage? "Slave of sense" or "slave of thought"? Empedocles' balance of bodily against mental servitude points to a reader's dilemma: Which addiction is the more despotic, to sensuous imagery or to conceptual ideation? The image can enthrall us, making us "slaves of sense," but Empedocles discerns that the idea, even as it liberates us from the image, can enthrall us just as stubbornly to itself. No one has "been always free," and certainly not Empedocles, estranged from his "own soul."

Bad news for the critic, the alienated modern exegete whom Arnold clearly means Empedocles to portend. And yet just here Empedocles saves himself for criticism, and saves for criticism a modicum of self-respect that is even,

---

ern resourcefulness with "the mysteriously difficult lyric project of saying things as they are" (764).

in a way peculiarly Arnoldian, exhilarating. Things may be bad, yet the critical intellect takes a residual pride in the ability to announce just how bad they are:

> But I have not grown easy in these bonds—
> But I have not denied what bonds these were.

"Far from warmth and light," these blank lines occupy a zero point of frigid darkness. But they also straddle the turning point of a sonnet however twisted, and the dash between them sparks a difference that belies their syntactic parallelism, activating the ambiguity whereby the second "But" may betoken not reinforcement of the first but a dissenting departure into fresh matter worthy of a sestet. This difference corresponds to a difference between the orders of affect and of discourse—between how you are doing and what you may nevertheless rise to the occasion of saying on that dreary topic—a difference which the passage also reflects in its verb tenses: the only places Empedocles does not suicidally speak of himself as a has-been are references to his own present speech ("who can say," "I take myself to witness"). Granted, says Empedocles, I am a slave to my own mind, and to its reciprocating tyrannies of image and idea. But I know that is what I am; I reserve the right to say so, and I hereby exercise the power. The sign of this power is the way Empedocles' hard-won victory in the order of discourse flows back into the order of affect to lighten his mood after all. His sonnet sestet grows positively cheerful through the mediation of the double negative, where the reiteration of "no" means "Yea."[13]

We approach here a Cartesian point of origin for the Arnoldian critical impulse at its purest. It is much the same point, incidentally, around which movements in interpretation like new historicism and cultural studies have recently spun cycles of critique, gleaning what cheer they can from bleakly over-determined textual fields. And it is much the same point at which the greatest English critic of all, Samuel Johnson, arrived during his seventy-fifth year, in what is my hands-down favorite anecdote in illustration of the critical mind.

> On Monday, the 16th, I sat for my picture, and walked a considerable way with little inconvenience. In the afternoon and evening I felt myself light and easy, and began to plan schemes of life. Thus I went to bed, and in a short time waked and sat up, as has been long my custom, when I felt a confusion and indistinctness in my head, which lasted, I suppose, about half a minute. I was

---

[13] Writ large, double negation underlies Arnold's justly famous irony; writ small, and apparently off-guard, it produces the following enigmatically toned phrase, which a new scholarly edition lets us cite more pointedly than heretofore: "the modern situation in its true *blankness* and *barrenness*, and un*poetrylessness*" (Arnold's letter to A. H. Clough, 14 December 1852, in *Letters*, ed. Lang, vol. 1 [1996], 250). Italics and all, that word "un*poetrylessness*" puts my thesis about Arnold's criticism in a nutshell.

alarmed, and prayed God, that however he might afflict my body, he would spare my understanding. This prayer, that I might try the integrity of my faculties, I made in Latin verse. The lines were not very good, but I knew them not to be very good: I made them easily, and concluded myself to be unimpaired in my faculties.[14]

As Johnson, so Empedocles: uneasy in his bonds, yet not about to deny what bonds they are; facile in composition (the chant to Pausanias is lethally fluent), yet in judgment swift, tough, and most vital. Reviewing the record of his life as a critic might a book, Empedocles declares it unsatisfactory, pans it in effect; and yet by doing so, like the stricken yet still exacting petitioner Dr. Johnson, he upholds with satisfaction a criterion that, even when it is disappointed, suffices to "inspirit and rejoice the reader" (1853 Preface, 665). Empedocles' confession of failure in life constitutes his profession of faith as the prototypical Arnoldian critic, for whom it is less the case that the truth shall make you free than that a certain neurotic vacillation about the truth may keep you out of the grosser traps.

Self-discomfiture thus offers a margin of independence that you can live on—but only, it appears, if you stand ready to live as a critic rather than a poet.[15] Empedocles does not stand thus ready. Having always conceived himself as a sort of shaman, statesman, and bard in one, he finds the examined life of an alienated intellectual not worth living, so within twenty lines he does the glamorous thing and topples into the magma. Arnold's first hero actualizes himself poetically only over his own dead body; and thus, taking himself out, he anticipates what Arnold would do in 1853 by taking *Empedocles on Etna* out of his *Poems*. It is as if, in order for Arnold to survive on the terms modern life had made available, the poet in him had to give way to the critic. And, before the critic in him had concluded his career, he would establish that for the sake of modern culture the institution of literature—which is what he meant by the term *poetry*—was going to have to give way to the institution of criticism.

Arnold's poetry is about to give way to his criticism in this essay, as well. But first, one glimpse more at the poetry, if only to suggest that the dead end at which Empedocles arrives marks a cul-de-sac into which Arnold's poetry kept leading him, even in the poems he did not suppress, and indeed in the

---

[14] Letter of 19 June 1783 to Hester Thrale, quoted in James Boswell, *Life of Johnson*, ed. R. W. Chapman (London: Oxford University Press, 1970), 1241.

[15] The divide between these two walks of literary life has been much muddied, of course, and by shoes from both sides. Arnold's systematic trespass, most clearly marked in "The Function of Criticism," has invited a host of successors. See Geoffrey Hartman, *Criticism in the Wilderness: The Study of Literature Today* (New Haven: Yale University Press, 1980), and the forum of responses to Hartman's book by Eugene Goodheart, George Levine, Morris Dickstein, and Stuart Tave published in *Critical Inquiry* 9 (1983); see also Mary W. Schneider, *Poetry in the Age of Democracy: The Literary Criticism of Matthew Arnold* (Lawrence: University Press of Kansas, 1989).

poems that are his best. I might cite "The Scholar-Gipsy" and "Stanzas from the Grande Chartreuse," where Arnold fondly seeks an alliance with some poetic and religious alternative to the world of reason, commerce, and technology. But he cannot, for the poetic life of him, manage more than a nostalgic allegiance to imaginative powers that his better judgment tells him are impotent. His poetry's inability to believe in itself comes most stunningly into focus at the close of "Dover Beach," where the Empedoclean word *true* peals its iron note over one of the most disturbing *carpe diem* poems in the canon.

> Ah, love, let us be true
> To one another! for the world, which seems
> To lie before us like a land of dreams,
> So various, so beautiful, so new,
> Hath really neither joy, nor love, nor light,
> Nor certitude, nor peace, nor help for pain;
> And we are here as on a darkling plain
> Swept with confused alarms of struggle and flight,
> Where ignorant armies clash by night.
>
> (29–37)

He fables, yet speaks truth. Arnold's ignorant armies are fabulous enough to distract us from the homely truth in the lines that precede them, but those are the lines that harbor this anthology piece's really shocking intelligence. Their point is a meta-hermeneutic inquiry into the truth about troth. What does "true" mean in the first line, exposed by enjambment as it is? Does it mean loyal, or candid? Faithful, or frank? What, for that matter, is meant in this ostensible love poem by "love"? Even when love is evoked as merely a "mournful cosmic last resort" (thus Anthony Hecht's shrewd parody "The Dover Bitch")—what does it mean, within four lines of that evocation, to find "love" not just quarantined but disappeared, withdrawn like the Sea of Faith from a world that "really" (*truly?*) has "neither joy, nor love, nor light"? Arnold's proposal to his lady, if that is what "Dover Beach" is, reduces to a proposition, and not the kind Hecht would have us think: I mean the bleak proposition that he respects her too much not to trust her with the whole sorry truth about love affairs, which looks suspiciously like the whole sorry truth about human affairs at large. If these yearning bodies are to unite after all, they won't have poetry's sweet nothings to thank for it. With the recession of the Sea of Faith, and the onset of ignorance militant, such salvation as may subsist lies in the astringent fellowship of critique.

It did not have to be that way. Even during Arnold's poetically active decade the 1850s, Tennyson in *In Memoriam*, Browning in *Men and Women*, and Barrett Browning in *Aurora Leigh* not only were plucking love and beauty and God from the ashes of analytic critique but were showing how a modern poetry might warm to the same conflicts that stopped the poet in Arnold cold: the conflicts between image and idea, belief and skepticism, which under-wrote the handful of fine poems he did manage yet also kept such poems few and far between. Looking ahead to our century, we could even say that what paralyzed the poet in Arnold galvanized some of his most conspicuous suc-cessors. W. B. Yeats, for one, positively throve on the vacillations that gave Arnold cramp; and for Wallace Stevens, whose modernist man on the dump might stand comparison with the Victorian's pre-Socratic man on the vol-cano, the dialogue of the mind with itself became poetry's sine qua non. I cannot explain this deficiency in Arnold beyond saying that in identifying poetry with a single-minded brand of creative affirmation—a vulgar Romanticism that he was never able to stomach intellectually—he confined his poems to a narrow gamut of melancholy and embitterment and doomed himself to poetic minority.[16]

II

Another minor Victorian poet is all Matthew Arnold would be for us today if he had not made the momentous career change into criticism that is fore-cast in *Empedocles on Etna,* that is broadcast in the 1853 preface, and that, I shall now argue, left its traces on his most important essays. Having taken his critical origin from the defeat (or betrayal) of poetry, he returned to the scene of that contest (or crime) in each of his major critical manifestos and enacted it afresh. I offer now a highly abbreviated tour of those essays, with a view to showing how they add up to a vindication of criticism as, in Arnold's developing thought, criticism takes more and more advantage of poetry.

Three steps are to be discerned in this gradual development. In the first Arnold meekly submits that criticism may become, under certain conditions, not merely ancillary to poetry but an activity of equivalent interest and worth. The second step promotes the critical handmaid to midwife and presses the initial assertion of *equality* into something more: an assertion of criticism's actual *priority.* With his third and final step Arnold seems to fall back and defer again to the poet. But it seems thus only because, by this point in the evolution of his criticism program, Arnold can produce the poet as a hostage indemnifying criticism against all methodological or conceptual constraint whatsoever. This last step, which did much to provide English studies with their disciplinary charter when they took firm root in the academy a hun-dred years ago, is represented by the amazing passage on "touchstones" from

---

[16] The most ambitious recent account of this doom is Riede's. Comparing Arnold's output to his contemporaries', Riede links the exceptional inhibition of poetry in his case with an ex-ceptionally strong commitment to "empirical rationalism" (Reide, *Matthew Arnold,* 27) and the denotative language theory that accompanied it.

Arnold's late essay "The Study of Poetry" (1880). The other two are both present in what seems to me the finest thing he ever wrote, the 1864 essay wryly entitled "The Function of Criticism at the Present Time." But, since the first step is more premised than argued for in that swift and cunning piece, it will help if we back up from 1864 to 1857 and note a couple of sentences that Arnold put into the lecture he delivered that year when inaugurating his tenure as Professor of Poetry at Oxford.

The lecture is called "On the Modern Element in Literature," and no attentive reader of the preface of 1853, published just four years before, should be surprised to find that by "modern" Arnold does not mean "contemporary." Having despatched *Empedocles,* Arnold had devoted the bulk of the preface to defending classical topics and principles for literary art against the lure of the transitory, with which for rhetorical reasons he made the "modern" more or less synonymous. This concession he has thought better of by 1857, and his Oxford lecture sets about rescinding it. What he does mean by "modern" it takes Arnold most of the lecture to establish, but the pith of it is that a "modern" literature—be it from Periclean Athens, late republican Rome, Elizabethan or Victorian England—is one in which a rich and complex society finds itself reflected *and comprehended.* I shall not rehearse Arnold's argument but merely underscore the consequences, for mine, of his declaration that it is the function of literature to *comprehend* the spectacle of its own day:

> He who has found that point of view, he who adequately comprehends this spectacle, has risen to the comprehension of his age: he who communicates that point of view to his age, he who interprets to it that spectacle, is one of his age's intellectual deliverers. (1:20)[17]

Arnold's "He" here is the poet, the Sophocles or Shakespeare or Goethe who sees life steadily and whole. But whose job does Arnold actually have him doing? Ask Empedocles: the job of comprehension and interpretation belongs to that "slave of thought" the critic. Sure enough, before the lecture is over Arnold will couch his highest praise of literature in terms of "the interpreting power, the illuminating and revealing intellect" (1:22), and finally, in a phrase we should be waiting for, "the critical power" (1:28).[18] The Arnoldian poet of 1857 is not a maker or seer or singer but an *interpreter,* one who occupies vis-à-vis life a position quite analogous to the critic's vis-à-vis literature. This analogy is already wound into the sentence indented

---

[17] All citations of "On the Modern Element," "The Function of Criticism," and "The Study of Poetry" refer by volume and page to the *Complete Prose Works,* ed. R.H. Super, 11 vols. (Ann Arbor: University of Michigan Press, 1960–77).

[18] Schneider observes that in this lecture Arnold attempted "to make a way for the poet by making the poet share the functions of the historian.... Arnold, however, found the place for poetry at a great cost to poetry" (60), inasmuch as the "modern" element proved there to equal "a critical or rational habit of mind" (129).

above, with the term "adequately": the lexicon of *adequacy* is ubiquitous in Arnold's 1857 lecture, and it presupposes the existence of some standard of comparative measure that lies outside the literary work it calibrates, and that is in the first instance accessible to the critic—to whom, or into whom, the poet seeking an adequate comprehensiveness must turn for ratification. The truly modern poet, therefore, is a model of cultural intelligence and health who obeys the same critical imperative that drove Empedocles to the edge yet is cured of the Romantic spasmodism that drove Empedocles over it. Art is refigured, along a line that will lead from Arnold through Walter Pater to Oscar Wilde, as a criticism of life.[19]

Working out this analogy, or adequation, in such a way as to put criticism on top becomes the business of that dextrous essay one cannot read too often, "The Function of Criticism at the Present Time." If a touchstone were needed for distinguishing the helplessly, congenitally susceptible literary critic from the common reader, it might be found in the degree of thrilled responsiveness with which candidates for that office come upon Arnold's declaration about "the free play of the mind upon all subjects being a pleasure in itself, being an object of desire, being an essential provider of elements without which a nation's spirit, whatever compensations it may have for them, must, in the long run, die of inanition" (3:268). This is stirring stuff, and the life of literary scholarship would be the poorer without it. But the free play of the mind upon our present subject gravitates toward the metaphor in which Arnold figures criticism as, more than a parasite or plaything, a "provider" of spiritual staples. This trope discloses a subversive logic whose near Victorian analogue, in economic practice and theory alike, was the preemption of production by consumption, wherein advertising and marketing circa 1870 started to drive the manufacture to which they had formerly been subordinate; and it is intriguing to reflect that at such a time, under conditions of advancing literacy and systematic overproduction of cultural wares, Arnold should have represented as a needful *provision* the consultancy service that criticism supplied to market-addled readers. This trope, and this logic, lead to a newly telling formulation: "Criticism first; a time of true creative activity, perhaps—which, as I have said, must inevitably be preceded amongst us by a time of criticism—hereafter, when criticism has done its work" (3:269).

"Criticism first": Arnold's priorities could not be clearer. Elsewhere in these pages he calls criticism poetry's "true basis" and "means of prepara-

---

[19] The famous phrase "criticism of life," adumbrated in *On Translating Homer* (1861), arrives with éclat in the essay "Joubert" (1864), where Arnold discriminates between literary "genius" and "ability," only to affirm that "The work of the two orders of men is at bottom the same, a criticism of life." The essay was collected in the 1865 *Essays in Criticism*, which also included, in "Maurice de Guérin," the cognate claim that "Poetry is the interpretress of the natural world, and she is the interpretress of the moral world" (*Essays in Criticism, First Series* [London: Macmillan, 1903], 302–3, 106–7). On Arnoldian "adequacy" see A. Dwight Culler, "Matthew Arnold and the Zeitgeist," in Bloom, *Matthew Arnold: Modern Critical Views*, 115–116.

tion," even poetry's happy source of "inspiration," as if the critic were not only a prophetic herald but in some sense a muse: significantly passive, the poet's "gift lies in the faculty of being happily inspired by a certain intellectual and spiritual atmosphere, by a certain order of ideas," which order it is the critic's work to create (3:260). *Criticism first.* This is the place, too, where Arnold clucks his tongue over the regrettable impetuosity of the Romantic poets, whose work was "premature" (3:262), it seems, because, like Thyrsis in the 1866 elegy, they could not stay, could not wait for Arnold and criticism to steer them right. Arnold's argument here is strictly speaking contingent on history: he purports to describe "the present time," the nineteenth-century scene, and he hangs his remarks on a conviction that under culturally optimal conditions—such as obtained in fifth-century Athens—literature can safely make its way without a critical chaperone. The only trouble is that, according to Arnold's vision of cultural history, these ideal conditions have never occurred *since* fifth-century Athens. The Age of Pericles is the exception that proves the rule; and the rule is, let us say it again, *Criticism first.* Leaving no doubt that if ever an epoch has needed critical guidance, that epoch is the Age of Victoria, Arnold secures to criticism at the present time a vigorously functional role.

We have come a long way already to this indispensable cultural functionary, from the analytically muscle-bound, creatively impotent Empedocles with whom we began. Yet Arnold has another giant step in prospect, one that pushes off from the instrumental model which conceives criticism as a means to a cultural and creative end, into a headier sphere where criticism may shed such duties and become an aestheticized end in itself. For the weakness of the position we have seen Arnold stake out thus far in "The Function of Criticism" is the one betrayed by that word "function." The very word, which Arnold deploys with more irony than is ordinarily noted, savors of utilitarian machine-oil: the notion that criticism draws its justification from ministering to some ulterior cause leaves the critic at the mercy of that cause. And from political, social, even intellectual causes Arnold in the 1860s is increasingly ambitious to set criticism free. It is to this end—the end of exalting criticism as an end in itself—that Arnold invokes during the second half of the essay the notion of "disinterestedness."

Even after patiently discriminating "disinterested," as must be done these days, from its blasé tag-along "uninterested," it is not easy to say what "disinterestedness" is. I infer from Arnold's own handling of the question that he thought it unwise to try. He treats the term thaumaturgically, in fact; as with sacralized terms generally, the discourse it attracts is either tautologically circular or negatively prophylactic. Criticism asserts its disinterestedness, says Arnold, "by resolutely following the law of its own nature"; smartly Victorian, it minds its own "business" (3:270); shunning the practical interests of sect and party, it becomes "a criticism, not the minister of these interests, not their enemy, but absolutely and entirely independent of them" (3:271).[20] To which Arnold then adds, revealingly, "No other criticism will ever attain any real authority." It is just this co-presence of practical independence with "real authority" that weaves the Arnoldian critical ideal, whereby the modern English department arose in the late nineteenth century, and whereby it has been sustained ever since in crises of self-doubt—which is to say, given the disposition to crisis from which the critic is seldom reprieved, more or less all the time. The same logic that led Arnold on from *Criticism too* to *Criticism first* now culminates in *Criticism only*. Cultural command without political compromise or social astigmatism: such is the ideal, or the deal, which Arnold offered, and which his heirs on the right and left alike continue to offer to the aspiring intellectual in industrial culture at large, nowhere more pointedly than in the English department. For Matthew Arnold is still the tutelary patron of English studies, despite the fact that he kept aloof from the institution of English as a university discipline, a prospect he actually discountenanced when it was suggested at Oxford. He devoted his paid professional life instead—admirably, unflaggingly—to the more basic project of setting up a system of British national education at the primary and secondary levels. In this respect, as in the social and political reach his practice implicitly claimed for criticism—obviously in *Culture and Anarchy* (1869) but by no means only there—Arnold was doing cultural studies well *avant la lettre*.[21] Still, those who did on a much narrower basis organize postsecondary departments of English near the close of the nineteenth century drew liberally on Arnold's ideas about criticism. If not a founding father of English, Arnold was its godfather: the whispering forebear who made me for one, during the late 1960s, an offer I couldn't refuse.

To institutionalize disinterestedness was a tricky business, and never more than at a time when free-trade rhetoric so dominated national discourse as to polarize the light in which readers might regard Arnold's proposed antidote to that dominion, "the free play of the mind upon all subjects." One precipitate of this cultural pressure was Carlyle's fascination with the inspired supra-partisan dictator who, as Napoleon (1837) or Cromwell (1845) or Friedrich (1858), typified an individual freedom awkwardly premised on mass subjugation; another and more surprising precipitate, at the bureaucratic security-systems level, was Mill's flirtation at the end of the book he entitled *On Liberty* (1859) with a Victorian FBI or CIA whose benign data control might, in both senses of the verb, *make* everyone free. When such ti-

---

[20] For Douglas Bush, *Matthew Arnold: A Survey of His Poetry and Prose* (New York: Macmillan, 1971), 103, "It was Arnold who, while setting criticism below creation, raised it from a camp follower of literature to the vanguard of thought." Goodheart goes further: "The fact is that for Arnold criticism as a speculative function is not a dependent activity. On the contrary, it is imaginative literature that depends on the prior activity of criticism" ("Arnold at the Present Time," *Critical Inquiry* 9 [1983]: 466).

[21] Stefan Collini measures Arnold's extended sense of "literary criticism" against that of his diminished twentieth-century successors in *Victorian Thinkers*, ed. Keith Thomas (Oxford: Oxford University Press, 1993), 257.

tanic minds had foundered on the problem of modern authority, the fin-de-siècle fathers of English studies needed as much godfathering as they could get. The one piece of Arnold's that they found most influential is "The Study of Poetry" (1880). This essay does the same introductory honors for the second (posthumous) series of *Essays in Criticism* (1888) as "The Function of Criticism" does for the first, but it is a piece of writing less theoretical and more practically pedagogical, because here Arnold addresses the studious culture-hunter, the person bent on self-improvement who will buy the poetry anthology that the essay was commissioned to introduce.[22] Think of Leonard Bast in his apartment in London, from Forster's *Howards End,* who reads Ruskin but for Arnold's reasons.

Or, if you like, think of me in my apartment in Minneapolis in the early 1970s, a conscientious objector out of college, out of prospects, taking consolation and sustainment where I might. I found it, among other places, in Arnold on "The Study of Poetry":

> More and more mankind will discover that we have to turn to poetry to interpret life for us, to console us, to sustain us. Without poetry, our science will appear incomplete; and most of what now passes with us for religion and philosophy will be replaced by poetry.... But if we conceive thus highly of the destinies of poetry, we must also set our standard for poetry high, since poetry, to be capable of fulfilling such high destinies, must be poetry of a high order of excellence. We must accustom ourselves to a high standard and to a strict judgment. (9:161)

The clarion of Arnold's opening, which still calls out to those he meant it to find, will not be muted if we find it a place within the orchestrated development we have traced thus far. We can see by now that the challenge Arnold braces literature to face is really a double one. First, there is the challenge posed by its weightiest rivals on the Victorian scene: science, religion, philosophy must all yield, if Arnold is right, to poetry; and around this time he says as much, at length, in *Literature and Dogma* (1873) and "Literature and Science" (1882). But then poetry has a subtler challenge to withstand, the one posed by its bodyguard/spy criticism—the one, indeed, that is named in the essay's title: not "Poetry," but "The Study of Poetry."

Casting poetry in criticism's image ("to interpret life for us"), and vowing to judge poetry by the highest of standards (lodged with the critic), Arnold lays great stress on the principle of critical judgment. But about the criterion itself, as distinct from its important operation, he discloses next to nothing.

---

22 R. H. Super, "Arnold's Literary Criticism (II)," in *Matthew Arnold,* ed. Kenneth Allott (London: Bell, 1975), 165–69, shows how in "The Study of Poetry" Arnold accommodated an exceptionally broad public by eschewing his elite allusiveness and banter; what replaced these practices, we should add, and evidently suited Arnold's conception of an expanded public, was a generous helping of sheer rhetorical conjuration.

It is decidedly an in-house derivative of great literature and not an import from outside areas like religious morality, philosophical aesthetics, linguistic or psychological science. But beyond that? Arnold leaves us—me and Leonard Bast—nearly on our own as regards the one thing needful: a critical standard for evaluating that poetry which is to sustain and console us. Nearly on our own, but not quite. For Arnold does equip us with a prospector's kit, consisting of some dozen "touchstones," and he commends them to our use when assailed by anxiety over the excellence of what we may be independently tempted to prize. He displays these touchstones for our guidance, with the most perfunctory of captions and no explanation at all. And then he goes on to write two of the most extraordinary paragraphs I know in literary criticism, grave parodies of circumlocution that might have been inserted into the text by David Lodge, if not Monty Python. Take these sentences slowly, please:

> Critics give themselves great labour to draw out what in the abstract constitutes the characters of a high quality of poetry. It is much better simply to have recourse to concrete examples;—to take specimens of poetry of the high, the very highest quality, and to say: The characters of a high quality of poetry are what is expressed *there*. They are far better recognised by being felt in the verse of the master, than by being perused in the prose of the critic. Nevertheless, if we are urgently pressed to give some critical account of them, we may safely, perhaps, venture on laying down, not indeed how and why the characters arise, but where and in what they arise. They are in the matter and substance of the poetry, and they are in its manner and style. Both of these, the substance and matter on the one hand, the style and manner on the other, have a mark, an accent, of high beauty, worth, and power. But if we are asked to define this mark and accent in the abstract, our answer must be: No, for we should thereby be darkening the question, not clearing it. The mark and accent are as given by the substance and matter of that poetry, by the style and manner of that poetry, and of all other poetry which is akin to it in quality.
>
> Only one thing we may add as to the substance and matter of poetry, guiding ourselves by Aristotle's profound observation that the superiority of poetry over history consists in its possessing a higher truth and a higher seriousness (φιλοσοφώτερον καὶ σπουδαιότερον). Let us add, therefore, to what we have said, this: that the substance and matter of the best poetry acquire their special character from possessing, in an eminent degree, truth and seriousness. We may add yet further, what is in itself evident, that to the style and manner of the best poetry their special character, their accent, is given by their diction, and, even yet more, by their movement. And though we distinguish between the two characters, the two accents, of superiority, yet they are nevertheless vitally connected one with the other. The superior character of truth and seriousness, in the matter and substance of the best poetry, is inseparable from the superiority of diction and movement marking its style and manner. The two superiorities are

closely related, and are in steadfast proportion one to the other. So far as high poetic truth and seriousness are wanting to a poet's matter and substance, so far also, we may be sure, will a high poetic stamp of diction and movement be wanting to his style and manner. In proportion as this high stamp of diction and movement, again, is absent from a poet's style and manner, we shall find, also, that high poetic truth and seriousness are absent from his substance and matter. (9:170–71)

It is not that Arnold's elegant sentences state and restate the obvious, because they hardly do even that. Rather, they execute a set of permutations, full to the point of redundancy, on the proposition that poetry has a form and also has a content; that poetry is composed of words, which have meanings, and which are organized in rhythmical patterns. The circularity of this stupefying nonexplanation can feel like mere filibustering, but it is, in effect, the circularity of the prayer-wheel or hypnotic mantra; for Arnold designs here to work some magic.[23] Notwithstanding an imperturbable manner that seems the reverse of enthusiastic—judicious, approving, anything but overwhelmed— the passage makes a quite Longinian appeal to the knockout power of great writing. Arnold means to forbid all appeal to techniques or rules for reading, and to throw us back, on the shortest of rations, toward those critical resources summed up in the curt word "tact." In a virtually survivalist exercise in intellectual deprivation, reprising the sublation of religion and science into poetry announced as a fait accompli at the head of the essay, Arnold by playing grandiloquently dumb urges us to own that art is its own interpreter and will make all things plain.

In abandoning us like this Arnold is, in his way, dead right: if criticism were less a matter of spontaneous response and lucky hunch, it would be a game few of us cared to play. Yet if Arnold's all but self-parodic disavowal of critical principle and method conjures a charmed space for the privacy of literary response, it also creates an ideological vacuum. And, since culture abhors a vacuum, what rushes in to fill the space Arnold has created is the authoritarianism of a cult of personality.[24] "If we have any tact"—and what

---

[23] On the calculated, thaumaturgic "emptiness" of Arnold's writing see the introduction to Riede's book, especially 1–7. Schneider, 138, makes a nice bibliographical point about how, in revising these sentences, Arnold literally emptied his phrasing of ideas: "On Poetry," an earlier essay Arnold cannibalized in composing "The Study of Poetry," had rendered plainly Aristotle's "profound observation" that poetry differed from history in being "more philosophical" as well as nobler; but in 1880 this latter phrase was dropped, lest poetry's "higher truth" be subordinated to its propositional content.

[24] See Francis Mulhern, "Culture and Authority," *Critical Quarterly* 37 (1995): "Criticism, the free play of the mind upon the underlying issues, must respect a limit, the overarching norms, the indefinable 'touchstones' of culture. Criticism is not the test to which authority must submit; it is the agent of authority" (78), and its agency, "however modestly and convivially, is to relay a culture that is less critical than authoritarian" (82). The ambivalence prompted by this recognition, and expressed one way or another by every commentator worth reading, shows better than anything else how the Arnoldian instance has saturated anglophone literary culture.

imaginable reader of this essay will not claim at least a little?—then it looks very much as though we had better find ourselves in agreement with Matthew Arnold. Where there are no reading rules and the criteria of value are completely dissolved into the examples, the authority those examples bear devolves on the criteriarch who has produced them. Here may be glimpsed the seamy side of the godfather's offer: we get a permit to read with utmost liberty, but the silently stipulated fee is a loyalty oath.[25]

III

The best way to resist this authoritarian edict of Arnold's lies through consideration of the touchstones themselves. Arnold claims that "the specimens I have quoted differ widely from each other" (9:170), but in important respects they do not. Each is written in the grand style of its respective language: Greek hexameter, Italian hendecasyllabic, English blank verse. Not only that, but nearly all record the inevitability of human suffering, registered in a mode of either tragic resistance or resigned submission—the very modes, come to think of it, that typify Arnold's poetry from *The Strayed Reveller* through *New Poems* (1867). The marked family resemblance among the touchstones pleads strongly for Arnold's own susceptibility to what in this same essay he identifies as a "fallacy in our poetic judgments—the fallacy caused by an estimate which we may call personal" (9:164). Insofar as the touchstones constitute a pocket anthology as personal as a fingerprint, Arnold has broken his own rule.[26]

And a good thing too. With the practical recommendations of "The Study of Poetry" the edifice that we have watched Arnold construct across the years, building for criticism a room of its own, collapses under its own weight. Emancipating modern criticism one step at a time from primitive poetic imagination, from ignorant creativity, from extraliterary agendas, and lastly from principle and method themselves, Arnold stranded the critical mind in a bell

---

See George Levine, "Matthew Arnold: The Artist in the Wilderness," *Critical Inquiry* 9 (1983): 469–482.

[25] Keeping faith with the touchstones paragraphs I have quoted usually means, among the Arnoldians it cannot but confound, either keeping mum about its want of principle or contriving a brave new paraphrase, e.g., to the effect that the inexplicit criteria "clearly comprehend… the coherent ordering of significant experience" (Bush, 116). Arnoldian loyalty attains a climax of sorts in E. K. Brown, *Matthew Arnold: A Study in Conflict* (Chicago: University of Chicago Press, 1948), when the critic celebrates Arnold's rhetorical necromancy as a triumph of the very truisms its touchstone passage recites: "The strategy of the essay is in perfect keeping with the disposition it exalts and is intended to serve: the evolution moves with a spacious ease, and the style has a sober and almost colorless beauty, a perfect unity of texture…" (159–160). Leonard Bast take note.

[26] On the personal plangency of the touchstones see John Shepard Eells Jr., *The Touchstones of Matthew Arnold* (New York: Bookman, 1955), and David J. DeLaura, "Arnold and Literary Criticism (I)," in *Matthew Arnold*, ed. Allott, 132.

jar where it could only explode. It had to lie down, as Yeats would say, where all the ladders start, in the abyss of personality for which the post-Romantic Arnold felt so modern a horror. "The calm, the cheerfulness, the disinterested objectivity have disappeared; the dialogue of the mind with itself has commenced" (654). These are Arnold's famous words about Empedocles, from the preface of 1853, where they delineated the fate from which a renewed poetry, and a culture-renewing criticism, were to deliver the modern world. Yet "The Study of Poetry," if I am right about its authoritarian appeal to the expertise of personality, brings Arnold's thought full circle and spins us loose from what is merely idiosyncratic in his specific kind of gravity. The touchstones are so many relics of this particular critical self, fragments suggestive of what he formerly urged his reader to scorn as "a true allegory of the state of one's own mind" (662). Arnold's sweeping charisma is not so fine, after all, that no idea can violate it. Scratch the authoritarian and you can sniff the needy brother, your semblable, your ideologue.

Modern literature and criticism have not realized the dreams that Arnold cherished for them, because they cannot. Disinterestedness is a fantasy: at best a calisthenically useful ideal for keeping critics on their toes, at worst a drug impounding critics in their ivory tower. What that last sentence of mine just said is no longer news, of course; the interesting fact now is that the critique of disinterestedness should have become an attractive maneuver to parties of all stripes as they debate the place of literature, and its study, in contemporary culture.[27] It has become binding on any moderately engagé commentator to disavow an Arnoldian posture, in more or less earnest reproof of the headmaster's son from Rugby with the incredible sideburns. So let me pay my dues too: Criticism is, like the literature to which it belongs and contributes, an activity that is always contexted, politically contested, and therefore, despite what Arnold says, inescapably interested. Checking your agenda at the door of criticism is the surest way to ensure its return through the back once you have been happily distracted by something else. Your touchstones of ostensibly impersonal, disinterested literary value will prove to be the fragments you have shored against your ruin; and your ruin, as Empedocles might aver, is the most personal, least disinterested thing about you. Disinterestedness is interpretation by other means.

And that is precisely why the vital need for criticism will never go away. "Poetry attaches its emotion to the idea" (9:161); criticism does otherwise. By 1880 Arnold knew the ins and outs of disinterestedness well enough to *de*tach criticism from the idea, which is to say from interpretation and its

---

[27] See Dickstein and Mulhern, previously cited; also David Bromwich, "The Genealogy of Disinterestedness," *Raritan* 1 (1982): 62–92; Joseph Epstein, "Matthew Arnold and the Resistance," *Commentary* 73, no. 4 (1982): 53–60; Steven Marcus, "*Culture and Anarchy* Today," *Southern Review* 29 (1993): 433–452; Eugene Goodheart, "Arnold among the Neoconservatives," *Clio* 25 (1996): 455–458; Bill Bell, "The Function of Arnold at the Present Time," *Essays in Criticism* 47 (1997): 203–19.

agendas. He attached criticism instead to a canon; or, if the paradox will be tolerated, to the *idea* of a canon, since as we have just seen from the pocket version that his touchstones represent, Arnold's own canon turns out to be as selfishly, uncritically cathected as any of ours. The *idea* of a canon—the reading mind's appointed refuge from the tyranny of understanding; a taste-tested, constantly revised and collectively maintained resistance to transient fashions in ambient meaning—is something else again. It is where Arnold's best self awaits us: in criticism rather than interpretation, in quest of an ideal order of writings through which a current of fresh ideas may flow, rather than (since what flows in fresh tends to flow out stale) in the business of decoding or explaining or purveying ideas in their own right.[28]

Without planning to do so, I have written here an essay that equivocates reading-as-interpretation (the focus of the collectively authored book that contains it) with reading-as-criticism (the focus of the curiosity in me that motivates it). To this extent Arnold has had his way with me. For the equivocation of criticism with interpretation is Arnold's. In an age that anxiously demanded new meanings to live by, Arnold's genius lay in making criticism pass for and thus usurp interpretation. The gift that he received from Romanticism via Carlyle, Emerson, and Newman, and that he transmitted to modernism via Pater, Wilde, and T. S. Eliot, lay in grasping that this usurpation or elision of meaning was what the age would prove to have actually needed. About the most urgent Victorian questions Arnold the sage had, as we say, no idea. This is not to call him clueless, but to credit him with a key to all the mythologies. When we apply to this sage for a dispensation of truth, he graciously consents to bestow it; what we come away with, though, turns out to be a syllabus—that, and a license to read in it as freely as we can. Our ears buzz a while with rich phrases about the sweetness and light of the best that has been thought and said, about the power not ourselves that makes for righteousness. Yet all we remember when we get home is that he told us to read Homer and Wordsworth and the Bible, and warned us against taking either them or their conveyancers at face value. Arnold's legacy is not propositional but curricular, because he believed criticism would outlast interpretation every time.

---

[28] On this question Suleri is witheringly provocative. Arnold emerges in her reading as a "cultural mobile" I imagine a suspended structure of deliberation à la Calder answering despair "with the sharp edge of an intelligent choice, compensating for an absence of belief by summoning up previous modes of believing, and taking a reader's revenge in the judgments it passes on them" (142); "the loss of belief that the poems mourn becomes a background against which Arnold can move freely and efficiently between beliefs" (141). *Empedocles* was banished, then, because it threatened to forestall this Arnoldian project of cultural mobility, mocking it in advance through the rendition of a spectacularly "failed reader" (145). All true, and yet so is the dialectical completion of this thought in Dickstein: "The detachment Arnold commends...is the subtler language of an intense commitment" (505).

6. Aesthetics, Ethics, and Unreadable Acts in George Eliot

JONATHAN LOESBERG

Feeling George Eliot's ethical claims upon us and simultaneously suspecting that those claims are incoherent, unearned, and possibly both,
seem to form an enduring part of the reading experience her novels either afford or threaten. Once it became clear that the sympathy in her depiction of clergy in *Scenes from Clerical Life* and *Adam Bede* accompanied
a distancing analytic consciousness that contrasted with their religion, her
Victorian reviewers of novels from *The Mill on the Floss* on regularly noticed and rebelled against what they took to be the ethical stance of the novels.[1] And those who did not rebel at least questioned its aesthetic effect. Thus,
famously, Henry James objected to the intrusive idealism of *Daniel Deronda*
even as he implicitly recognized what later critics have also recognized, that
his objections to the character of Deronda derive from that figure's being an
attempt to embody as a consciousness within the novel the moral stance of
the narrator of *Middlemarch*.[2] And contemporary critics, with less of the
sense of immediate challenge that Victorians felt in response to the ethics that
shaped her fiction, still have a similar sense of a problem, expressed in the
claim that her ethics, aesthetics, and realism are in some unresolvable contradiction.[3] These three concepts in particular figure in the contradiction

[1] Dinah Mulock, in her review of The *Mill on the Floss*, noticeably defined a moral significance in its depiction of Maggie to which she claimed one should object, even as she praised the
novel's literary qualities. And Mulock's is only the most intelligent version of a kind of objection that critics regularly registered against Eliot's work. David Carroll, ed., *George Eliot: The
Critical Heritage* (New York: Barnes and Noble, 1971), 154–61.

[2] Ibid., 417–434; Neil Hertz, "Some Words in George Eliot: Nullify, Neutral, Numb, Number,"
in *Languages of the Unsayable: The Play of Negativity in Literature and Literary Theory*, ed.
Sanford Budick and Wolfgang Iser (New York: Columbia University Press, 1989), 288.

[3] In its most formal register, Eliot's deconstructive critics have done most of the analysis of
the contradictions in Eliot's realism and between it and her ethics. See J. Hillis Miller, "Narrative

Eliot's fiction presents first because she claimed an ethic to her realism that not everyone has felt to be self-evident, second because the realism itself has always been a matter of question, more in the case of some novels than others perhaps but more or less throughout, and finally because both realism and the ethic she attached to it can seem commitments at war with other aesthetic criteria. All of these problems, though, arise only if one assumes that Eliot follows the eighteenth-century empirical aesthetics of sympathy, most clearly articulated by Edmund Burke, in which the spectacle of human sensation has sympathy as an automatic response. In this article, I will argue that despite her realism, or our understanding of it at any rate, Eliot's aesthetic was more nearly German idealist, that through her reading of Hegel or his secondary commentators and of the exemplary Young Hegelian, Ludwig Feuerbach, she saw aesthetics not in terms of the forming of literary objects but as a form of consciousness that created the significance, ethical and otherwise, of the objects it construed. The contradictions critics read in Eliot are the content of that consciousness and part of what it comments upon. Thus the formal and ideological conflicts of Eliot's critics, from her contemporaries to ours, are conflicts she analyzes as well as embodies.

In turning from eighteenth-century British aesthetics to Hegel's theory of realism, the role of tragedy in Hegel and Eliot and then the ethical manifestation of this aesthetic in the Feuerbachian symbolic interpretation of Christianity to which Eliot subscribed, this essay intends to outline a theory of realism that claims an ethical transformation occurring as an immediate element in the aesthetic spectacle offered rather than as a causal consequence of it as in the British aesthetics that argued a sympathy resulting from accurate imitation. Eliot does not, I will argue, think sympathy to be an automatic result of mimesis, as for instance Burke did. And while she did not share Hegel's justification of realism in terms of its idealist transfiguration of the ordinary, she did share his irony at an ethics of realism that justified the quotidian either by reveling in social success or at least resigning oneself to social norms. Her response, in a theory of realist tragedy that also bears comparison with Hegel, was to pose a spectacle of collision between social

and History," *ELH* 41 (1974): 455–473, and "Optic and Semiotic in *Middlemarch*," in *The Worlds of Victorian Fiction,* ed. Jerome H. Buckley (Cambridge: Harvard University Press, 1975), 125–145; and Neil Hertz "Recognizing Casaubon," in *The End of the Line* (New York: Columbia University Press, 1985), 76–87 and "Some Words in George Eliot" for the most influential of these essays. But the sense of contradiction and conflicting impulse in Eliot's fiction permeates feminist treatment, dating at least from Sandra M. Gilbert and Susan Gubar's chapters on Eliot in *The Madwoman in the Attic* (New Haven: Yale University Press, 1979), 443–535, and is a matter of close attention in Alison Booth's *Greatness Engendered: George Eliot and Virginia Woolf* (Ithaca: Cornell University Press, 1992) as well as historicist readings (see, for instance, Elsie Michie's discussion of *Middlemarch* and the gendering of culture in *Outside the Pale: Cultural Exclusion, Gender Difference, and the Victorian Woman Writer* [Ithaca: Cornell University Press, 1993], 142–71.)

norm and individual obligation whose ethical charge was not any tragic resolution offered but the spectacle of collision itself. A consequent reading of
Feuerbach will show the larger implications of this aesthetic for Eliot's ethic
of a desacralized, symbolically apprehended Christianity.

Although the problem of historical observation and historical relativity
will not be an explicit element in my discussion, the implications of a realist
apprehension that transforms what it depicts for that historical debate hover
just below the surface. The problem we will see Feuerbach outlining, for instance, when he notes that no one who is religious can be aware of the projective and anthropomorphic nature of religion without ceasing to be religious, may not quite be one of historical relativism, the question of whether
we can see the past as it actually was. But that problem does pose a question: If we saw the past as it actually was,would we be seeing it as the people
of the past saw it, and would not our perspective, even if absolutely accurate, be therefore a transformation of it? Arthur Danto's *Narration and
Knowledge,* because it offers an analytical philosophy of history, poses the
problem usefully for us precisely in the distance of its philosophical tradition
from Feuerbach's Hegelianism. Danto proposes that historical sentences are
what he terms "*narrative sentences:* sentences the truth of which entails that
at least two time-separated events have happened. Thus 'Washington became
first president of the United States,' taken literally, entails at least the two
events of the advent of Washington and the advent of some later president."
This lexical analysis has as its consequence that "events under narrative descriptions could not have been experienced as such by those who lived
through them—unless those people had a knowledge of the future we would
very likely impugn as impossible."[4] This formulation is striking precisely in
the way it makes a logical necessity of a formal contradictoriness Feuerbach
recognizes and Eliot consciously uses. For Danto, the formal possibility of
historical knowledge entails seeing the past as it could not see itself; for
Feuerbach, seeing religion entailed seeing religious belief as no religious person could; for Eliot, seeing an event with sympathetic understanding entailed
seeing its status as event as unreadable.

But this traversing of German idealism to arrive at Eliot's theories of realism and sympathy will seem at first glance to oppose, quite counterintui-
tively, the apparently obvious empirical connection between the two in her
texts. Critics have not needed any English or Burkean aesthetic tradition to
determine that Eliot founded her realism's moral value on its being able to
elicit sympathy with the spectacle of human daily life. It is virtually a truism
of Eliot criticism that "what we gain through being forced to feel real kinship with someone to whom we had first felt aloof and superior should be

---

[4] Arthur C. Danto, *Narration and Knowledge (including the integral text of Analytical
Philosophy of History)* (New York: Columbia University Press, 1985), 293, 294. (Danto's emphasis.)

nothing less than a revelation of our essential, shared human nature at once pitiful and sublime."[5] In the context of this tie between seeing humanity and sympathizing with it several critics have recently charted a problem with the mimetic claims of realism dating back to the eighteenth-century assertions of correspondence between word, internal sensation, and image.[6] Prior to the problems of mimesis, however, is the problem of how one gets from the spectacle of human experience to an identification with it. Burke's route was considerably less than straightforward. Like Eliot, Burke saw the value of literature in the sympathy with suffering it created in the reader, and this sympathy has much the same moral value that critics assert it has in Eliot. But it more nearly arises from divine intervention than from any self-evident associational psychological construction: "As our Creator has designed we should be united by the bond of sympathy, he has strengthened that bond by a proportionable delight; and there most where our sympathy is most wanted, in the distresses of others."[7] Denying the usual contemporaneous view that we are repulsed by the spectacle of actual pain, Burke arrives at the moral view of sympathy only by asserting its universal occurrence and divine causation.

Eliot, while assenting to Burke's view that the bond of sympathy unites us and that it is most wanted in cases of distress, nevertheless had no more faith in its universality than in its divine causation. Although her fictions are frequently about characters who learn this sympathy, they also depict quite fully its more usual failure to occur. For every hero, from Tryan in "Janet's Repentance" through Adam Bede to Dorothea Brooke and Daniel Deronda, who exemplifies this sympathy, her novels are filled with numberless more who, namelessly as part of the vaguely thoughtless and prejudiced community, or pointedly in their egoism, either refuse sympathy or repress it when it occurs. Thus Eliot's famous appeal in *Adam Bede* veils an aesthetic problem that she treats explicitly as a moral one: "Do not impose on us any aesthetic rules which shall banish from the region of Art those old women scraping carrots with their work-worn hands....In this world there are so many of these common coarse people, who have no picturesque sentimental wretchedness! It is so needful we should remember their existence."[8] We may be able to create an artifice of sympathy through picturesque sentimentality,

[5] Derek Oldfield and Sybil Oldfield, " 'Scenes of Clerical Life': The Diagram and the Picture," in *Critical Essays on George Eliot*, ed. Barbara Hardy (London: Routledge and Kegan Paul, 1970), 5.

[6] The best discussion of the problem with this aesthetic tradition and Eliot's adherence to it is Marc Redfield's chapter on Eliot "The Aesthetics of Sympathy: George Eliot's Telepathy Machine," in *Phantom Formations: Aesthetic Ideology and the "Bildungsroman"* (Ithaca: Cornell University Press, 1996), 134–70.

[7] Edmund Burke, *A Philosophical Enquiry into the Origin of Our Ideas of the Sublime and Beautiful*, ed. J.T. Boulton (Notre Dame: University of Notre Dame Press, 1968), 46.

[8] George Eliot, *Adam Bede* (New York: Signet, 1961), 177. Further references cited in the text as *AB*.

but we need to experience real sympathy at the spectacle of common suffering. But if sympathy does not arise automatically from that spectacle, how will a pure realist evocation of the quotidian evoke it?

If Eliot does not follow Burke in believing that the miming of pain automatically evokes sympathy, neither is she unaware of the possible aesthetic problems with realism's epistemic claims to recreate reality in art. Turning from British aesthetics to an idealist one, we can immediately see the theoretical problems with realism that Eliot quite consciously meant to respond to. The first question a realist depiction must face is not the contemporary one of whether accurate mimesis is possible but the much older one of what need it serves. Hegel asks this question most directly and his version is relevant since, whether or not she was aware of Hegel's *Aesthetic* directly, Eliot often seems to be dealing with its issues.[9] Hegel says of the view of art as an imitation of nature that, by this definition, art "can be seen at once to be.... *a superfluous* labour.... And looked at more closely, this superfluous labour may even be regarded as a presumptuous game...which falls far short of nature."[10] If we measure realism by its accuracy in imitation—and Eliot constantly opposes to her putative reader's desire for idealized characters her depiction of human nature and appearance as she at least actually sees it (*AB*, 174)—then the purpose of such accuracy remains in question since the original is already there for us to refer to and the depiction will always, as Plato first claimed, be secondary to the original. Hegel discusses two justifications for realism, one of which Eliot would not accept, the other of which neither of them could. In a general discussion of contemporary art, which he thinks to be no longer in touch with the ideal, Hegel makes clear the transcendental value to seeming realism: "To grasp this most transitory and fugitive material, and to give it permanence for our contemplation in the fullness of its

---

[9] Eliot's letters establish explicitly an awareness of some of Hegel's works, but the amount of her direct knowledge of the *Aesthetics* is hard to know. The general point of connection is the clear correlations between her theories of tragedy and Hegel's discussion of it. Mansell argues for a direct connection. Darrell Mansell Jr., "A Note on Hegel and George Eliot," *Victorian Newsletter* 27 (1965): 12–15. Joseph finds Mansell's claim unconvincing but nevertheless finds Hegel pertinent since "such matters were certainly in the air, and her use of Böckh's formulation to buttress her own reading of [*Antigone*] demonstrates her debt to the Hegelians if not to Hegel directly." Gerhard Joseph, "The *Antigone* as Cultural Touchstone: Matthew Arnold, Hegel, George Eliot, Virginia Woolf, and Margaret Drabble," *PMLA* 96 (1981): 23–35. Ashton never discusses Hegel in her analysis of Eliot's reading of German idealism (147–77) but has a long discussion of Lewes's magazine article on Hegel's *Aesthetics* (115–19). Rosemary Ashton, *The German Idea: Four English Writers and the Reception of German Thought, 1800–1860* (Cambridge: Cambridge University Press, 1980). But Lewes wrote his article in 1842, years before he and Eliot met. Still, use of Hegelian formulations of tragedy are suggestive and, in view of Eliot's discussion of Dutch genre painting in chapter 17 of *Adam Bede*, Lewes's conclusion of his discussion of Hegel with extended quotation of Hegel on Dutch painting also seems significant. George Henry Lewes, "Hegel's Aesthetics," *British and Foreign Review* 13 (1842): 46.

[10] G. W. F. Hegel, *Aesthetics: Lectures on Fine Art*, 2 vols., trans. T. M. Knox (Oxford: Oxford University Press, 1975), 1:42. Further references cited in the text as Hegel.

life, is the hard task of art at this stage" (Hegel, 1:599). In other words, seeming realism has value in its capturing and giving an ideal permanence precisely to surface appearance for its own sake, without reference to either deeper truth or significance.

Eliot will have none of this justification of realism though. Whether or not she had read Hegel's discussion of it either directly or in Lewes's approximate translation, her discussion insists on a sympathy with ordinariness rather than a transfiguration of it: "It is for this rare, precious quality of truthfulness that I delight in Dutch paintings, which lofty-minded people despise. I find a source of delicious sympathy in these faithful pictures of a monotonous homely existence" (*AB*, 176). Again, she insists on accuracy or at least "truthfulness" and justifies it by its ability to evoke sympathy. And again, implicitly, the evocation of sympathy we know not to be a dependable effect of the accuracy since some people will despise the pictures rather than sympathize with their content. Since Burke posited sympathy as an effect of any spectacle of human pain, he could not have it rise from an aesthetic cause, but simply asserted it as a divine mechanism. Eliot, though, might have argued an aesthetic effect arising from identification between reader and character—the kinship that the Oldfields' article cited above refers to—by offering the incarnational justification of realism one often sees in the nineteenth century since at least Wordsworth. In this view, the realist particular contains within it, with greater or less adequacy depending on the theorist, the general significance that links spectator to aesthetic object. In her essay on "The Natural History of German Life," Eliot appeals to this justification more or less directly:

> The greatest benefit we owe to the artist, whether painter, poet, or novelist, is the extension of our sympathies. Appeals founded on generalizations and statistics require a sympathy ready-made, a moral sentiment already in activity; but a picture of human life such as a great artist can give, surprises even the trivial and the selfish into that attention to what is apart from themselves which may be called the raw material of moral sentiment. When Scott takes us into Luckie Mucklebackit's cottage, or tells the story of "The Two Drovers,"—when Wordsworth sings us the reverie of "Poor Susan" ... more is done towards linking the higher classes with the lower, towards obliterating the vulgarity of exclusiveness, than by hundreds of sermons and philosophical dissertations.[11]

Realist art may have the same message as "appeals founded on generalizations and statistics," but art evokes the sympathy those generalizations cannot by militating against exclusiveness, showing the linking of general humanity within the specific difference it accurately depicts.

---

[11] George Eliot, *Essays,* ed. Thomas Pinney (New York: Columbia University Press, 1963), 270–271.

But if idealist attitudes toward reality may be delusional in Eliot, the claims of incarnational realism may lead as easily to self-aggrandizing wish-fulfillment fantasies. Hegel's hilariously ironic description of what he calls "Romantic Fiction" (Hegel labels the modern period of art as the "romantic") is apt here:

> Now the thing is to breach this order of things, to change the world, to improve it, or at least in spite of it to carve out of it a heaven upon earth: to seek for the ideal girl, find her, win her away from her wicked relations or other discordant ties, and carry her off in defiance. But in the modern world these fights are nothing more than "apprenticeship," the education of the individual into the realities of the present, and thereby they acquire their true significance. For the end of such apprenticeship consists in this, that the subject sows his wild oats, builds himself with his wishes and opinions into harmony with subsisting relationships and their rationality, enters the concatenation of the world and acquires for himself an appropriate attitude to it. However much he may have quarrelled with the world, or been pushed about in it, in most cases at last he gets his girl and some sort of position, marries her, and becomes as good a Philistine as others. The woman takes charge of household management, children arrive, the adored wife, at first unique, an angel, behaves pretty much as all other wives do; the man's profession provides work and vexations, marriage brings domestic affliction—so here we have all the headaches of the rest of married folk.—We see here the like character of adventurousness except that now it finds its right significance, wherein the fantastic element must experience the necessary corrective. (Hegel, 1:593)

Although Hegel's use of the word "apprenticeship" clearly alludes to Goëthe's *Wilhelm Meisters Lehrjahre,* his description of the way realism may take the daily events of all lives and construe them as great victories, thus easing the passage into a philistine adulthood, has obvious relevance to Eliot's sense of realism as a universalizing corrective to a deluded belief in one's own exclusivity. Nor would a less positive outcome, one that did not lead to a prosperous philistinism, really make the situation appreciably better. Even if the necessary corrective to the fantastic element of adventurousness is a reduction of great expectations and a lesson in the hard realities of worldly limits, essentially the novel thus teaches a lesson of resignation to social reality as if it were natural reality.

But what is Hegel to Eliot? The English bildungsroman certainly did frequently construct maturation as entailing an acceptance of one's social surrounding, either in the mode of ironic resignation or of comic success and if Hegel's irony is apt, that does not mean it elucidates Eliot's particular fictive stance except as she shares it with any number of other nineteenth-century authors. Hegel's critique of the quietism and philistinism inherent in realism may touch upon an ethical failing of the realist novel in general, but its relevance to the particular problems of realism and ethics in Eliot seems less certain. There are two answers to the question of what Hegel is to Eliot and they will finally bring us to the role of an idealist aesthetic consciousness in connecting her realism with her ethics. The first is that Eliot does not always support resignation to the quotidian. Hegel's critique of realism and Eliot's occasional assent to that critique sheds light on a contradiction within Eliot's ethical attitudes that complexifies the contradiction we have been outlining between realism and its ostensible ethical consequence. Although Eliot's ethic of sympathy could certainly lead to a premature acceptance of social reality as unchangeable, and critics have certainly caught that strand in her, at other moments she shows an equal awareness of the self-aggrandizing potential in the position and a willingness to entertain quite virulent resistance to it.[12] The depiction of Bulstrode in *Middlemarch,* after all, precisely follows Hegel's parodic narrative, which transforms youthful idealism and wild oats into a self-satisfied philistinism that construes itself as an acceptance of divine will. And when Mrs. Cadwallader says to Dorothea, "Sitting alone in that library at Lowick you may fancy yourself ruling the weather; you must get a few people round you who wouldn't believe you if you told them. That is good lowering medicine," surely Eliot shares Hegel's irony at this advice.[13] In any case the narrator implicitly affirms Dorothea's refusal to be lowered here.

The second answer to the question of Hegel's relevance brings up the explicit connection between Eliot's theory of tragedy and Hegel's as manifested by their reading of *Antigone.* If Hegel's doubts about realism illuminate an ethical problem in Eliot, his view of tragedy as ethical conflict in turn illuminates her use of tragedy as a mode of imbedding an ethical significance directly within a realist spectacle. In her theory of realist tragedy, Eliot worked out the conflict between her resignation to hard reality and her frequent belief that that resignation could entail a premature acceptance of social reality. As well, through the form of tragic awareness, she closed the gap between a representation and any sympathy that is supposed to follow from it. For both Hegel and Eliot, then, *Antigone* represents a collision between an individual's sense of moral duty and the state's ethical and legal code. Seeming to refer to Hegel's concept of a "collision" in tragedy, Eliot in her discussion of *Antigone* says virtually the same thing: "Here lies the dramatic collision:

---

[12] The first feminist critics of Eliot, in particular, noted the conservative strain in an ethic of sympathy and acceptance (see Lee R. Edwards, "Women, Energy, and *Middlemarch,*" *Massachusetts Review* 13 [1972]: 223–238, as well as Gilbert and Gubar). Bodenheimer captures the contradiction between Eliot's resignation and her resistance nicely in her discussion of Eliot's resolution of her Holy War with her father in which Ruby Redinger sees Eliot learning the lessons of sympathy and resignation (125). Rosemarie Bodenheimer, *The Real Life of Mary Ann Evans: George Eliot, Her Letters and Fiction.* (Ithaca: Cornell University Press, 1994); Ruby V. Redinger, *George Eliot: The Emergent Self* (New York: Knopf, 1975).

[13] George Eliot, *Middlemarch.,* Norton Critical Edition, ed. Bert G. Hornback (New York: W. W. Norton, 1977), 371.

the impulse of sisterly piety which allies itself with reverence for the Gods, clashes with the duties of citizenship; two principles, both having their validity are at war with each" (*Essays*, 263).[14] The difference between the two is that there is no resolution to the tragic collision in Hegel because that resolution occurs in the higher form of comedy (Hegel, 2:1220), and particularly in classical comedy, in which the characters enact a "constant reconciliation" (2:1235) that sublates the tragic collision. For Eliot, in whom the tragic collision is a realist event rather than a surpassed formal manifestation of a spiritual conflict, no such sublation is available. And her response to the tragic collision, in the essay on *Antigone* at least, is the familiar sympathetic resignation: "Perhaps the best moral we can draw is that to which the Chorus points—that our protest for the right should be seasoned with moderation and reverence" (*Essays*, 265).

In another discussion of tragedy, however—in her notes toward the writing of "The Spanish Gypsy"—Eliot does outline where the tragic sublation occurs within a realist work. She proposes a conflict between hereditary obligation and a quotidian desire to "share in the ordinary lot of womanhood," marriage.[15] Since she still thinks that to be tragic, a subject "must represent irreparable collision between the individual and the general" (32), the general in this schema must have its embodiment in hereditary obligations while the individual exists in the desire to live out an ordinary life. By defining "the general" as hereditary obligation, though, Eliot has made the tragic collision effectively an internal one. Those obligations may well have an external manifestation, but the hold they have on one will be internal; they make up "what we call duty" (31). This tragedy is of course available to realist characters. But for the situation to be tragic, they must realize its tragedy and the audience must also realize it through them. Thus Eliot posits, "Suppose for a moment that our conduct at great epochs was determined entirely by reflection, without the immediate intervention of feeling, which supersedes reflection, our determination as to the right would consist in an adjustment of our individual needs to the dire necessities of our lot, partly as to our natural constitution, partly as sharers of life with our fellow-beings. Tragedy consists in the terrible difficulty of this adjustment" (31). Tragedy here occurs not with external conflict but with our recognition of that conflict as demanding difficult choices. The ethical dilemma is not in the situation but in our conscious recognition of it. The ethical significance of this dilemma, that which functions in the place of the Hegelian sublation, also involves consciousness, this time the audience's consciousness: "It is the individual with whom we sympathize, and the general of which we recognize the irresistible power.... A

<hr />

[14] Gerhard Joseph outlines the common grounds between Hegel's and Eliot's views and notes the concept of "collision" in Hegel (The *Antigone*, 24).

[15] J. W. Cross, *George Eliot's Life as Related in Her Letters and Journals*, 3 vols. (New York: Harper and Brothers, n.d), 3:30.

tragedy has not to expound why the individual must give way to the general; it has to show that it is compelled to give way" (32, 33). The sympathy that realist tragedy evokes here does not result from any mechanism connected with realist mimesis. It is in fact a formal necessity if the represented conflict is to be a tragic collision. That collision will be experienced first in the consciousness of the protagonist in the tragedy and then by the audience of it and this doubled awareness is the aesthetic effect of tragedy, the sublation it offers. Further, whatever ethic of sympathy results from this aesthetic, formal consciousness can only occur coincident with it and will be part of its workings.

A formal consciousness in Eliot's fiction, then, enacted both in characters and in a space of reading constructed by the narrative, thus in the audience of the spectacle in the novel, constructs the aesthetic effect both she and we delineate as an ethic. But this ethic is neither something added on nor something that obstructs or competes with the novel's aesthetics but is literally part of its generic working. For the tragic collision to occur in realism, the awareness in which it takes place must also occur and that awareness is always ethical in content as well, involving sympathy with suffering and recognition of its necessity, involving resistance to hereditary obligation and external law and a realization of their exigency and resignation to it. The contradictions, as well, are as we will see, part of the form of this awareness and not a consequence of it indicating either a problematic ontology or a problematic ideology (that awareness may be wanting either ideologically or ontologically, of course, but contradiction cannot be evidence of that lack since it does not result from the awareness but just is part of it). To show the working of this aesthetic consciousness in Eliot, then, the balance of this paper will first verify its grounding in German idealism by tracing its working to Eliot's translation of Feuerbach's *The Essence of Christianity,* then by showing its working on a narrative in The *Mill on the Floss* and in a narrative in *Daniel Deronda.* Feuerbach is particularly pertinent here as his theory of Christianity's genealogy as well as of its essence highlights the implicit view of historic interpretation in Eliot's aesthetics. Just as for Feuerbach a historically accurate view of Christianity's essential significance entails seeing it as no Christian can, and thus standing outside of Christianity, it would follow that the most scrupulously accurate historical knowledge is always a presentist revision of the past as well.

Although Eliot's translation of Feuerbach has generally been taken as a step in the path toward her adoption of the religion of humanity, one might as easily take her stated adherence to Feuerbach as a connection back to Hegel, who was a direct influence on him.[16] Indeed, if there were no evidence

---

[16] Eliot's letter to Sara Hennel stating that "With the ideas of Feuerbach I everywhere agree" is everywhere cited. Gordon S. Haight, ed., *The George Eliot Letters,* 9 vols. (New Haven: Yale University Press, 1954–74), 2:153. Critics who see Feuerbach as the source of a renewed, humanistic Christianity include Bernard J. Paris, *Experiments in Life: George Eliot's Quest for Values* (Detroit: Wayne State University Press, 1965), 92–95; U.C. Knoepflmacher, *Religious*

that Eliot had any knowledge of Hegel, her connection with Feuerbach would be enough of a basis from which to articulate the workings of a transformative aesthetic consciousness. In order to see the workings of that connection, though, we need to restore the nineteenth-century sense that Feuerbach in *The Essence of Christianity* was writing as an unbeliever rather than a humanizer looking to preserve Christianity's real moral content in the manner of Matthew Arnold and later Victorians.[17] Feuerbach's connection to the Hegelian view of human history as a matter of developing consciousness is clear enough:

> But when religion—consciousness of God—is designated as the self-consciousness of man, this is not to be understood as affirming that the religious man is directly aware of this identity; for, on the contrary, ignorance of it is fundamental to the peculiar nature of religion. To preclude this misconception, it is better to say, religion is man's earliest and also indirect form of self-knowledge. Hence, religion everywhere precedes philosophy, as in the history of the race, so also in that of the individual.[18]

The link between the development of individual consciousness and the development of human understanding throughout history, of course, forms Hegel's *Phenomenology of Mind*. And Feuerbach follows Hegel in seeing religion as a form of knowledge that will be replaced by the more complete understanding that philosophy will bring.

One should also note that while the above passage describes the essence of religion in terms of human self-consciousness, and Feuerbach equates all consciousness with a consciousness of the infinite (Feuerbach, 2), which is the essential value of religion, it also insists that human consciousness, while being religious, cannot recognize this truth about itself. For Feuerbach, religion occurs when human consciousness, recognizing its own infinitude, objectifies that infinitude in the false conception of god. But religion can never recognize the difference between its essence and its resulting conceptions:

Humanism and the Victorian Novel: George Eliot, Walter Pater, and Samuel Butler (Princeton: Princeton University Press, 1965), 52–59; and her most recent biographer, Frederick R. Karl, *George Eliot: Voice of a Century* (New York: W. W. Norton, 1995).

[17] Lord Acton, in his review of Cross's life of Eliot, sums up the work this way: "*The Essence of Christianity* had been published more than twelve years, and expressed neither a prevailing phase of philosophy nor the last views of the author. More than any other work it had contributed to the downfall of metaphysics, and it contained an ingenious theory of the rise and growth of religion, and of the relation of the soul to God, while denying the existence of either. Feuerbach repudiated Christianity so decisively that Strauss was distanced and stranded for thirty years." Lord Acton, *Essays in Religion, Politics, and Morality,* ed. J. Rufus Fears (Indianapolis: Liberty Classics, 1988), 473. Although critics frequently cite Marx's critical "Theses on Feuerbach," they ignore that even in the midst of his most corrosive descriptions of Feuerbach's project, he nevertheless described the project as an attack on religion and not a restoration of it. Karl Marx and Friedrich Engels, *The German Ideology: Parts I & III,* ed. R. Pascal (New York: International Publishers, 1947), 5.

[18] Ludwig Feuerbach, *The Essence of Christianity,* trans. George Eliot (Buffalo, N.Y.: Prometheus Books, 1989), 13. All further references cited in the text as Feuerbach.

> Scepticism is the arch-enemy of religion; but the distinction between object and conception—between God as he is in himself, and God as he is for me—is a sceptical distinction, and therefore an irreligious one....If God were an object to the bird, he would be a winged being: the bird knows nothing higher, nothing more blissful, than the winged condition. How ludicrous would it be if this bird pronounced: To me God appears as a bird, but what he is in himself I know not. To the bird the highest nature is the bird-nature; take from him the conception of this, and you take from him the conception of the highest being.... Wherever, therefore, this idea, that the religious predicates are only anthropomorphisms, has taken possession of a man, there has doubt, has unbelief, obtained the mastery of faith. (Feuerbach, 17)

Eliot's critics usually identify the target of Feuerbach's irony as modern theologians who, instead of seeing its human values, try to give Christianity an intellectual framework it will not bear, thus generating skepticism. And certainly Feuerbach does say that here, and Eliot does generally share his irony at intellectually self-conscious Christian theology. But Feuerbach also claims quite clearly that any consciousness of how religion makes a divinity out of its own highest nature entails skepticism. And this skepticism includes the idea that "the religious predicates are only anthropomorphisms," the explicit thesis of *The Essence of Christianity*. Thus Feuerbach also states explicitly that "the essence of religion, thus hidden to the religious, is evident to the thinker, by whom religion is viewed objectively, which it cannot be by its votaries" (Feuerbach, 13). Feuerbach's work, with which Eliot everywhere agrees, is not a preservation of Christianity on new terms but a bringing to consciousness of Christianity's basic human and moral values, a bringing to consciousness that makes the task, of necessity, skeptical and not religious even as it lauds and seeks to preserve religious, moral awareness.

Thus Feuerbach's analysis of religion, like Hegel's discussion of aesthetics in general and tragedy in particular, proposes a conscious awareness of religion's essential value as, necessarily, a transformation of religion into a higher, non-religious significance. Again, the act of consciousness is a conflicted one, trying to preserve, as it does, the values of Christian love in particular, even as it realizes as part of its constitution that it can no longer identify with that in which it finds value. The direct application of this consciousness to the incarnational justifications of realism occurs in one of Feuerbach's most controversial passages, concerning the true significance of the sacraments of baptism and the eucharist, and this passage thus binds the controversy over Feuerbach's significance with the working of aesthetic consciousness in Eliot's realist fiction. Feuerbach concludes *The Essence of Christianity* by justifying baptism in terms of water's natural ability to clean and justifying the eucharist in terms of the ability of bread and wine to assuage hunger and thirst. He generalizes these values by seeing in baptism a recognition of our connection to nature (water is a natural element) and in the eucharist a recognition of nature's need of us to achieve a higher value (bread and wine are human productions), but he relentlessly holds the sacraments to their material values as well, ending the book with these words:

> Hunger and thirst destroy not only the physical but also the mental and moral powers of man; they rob him of his humanity—of understanding, of consciousness. Oh! if thou shouldst ever experience such want, how wouldst thou bless and praise the natural qualities of bread and wine, which restore to thee thy humanity, thy intellect! It needs only that the ordinary course of things be interrupted in order to vindicate to common things an uncommon significance, *to life, as such, a religious import.* Therefore let bread be sacred for us, let wine be sacred, and also let water be sacred! Amen. (Feuerbach, 277–78)

Feuerbach's contemporaries singled out this passage for scorn for its implicit atheism. Yet despite contemporary defenses of the passage as symbolic, a careful reading of Feuerbach's defense of it in his preface shows that he meant by it just what his contemporaries objected to.[19] And it thus may be taken to indicate the corrosive possibilities in Eliot's use of him. Here is Feuerbach's defense of his analysis:

> But while I thus view water as a real thing, I at the same time intend it as a vehicle, an image, an example, a symbol, of the "unholy" spirit of my work, just as the water of Baptism—the object of my analysis—is at once literal and symbolical water. It is the same with bread and wine. Malignity has hence drawn the conclusion that bathing, eating, and drinking are the *summa summarum,* the positive result of my work. I make no other reply than this: If the whole of religion is contained in the Sacraments, and there are consequently no other religious acts than those which are performed in Baptism and the Lord's Supper; *then* I grant that the entire purport and positive result of my work are bathing, eating, and drinking, since this work is nothing but a faithful, rigid, historico-philosophical analysis of religion—the revelation of religion to itself, the *awakening of religion to self-consciousness.* (Feuerbach, xx–xxi)

Although Feuerbach claims two symbolic activities, neither of them lifts the meaning of water from its material base. The first symbol is the analysis itself in that it symbolizes the "unholy" spirit of the work, its insistence on finding the essence of Christianity in that to which no Christian can assent. The second symbol is baptism's symbolization of water's ability to clean, the material significance that his critics scorned in the first place. In effect, Feuerbach fully embraces the significance of the quotidian that Hegel looked askance on in his reading of *Wilhelm Meister* and that Eliot could also be

---

[19] Ashton quotes James Martineau on Feuerbach as a Hegelian atheist and defends the passage as meant symbolically (*German Idea,* 162, 164).

suspicious of. He also gives it its resistance to the complacence Hegel and Eliot questioned by embracing the corrosive view of religion it entailed. He will only refuse to say that bathing, eating and drinking are not the whole of religion to the extent that there is more to religion than these sacraments. But the course of the book shows, and this passage implicitly asserts, that his treatment of all aspects of religion do follow the method of his analysis of these sacraments. The work reveals religion to itself, awakens itself to a self-consciousness. But this consciousness does not leave it still religious as religion had understood itself. The spirit of the work is " 'unholy,' " even if only in quotation marks because its support of incarnational significance in its own writing disputes the need of that significance in the valuing of the real. For Feuerbach, to see Christianity's essence accurately is to see it as no Christian can because, to preserve Christianity's moral content, Feuerbach sublates it into a contemporary, skeptical viewpoint. Again, as in Eliot's view of the aesthetics of tragedy, the moral value occurs as part of the awareness the theory induces by enacting.

There have been two problems for Eliot's realism we have been discussing: first while its ethical end can only occur when it evokes sympathy, no necessary link exists between a realistic reflection of the quotidian and sympathy with it; and second, from the perspective of its aesthetic significance, realism, at least as Hegel argued, tends toward a complacent affirmation of any existent social state. The Feuerbachian critique of Christianity, which works by bringing to awareness a humanist essence to Christianity, an essence which it affirms even as it thereby, in the very fact of its awareness becomes an unholy spirit, responds directly to these two problems and thus forms the model for Eliot's aesthetic stance and its operation. The recognition that the sacramental material base in water, wine, and bread gives them their entirely sufficient value occurs not with a simple depiction of that physical base but with the claim that their lack will teach us their value. In the same way, sympathy occurs not in automatic coincidence with realist depiction but with a conflict, in both Eliot's and Hegel's term for tragic conflict a "collision" between what we see and our sense of its meaning. In Eliot's fiction, moral sympathy, either as evoked in its readers or as arising in its characters, occurs in a moment of conflicted awareness in which the meaning of what one brings to consciousness, perhaps for the first time, cannot be satisfactorily interpreted or understood. It occurs in a moment in which reality is seen as in some sense not real enough to be immediately understood. We recognize, in a sense, that our accurate apprehension changes the significance of what we apprehend in some way.

This same collision works against the threat of complacency since it works only in the absence of a satisfactory understanding of the object of one's awareness. In Feuerbachian awareness, this collision involves simultaneously recognizing both Christianity's insufficiency and its essence in the Christian love one values. Thus, for instance, the affirmation of the materiality of the sacraments does not really affirm their simple materiality as water, wine, and bread. It affirms their value as sacraments in their being of that materiality rather than some other thing. One learns their value when one lacks them, thus learning both what value the material has and what value it has only by being precisely less than what religion would claim for it. The wateriness of water matters only as it also contests Christian baptism as well as explaining it. Again, we will see how this contesting of complacency through an unresolved doubleness in one's recognition of the material works in Eliot in her depiction of how characters learn to question their own tendency to see life in terms of their own desires, and thus learn to question the value of those desires. Questioning occurs not by having desires obstructed necessarily but by an awareness that cannot determine whether an event counts as a fulfillment of a desire or not, an awareness of materiality that cannot determine what significance it might have. We will see this awareness that foregrounds the conflict it automatically causes, causing a simultaneous moral sympathy and epistemological doubt, first as the aesthetic effect of Eliot's narrative form in *The Mill on the Floss* and finally as the psychology of learning through guilt in *Daniel Deronda*.

The entrance of Stephen Guest into the plot of *The Mill on the Floss*, Maggie Tulliver's attraction to him, their near-elopement, her resistance to it, and the resultant social condemnation of Maggie, combined with the novel's affirmation of her higher moral position, has long been an ethical and formal crux for readers of the novel. And the problem readers have faced—How should one judge the ethics of both Maggie's elopement and her return?—produces readings equally as unsatisfactory as the immediate responses of the gossips in St. Ogg's, a coincidence that will make their failure to comprehend Maggie look to have a deeper cause than their provincial narrowness. Because the failure of the gossips to see Maggie's moral value comes not merely from their narrowness of sympathy but from their literal failure to provide a narrative that adequately accommodates the action they are trying to explain, the narrative-free indirect reproduction of that local response needs a fairly close look:

If Miss Tulliver, after a few months of well-chosen travel, had returned as Mrs. Stephen Guest with a post-marital trousseau and all the advantages possessed even by the most unwelcome wife of an only son, public opinion...would have seen that the two handsome young people—the gentleman quite the first family in St. Ogg's—having found themselves in a false position, had been led into a course which, to say the least of it, was highly injudicious and productive of sad pain and disappointment, especially to that sweet young thing, Miss Deane. Mr. Stephen Guest had certainly not behaved well, but young men were liable to those sudden infatuated attachments; and bad as it might seem in Mrs. Stephen

Guest to admit the faintest advances from her cousin's lover ... still she was very young. ... Society couldn't be carried on if we inquired into private conduct in that way, and Christianity tells us to think no evil.

But the results, we know, were not of a kind to warrant this extenuation of the past. Maggie had returned without a trousseau, without a husband, in that degraded and outcast condition to which error is well known to lead.[20]

Effectively the gossips imagine two stories here, one the successful love story of the "potboiler romance," in which Stephen, overcome by love, overrides Maggie's objections and "sweeps her away," the second the melodrama of the fallen woman, in which Maggie is the unsuccessful temptress.[21] The failure of the gossips to account adequately for what has happened comes not merely from their moral narrowness, though, but from the simple inability to recount what actually happened, and that inability, it turns out, will have larger implications. In condemning Maggie on her return, they do not credit the story the novel tells and Stephen admits to, that Maggie had successfully swept Stephen away against her will and then herself resisted eloping at the last moment. If her resistance is Maggie's moral triumph, it is also a narrative anomaly for more than the gossips of St. Ogg's, though, as we can see by looking at some critical responses. For instance, there is an obvious similarity between Maggie's near-elopement with Stephen and Eliot's own elopement with George Henry Lewes that seems to cry out for an ethical conclusion, but which one? Critics have seen Eliot as affirming her own elopement by contrasting its freedom from harming others with the pain that Maggie's elopement would have caused others. In contrast, other critics have seen the narrative as self-criticism, Eliot's affirmation of Maggie's return as a condemnation of her own willingness to brook social disapproval in making unconventional choices. Both these positions at least agree that Maggie was morally right in returning. But critics have also wondered why Maggie did not in fact assent to Stephen's desires since she shared them, thus in effect wondering why she did not just reproduce the more readable first narrative after all.[22]

---

[20] George Eliot, *The Mill on the Floss* (New York: Signet, 1965), 512–14.

[21] I am indebted to Bodenheimer for the characterizations of the gossip's narrative in terms of standard Victorian plots. Bodenheimer's further claim that these narratives are "crass distortions of the two sides of Maggie" suggests the resistance of this passage to easy ethical conclusion that I will be arguing (*Real Life*, 147).

[22] Barbara Hardy argues that Eliot affirms her own choice by contrasting her situation with Maggie's. " 'The Mill on the Floss,' " in *Critical Essays on George Eliot*, ed. Barbara Hardy (London: Routledge and Kegan Paul, 1970), 51. Janice Carlisle sees Eliot as condemning herself. "The Mirror in *The Mill on the Floss*: Toward a Reading of Autobiography as Discourse," *Studies in the Literary Imagination* 23 (1990): 195. Bodenheimer affirms the basic analogy between the two situations but argues that Eliot is "dramatizing the hopelessly tangled stresses of competing claims which contaminate acts of choice" (*Real Life*, 103). Welsh outlines how one may sympathize with Stephen in his debate with Maggie over whether to continue their elope-

All these positions, in one way or another, either run athwart or try to elide the same narrative that the gossips of St. Ogg's won't credit, a plot that both depicts an elopement and then poses it as having been renounced. Seeing Maggie as a contrast to Eliot's situation with Lewes and thus as an affirmation of her choice is not merely unlikely because it is such an odd way to construct a narrative affirmation of that choice (why not merely dramatize it directly?). It must also ignore the narrative of elopement and return in order to construct one of clean self-sacrifice on Maggie's part. As a contrast with Eliot's elopement with Lewes, surely a simple refusal would have been a superior fable. But the view that Eliot condemns herself runs afoul of the same problem. If Eliot wanted a narrative of self-sacrifice to contrast with her own resistance to public convention, she constructed an odd fable in which Maggie still managed to affront social convention and hurt at least Lucy as much as she might have done if she had completed the elopement since Stephen's affections were just as manifest. Thus the third critical view seems to have a point in arguing that, insofar as Maggie's reason for returning was to avoid harming the feelings of Lucy and Philip, by the time she argues for returning the damage has been done, and she might as well have continued on. In effect, both St. Ogg's condemnation of Maggie and the critical affirmation of her cannot quite comprehend the events that the novel puts before us in a coherent moral narrative.

But the failure of both the critics and St. Ogg's gossips to construct a coherent narrative may not be entirely one of imagination. In effect, Eliot's narrative runs counter not merely to what the gossips want to see, but to the conclusions it draws. Although Maggie's refusal to elope with Stephen is surely her moral triumph, in narrative terms, it is not clear that her last-minute renunciation effects the ends the novel claims for it. In Victorian terms, Maggie may be no less fallen merely because she returns before the elopement with Stephen has led to sexual intercourse. Edith Dombey, for instance, refuses sex with Carker even after running off with him, knowing that she will be seen as guilty of adultery, indeed desiring that judgment, and in these terms, Maggie's renunciation may be seen as too little, too late. Nor is this view merely narrow Victorian sexual ethics. In effect, the contemporary critic who agrees that Maggie might as well have continued the elopement draws a version of the same conclusion. Any damage Maggie might have done by marrying Stephen or running off with him, she has in effect already done. And Sir Edward Bulwer-Lytton, in a contemporary response to the novel, puts this ethical judgment in aesthetic terms:

> It may be quite natural that [Maggie] should take that liking to [Stephen], but it is a position at variance with all that had before been Heroic about her. The

---

ment or not. Alexander Welsh, *George Eliot and Blackmail* (Cambridge: Harvard University Press, 1985), 144–145.

indulgence of such a sentiment for the affianced of a friend under whose roof she was, was a treachery and a meanness according to the Ethics of Art, and nothing can afterwards lift the character into the same hold on us. The refusal to marry Stephen fails to do so.[23]

By shifting the issue from what guilt an actual person might bear for what Maggie does to what effect Eliot's depiction has on a reader, Bulwer-Lytton makes the judgment of St. Ogg's a narrative one. Even if, realistically, someone in Maggie's position might have felt what she did, still her indulgence in the feeling transgresses "the Ethics of Art," and thus Eliot has not constructed the plot well, has not evoked for Maggie the sympathy the narrative demands.

Eliot knows that her narrative affronts at just the moment it demands ethical approval, but she also clearly intends just that contradiction. She comments on one of Tom's rare insights about Maggie that it was "that hard rind of truth which is discerned by unimaginative, unsympathetic minds." And her reply to Bulwer-Lytton also criticizes his narrowness:

> The other chief point of criticism—Maggie's position towards Stephen—is too vital a part of my whole conception and purpose for me to be converted to the condemnation of it. If I am wrong there—if I did not really know what my heroine would feel and do under the circumstances in which I deliberately placed her, I ought not to have written this book at all, but quite a different book, if any. If the ethics of art do not admit the truthful presentation of a character essentially noble but liable to great error—error that is anguish to its own nobleness—then, it seems to me, the ethics of art are too narrow, and must be widened to correspond to a widening psychology.[24]

Bulwer-Lytton does not argue that it is not verisimilitudinous for Maggie to be attracted to Stephen but that the attraction mars the narrative. From this perspective, Eliot's familiar defense of the realism of her depiction of Maggie seems beside the point until she forcibly makes it the point by arguing that Bulwer-Lytton's artistic criteria are as narrow as Tom's ethical ones. Her point is to evoke sympathy not merely in the face of error but precisely as a result of the connection of error with nobleness, in this case of Maggie's near-elopement with her return. No character in the novel can make a narrative of this conflict, not Maggie, not Tom, not the gossips of St. Ogg's, not merely or always because their ethics are too narrow, but because they look for a coherent narrative while Eliot insists on an aesthetics that creates sympathy out of just the moments of unreadability from which Tom, insisting on the hard rind of truth, recoils. Just as Feuerbach's secular analysis of Christianity's essence becomes a sympathetic one at the moment it recognizes simul-

---

[23] *George Eliot: The Critical Heritage*, 121.
[24] Ibid., 123.

taneously Christianity's insufficiency and its value, Eliot constructs a sympathy for Maggie that grows out of our awareness that her elopement and return cannot be read in any narratively satisfactory manner. If the narrative depiction corresponds with actual psychology, as Eliot insists, realism here results not in the affirmation of the quotidian and commonplace but in an unreadability that creates the wider sympathy that such a coherent affirmation could not.

The Mill on the Floss may still appear to see sympathy growing out of realistic mimesis inasmuch as it constructs its aesthetic artifice—in which a blocked awareness grows out of an unreadable object of that awareness—from the narratively supposed audience awareness of Maggie's near-elopement and return and its significance. Even here, the constant objections to this element of the plot, and even more to its consequence in Maggie's and Tom's drowning, manifest a real audience's resistance to the aesthetic perspective the novel asks from them. *Daniel Deronda,* famously, makes the status of Eliot's realism an issue, either, depending on the view of the critic, by blatantly failing to live up to its dictates or by consciously calling its limitations into question. Usually critics pose the problem of realism in *Deronda* in terms of the section of the plot dealing with Deronda, seeing the section dealing with Gwendolen Harleth as a further extension of Eliot's domestic realism. If critics regularly remark on the odd wish-fulfilment aspect of the Deronda plot, however, few remark on the narrative convenience of Grandcourt's death, possibly because, turning our attention to Gwendolen's response to her part in that death, that element in the novel so clearly asks Eliot's constant question about the criminal acts guilty wishes may cause.[25] But Gwendolen's response, we will see, is as vexed and conflicted as the incident it reflects on is narratively convenient. In that response, I will argue, Eliot constructs the psychological equivalent of her conflicted narrative awareness in *Mill on the Floss,* and also the justification for the narrative wish-fulfillment in the Deronda plot.

Although critics frequently mark Feuerbach's influence on Eliot's early fictions, one can note quite explicit recalls of Feuerbach's theories of the construction of religion and religious imagery in *Daniel Deronda,* applied with quite dizzying irony to the passages on which they comment. They indicate not merely Eliot's awareness of the way her plot breaks realist convention but the role of Feuerbachian awareness in that transgression. Thus, for instance, we see the development of Gwendolen's concern for Deronda's judgment of her:

---

[25] Although the critiques of the Deronda plot are myriad, perhaps the best comment on the way in which it constructs narrative origins to achieve thematic effects that really cause their constructions, thus on the formal aspect of the plot's wish-fulfillment element, is Cynthia Chase's "The Decomposition of Elephants: Double-Reading *Daniel Deronda,*" *PMLA* 93 (1978): 215–27. Redfield (*Phantom Formations,* 154) and Hertz ("Some Words," 281) also note wish-fulfillment elements in the plot.

Her anger towards Deronda had changed into a superstitious dread—due, perhaps, to the coercion he had exercised over her thought—lest that first interference of his in her life might foreshadow some future influence. It is of such stuff that superstitions are commonly made: an intense feeling about ourselves which makes the evening star shine at us with a threat, and the blessing of a beggar encourage us. And superstitions carry consequences which often verify their hope or foreboding.[26]

This passage recapitulates Feuerbach's argument that we construct our religions by imposing our own needs and sensibilities on an external object, taking our image-making as information about reality. And as in Feuerbach, it also sees the value in the activity it debunks since Gwendolen, like Feuerbach's Christians, fetishizes a saving aspect of herself and the consequences of her superstition will not be entirely undesirable.

Gwendolen's image-making here operates in a way that corresponds to a reading of Feuerbach as grounding a religion of humanity. Indeed since she is literally making a religion of a human being, Deronda, and since that superstition works beneficently for her, one can easily see in this passage a near literal enactment of that religion. If this reading places the passage as another in a long line of Eliot's unbelieving but approving treatments of religious sensibility, dating back to her depictions of Tryan in *Scenes From a Clerical Life* and Dinah in *Adam Bede,* though, Gwendolen's literal making a superstition of a human being looks at least somewhat odder than past examples of Christians whose moral essence was humanist. It has all the elements of believing in the reality of one's desires for which the novel is frequently criticized. Deronda's discovery of his own Judaism, for instance, is famously vexed because of both its moral centrality to the novel and its at least seemingly unrealistic, wish-fulfillment element. And that wish-fulfillment may be Deronda's as well as Mordecai's. Indeed, much of what Eliot has to say about the wish-fulfillment in the "mind-and-millinery" school of "Silly Novels by Lady Novelists" can be applied, only slightly harming Eliot's jaundiced irony, to *Daniel Deronda.* Thus, for instance, Eliot hilariously recounts in that essay the plot of a novel that turns on a heroine falling in love with a prime minister through newspaper accounts of his activity, suddenly being ennobled and meeting the prime minister, who of course turns out to be young and handsome so that she can fall in love with him and marry him in person (*Essays,* 307–308). Is Deronda's discovery of his own Jewishness, an outcome which aligns him with Mordecai's prophetic vision and allows him to marry Mirah, really any more narratively convenient and unlikely?

This application of Eliot's essay to the novel harms the essay's irony only because of Eliot's greater awareness of her narrative's affront to realism. She

---

[26] George Eliot, *Daniel Deronda,* ed. Barbara Hardy (Harmondsworth: Penguin, 1967), 374–375. Further references cited in the text as *DD.*

stresses rather than trying to elide the narratively willful element of this plot turn. When Deronda starts to consider seriously Mordecai's belief without evidence in his Jewishness, even while imagining its possible truth, he also labels its sources ruthlessly: "And now, suppose that wish begotten belief in his Jewish birth, and that extravagant demand of discipleship to be the fore-shadowing of an actual discovery and genuine spiritual result: suppose Mordecai's ideas made a real conquest over Deronda's conviction?" (*DD*, 570). This passage imagines Mordecai's "wish begotten belief" making a conquest over Deronda's conviction by its moral and visionary force, not by any inherent likeliness or verisimilitude in the claim. Even as he connects Mordecai's visionariness with that of Columbus, Deronda recognizes that he cannot adhere to it as a result of any material element in their connection. Although Deronda immediately goes on to suppose Mordecai to be correct, he never thinks that Mordecai's belief has any evidentiary basis.[27] And by implication, the narrative that winds up affirming Mordecai's and Deronda's wish here calls its own realism into question. Deronda simply denies that his and Mordecai's connection can have other than the validity of a correspon-dent image: "Suppose, in spite of all presumptions to the contrary, that his impression should somehow be proved true, and that I should come actually to share any of the ideas he is devoted to? This is the only question which really concerns the effect of our meeting on my life" (*DD*, 573). His suppo-sition, based on coincidence giving a material image to a wish, however, makes the novel's fictive narrative, which enacts that coincidence, literally a wish-fulfillment.

The narrative of Deronda's discovery of his origin enhances the effect I have outlined in *The Mill on the Floss*. As there, we see here an aesthetic in Eliot that first presents a narrative whose self-awareness creates conflicting values—here Mordecai's visionary claims on Deronda's future, the realism of lowered expectation that Deronda still uses to evaluate that vision and the narrative's realist recognition of its own extravagance. The aesthetic of nar-rative contradiction then questions a reader's modes of evaluating what that

[27] Deronda's refusal here and throughout to see Mordecai's and his wishes about his birth as having any antecedent likelihood I think undercuts attempts to recuperate the realist element in Eliot's narrative by posing Mordecai's claim that Deronda is a Jew as a scientific hypothesis that the narrative will test. The model formulation of this view is in George Levine, "George Eliot's Hypothesis of Reality," *Nineteenth Century Fiction*, 35 (1980): 5. Sally Shuttleworth follows Levine in connecting Mordecai's transformative supposition with an enlarged view of science. *George Eliot and Nineteenth-Century Science* (Cambridge: Cambridge University Press, 1984), 181. While in moral quality Mordecai's visions are nothing like Gwendolen's, on an epis-temological basis I do not think they are very different. So far from being a hypothesis, Mordecai's belief, if it did not exist in a novel that offered a fictively constructed affirmation of it, would not even be falsifiable enough to be tested at all: What kind of evidence would he ac-cept that Deronda was not a Jew? Any disconfirming evidence about his birth would surely be as easily gotten around as the wild unlikeliness of it at this point in the novel. What differenti-ates Deronda and Eliot from those vulgar critics is not any greater science but their attempt to deal with Feuerbachian image-making with Feuerbachian awareness.

narrative recounts. This aesthetic, drawn from Hegel possibly indirectly but from Feuerbach quite directly, has always run deeper than Eliot's commitment to realism and here seems to overpower it. But the novel reconnects the narrative of Deronda's origin and its ethical impulse to Eliot's realism in the moment in which Gwendolen comes to the kind of ethical awareness that a confrontation with one's actual desires and their consequences regularly creates in Eliot, and this moment, her attempt to evaluate her responsibility for Grandcourt's death, shows how the transforming awareness that shapes Eliot's narrative may be figured as part of a character's psychology.

Gwendolen's role in Grandcourt's death bears a certain resemblance to Bulstrode's murder of his blackmailer, Rigg, in *Middlemarch*. Certainly, as Bulstrode intensely desires Rigg's death, Gwendolen comes to hope for Grandcourt's in full and explicit awareness. In the event, Grandcourt falls from a yacht at the exact moment that Gwendolen most intensely wishes his death. Gwendolen, confessing to Deronda, leads up to Grandcourt's drowning by noting, "I knew no way of killing him there, but I did, I did kill him in my thoughts" (*DD*, 760). Thus when Grandcourt is thrown from the yacht, she says "I only know that I saw my wish outside me" (*DD*, 761). Learning to see the egoism of one's desires by seeing them outside oneself, outside the veils of ego, is, of course, a seminal ethical moment in Eliot. But to recognize her guilt, it seems, Gwendolen must go much further than this in finding a way to see herself as complicitous in Grandcourt's death:

> It was all like lightning. "The rope!" he called out in a voice—not his own—I hear it now—and I stooped for the rope—I felt I must—I felt sure he could swim, and he would come back whether or not, and I dreaded him. That was in my mind—he would come back. But he was gone down again and I had the rope in my hand—no there he was again—his face above the water—and he cried again—and I held my hand, and my heart said "Die!"—and he sank; and I felt "It is done—I am wicked, I am lost!"—and I had the rope in my hand—I don't know what I thought—I was leaping away from myself—I would have saved him then. (*DD*, 761)

At this point Gwendolen jumps in the water according to the earlier testimony of the fishermen, perhaps in an attempt to save Grandcourt.[28] The narrative presses hard to inculpate Gwendolen for Grandcourt's death, which perhaps accounts for a certain critical eagerness to convict her. But it then presses equally hard to exculpate her. The only event that actually attaches

---

[28] As a result of this description of the scene, both Simon During and Henry Alley come close to Welsh in describing this as a murder, though both realize the case to be ambiguous. Simon During, "The Strange Case of Monomania: Patriarchy in Literature, Murder in *Middlemarch*, Drowning in *Daniel Deronda*," *Representations* 23 (1988): 86–104; Henry Alley, "George Eliot and the Ambiguity of Murder," *Studies in the Novel* 25 (1993): 59–75.

her wish to his death is the second moment in which she does not throw the rope while saying in her heart "Die!" Deronda, in contrast to most of the novel's critics, immediately finds her not only legally guiltless but actually so: "'With your quickest, utmost effort, it seems impossible that you could have done anything to save him. That murderous will cannot, I think, have altered the course of events. Its effect is confined to the motives in your own breast'" (DD, 764). Nor does Deronda seem to be rationalizing here. Only the virulence of Gwendolen's wish makes us want to construe her not throwing the rope as a consequential act having Grandcourt's death as an effect.

Gwendolen does experience an intention to kill—or at least a quite vibrantly expressed wish—coupled with an act that certainly could, under some circumstances, have had Grandcourt's death as its consequence. But not only did the act not, in all probability, have the death as its consequence, within the entire concatenation of acts surrounding the drowning, its momentariness reduces any tie it might have had to the event almost to nothing. In other words, even if we imagine that Grandcourt drowned because he did not have a rope to grasp at the second time he came up, not merely the fact that he was already drowning but the alacrity with which Gwendolen would have had to act to get him the rope before he finally drowned all tend to split her moment of withholding action from the event to which she ties it. Up to a point, one could say that the relationship between Gwendolen's act and her guilt matches the relation critics complain about between Deronda's wishes for himself and the narrative granting of that wish in giving him a Jewish origin. In each case, the external situation matches the internal state to which it is taken to correspond in the manner of a symbol rather than as a cause or effect: just as Deronda's Jewishness is more the symbol of his status as inheritor of Mordecai's prophetic role than a causal element of his identity, Gwendolen's act of withholding the rope gives her a material image on which to hang her guilt, a way for her to say meaningfully not only that she has seen her wish outside herself but also that she has acted on it.

From Gwendolen's perspective and perhaps from that of many readers of the novel—particularly those who think that Gwendolen murders Grandcourt—this definition of Gwendolen's act as symbol may seem too subtle by half. Unlike Deronda's sudden discovery of Jewishness, Grandcourt's death follows upon her wish and upon an act that has some obvious possible connection to it. And although the drowning is as conveniently constructed by the narrative as is Deronda's Jewishness, the death itself, split from its circumstances, is at least a narratively expectable outcome of the bitter power struggle their marriage has become. More importantly, Gwendolen's guilt is vital to her moral redemption in the novel: "Her remorse was the precious sign of a recoverable nature; it was the culmination of that self-disapproval which had been the awakening of a new life within her; it marked her from those criminals whose only regret is failure in securing their evil wish" (*DD*, 762).[29] And Gwendolen specifies the moment with the rope quite explicitly as the connection she cannot blink: "But if I had not had that murderous will—that moment—if I had thrown the rope on the instant—perhaps it would have hindered death?" (*DD*, 762). But of course it is also vital to Gwendolen's moral regeneration that she has not committed murder, that she has in fact consciously resisted her impulse regularly in the scenes leading up to the drowning. Finally, although Gwendolen's awareness of her unreadable act brings guilt as well as moral improvement, she is in the position of the audience to Maggie's return from her journey with Stephen. Although Maggie's return comes too late to avoid giving the pain to others, it still has the shape of renunciation leading to the sense of it as morally significant. The narrative awareness may construct that approval about which others in the novel are less sure, but it is an approval that occurs ineluctably and consequentially with that aesthetically constructed awareness. In the same way, Gwendolen's awareness changes her act from one of guilt to moral redemption precisely in the ambiguity of the act it regards and the way that ambiguity allows its symbolism to function consequentially for her. This moment of regarding an act as a consequence even as she knows its relation to her intent is symbolic is her Feuerbachian moment of transforming awareness and is, like Deronda's recognition of his origin and the narrative's affirmation of Maggie's renunciation, dependent on the way that awareness recognizes and enhances the unreadableness of the act it regards.[30]

Critical discussions of the way *Daniel Deronda* questions the realism of Eliot's previous fiction have mostly considered the character of Deronda and

[29] This sentence describes Deronda's thoughts and it is perhaps not entirely irrelevant in this context that he seems to identify in the space of three clauses "sign," "culmination," and causal "mark" as if they were equivalent. The distinctions this essay worries and other readers have tried to sort out for the purposes of both aesthetic evaluation and thematic interpretation seem for Deronda, and perhaps for the narrator, quite permeable ones.

[30] Since this essay connects an ethical consequence with an unreadable moment in literary texts, it obviously has some affinity with J. Hillis Miller's argument for a deconstructive ethic in *The Ethics of Reading: Kant, de Man, Eliot, Trollope, James, and Benjamin* (New York: Columbia University Press, 1987). But the differences between Miller's theory and the one I outline in Feuerbach and Eliot are also significant. Miller discusses primarily an ethical obligation he sees a reader as owing to a text (4). This obligation entails an experience of textual unreadability that is necessary in the ethical as well as the epistemological sense (59). Because Miller's situation is a generalized one, his reading of this situation in Eliot entails a deconstruction of Eliot's realism, construed as entailing primarily a presumption of accurate mimesis (61–80). In contrast, I am arguing not for any ethics of unreadability but for an ethical realization consequent upon the experience of unreadability. Because it is not a general ethics of reading but a very specific construct within her aesthetic of the problems that a deconstruction would use to call her narrative into question, this essay cannot enact a deconstruction of Eliot's realism. Still, as should be clear, my argument owes to such deconstructions as Miller's and Hertz's precisely in terms of this consideration of the epistemology, ethics, and aesthetics of that which cannot be read coherently as opposed to that which can.

the strangeness of the Jewish sections of the novel as a whole. The Gwendolen section of the novel has seemed more in line with the author's past realism. But, I have argued, Gwendolen's reflection upon her own guilt, and the moral recuperation that reflection brings—the moral narrative Eliot is supposed to be telling in her previous fiction—rests on an awareness of an act that has all the symbolist questioning of the limits of realism that critics find in Deronda's discovery of his origin or in his mother's self-dramatizing that also dramatizes the ills of mimetic representation. Gwendolen's ambiguous awareness, however, differs from the realist narrative's evocation of sympathy in its depiction of Maggie's return, or in the numbers of near-violent events that critics regularly connect with Grandcourt's drowning, only in that it moves the form of awareness, as I said, from that offered by the narrative in its depiction of events to Gwendolen's own awareness as represented by the narrative. Eliot's creation of a psychological representation of the ethical working of her aesthetic, then, instead of cementing its ostensible realist base, connects her psychological realism with an idealist mode of aesthetic figuration.

But my point in showing how a moment of ostensible psychological realism operates with a decidedly idealist aesthetics of a transforming awareness has not been to deconstruct Eliot's realism. Instead I have wanted to question if our usual understanding of that realism has really been sufficient to deal with the moments of ethical or ideological contradiction in any of her novels. We usually think of an ethical analysis in art as growing out of an organic wholeness of vision that gives it its validity. When various critics, Victorian or contemporary, find that organic wholeness wanting, they either conclude that Eliot's ethical ends have disrupted her aesthetic integrity or that her sharing in the values of organicism are the more fundamental problem, depending on their own ethical and aesthetic presumptions. Instead, through a discussion of her own statements about her art in the context of Feuerbach and his idealist precursors, I have tried to outline a view of aesthetic form as bringing to a full emergence, without offering any resolution, various contradictions both in the material it regards and in its own regard of that material. From this perspective, the ethical effects that Eliot's fiction quite evidently aim at depend on these contradictions rather than on any organic formalism, and our notice of them is part of how that disruptive aesthetic awareness works. While her development of such an awareness—first in her narrative, then in *Daniel Deronda*'s depiction of psychology that finally made the disruptive form of that awareness manifest—will not make her novels in any sense invulnerable to the kinds of Victorian, deconstructive, and historicist critique whose arguments I have so regularly used here, it will demand a redirection of those arguments and a questioning of what they presume Eliot represents and what her realism meant to be and do.

In terms of the surrounding debate on historicism and historical relativity in which this essay participates, Eliot's aesthetic suggests, I would argue, that the oppositions usually posed are far too bald. We see Arthur Danto's distinction between seeing history accurately and seeing it with no revision of the historically lived experience in Feuerbach's symbolic history of Christianity, out of which Eliot constructed her defining moments of narrative symbolism and significance. Both Feuerbach and Eliot recognize the essential contradiction of a symbolic interpretation that defines an essence by radically changing an appearance. While Eliot uses that recognition toward an ethical end, its historical signficance would be a version of the same: a historical interpretation will always be an artificial historical reconstruction, not because of some epistemological limit (whether such limits do or do not exist is a matter of indifference to this argument) but because of the necessary form of historical awareness. For this reason, while I have at times suggested that Eliot's aesthetic does not evade its contemporary deconstructions but captures their form within itself, that aesthetic would also capture the discursive form of historicist critiques of her work.

While the full analysis of that effect of her form would be well beyond the purview of this paper, one may see how this invasion of Eliot's aesthetic into a historicist critique of her occurs by considering how such a critique might grow out of her encounter with Feuerbach. Marx's fourth thesis on Feuerbach offers itself as a starting point for such a critique:

> Feuerbach starts out from the fact of religious self-estrangement, of the duplication of the world into a religious and a secular one. His work consists in resolving the religious world into its secular basis. But that the secular basis raises itself above itself and establishes for itself an independent realm in the clouds can be explained only through the cleavage and self-contradictions within the secular basis. The latter must therefore in itself be both understood in its contradiction and revolutionized in practice. Therefore after, e.g., the earthly family is discovered to be the secret of the heavenly family, one must proceed to destroy the former both in theory and in practice.[31]

Marx, in effect, outlines the beginnings of a historical analysis that would be an ideological critique. In showing that religious belief is inappropriately transformed secular apprehension, Marx argues, Feuerbach nevertheless also means to give the secular a newly understood value that in effect makes it a renewed spiritual belief: "[T]he secular basis raises itself above itself and establishes for itself an independent realm in the clouds." And whether Feuerbach meant to do this, certainly Eliot quite explicitly did, as we have seen in her treatments of Deronda's and Gwendolen's image-making. When Marx then turns from the transformation of the heavenly family to the earthly family, asking for the theoretical destruction of that concept, he pre-

---

[31] Marx, *German Ideology,* 198.

dicts the line of argument taken by recent historicist analysis of Victorian fiction in general and of Eliot in particular.[32]

But if Feuerbach and Eliot are guilty of this particular secular theology, the compression of Marx's thesis rests on its assumption of the modes of critiquing that belief merely by articulating it that, as we have seen, those two authors outlined. In effect, one knows the error of spiritualizing the earthly family, almost without saying, only because Feuerbach has already shown the error of spiritualizing at all. Moreover, Marx's historical undercutting of the notion of a sacralized secular family works by merely mentioning the fact of that sacralization precisely in the way that Feuerbach's transformation of religion by defining its essence works, via a historical understanding that changes what it understands through the form of its understanding. If the aesthetic of conflicted awareness that I have analyzed here entails some transfiguration of the material into image-making, it simultaneously shows, as part of its formal working, how that transfiguration may be recognized in its own contradictoriness. As such, it has made itself logically necessary for the ideological and historicist critiques that have recently intended to destroy it in theory and in practice.

[32] Graham Martin offered a first pass at considering Eliot through the rubric of Marx's thesis on Feuerbach some years ago in " 'Daniel Deronda': George Eliot and Political Change," in *Critical Essays on George Eliot,* ed. Barbara Hardy (London: Routledge and Kegan Paul, 1970), 133–50. But he treated the issue entirely in terms of the contradictions Eliot's characters experience or represent. Although I do not know of explicit historicist applications of Marx on Feuerbach, one can see the shadows of his thesis not only in Nancy Armstrong's general argument in *Desire and Domestic Fiction* (New York: Oxford University Press, 1987) but in Jeff Nunokawa's project of undercutting the idea that commodity was an intrusion into domesticity in *The Afterlife of Property: Domestic Security and the Victorian Novel* (Princeton: Princeton University Press, 1994), 77–99.

PART III

CONTINUITIES

7. The Structure of Anxiety in Political Economy and Hard Times

MARY POOVEY

Inspired by the success of natural and physical scientists, British moral philosophers began trying to develop systematic accounts of society and human behavior as early as the middle of the eighteenth century.[1] By the first decades of the nineteenth century, advocates could claim some progress for political economy in particular: Dugald Stewart had begun to teach the subject at Edinburgh in the last decades of the eighteenth century, and in 1805 Robert Malthus was awarded the first university chair in the fledgling science. Despite economists' success in winning institutional recognition for their enterprise, however, efforts to refine the sciences of wealth and society introduced theoretical problems that natural scientists rarely had to face. Whereas the latter could claim, as Bacon had, that empirical observations of material phenomena could be used to induce reliable generalizations, would-be social scientists had to construct abstractions before they could make empirical observations or formulate general knowledge claims. This methodological imperative emanated from the very nature of the social-scientific project: to produce systematic knowledge about society, human nature, or the market, social scientists first had to generate an abstraction—"society," "human nature," or "the market"—that somehow stood in for, but did not refer directly to, whatever material phenomena it was said to represent.

---

[1] For accounts of the eighteenth-century social sciences, see the essays included in *Inventing Human Science: Eighteenth-Century Domains,* ed. Christopher Fox, Roy Porter, and Robert Wokler (Berkeley: University of California Press, 1995). See also Mary Poovey, *A History of the Modern Fact: Problems of Knowledge in the Sciences of Man and Society* (Chicago: University of Chicago Press, 1998), chaps. 4–6.

Because they wanted to consolidate their own social authority, nineteenth-century social scientists sought to naturalize these abstractions, to make them seem as ontologically stable as the material phenomena natural scientists claimed to observe. Despite the relative ease with which the social-scientific use of abstractions was able to piggyback on a more general acceptance of immaterialities, however, early nineteenth-century scientists of wealth and society both provoked and betrayed a certain discomfort with the methodological, epistemological, and ontological questions raised by their reliance on abstractions. In this essay, I argue that this discomfort manifested itself not only in skeptical responses to political economy, but also in formal features that appear in political economists' texts. I call the paradigm that organizes these features the "structure of anxiety" because when it was explicitly theorized in 1926, Freud called it anxiety. As he theorized anxiety, moreover, Freud described it as a formal or structural relation rather than assigning it a specific emotional content. The inability of nineteenth-century political economists to articulate what motivated certain formal infelicities in their own writing is consistent with what Freud described as anxiety's resistance to transparency: one cannot say—or know—what causes anxiety or what anxiety is about because anxiety protects by obscuring what would otherwise be intolerable to contemplate.

My essay proposes a model for knowing the past that repeats the structure of anxiety, as I derive this paradigm from Freud. This model assumes that we cannot know the past as it was in and for itself (or on its own terms) because, like the source of anxiety, a past "event" only manifests itself as meaningful to the present reader through, and in the terms provided by, the interpretive response it occasions.[2] Thus part of (what can only retrospectively be constructed as) the meaning of a past text or event appears belatedly, in attempts to make the text or event meaningful now—just as whatever event in the past occasions present anxiety can only be known as anxiety-provoking after it is over and through the anxiety it occasions. What I have just stated about meaning holds true for identity as well. Part of what can only retrospectively be constructed as the identity of a past text or event appears belatedly because the way we delineate the beginning and ending of a text or an event—the way we identify the "text" or the "event" itself—derives from our present sense of its meaning *in relation to our own interpretive categories,* which exist to make the past meaningful to us now.

In terms of my account of political economy, this model implies that what I call the structure of anxiety is only visible now because Freud, who was another scientist of human nature, made this structure—and, by extension, this interpretive paradigm—explicit. Yet Freud did not use the phrase "the struc-

---

[2] A relevant discussion of this ontology of the event can be found in Jacques Lezra, *Unspeakable Subjects: The Genealogy of the Event in Early Modern Europe* (Stanford, Calif.: Stanford University Press, 1997), esp. chap. 1.

ture of anxiety," nor did he think of his analysis as providing an account of political economy or interpretation. I can draw a connection between Freud's theorization of anxiety and certain formal features in nineteenth-century political economists' work only because of the development of new interpretive paradigms, which provide vocabularies that assign names to what had previously been incomprehensible. Thus sociology provides a way to understand (what we now call) professionalization, and psychoanalysis offers a vocabulary with which we can describe (what we now interpret as) the dynamic of deferral. As I argue in the second part of this essay, however, some nineteenth-century writers were able to mobilize the productive capacity of anxiety even if they could neither name nor theorize its content or structure. In Charles Dickens's *Hard Times* we see how the structural relationship that Freud called anxiety could produce different effects in different genres, especially when one writer—in this case, the novelist—explicitly set out to criticize the way the other writer generated knowledge.

I

I return to these epistemological issues at the end of this essay. For now, I want to highlight the role that anxiety can be said to have played in organizing nineteenth-century political economy by beginning with Freud. The methodology I use here follows the logic of belated or deferred identity I have just described: in order to identify the discomfort that manifests itself formally in political economy as a manifestation of anxiety, it is necessary for me to work backwards, to read political economy through Freud's discussion of anxiety. This approach assumes that psychoanalysis was a late-nineteenth-century version of the social-scientific initiative first launched by eighteenth-century political economists. It also assumes that the appearance in political economy of formal infelicities that political economists could not efface made Freud realize that anxiety was a problem he needed to theorize, not just one among a series of affective states. I approach political economy through Freud's work not primarily to trace this genealogical connection, however, but to argue that we can only grasp what political economists could not know about their science with the assistance of what late-twentieth-century theorists have enabled us to know about Freud's science: that psychoanalysis enacts as well as describes an antimetaphysical model that implies the interpretive paradigm I use here.

In his most sustained discussion of the topic, the 1926 "Supplementary Remarks on Anxiety," Freud initially distinguishes two types of anxiety, which constitute responses to two types of danger. "Real danger is a danger that is known, and realistic anxiety [*angst*] is anxiety about a known danger of this sort," Freud explains. "Neurotic anxiety is anxiety about an unknown danger. Neurotic danger is thus a danger that has still to be discovered."[3] Almost immediately, Freud amends the distinction he has just established by asserting that, far from being an alternative to "realistic anxiety," neurotic anxiety is actually the prototype of all anxiety. As such, neurotic anxiety is characterized by two features: first, it bears some relation to expectation ("it is anxiety *about* something," Freud explains [*ISA,* 165]); and second, it often lacks an identifiable object (*ISA,* 165). This peculiar combination—expectation but of something that is not known—leads Freud to argue that neurotic anxiety may anticipate a repetition of something that once occurred. Even though we can make this assumption, Freud continues, we can never know what past event occasioned trauma because anxiety protects by a proleptic leap that obscures the past by anticipating a repetition that never occurs as such. "The signal of anxiety" is given, Freud explains, when the subject expects the repetition of a danger-situation.

> The signal announces: "I am expecting a situation of helplessness to set in," or: "The present situation reminds me of one of the traumatic experiences I have had before. Therefore I will anticipate the trauma and behave as though it had already come, while there is yet time to turn it aside." Anxiety is therefore on the one hand an expectation of a trauma, and on the other a repetition of it in a mitigated form.... The ego, which experienced the trauma passively, now repeats it actively in a weakened version, in the hope of being able itself to direct its course. (*ISA,* 166–67)

As Freud describes it, neurotic anxiety protects through two devices: by splitting the subject into three parts and by establishing a relationship among these parts that is capable of opening a gap in time as well as identity. The result is a triangle, in which the first position is occupied by the part-object that is presently endangered, the second by the past danger, and the third by the part-object in charge of exaggerating the distinction between past, present, and future through repetition. Repetition has the ability to exaggerate temporal distinctions and thus to protect the endangered subject, because it replaces the real danger that presumably occurred in the past with a representation, which "mitigates" the original danger situation. This "mitigation" involves two variants of abstraction, which substantially *revise,* so as to *efface,* the danger that once threatened the subject. In the first phase of abstraction, the ego abstracts an affect from the initial danger-situation; the ego *separates* the affect of helplessness from the danger-situation in order to control it. The affect can be controlled, in turn, because it is weaker in its

---

[3] Sigmund Freud, *Inhibitions, Symptoms, and Anxiety,* in *The Standard Edition of the Complete Psychological Works of Sigmund Freud,* trans. and ed. by James Strachey et al., vol. 20 (Toronto: Hogarth Press, 1964), 165. Future references to this text will be cited by the abbreviation *ISA.*

This triangle simultaneously manages anxiety and produces it.

The blocking agent (abstract theory or narrative) manages anxiety by converting the source of danger into an image or concept and by abstracting its affect.

The blocking agent produces anxiety because it prevents the endangered subject from seeing and knowing the source of danger for what it is.

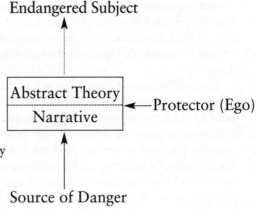

Figure 7.1. The Structure of Anxiety

isolated form, and because an image of the object that once provoked the fear replaces the actual source of danger in a narrative that allows the subject agency. In the second phase of abstraction, the analyst *theorizes* the abstracted affect by constructing new abstractions that explain it scientifically ("the ego," "the psychical apparatus," and so on). Thus, imaginatively triangulating the danger-situation protects the part of the subject that is presently endangered by obliterating whatever past event occasioned trauma and by giving future agency to another part of the subject—the part that abstracts affect and that, in so doing, either provokes action or provides the materials from which psychoanalytic theory can be generated.

The account I have just given of Freud's theory can be rendered by an abstraction of my own (fig. 7.1). At the top of the triangle, we find the endangered subject, and at the bottom we find the source of danger, which is rendered obscure by the agency of the figure on the right, which Freud calls the ego. What obscures the source of danger (which belongs to the past) is the process of representation, which is also a process of abstraction, and which entails the two phases I have just described: the initial abstraction of affect from its (past) cause and the subsequent arrangement of new abstractions into narratives or theories, which function both to obliterate the past and to anticipate a mitigated return. Thus the figure on the right (the ego) protects the figure at the top (the endangered subject) by a twofold process of abstraction that creates a spatial and temporal barrier between the endangered subject and whatever objects might once have endangered it.

Even if this defense protects the subject from a literal return of whatever once endangered it, the anxiety the subject experiences in the present reveals that the barrier that protects the subject from the past also produces a new relation to it, one that "anticipates" the return of something whose identity is obscured by the barrier of anxiety. Thus even though the barrier manages the helplessness that the danger-situation (presumably) once provoked, it also generates a new version of helplessness because the barrier makes it impossible for the endangered subject to know what once endangered it.

This double, or self-contradictory, tendency of abstraction simultaneously attracted and alarmed nineteenth-century writers trying to produce knowledge about abstractions like society, human nature, and the market. Like the abstracted anxiety by which the ego proleptically forecloses the possibility that the past will return in anything but a mitigated form, the abstractions with which nineteenth-century social scientists represented their analytic objects foreclosed the possibility that skeptics could know the actual particulars that political economists claimed to analyze except through the representations that took their place. Obliterating the particulars represented by abstractions like "the market" thus tended to prevent critics from being able to judge the accuracy or adequacy of political economy itself. For J. R. McCulloch, one of the leading practitioners of the science of wealth, abstractions were attractive for precisely this reason: in making visible something that could not exist except as a construct created by political economists, abstractions promised to make critics' skepticism irrelevant. As McCulloch discovered, however, the skepticism political economy's abstractions were intended to control had a nasty way of returning—as suspicion about the science of political economy itself. This suspicion also has a formal counterpart in McCulloch's own writing. In his attempts to promote political economy, we can identify not only his eagerness to forestall objections to his science's reliance on abstractions but also the infelicitous traces of his inability to do so.

As a branch of moral philosophy, political economy was the first, as well as the prototypical, science of society, for its eighteenth-century incarnation constituted the first systematic attempt to link sociality with impulses deemed to be quintessentially human—what Adam Smith called the universal desire "to truck, barter, and exchange one thing for another."[4] Smith's version of political economy built an account of human sociality on abstractions like "the market," but Smith's work did not foreground or arouse anxiety because his emphasis on wealth tended to defuse questions about his method in readers who were gratified by his optimism. In the text that gave Victorian political economy its distinctive cast, by contrast, Robert Malthus stressed scarcity instead of plenty, and the abstractions he used to represent what could not be seen alluded to controversial figures in the social landscape (the poor). As a consequence of the authority political economists tried to claim for their science, moreover, anxiety both radiated from

[4] Adam Smith, *An Inquiry into the Nature and Causes of the Wealth of Nations,* ed. Edwin Cannan (1776; New York: Modern Library, 1937), bk. 1, pt. 1, chap. 2, p. 13.

and greeted Malthus's *Essay on the Principles of Population*. When nineteenth-century political economists like Thomas Chalmers and David Ricardo elaborated Malthus's thesis that poor bodies breed faster than nature can supply food, they brought the anxiety that Smith's optimism had allayed to the surface of the dismal science, for they specifically raised questions about how society would survive if the poor continued to eat and reproduce. In so doing, they inadvertently encouraged critics to raise questions about political economy itself, because readers who did not agree with Malthus's conclusions sought ways to impugn a methodology that seemed to substitute interpretive abstractions for more tolerable accounts of what everybody thought they knew.[5]

In the first instance, then, nineteenth-century political economy can be said to have been an expression of and defense against anxiety about the poor. This defense can be mapped onto the triangular structure I have extracted from Freud's 1926 essay. In nineteenth-century political economy, the position of the endangered subject is occupied by members of the middle class, the dangerous object's position is occupied by the copulating poor, and the position of the ego is occupied by the political economist, who tries to ward off the twin threats of overpopulation and starvation by devising theories about how to curtail reproduction and enhance wealth.

Like Freud's ego, nineteenth-century political economists performed their protective function by a two-phase process of abstraction—by separating the fear they attributed to the middle class from its putative cause (the bodies of the copulating poor), and by positioning this fear in relation to theories based on abstractions like "wealth" and "the population." We can see how this process of abstraction sought to manage anxiety in McCulloch's 1825 *Discourse on…Political Economy*. To make the science of wealth palatable to a middle-class audience, McCulloch obliquely denominated the threat that political economy was devised to counter: Malthus's copulating poor. In the way McCulloch invokes this threat and treats the poor, we see how abstraction separated fear from the poor bodies that supposedly aroused it, then transformed the fear-inducing threat into abstractions embedded in narratives designed to console the middle-class reader by promising a future change. "Make the body of the people once fully aware of the circumstances which really determine their condition, and you may be assured that an immense majority will endeavour to turn that knowledge to good account....

---

[5] See Thomas Chalmers, *On the Christian and Economic Polity of a Nation*, vol. 14 of *The Works of Thomas Chalmers*, ed. A. C. Cheyne (Glasgow: William Collins, 1836–1842, 1845), 65–83; David Ricardo, *The Works and Correspondence of David Ricardo*, ed. Piero Sraffa and H. M. Dobb (Cambridge: Cambridge University Press, 1951–1973). For an explicit critique of what Carlyle called Malthus's "dismal science," see Robert Southey, "On the State of the Poor, the Principle of M. Malthus's Essay on Population, and the Manufacturing System, 1812," in *Essays, Moral and Political*, vol. 1 (London: John Murray, 1832). This essay was originally published in the *Quarterly Review* (1812).

The harvest of sound instruction, though late, will, in the end, be most luxuriant."[6]

In this passage, the central abstraction—"the body of the people"—simultaneously reminds the middle-class reader of Malthus's dire prediction (that poor individuals obey their bodily drives) and, by placing it in a narrative of cause and effect, neutralizes its threat. At the same time, the reference to "the harvest of sound instruction" invokes the other half of Malthus's warning (that the earth cannot produce sufficient harvests), only to translate this specter into another consoling narrative, which culminates in a vision of the future rewards of education. Of course, shifting the emphasis of these images from the threat to the consolation turned on McCulloch's ability to make middle-class readers embrace the abstractions instead of remembering the bodies and crops they might actually have seen. In essence, this was the task McCulloch's text was designed to perform: to make abstractions and the narratives they populated seem more credible than what readers could see or had seen with their own eyes.

Even if McCulloch's platitudes stress the protective capacity of abstraction, many of his readers objected to both the specific abstractions he used and the method that underwrote them. If individual members of "the poor" could be observed not to have excessively large families, readers charged, or to eat more than they could produce, then how could political economists claim that laws about abstractions more accurately foretold the future than what Englishmen actually witnessed or believed? If laws about abstractions were true, they complained, didn't this obliterate the possibility of free will? Didn't it constitute a pernicious determinism? In addition to the explicit criticisms of political economy we find in contemporary writing, we can also see this skepticism reflected in John Stuart Mill's concern that readers unsympathetic to political economy were apt either to dismiss the political economists' abstractions or to insist that political economic laws must always come true. Thus Mill worried about readers who thought that if a political economist said that twenty murders occurred each year in Hertfortshire, then at the end of a year with only nineteen murders, someone would have to make up the shortfall by murdering someone else.[7]

Political economists articulated their own version of this anxiety about the relationship between abstractions and the particulars of a phenomenal (or

---

[6] J. R. McCulloch, *A Discourse on the Rise, Progress, Peculiar Objects, and Importance of Political Economy: Containing an Outline of a Course of Lectures on the Principles and Doctrines of that Science* (Edinburgh: Archibald Constable, 1825), 87. All future citations will be abbreviated as *Discourse*.

[7] John Stuart Mill, *The Logic of the Moral Sciences*, ed. A.J. Ayer (La Salle, Ill.: Open Court, 1987), 123. This is a reprint of the sixth book of Mill's *System of Logic Ratiocinative and Inductive*, which was initially published in 1843. The relevant passage appears in chapter 11, section 2. For additional explicit contemporary criticisms of political economy, see Robert Southey, "On the State of the Poor," and the discussions of this subject in Donald Winch, *Poverty and Riches: An Intellectual History of Political Economy in Britain, 1750–1834* (Cambridge: Cambridge University Press, 1996), chap. 11; and Poovey, *A History of the Modern Fact*, 293–95.

God-governed) world. Instead of specifically interrogating how abstractions could represent what they claimed to replace, however, political economists tended to react defensively—proleptically, in fact—to the skepticism they anticipated. We see a formal sign of this defensive anticipation in McCulloch's eagerness—and inability—to align political economy with its counterparts, the natural and physical sciences. If McCulloch could demonstrate that political economy was a science, after all, he would be able to capitalize sufficiently on the authority the physical and natural sciences had come to enjoy to set aside the kind of objections that greeted methodological differences. As he was forced to acknowledge, however, political economy was both like and unlike other sciences: the science of wealth could generate systematic knowledge, as physics did, but, because political economy had to rely on abstractions, the economist's accounts of wealth did not obtain in every instance, as did the mathematical description of motion.

We see McCulloch's discomfort with the misalignment between political economy and the other sciences in his tendency to return repeatedly to their relationship. Thus early in the *Discourse*, McCulloch draws the connection—and distinction—between physical science and political economy; then, barely a page later, he reiterates the same point. Whereas the conclusions of physicists "apply in *every* case," McCulloch initially explains, the conclusions of the political economist "apply only in the *majority* of cases. The principles on which the production and accumulation of wealth depend are inherent in our nature, and exert a powerful, but not always the *same* degree of influence over the conduct of every individual; and the theorist must, therefore, satisfy himself with framing his general rules so as to explain their operation in the majority of instances, leaving it to the sagacity of the observer to modify them so as to suit individual cases" (*Discourse,* 10). One page later he restates this point: "it is not required of the economist, that his theories should quadrate with the peculiar bias of the mind of a particular person. His conclusions are drawn from observing *the principles which are found to determine the condition of mankind,* as presented on the large scale of nations and empires" (*Discourse,* 11).

For a nineteenth-century political economist, the "large scale" was precisely the problem, for McCulloch and his contemporaries had no way to theorize the relationship between abstractions constructed on this "large scale" and individual instances. For modern social scientists, this relationship no longer seems problematic because, as professionals who can establish and defend the methodological conventions of their disciplines, they have tacitly agreed not to belabor this relation. Typically, moreover, the conventions professional social scientists use to connect the large scale to particulars are based on mathematical principles, and this tends to bolster the authority of social scientists because it strengthens the affinity McCulloch was so eager to assert—between the social and the physical sciences. Thus, statistical sampling is a mathematics-based method that grounds generalizations about "populations" on small numbers of observations, and the concept of a "social fact" helps substantiate claims about numerically demonstrable regularities even when personal experience seems to contradict these claims.[8] In the mid-nineteenth century, as we have seen, when the fledgling social sciences could not yet draw social authority from professionalization or mathematics, it was impossible to determine what the basis of social scientific abstractions was—whether political economists' abstractions, for example, were mathematically derived from observed particulars or expressed only the *a priori* assumptions with which the theorist set out, as McCulloch's reference to "principles...inherent in our nature" might suggest.

McCulloch's admission that the regularities political economists describe do not account for every instance can thus be seen as anticipating—and attempting to manage—a threat to the credibility this new social science was struggling to establish. This is the source of danger—which was located in remembered objections as well as in anticipated scorn—that McCulloch could not contemplate. Even if McCulloch's attempt to connect the social and the physical sciences tried to manage such objections without naming them, however, the infelicities that distinguish his effort—the repetitions and the fineness of the distinctions he asserts—also announce his own anxiety that assertions will not suffice. Just as political economists tried to assuage the anxieties raised by the poor with abstractions that displaced poor bodies, so McCulloch struggled to manage worries about political economy by insisting that his practice was a science. His repeated acknowledgments that, in some sense at least, political economy was *not* a science like others betrayed in himself the anxiety he struggled to assuage in others, as a return, in mitigated form, of the danger he wanted to neutralize.

II

Political economists like McCulloch were willing to acknowledge only obliquely the epistemological problems their method introduced, but critics of the dismal science were explicitly skeptical about the economists' efforts to systematize human behavior with abstractions. Charles Dickens, one of political economy's most outspoken critics, insisted, for example, that abstractions like "the population" threatened to undermine personal responsibility, which could otherwise help keep society intact. In *Hard Times,* char-

---

[8] My argument here is not that statistical sampling or the concept of the social fact actually *answers* all of the questions raised by what can always be construed as a problematic relationship between individual instances and general theories. Instead, I intend to refer to the *professionalization* of the social sciences. Among the conditions that modern sociologists argue make professionalization possible (and, as an extension, one of its effects) is a general agreement among practitioners about the conventions and methods that are necessary for scientific validity. In the case of statistical sampling, professional agreement has naturalized this method, although, as we see in the political argument over its use in the 2000 census, professional agreement may not always convince politicians or the public.

acters like M'Choakumchild (whom some editors equate with McCulloch) and the Gradgrind of the opening chapters lampoon the purported superiority of abstract knowledge; and the sniveling rationalization Tom Gradgrind offers at the novel's end—"How can I help laws?"—refers directly to the challenge Dickens thought the law of large numbers posed to personal accountability.[9]

If *Hard Times* can and should be read as an explicit criticism of political economy, its portrait of the anxiety associated with this science suggests a more complex engagement with this subject. In particular, *Hard Times* takes up and explores the triangular structure by which political economists sought to manage the anxiety they associated with the copulating poor. We have already seen that Freud's discussion of anxiety clarifies the defensive function this triangle plays in political economy. In *Hard Times,* where questions about authority and epistemology take a slightly different form, we can see the productive capacity of the barrier that supposedly shields the endangered object from the source of danger. Late in his life, in texts like "Analysis Terminable and Interminable," Freud also elaborated the tendency of the protective barrier to produce new and unresolvable affects, but in the nineteenth century this tendency was most thoroughly explored by novelists. Whereas both Freud and political economists emphasized the ability of abstractions to assuage anxiety by displacing the source of threat, Dickens elaborated the capacity of this displacement to generate a form of anxiety that enhanced the appeal of his fiction. As we will see in a moment, Dickens finally did allay the anxiety he cultivated for much of *Hard Times,* but when he did so it was to protect the ethical function of the novel and his own reputation as a moralist.

In *Hard Times,* Dickens's explicit criticisms of political economy are ratified by a subtler critique, which both targets and exploits the structure of anxiety. We can identify this critique in Dickens's repeated use of situations in which a third character is summoned to observe a contract two characters are about to make. When Gradgrind wants to apprentice Sissy Jupe, for example, he insists that Bounderby witness the apprenticeship, as if having Bounderby present will ensure Sissy's future tractability (*HT,* 52–54). In this triangle, Gradgrind is the endangered subject, Bounderby is the protective ego, and Sissy's past frivolities constitute the source of danger, which Bounderby binds by witnessing. This triangle appears again in the episode that exposes the mysterious old woman as Bounderby's mother. In this scene, Bounderby is the endangered subject, the old woman and her hidden past constitute the source of danger, and the protection is afforded by the twenty-five "chance witnesses" who crowd into Bounderby's dining room to attest to the woman's unmasking (*HT,* 260).

---

[9] Charles Dickens, *Hard Times, for These Times,* ed. Kate Flint (London: Penguin Books, 1995), 284. All future references will be cited in the text as *HT.*

If witnesses occupy the position of the protective ego in these scenes, then witnessing must constitute the protection, the barrier that shields the endangered subject from the source of danger. These episodes suggest that witnessing works this way because, like an abstraction, a witness establishes the conditions for an imaginary narrative that seeks to obliterate the past with promises of a favorable future. This imaginary narrative, which seeks to bind the future to the present, is the object of Dickens's scorn, for, like abstractions, it obliterates free will and, with it, the personal responsibility Dickens assumes will protect society.

In his most elaborate dramatization of this process, the scene in which Mrs. Sparsit spies on Louisa and Harthouse, Dickens exposes both the futility of such devices and their ability to generate unintended effects. In this scene, Dickens narrates Mrs. Sparsit's witnessing in such a way as to place the reader in Mrs. Sparsit's position. As Mrs. Sparsit gets drawn into the action she observes, the narrative reproduces for the reader the fantasy that witnessing unleashes.

> Mrs Sparsit saw him detain her with his encircling arm, and heard him then and there, within *her (Mrs Sparsit's)* greedy hearing, tell her how he loved her, and how she was the stake for which he ardently desired to play away all that he had in life. The objects he had lately pursued, turned worthless beside her; such success as was almost in his grasp, he flung away from him like the dirt it was, compared with her. Its pursuit, nevertheless, if it kept him near her, or its renunciation if it took him from her, or flight if she shared it, or secrecy if she commanded it, or any fate, or every fate, all was alike to him, so that she was true to him—the man who had seen how cast away she was, whom she had inspired at their first meeting with an admiration, an interest, of which he had thought himself incapable, whom she had received into her confidence, who was devoted to her and adored her. All this, and more, in his hurry, and in hers, in the whirl of *her own gratified malice,* in the dread of being discovered, in the rapidly increasing noise of heavy rain among the leaves, and a thunder-storm rolling up—Mrs Sparsit received into her mind, set off with such an unavoidable halo of confusion and indistinctness, that when at length he climbed the fence and led his horse away, she was not sure where they were to meet, or when, except that they had said it was to be that night. (*HT,* 212; emphasis added)

In this passage, Dickens explicitly distinguishes the referent of the second *her* (Mrs. Sparsit) from that of the first (Louisa), but he does not mark the point at which the series of pronominal references to Louisa gives way again. As a result, Mrs. Sparsit becomes the *her* in question, and the reader experiences firsthand the rivalry with Louisa that fuels Mrs. Sparsit's obsessive attention. Indeed, Dickens's use of free indirect discourse encourages the reader to feel Mrs. Sparsit's anxiety as an energy so distorting that it undermines her stated reason for eavesdropping—to discover where and when the lovers will meet.

If this passage is a critique of the unpredictable affect abstractions can provoke, then it also shows how Dickens could use the ambiguity abstraction generates to rivet the reader's attention. This is a benefit novelists could reap from the structure of anxiety that was unavailable to political economists, for whereas doubts about the mimetic nature of abstractions led to questions about the validity of political economy, this and other uncertainties helped make reading novels a pleasurable experience. In *Hard Times*, Dickens's most creative use of such ambiguity occurs in his representation of Louisa. By repeatedly blocking the reader's access to Louisa's feelings, Dickens keeps us guessing about whether she will fall to Harthouse. Obscuring Louisa's motives while insisting on the danger her immorality would represent keeps the reader in the position Mrs. Sparsit occupies in the passage just quoted. Thus the anxiety generated in that passage by free indirect discourse is maintained elsewhere by Dickens's refusal to tell us what Louisa feels. In the triangle that is set up by this refusal, the reader is the endangered subject who cannot judge the magnitude of the threat Louisa seems to pose.

Typically, Dickens manipulates the reader's relation to Louisa simply by limiting our point of view to that of the characters who try, but fail, to "penetrate" her. "There were times when Mr James Harthouse was not sure of her," the narrator tells us. "There were times when he could not read the face he had studied so long; and when this lonely girl was a greater mystery to him, than any woman of the world with a ring of satellites to help her" (*HT*, 206–7). Similarly, what the narrator describes as Louisa's "curious reserve" "baffles[s], while it stimulate[s]" Mrs. Sparsit (*HT*, 206). The imaginary stairway Mrs. Sparsit conjures to monitor Louisa's moral descent is the result of this stimulation; as the narrator tells us, Louisa's "impenetrable demeanour, which keenly whetted and sharpened Mrs Sparsit's edge, must have given her as it were a lift, in the way of inspiration" (*HT*, 202).

In several passages, the "inspiration" provoked by Louisa's "closed heart" infects the narrative voice as well (*HT*, 197). In these passages, when the narrator begins to speculate about what Louisa must feel, we can see more clearly what was at stake in Dickens's attempt to use—as well as control—the triangular structure of anxiety. When Louisa approaches her parents' home for the first time after her marriage, for example, the narrator waxes eloquent about what Louisa does *not* remember. In this passage, the volubility of the narrative voice seems directly proportional to Louisa's silence, as if what Dickens describes as her "heavy, hardened kind of sorrow" provokes compensatory elaboration, the expression of sentiments that are specifically not hers but the narrator's.

Neither, as she approached her old home now, did any of the best influences of old home descend upon her. The dreams of childhood—its airy fables; its graceful, beautiful, humane, impossible adornments of the world beyond: so good to be believed in once, so good to be remembered when outgrown, for then the least among them rises to the stature of a great Charity in the heart, suffering little children to come into the midst of it, and to keep with their pure hands a garden in the stony ways of this world, wherein it were better for all the children of Adam that they should oftener sun themselves, simple and trustful, and not worldly-wise—what had she to do with these? Remembrances of how she had journeyed to the little that she knew, by the enchanted roads of what she and millions of innocent creatures had hoped and imagined; of how, first coming upon Reason through the tender light of Fancy, she had seen a beneficent god, deferring to gods as great as itself: not a grim Idol, cruel and cold, with its victims bound hand to foot, and its big dumb shape set up with a sightless stare, never to be moved by anything but so many calculated tons of leverage—what had she to do with these? Her remembrances of home and childhood, were remembrances of the drying up of every spring and fountain in her young heart as it gushed out. The golden waters were not there. (*HT,* 198)

The movement of this passage—from its initial "airy fables" to the sadistic image of the Idol—reveals the problem introduced by attempts to use the ambiguity associated with abstraction, even for novelists who dealt self-consciously with fictions. The progression from those "dreams of childhood" that Louisa does not have to the sadistic Idol belongs to the narrative voice, and the narrator's tendency to devolve to darker thoughts when his fantasies are allowed free rein suggests that the salaciousness that spews from Mrs. Sparsit is but one propensity of an unleashed imagination. It also suggests that such excesses are not limited to jealous old women. The occlusion of Louisa's feelings, in other words, which creates speculative activity in the other characters, the reader, and the narrator as well, also threatens the optimistic picture of childhood the narrator claims to want to present, for blocking Louisa's feelings invites the narrator, who ought to be the reader's protective ego, to divulge a range of associations, not all of which are as sunny as the "fable" of a "graceful...world beyond."

Hard Times can be read as a contest between Dickens's cultivation of the positive effects such narrative obscurity generates and his attempts to halt the flow of contaminating associations epitomized by the sadistic image of the Idol. On the one hand, for the sake of narrative engagement, Dickens seeks to exploit anxiety's ability to sustain the reader's attention. On the other hand, however, exploiting the anxiety that uncertainty arouses poses a threat to the moral lesson Dickens wants to convey. As long as Dickens leaves the reader in Mrs. Sparsit's position, he can sustain the titillating sense of danger that keeps the reader reading; but he also risks losing control of the reader's own imagination, which is aroused by Sparsit's provocative example and by the narrator's uncensored associations.

The only way Dickens can ward off the moral decline that responses to Louisa seem to invite is to remove the block that has thus far obscured Louisa's feelings. In terms of my diagram, this entails substituting an explanatory abstraction for the refusal that has thus far obscured Louisa. In the passage where this substitution occurs, Dickens offers for the first time an explicit explanation for why Louisa responds to Harthouse as she does.

> It was even the worse for her at this pass, that in her mind—implanted there before her eminently practical father began to form it—a struggling disposition to believe in a wider and nobler humanity than she had ever heard of, constantly strove with doubts and resentments. With doubts, because the aspiration had been so laid waste in her youth. With resentments, because of the wrong that had been done her, if it were indeed a whisper of the truth. Upon a nature long accustomed to self-suppression, thus torn and divided, the Harthouse philosophy came as a relief and justification. Everything being hollow and worthless, she had missed nothing and sacrificed nothing. What did it matter, she had said to her father, when he proposed her husband. What did it matter, she said still. With a scornful self-reliance, she asked herself, What did anything matter—and went on. (*HT,* 168–69)

In this passage, Dickens explains Louisa's action by means of a formulaic account: Louisa feels hollow and worthless because her father has induced a dynamic of self-cancellation, in which her resentments and doubts erase the truths and beliefs with which she was presumably born. This explanation seems to justify the narrative technique by which the character has thus far been presented: she is represented as impenetrable because there is nothing inside her to see. Yet even as it explains Louisa and her narrative presentation, Dickens's use of this abstract account also halts the novel's plot, for it converts Louisa from an enigma that solicits (re)action into the formula that obliterates the puzzle. At this moment, Dickens abandons the generative capacity of the barrier Freud associated with anxiety and embraces its defensive function instead. It is as if Dickens suddenly reverts from the novelist's cultivation of ambiguity to the political economist's proclivity for summary abstraction. Even though the explanation Dickens offers departs radically from abstractions like "the market," his use of an explanatory formula serves the same function as political economic abstractions: with Freud's model in mind, we can see that all of these abstractions seek to contain anxiety by protecting the endangered subject from some danger that one cannot see.

Given the nature of the temptation Louisa has faced, the salaciousness of Mrs. Sparsit's "greedy" eavesdropping, and the sexual connotations of the sadistic Idol, modern readers assume that the danger Louisa simultaneously masks and incarnates has something to do with what was still for Freud the "dark continent" of female sexuality. In *Hard Times,* as in so many nineteenth-century works, female sexuality both attracts and repulses; it provides the occasion for male writers' bravura performances, but it also forecloses explicit naming and often causes the same kind of formal discomfort that we see in McCulloch's repetitions and assertions. By the same token, Dickens's turn to an abstract explanation to expose Louisa's otherwise impenetrable interior resembles McCulloch's use of abstractions to manage fears about the copulating poor. Dickens tries to master the associations Louisa provokes by an abstract formula that shifts the power back to the knowledgeable narrator, just as McCulloch tries to shift authority to assertions when his claim to be a scientist falters. Whereas the authority of political economy was jeopardized by the uncertain relation between actual particulars and social-scientific abstractions, however, the authority of the novel was threatened by this genre's ability to provoke in readers the kind of immoral associations Dickens dramatizes in Mrs. Sparsit and the narrator. If we entertain for a moment the notion that political economists and novelists both sought to produce useful knowledge about something no one could see, we can see how criticisms about the two modes of knowledge production provoked different but parallel attempts to defend the use of abstractions in the production of what could count as truth.

Nineteenth-century political economists wanted to illuminate the human propensity to "truck, barter, and exchange," the economic laws of accumulation and waste, and the appearance of regularities in social phenomena like population increase and suicide. Nineteenth-century novelists wanted to illuminate human propensities too, but instead of constructing abstractions with which to generalize laws and regularities, novelists deployed fictional characters whose behaviors could mimic or comment upon the behaviors of observable people. Whereas political economists provoked the charge that the abstractions they generated misrepresented actual human beings or reduced them to automatons, novelists too often heard that their attempts to fictionalize real life were insufficiently moral—that novels elicited imaginative indulgences their moralizing could not contain. During the second half of the nineteenth century, political economists gradually countered the charge levied against them by adopting professional standards that helped naturalize methodological conventions, including conventions that linked abstractions to observable phenomena through mathematical models.

By the end of the century, British novelists had begun to defend their mode of knowledge production too. Even though they were never able to agree on terms for professionalization or on a single methodology, novelists who considered themselves serious and who cared about the social authority of the genre did try to establish standards for their work. These standards, while always informal, were intended both to distinguish good novels from bad and to specify the relationship between the stories novelists made up and the truths they tried to convey. Whether by chastising "lady novelists" for overtly moralizing in "silly novels," as George Eliot did, or by theorizing the relationship between a novel's organic unity and the moral world, as Henry James did, nineteenth-century novelists and critics gradually established principles that would enable readers to recognize some novels as good and, more importantly, to understand that the fictions they read were moral even when they did not seem to be so.[10]

Dickens's willingness to capitalize upon but then curtail anxiety's capacity to engage belongs to this nineteenth-century process of disciplinary—or, more properly, generic—self-regulation. Like McCulloch's retreat from the claim that political economy was like the natural sciences, Dickens's retreat from the imaginative allure of anxiety sought to anticipate the criticism that the knowledge his writing produced was suspect: in the case of political economy, knowledge seemed suspect because it substituted deterministic abstractions for people who had free will; in the case of novels, knowledge seemed suspect because the imaginative engagement this form of writing elicited was somehow morally volatile. Even though they openly scorned each other's methods and conclusions, J. R. McCulloch and Charles Dickens both struggled with the structure of anxiety because each writer wanted to produce useful knowledge about something no one could see. Just as the two writers can be said to have engaged in a variant of the same epistemological campaign, moreover, they also resemble each other in having failed to allay the anxiety they sought to manage, as reading their texts though Freud's paradigm reveals.

III

The epistemological and ethical similarities between political economy and novels like *Hard Times* remained invisible for much of the nineteenth century, of course. Indeed, the bitter caricatures by which political economists and novelists lampooned each other suggest that practitioners of each kind of writing defined their mode of knowledge production partly by its difference from the other. Not until Freud began to theorize anxiety did the similarities between political economy and nineteenth-century novels begin to become apparent. Even in the 1920s, however, Freud did not draw an explicit connection between psychoanalysis and political economy, nor did he connect what Dickens exploited as the productive capacity of anxiety to a model of identity that potentially imperiled the positivist epistemology upon which all social scientists—including Freud—sought to anchor their professions' authority. In order to elaborate the epistemological implications that Freud did not explore—and that ground the method I have been using in this essay—I move now to discuss more explicitly both my own method and the

---

[10] George Eliot (Mary Ann Evans), "Silly Novels by Lady Novelists" (1856), reprinted in *Victorian Criticism of the Novel*, ed. Edwin M. Eigner and George J. Worth (Cambridge: Cambridge University Press, 1985), 159–80; and Henry James, "The Art of Fiction" (1884), in *Victorian Criticism*, 193–212. James actually deflected the argument about morals by insisting that novels did not have to be morally constructive as long as they were aesthetically pleasing.

assumptions about identity implied by what I have called the structure of anxiety.

In order to link Freud's discussion of anxiety to political economy and *Hard Times,* I have used two narratives, a pair of abstractions, and a diagram that maps a structural relation between three positions that are also abstract, in the sense that they can be occupied by various figures. The abstractions I have used—the "copulating poor" and "female sexuality"—do not appear in the primary texts I discuss in the essay, just as "the structure of anxiety" never appears as a phrase in Freud's writing. The two narratives I have invoked are also analytic constructs: the story of the professionalization of the social sciences, which I use to explain how twentieth-century social scientists "solved" the problem of abstraction, is only available now because sociologists have provided an account that naturalizes "professionalization" as a series of collective accomplishments recognized institutionally and socially. By the same token, I can elaborate Freud's work as I do only because of interpretations by twentieth-century theorists like Jacques Lacan and Shoshana Felman that emphasize the turns by which Freud qualified distinctions he initially presented as absolute.[11] If the primary terms of my analysis do not appear in the materials I discuss, my diagram is not included in Freud's essay, and my explanatory narratives are twentieth-century constructs, then can I really claim that this essay is "about" nineteenth-century political economy, *Hard Times,* or even Freud's theories? In what sense, if at all, can I say that "the structure of anxiety" existed in the nineteenth-century texts in which I claim to find it? To phrase these questions another way, which highlights their stakes for the authority of literary critical interpretations like this one: how can I claim that this "structure," which I derive from my interpretation of other interpretations of an interpretation that was never "about" political economy or *Hard Times* at all, is not simply a projection, which I have imposed upon the past texts from which I purport to derive it?

In order to answer these questions, I need to offer a more elaborate version of the ontological model I introduced at the beginning of this essay. If one takes seriously—as I do—the implications of Freud's discussion of anxiety, then identity is not a self-evident property of a text or event but the product of an interplay between something that is retrospectively designated the "original" text or event and the recipient who makes this designation, in

[11] Among the contemporary theoretical essays that have influenced my thinking for this article, two by Shoshana Felman have been particularly important. See "Beyond Oedipus: The Specimen Subject of Psychoanalysis," in *Lacan and Narration: The Psychoanalytic Difference in Narrative Theory,* ed. Robert Con Davis (Baltimore: Johns Hopkins University Press, 1983), 1021–53; and "Education and Crisis, or the Vicissitudes of Teaching," in *Testimony: Crisis of Witnessing in Literature, Psychoanalysis, and History,* ed. Shoshana Felman and Dori Laub (New York: Routledge, 1992), 1–56.

her effort to make the text or event meaningful now. In Freud's account, a past event is designated the "source of danger" only retrospectively, because of the anxiety it generates in the present; by the same token, I designate a certain pattern, which I see "in" McCulloch's text and *Hard Times,* "the structure of anxiety" because this pattern can, with hindsight, be said to resemble a pattern I see in Freud's essay on anxiety. Of course, just as Freud used theoretical assumptions about trauma to guide his delineation of anxiety, so I use theoretical assumptions about how to read Freud's essay to construct the model that allows me to see this pattern in all of these texts. According to this model, the identity of "the source of danger" or even of the "texts" by Freud, Dickens, and McCulloch is not equivalent to the event or book itself but is the product of a dynamic interaction, which, theoretically, has as many manifestations as a book has readers.

Let me be clear about a couple of points. First, this ontological model implies that "identity" is partly a function of the meanings and significance assigned to a text or event by its reception—by readers or by people seeking to remember or make sense of an event. Reception, in turn, is not simply the additive compilation of individual readers' or interpreters' responses but a social force, composed on the one hand of the social and historical conditions that make reading and experience possible, and, on the other hand by the material effects of collective reading practices and interpretations of experience. We can see the implications of this model if we take the case of a single text—say, *Hard Times.* When it was initially published, in parts and then as a bound volume, *Hard Times* was read by readers whose responses helped constitute the novel's meaning(s), the text's significance, Dickens's reputation, and the reputation of the novel as a genre. This consolidation, in turn, encouraged publishers to reprint *Hard Times;* it encouraged readers to read novels like (and including) *Hard Times;* and the reprinting, reading, and ratification of the reputation of novels like *Hard Times* helped establish the conditions that enabled journalists (who were often novelists too) to discriminate between kinds of reading practices—to establish, in other words, the rudimentary terms for what I now practice professionally in relation to *Hard Times:* literary critical analysis. This is the process to which I alluded at the end of the previous section. Given the fact that professional literary critics like myself can now only read novels like *Hard Times* for determinate institutional occasions (writing an article for a volume of academic essays), and through both the assumptions about genre that help mark such occasions as professional and the theoretical paradigms that now govern professional literary reading, then what I know of *Hard Times—what I know* as Hard Times—is only available through the categories and social/material conditions that enable me to understand now.

My second point is that the claim I have just made about the meaning and significance of a text or event also holds true for the text or event "itself."

That is, just as we can only discuss "political economy" through a theoretical paradigm that retrospectively assimilates certain readings of certain historical texts to an abstraction (which is often abstracted even more, into a "discourse"), so I can only discuss *Hard Times* through a theoretical paradigm that silently effaces the difference between the serial and bound versions of the novel and that equates all of the editions and copies of this novel to a single entity, *Hard Times*. The work of this theoretical paradigm, which establishes boundaries around a text the way a name delineates the beginning and end of an event ("the French Revolution"), is even clearer in the case of Freud's essay: in this instance, the theoretical paradigm enables me to efface whatever difference translation introduces and to marginalize the consequences of this essay's supplemental nature—its claim to comment on and elaborate another essay, which was, in turn, an elaboration of theories Freud had introduced in much earlier writing.

If one accepts the ontological model implicit in (a certain interpretation of) Freud's late writing, then it makes no sense to ask whether we can know the past on its own terms or whether my interpretation is only a projection. We cannot know the past on its own terms because the terms that make sense to us now—the terms that enable us to make the past sensible as a meaningful collection of texts and events—are derived from interpretive paradigms that make sense to us now. Modern interpretations of past events or texts can never be "merely" projections because what we know as a text or event is partly an effect of the interpretive paradigms that allow us to know these texts and events as "past" but also as related—or meaningful—to us.

My third point concerns the limitations of the license this model grants modern readers. To say that what counts as a text or event is partly a function of the theoretical categories through which we now make the text or event meaningful is not necessarily to embrace relativism or to sanction every interpretation every reader offers. Just as the categories and conditions that delimit how I read set limits to what I can know of and as the past, so I believe that past texts and practices ought to set limits to what I can say about the past. I must emphasize that this is a belief I hold; the choice between trying to discipline my interpretation by (what my theoretical paradigms allow me to construe as) the texts I read or treating these texts as an occasion for creative self-expression is an *ethical* choice, not an expression of different assumptions about ontology.[12] Both my (relative) respect for the pastness of the past and the indifference to that otherness that I associate with creative criticism endorse the antimetaphysical ontology I have described here. The difference between these stances can only be described as ethical because it

---

[12] For a discussion of what I call "creative criticism," see Mary Poovey, "Creative Criticism: Adaptation, Performative Writing, and the Problem of Objectivity," *Narrative* 8, no. 2 (2000): 109–33.

concerns behavior—beliefs about the comportment, if you will, that should govern one's professional relationship to the past.

The theoretical stance I have taken in this essay constitutes something like a moderate (or compromised) objectivism. I interpret these texts in the light of an assumption that the meanings I ascribe to past texts are partly a function of the theoretical paradigms that postdate them and partly a function of the language of these nineteenth-century texts. In so doing, I am not alone. Many of my peers share my ethical commitment to respecting the otherness of the past; all of us see that past through some theoretical paradigm that makes sense now. No wonder we, as a professional group, chronically feel anxious about the status of the knowledge we claim to produce. This anxiety articulates the ambivalence generated in and by the structure of belatedness that Freud associated with anxiety: our theoretical paradigms enable us to make sense of the past and thus to neutralize the threat of its otherness; but as we make the past meaningful, we inevitably obscure, and thereby disrespect, the past that constitutes one condition of our attempts to know. Of course, as Freud's essay also allows us to realize, the anxiety that signals our vexed relation to a past we partly construct also provokes us to write. It is this agitated writing that promises that the future will never simply recapitulate the past we cannot contemplate.

8. How to Be a Benefactor without Any Money

The Chill of Welfare in Great Expectations

BRUCE ROBBINS

A 1997 article in the *New York Times* contrasted Sophocles' *Oedipus the King,* where the hero puts his eyes out after learning he is married to his mother, with John Sayles's movie *Lone Star,* whose reunited lovers, "after learning that they have the same father, continue their affair." Adding the evidence of "a dozen movies, television dramas and memoirs," the article concluded that "incest, one of humanity's last taboos, is taboo no longer. Incest is the plat du jour in the 90's marketplace." Needless to say, this was newsworthy. Film scholar Tom Gunning was quoted as follows: "Incest is in the foundations of Western drama. But to discover a familial relationship and go, 'So what?' That's relatively new."[1]

Up to this moment, the Western narrative tradition has found no more effective answer to the "So what?" question—for narrative, the make-or-break question—than the discovery of familial relationship. Again and again disclosure of hidden kinship has been coupled with narrative closure, hence with narrative itself. The decisiveness of this coupling is assumed to be self-evident in Aristotle's offhand remarks about tokens and recognition scenes, and it is still going strong in the greatest nineteenth-century novels, like *Jane Eyre* and *Bleak House.* If the blood/plot connection has now been broken, therefore, this break would seem to offer compelling evidence in the case for radical epistemological discontinuity, the pervasive discouragement about the possibility and/or desirability of knowing others, that has pressed heavily if often

---

[1] Karen De Witt, "Incest as a Selling Point," *New York Times,* Sunday, 30 March 1997, "Week in Review," 6.

obscurely upon recent literary scholarship. When the revelation of incestuous relationship is no longer capable of bestowing resolution on a narrative, the rules of interpretation would seem to have changed, and changed absolutely. Reading across an apparently unbridgeable gulf of incomprehension and indifference, we would seem obliged to echo Matthew Arnold's judgment that in *Antigone,* "the conflict between the heroine's duty to her brother's corpse and that to the laws of her country, is no longer one in which it is possible that we should feel a deep interest."[2] Like Arnold, or like early Christians reading the Old Testament, or like later Christians reading both Old and New Testaments, we would seem unable to insist on literal historical connections between these narratives and our own situation. We would seem forced into salvaging them only as true allegories of the state of our own mind.

One reason for not jumping to this conclusion is already peeking out of my analogies. If we have been there before, then we are not there yet. If the perceived loss of direct historical continuity with past texts and its replacement by an indirect allegorical bond have both been more or less permanent facts of textual interpretation, as well known to Arnold and to early Christian hermeneutics as to postmodern academic criticism, then it makes no sense to celebrate the present for its unique acknowledgment of historical discontinuity. Nor does it make sense on the contrary to accuse the present of a uniquely patronizing presentism. Rather than taking sides for or against discontinuity, it would seem more useful to inquire into when and why readers have felt suddenly or singularly distanced from the past, addressed by it only in an alien tongue, forced to impose their concerns on it. What needs exploring, in other words, is those particular histories in which the present is or is not ready to recognize its own concerns—an inquiry that is only coherent if it is assumed that the *refusal* of such recognition may be just as reasonable and desirable in any given instance.

Discontinuity has been the dominant emphasis in recent Victorian studies in large part because of the influence of Michel Foucault. But this influence, I would argue, has less to do with ultimate philosophical positions (hence Foucault's puzzlement at being considered a *champion* of discontinuity) than with a politically motivated twentieth-century estrangement from nineteenth-century narratives of scientific rationality, human liberation, the extension of democracy, and the reform of government.[3] Foucault saw the present as unfortunately all too continuous with the nineteenth century; his choice of

[2] Matthew Arnold, "Preface to *Poems* (1853)," in *Poetry and Prose of Matthew Arnold,* ed. A. Dwight Culler (Boston: Houghton Mifflin, 1961), 212.

[3] Michel Foucault, "Truth and Power," interview with Alessandro Fontana and Pasquale Pasquino, in *Power/Knowledge: Selected Interviews and Other Writings 1972–1977,* ed. Colin Gordon, trans. Colin Gordon et al. (New York: Pantheon, 1980). Being told that he "founds his theory of history on discontinuity," Foucault says, "leaves me flabbergasted" (111).

Nietzsche over Hegel was an imperative to break with a legacy of panoptical surveillance, multiplying bureaucratic apparatuses, the illusion of progressive reform. It is of course a defensible choice. Indeed, it is anticipated by, among others, Matthew Arnold, a hidden antiprogressive continuity that helps explain the relatively smooth transition from an Arnoldian to a Foucaultian regime in Victorian studies and that might also raise some suspicions about the new dispensation. If I am more inclined here to take Hegel's side, it is not on philosophical grounds, but because still more recent history, especially in the United States, has revealed unsuspected virtues in the object Foucault taught us to look at so critically: Victorian reformist governmentality. Hegel, who shared Arnold's sympathy for Creon and statism, embraced *Antigone* nonetheless, and he did so in part because he saw the collision between the demands of the state and those of an older family-based ethics as an extremely long-term event, an event that has not yet exhausted its historical energies and that entailed a new synthesis of these apparently opposed terms.[4] Paradoxically, he is more interested in *Antigone* than Arnold is because he is more positively invested in the prospects for his own present.[5] A similar investment will also be my excuse for trying to read the nineteenth-century novel, the domain of ethics and the family, from the perspective of that project of social engineering—then emergent, at present endangered and still very incomplete—called the social welfare state.

Giving collective social substance to the spiritual education or *Bildungsbiographie* he had offered in the *Phenomenology,* Hegel in the *Philosophy of Right* tells the story of the rise of civil society and the modern state.[6] A social solution to epistemological dilemmas (this is Hegel's circuitous answer to Kant), his state-centered upward mobility story also provides a context, I argue, for the cool indifference to incest in *Lone Star.* In Hegel's narrative, the decreasing ability of the biological family to represent society in general is explained not by a weakening of primal taboos so much as by a strengthening or invention of social bonds other than those of the family. For the novel, this will mean a displacement of interest away from the metaphorics of familial reproduction and toward social units and linkages that can be expressed only with difficulty in the conventions of marriage and other reproductive rites. This shift is visible in the strange preeminence of a category of characters who stand on the margins of the family and are defined largely by their narrative function. Benefactors, mediators, donors,

[4] Gerhard Joseph, "The *Antigone* as Cultural Touchstone: Matthew Arnold, Hegel, George Eliot, Virginia Woolf, and Margaret Drabble," *PMLA* 96, no. 1 (1981): 22–35.

[5] As David Lloyd and Paul Thomas point out in *Culture and the State* (New York: Routledge, 1998), Arnold, like Hobbes, "views civil society as the site of the war of each against all" (117), hence is driven to find a compensatory principle in an authoritarian notion of the state. It is Hegel's more positive view of civil society, the development of which is crucial to rather than opposed to that of the state, that allows him such a different view of *Antigone.*

[6] The phrase is from M. H. Abrams's brilliant reading of the *Phenomenology* in *Natural Supernaturalism* (New York: W. W. Norton, 1971), 229.

patrons, responsible for managing and conveying the meaning of upward mobility, they occupy the true extrafamilial center of a narrative that aims beyond the reproduction of the status quo. Yet they are also charged with giving emotional flesh and blood to this coldly unprecedented, frighteningly empty social terrain. In *Great Expectations*, the classic narrative of chastened, self-critical upward mobility, they are of course Abel Magwitch and Miss Havisham, the Male Criminal and the Older Woman. In pushing the novel beyond the thematics of domesticity, I suggest, these benefactors point the upward mobility story toward a more capacious if still historically limited social vision.

This argument proceeds, in other words, by offering the social welfare state as literal and pertinent common ground between the nineteenth century and the present day. The positing of common ground as a solution to alterity has been tried before, and there are reasons for treating this move with skepticism. Let me therefore preface what follows with a story about where the skepticism itself comes from.

Alterity in the strong or absolute sense is of course a social construction. But it is a social construction that denies its constructedness. As Judith Butler showed in *Subjects of Desire*, her book on twentieth-century French rereadings of Hegel, the dialectic of Lord and Bondsman from Book 4 of the *Phenomenology* is the source for most if not all significant twentieth-century discussions of Self and Other.[7] Hegel's narrative of a heretofore undefined being coming to self-consciousness by way of a life-and-death struggle with another, the two thus becoming Herr and Knecht, Lord and Bondsman, does not stop, of course, when Self and Other have taken shape. It points famously at a reversal, and later still at an eventual endpoint (though one that is never achieved in the *Phenomenology*) of equality and intersubjectivity. Both this endpoint and the originally unshaped, common human substance that it in a sense recapitulates are abandoned in the most influential subsequent readings, even those that preserve the moment of the Lord's overthrow by the Bondsman. When Nietzsche retells Hegel's story in his *Genealogy of Morals*, for example, the identities of Lord and Bondsman are given at the outset. Some are lambs, and some are birds of prey; some are strong, and some are weak. As a result, the projected endpoint of Nietzsche's story is also a reconfirmation of this initial and absolute alterity. In Nietzsche's version of the Hegelian reversal, the successful slave rebellion against the natural aristocrats, otherwise known as Christianity, has produced a morass of indistinction and sick self-consciousness. Nietzsche's solution is of course notoriously difficult and controversial, but one of its most compelling imperatives is the return to a nature of integral, previously given, incommensurable identities: respect for absolute alterity.

[7] Judith Butler, *Subjects of Desire: Hegelian Reflections in Twentieth-Century France* (New York: Columbia University Press, 1999).

This could be described as a truncation of the Hegelian dialectic, for it allows Hegel's narrative both to set out and to stall at the middle stage, trapped forever in an alterity that for Hegel was only provisional. This truncated dialectic defines not only what Foucault took from Nietzsche, but what Sartre took from Kojève's lectures on Hegel: the unidirectional "look" that defines power and that cannot be returned. It also defines what Sartre passed to Fanon and what passed via Fanon into the "otherness" theme of postcolonial studies. Distrust of the appropriative imperial Self and affirmation of the Other's desire to stand resolutely apart from it thus became a part of the new common sense, even though both were complicated in Fanon as well as in Lacan (another member of the audience for Kojève's Hegel lectures) by a residual Hegelian commitment to the hypothesis of ultimate commonality and reciprocity.

Perhaps surprisingly, absolute otherness is less consistent with contemporary common sense than the Hegelian narrative it so dramatically departs from. For it depends on just that essentialism that Hegel himself is at such pains to avoid: the positing of initial identities for the Lord and the Bondsman. Anti-essentialism aligns us with Hegel here—aligns us, that is, against the notion that others are radically unknowable or should be treated as if they were, protected from the invasive, mastering incorporation that is the aim of the will to power/knowledge. The same logic would also suggest that the epistemological and ethical problem of alterity is much the same at different scales and across discursive genres. Concern for standards or protocols of knowledge about works of literary imagination, seen as endangered by the aggressiveness of readings less grounded in a perhaps unknowable past than in the pressing interests of the present, might look to a philosopher like a special case of hermeneutic controversy about history. Both the problem of knowledge across distance in time and the problem of knowledge across distance in space—First World knowledge of Third World peoples, for example—might look like special cases of a still more general problem of epistemology. The more general the problem gets, however, the less one has to worry about it. If "Je est un autre," as Rimbaud so wonderfully put it, then solipsism is no longer an issue; the problem of knowing the Other is not solved, but neither is it absolutely or qualitatively different from the problem of knowing anything, including oneself. When we acquiesce in the notion that there exists a crisis of cross-cultural, cross-historical understanding, we tacitly accept that, up to the moment when it tries to cross the gulf around it, the self exists, and exists in a state of relatively competent or unproblematic self-knowledge. Take away that implied contrast, and the crisis of the "cross" remains, but only as a much diminished thing—hardly an adequate reason for forsaking the project of acquiring knowledge.

This is again a matter of common sense. Consider what follows if the self in question is, to pick two pertinent units, a period or a nation. Either of these entities can immediately be broken down further, of course—we all know the drill—into still smaller entities, each of them justly protesting that it is being homogenized and silenced by the false universalism of the larger unit. And so on, in an unstoppable anti-essentialist regress. The project of finding a common voice one can legitimately assign to any given period or nation is no less impossible, theoretically speaking, than the project of finding common ground *between* different periods or different nations. And no less impossible to avoid, if any intellectual work is to be done.

❧

In discussing Propp's *Morphology of the Folktale,* Fredric Jameson singles out "the donor," a figure "who after testing [the hero] for the appropriate reaction (for some courtesy, for instance) supplies him with a magical agent...which enables him to pass victoriously through his ordeal."[8] Jameson argues that "wish-fulfillment" (66) is not sufficient to explain what makes a string of episodes into a story. Nor is the defeat of the villain. Using Arthur Danto's definition of historical narrative as any " 'causal' explanation of how a given state of affairs A turned into a given state of affairs B" (66–67), Jameson argues that the real "explanation of the change" is located in the donor. "The donor is...the element which explains the change described in the story, that which supplies a sufficiently asymmetrical force to make it interesting to tell, and which is therefore somehow responsible for the 'storiness' of the story in the first place" (67).

Jameson gives this suggestive insight some historical grounding by relating it to René Girard's hypothesis, in *Deceit, Desire, and the Novel,* "that in modern society desires are not natural but learned" and that "the story the novel tells is the learning of desire from some mediator or third party."[9] The history Girard offers, roughly since the French Revolution, involves a transition from external to internal mediation—that is, from desire mediated by models who cannot also be rivals, like idolatry of the king by divine right, to desire in which the mediator is also a rival, as in Stendhal. Mediation that is also rivalry comes with increasing equality; for him, as for Nietzsche, it is a disease of democracy. Girard describes the mediated or triangular desire that accompanies democratic indistinction in the resonant phrase "cerebral love" (78). Two of his examples of cerebral love involve younger, upwardly mobile men and mediator/donors who are older, more powerful women: Gina in Stendhal's *The Charterhouse of Parma* and Mme. de Warens, the woman Rousseau called "Maman," in the *Confessions.*

[8] Fredric Jameson, *The Prison-House of Language: A Critical Account of Structuralism and Russian Formalism* (Princeton, N.J.: Princeton University Press, 1972), 65.

[9] René Girard, *Deceit, Desire, and the Novel,* trans. Yvonne Freccero (Baltimore: Johns Hopkins University Press, 1965), 68 n. 21.

Democracy, the endpoint of the story in which these donor or mediator figures intervene, also helps explain the characteristic lowering of the emotional temperature that marks "cerebral love." This relationship between Rousseau and Mme. de Warens in the *Confessions* (written in the 1760s and 1770s) is by no means the prototype for the many pairs of younger men and older women that go on to populate the nineteenth-century novel. But it does throw light on certain absences of heat, patterned zones of coolness or relative indifference that seem to attend the theme of upward mobility. Rousseau is bewildered by the somewhat dispassionate style in which Mme. de Warens proposes that they become lovers, as well as by his own sudden lack of eagerness for that which he has long desired.[10] Reflecting back, he denies that her speeches to him were "froids et tristes" (231), but he calls her "peu sensuelle" (235) and ascribes to her, despite a warm sensibility, a "tempérament de glace" (237). This is love, but love of a distinctly chilly sort. Rousseau's own coolness might result, he thinks, from the fact that she is already "possédé par un autre homme" (233)—the chill of the power of other men, of which she cannot help but serve as the mediator. Or perhaps it is simply because she is never erotically "interested" in him at all, inspired rather by motives that are generously pedagogical (she is more concerned, he says, with instructing than with seducing him) and altruistic: "elle n'a connu qu'un seul vrai plaisir au monde; c'était d'en faire à ceux qu'elle aimait" (237).

The coldness seems to fit the somewhat impersonal motives. In literary tradition love outside marriage has often been associated with passion that was more rather than less fervent, for such passion did not have to pass the test of everyday social durability. Here too love stands outside the cycle of biological reproduction—indeed, incompatibility with reproduction is one important connotation of the age disparity. But this love is cooler rather than warmer, I would suggest, precisely because it *does* aspire toward compromise with a reproducible reality. In aiming elsewhere than marriage and progeny, "cerebral love" aims at something other than perpetuating the existing social order—hence its appropriateness to a story of social mobility. But it does seem to aim at *some* social order—hence the pedagogical and altruistic motives that are so visibly if ambiguously mixed into erotic self-interest. For the moment, a social order that would be more rational and more democratic than the cozy, customary, patriarchal bonds of the family remains nameless.

Consider now the centrality of the donor/mediator and the affective frigidity that accompanies it in another narrative of upward mobility, the 1991 film *Silence of the Lambs.* Many of the film's first viewers were shocked at how completely the erotic seemed to be banished from its plot. The Jody Foster character, Clarice Starling, is not romantically involved with anybody. Instead, she has intense and slightly ambiguous relations with two older men,

---

[10] Jean-Jacques Rousseau, *Les Confessions I,* ed. Michel Launay (Paris: Flammarion, 1968), bk. 5.

each of whom has power over her career: her boss at the FBI, and above all the serial killer Hannibal Lecter. To cut a long story short, you might say that instead of a master, as the upwardly mobile protagonist of *Jane Eyre* has, she has a mentor. The main difference between a master and a mentor is that the master presides over a domestic unit, which is to say over the family and biological reproduction, while the mentor does not. The mentor's power concerns the reproduction of social units other than the family, units that are *not* domestic—institutions, disciplines, teams, professions, corporations. Their reproduction, too, involves the eliciting and channeling of erotic energy, albeit not in the direct and literal way demanded by families and pro-creation; hence there is always some ambiguity as to whether the suggestive but subdued relationship of mentorship is finally erotic or not. But to set the mentor against the master is to suggest a different endpoint for the upward mobility story, and thus also a different meaning: a meaning that no longer involves mere substitutions of personnel within a domestic unit that is otherwise unchanged (and that would be paradigmatic of a power structure that also remains unchanged), but rather a change in the *kind* of society we are talking about, a society in which the domestic unit is no longer paradigmatic. Clarice Starling seeks her advancement within the U.S. government bureaucracy. Despite the strong ethical misgivings hovering around the particular agency that employs her, I think it is fair to call her a representative of the welfare state.[11] And what audiences experience, in following both her hunt for the killer and the self-searching therapy-like conversations with Hannibal Lecter that make the hunt successful, is a reworking of desire, an apprenticeship in the affective transformation that advancement within that institutional frame has come to require.

Set midway between the *Confessions* and *Silence of the Lambs*, *Great Expectations* helps buttress the historical narrative that links them: the displacement of erotic energies outside the reproduction of the family, the superseding of masters by mentors and of the problematic of what Spivak calls "companionate love"—the love story of marriage and inheritance, ending in domesticity—by a chillier problematic of what Spivak calls "soulmaking," a sort of nonbiological reproduction that is centered outside the family, in the institutions of civil society and the state.[12] And this narrative in turn helps make sense of the novel's own Hannibal Lecter and its own Mme. de Warens: Abel Magwitch and Miss Havisham.

Both the Male Criminal and the Older Woman occupy an intermediate zone between responsibilities to which the family is now inadequate and responsibilities the state has not yet taken up. It is the state, of course, that defines Magwitch as a criminal and deals with him accordingly. For Miss

[11] See my "Murder and Mentorship: Advancement in *The Silence of the Lambs*," *boundary 2* 23, no. 1 (1996): 71–90.
[12] Gayatri Chakravorty Spivak, "Three Women's Texts and a Critique of Imperialism," *Critical Inquiry* 12 (autumn 1985): 243–61.

Havisham, her identity self-defined around the traumatic moment of non-marriage, it is exteriority to the family that is most salient, yet the novel's gestures toward hypothetical state-affiliated identities are also worth mentioning: she *almost* solicits the state's attention first as the victim of a crime (the broken promise of marriage) and then as the perpetrator of one (the loveless raising of Estella as an instrument of revenge—in other words, dereliction of her duty as an adoptive parent). And but for her riches, she would be a potential object of the state's therapeutic agency: a madwoman. Sinister as the thought may appear in this context, it is only by caring about the course of the state beyond the nineteenth century that we can know how to care about these characters and their not entirely ironic hold over Pip's expectations.

Contemporary reviewers described Miss Havisham as evidence of "fancy run mad" (*Blackwood's Magazine*), a "galvanized puppet" (*Westminster Review*), and "too exceptional, too nearly bordering on the monstrous and loathsome, to be appropriately introduced in the midst of a story of ordinary English life" (*Saturday Review*).[13] These objections translate directly into a twentieth-century critique of the English novel's treatment of upward mobility. "So many 'monsters' in English fiction," Franco Moretti exclaims.[14] According to Moretti, English society was too conservative to acknowledge the upward mobility in its midst. Its fiction solves this problem by projecting mobility's disruptive dynamic onto monstrous figures at the narrative's margins who, for good or evil, will serve as exterior, unknowable causes. Monsters need not be villains. Moretti's reading overlaps with George Orwell's observations on "the Good Rich Man" in the early Dickens, "a superhumanly kind-hearted old gentleman who 'trots' to and fro, raising his employees' wages, patting children on the head, getting debtors out of jail and, in general, acting the fairy godmother. Of course he is a pure dream figure....Even Dickens must have reflected occasionally that anyone who was so anxious to give his money away would never have acquired it in the first place."[15] From this perspective Miss Havisham would be an early-Dickens fairy godmother displaced into a late novel that has lost its faith in whatever vision of power these providential patrons had once embodied. Thus she, like Magwitch, could be read as a subversive parody of the benefactor de-

---

[13] These quotations are taken from Janice Carlisle, "A Critical History of *Great Expectations*," in *Charles Dickens, "Great Expectations,"* ed. Janice Carlisle (Boston: Bedford/St Martin's, 1996), 450.

[14] Franco Moretti, *The Way of the World: The* Bildungsroman *in European Culture* (London: Verso, 1987), 200. The dynamic element of the British *Bildungsroman,* Moretti argues, can come neither from its protagonist, who is insipidly normal, nor from its society, which is too stable and thoroughly classified. Instead, it comes from the "the Other," the villain who "stands for social mobility" (200) in a world that does not acknowledge it. It is only by virtue of these monstrous others that "narrative becomes possible" (201). The formula for narrative is "a monster *inside* an unyielding system" (201).

[15] George Orwell, "Charles Dickens," in *A Collection of Essays* (New York: Harcourt Brace Jovanovich, 1946), 52.

vice and evidence for Orwell's case that *Great Expectations* is "definitely an attack on patronage" (Orwell, 53).

The only trouble with this line of argument is that it leaves out the presence within the novel of the contrasting term in whose name patronage is presumably attacked: the modern ideal of a reformed, impartial, impersonal government administration, which was just taking its first hesitant steps toward realization by means of meritocratic recruitment. Something like Weberian bureaucracy is not merely implied by Dickens's critique of patronage; it is written into the emotional and financial dealings between Pip and his patrons. At the same time, however, these dealings also warm up Weber's subzero notion of bureaucratic modernity. For, despite the reserve with which they are treated, Pip's relations with his two benefactors are eroticized; the homosocial bond with Magwitch is the most obvious instance. And these erotic bonds are clearly central to the direction of the ending. Certainly they add more to it than anything that happens between Pip and Estella, the more acceptable recipient of feelings generated by and displaced from her adoptive mother. (In a French novel a somewhat younger Miss Havisham would have been Pip's lover herself, with no need for the indignity of an appendage.) In short, these patrons are something more than object lessons in the objectionable institution of patronage. They are invested with emotion and desire that do not merely belong to an institutional archaism, but lead toward modern social arrangements we have not yet fully learned to inhabit or defend.

With this narrative in mind, we are encouraged to shift the focus of our interpretive interest away from the merit or talent of the upwardly mobile protagonist and such questions as what the protagonist has or has not "earned." In a very real sense the center of the narrative of social mobility is no longer the protagonist at all, but rather the mentor or mediator or benefactor. In an imperfect world, upward mobility does not happen to you without some endorsement, sponsorship, support, or merely acceptance from above, from the same power or order that has kept you down. And anyone who has the power to help you must also imbue that help with extreme moral ambiguity. This means that the narrative becomes ethically more devious; indeed, the identification with "transgression" and "crime" that Moretti finds lacking in the English *Bildungsroman* is precisely what one is encouraged to seek out there.

After all, *why* should the benefactors offer their assistance? What fissure or contradiction do their mixed, uncertain, perhaps not altruistic motives open up in the powers that be? Spivak's implicit answer to this question in *Jane Eyre* is that if Britain needed the stability of class structure and the bourgeois family, it also needed support for the state policy of imperialism, and the second could be played off against the first, making some room in which an upwardly mobile protagonist could maneuver. This suggestion seems useful for other nineteenth-century mediators as well, and for the nondomestic space they inhabit. In Balzac's novel *Le Père Goriot,* as in *Silence of the Lambs,* the ideologically central figure is again the mentor or mediator rather than the protagonist.[16] The meaning of Rastignac's rise is not contained in his character, which is unimpressive and rather banal; it is in the much more remarkable Vautrin, his fellow lodger at the Pension Vauquer, who turns out to be a master criminal, offers the chance of upward mobility to Rastignac, and explains in advance what Rastignac will then go on to do without him. The real endpoint of the story is in the middle, in the mediator. It seems more than a coincidence that Vautrin is once again an escaped convict not averse to murder, a figure of sexual as well as moral ambiguity, without any doubt an ineligible marriage partner and yet—like Hannibal Lecter—a very attractive figure. And it is this attractiveness that fills in the protagonist's ascent with unexpectedly ambiguous meanings.

If the death of fatherhood in Goriot's sense is the birth of Vautrin's style of mentorship, this shift also marks the birth of a distinctive nondomestic space. Lodging houses are the special abode of people outside or irrelevant to the cycle of biological reproduction, and Vautrin, who shows a marked sexual appreciation for Rastignac, is always associated with the quintessentially nondomestic space of Mme. Vauquer's pension, that lodging house whose nightmarish description takes up the memorable and much-discussed first pages of the novel. An in-between space, neither the "proper" domesticity of the provincial home nor the questionable domesticity of the aristocratic *hôtel*—inhabited by the older, married women who play the same role in a slightly more familiar form, mediating to Rastignac the power of their husbands—the lodging house represents how protagonists are seduced away from domesticity, or what they are seduced by. It is a midpoint that is also a new endpoint, pointing upward mobility away from domesticity.

It is in the lodging house that Vautrin makes his proposition to Rastignac. All Rastignac needs to do, in order to secure the ascent he so desires, is to acquiesce in the death of someone he need never see. Rastignac will famously rephrase this proposition (misattributed to Rousseau) as the temptation to will the death of an aged Chinese mandarin halfway around the world.[17] But this invocation of the imperial world system, the surge of power that comes of being systematically spared the sight of your distant victims, is also the social logic of the pension itself. By the face-to-face standard of domestic intimacy, distance *is* criminality. Thus the lodging house and the mediator who lives there are necessarily associated with crime.

---

[16] Honoré de Balzac, *Le Père Goriot,* ed. Philippe Berthier (Paris: Flammarion, 1995).

[17] Carlo Ginzburg, "Killing a Chinese Mandarin: The Moral Implications of Distance," *Critical Inquiry* 21, no. 1 (1994): 46–60.

Magwitch, a more demure parallel to Lecter and Vautrin, is of course the true and criminal source of the expectations Pip believes he owes to the genteel Miss Havisham, and once again he brings the money from away, out of sight, in a territory provided by the empire. The empire (which Disraeli sold to skeptics as a source of upward mobility for their sons) is again where the power of upward mobility in fact comes from. Again, but even more emphatically, this territory is defined by having to *stay* out of sight. Magwitch's benefaction has taken the form of an interdiction—thou must not ask where the money comes from. And yet the novel's plot is defined by Magwitch transgressing the interdiction to stay out of sight, and the moral center of the plot, as critics have largely agreed, has to do with Pip recognizing and valuing the criminal who is the source of his funds, face to face, even as he renounces or loses the funds.

To describe the plot in this way is to suggest that the novel is critical of social mobility in the name of domesticity. Attention to the novel's nondomestic spaces (other than prison and Australia, where Magwitch is never actually seen) might reinforce this reading. Magwitch is associated in particular with three nondomestic spaces. He is first seen shivering in the cold churchyard, where Pip in effect takes leave of his deceased family. He is next seen in the cold marshes, which can stand for the emptiness, bleak but also somehow inviting, in which Pip must now invent himself, and *can* now invent himself. Finally and perhaps most interestingly, he reappears in Pip's "chambers" in London, where he seems radically out of place and yet where, unlike Joe, he quickly makes himself at home. As Sharon Marcus notes in *Apartment Stories,* the all-male legal chambers at Temple and Lincoln's Inns, where unmarried men shared the servants of the building, were among the rare exceptions to the English rule: a refusal of large multihousehold dwellings that dramatically distinguished mid-nineteenth-century London from mid-nineteenth-century Paris. London grew horizontally rather than vertically; it had no apartment houses, and to foreigners it could thus represent the apotheosis of domesticity.[18]

The prejudice against public space and in favor of private, domestic space is one for which there is considerable evidence in *Great Expectations.* There is no doubt that the novel's nondomestic spaces are set off against Wemmick's happy domesticity, and for that matter against the forge. When Pip returns to his town, his moral failure is signaled by his going not to the forge but to the inn. From the viewpoint of the forge, which comes to look more and more ideal after the providential assault on Mrs. Joe, Pip's nondomestic dwelling is simply uninhabitable. Joe's somewhat inconsiderate comment is, "I wouldn't keep a pig in it myself, not in the case that I wished him to fatten wholesome and to eat with a meller flavor on him" (chap. 27).

---

[18] Sharon Marcus, *Apartment Stories: City and Home in Nineteenth-Century Paris and London* (Berkeley: University of California Press, 1999), 277.

This view of domesticity would seem to accord with a view of the novel that would make of Magwitch an ethical lesson about the dirtiness of money, and thus also about social aspiration. In this view, Miss Havisham's money is always really Magwitch's money—that is, money wrung from misery, hard labor, and injustice. One cannot take people's money because, however respectable it may look, it always comes from crime, indeed from theft. But this sort of moral, if it seems radical on one level, is not very helpful on another. It suggests that it is *possible* not to take people's money. It suggests, in other words, that there exists a (meritocratic) status quo in which social climbing, snobbery, and dependence could and should be avoided, in which people therefore could and should be allowed (or forced) to stay what they already are.

This is the vision of domestic self-reliance to which Dickens gives the unforgettable spatial form of Wemmick's Castle. The paradoxical villa of Jaggers's clerk at Walworth is an archaic fantasy of suburban self-containment, complete with fake battlements and a drawbridge. It has fowl, rabbits—and, conveniently for me, that very pig that Joe despaired of raising properly in Pip's chambers. Late in the novel, escaping to Walworth after learning that his own rooms, with Magwitch in them, are being watched, Pip is advised by Wemmick (who is off to work) to " 'have a perfectly quiet day with the Aged—he'll be up presently—and a little bit of—you remember the pig?'

> 'Of course,' I said.
>   'Well, and a little bit of *him*. That sausage you roasted was his, and he was in all respects a first-rater. Do try him, if it is only for old acquaintance sake....' "
> (342–43)

Pause for a moment over the pig. Even if it did not recall rather precisely a conversation Wemmick has just had with a prisoner about to be executed, the charming callousness of this little speech might well make one wonder at the Castle's humorous but nonetheless putatively idyllic domesticity. Politeness to a pig who has been more of a pet, politeness to a pig who, like the Aged P, both is and isn't a full member of the family, a pig who is still an "acquaintance" even now that he has taken the form of sausage—this politeness suggests that a domesticity that would truly be self-reliant would mean devouring your relations. I take it as a humorous argument in favor of distance—an argument in favor of not eating your pets, that is, or not keeping quite so close at hand anything you are *going* to eat. In short, I take it as a subversion of the pig-keeping model of domesticity by which Joe has judged Pip's "chambers."

The language of this passage also seems a convenient way of getting at the tricky question of Pip's "progress": whether there is any, and how to feel about it, or its lack. According to Moretti, the narrative standpoint adopted in *Great Expectations* and *Jane Eyre*—that of the protagonists themselves, now older and wiser—already commits each novel to the established order: "since point of view has its own logic—which compels the reader to appropriate the point of view that makes the text readable to him—when it coincides with a violated order, he inevitably desires the anomalies to cease, and order to be reestablished" (*Way of the World,* 202). Moretti also says that the characteristic hero of an English *Bildungsroman* speaks rather than acts, and that the manner of the speech serves as "a status symbol, a caste indicator" (195). In short, the old critical question of what progress Pip has or has not made ought to be obvious, for better or worse, as soon as Pip opens his mouth.

In a sense it is, and in the novel's opening pages. The answer is there as the distance between the adult narrator and the child crying in the churchyard in front of the tombstones of his parents and brothers. That distance is expressed, of course, in a style of speech:

> To five little stone lozenges, each about a foot and a half long, which were arranged in a neat row beside [my parents'] grave, and were sacred to the memory of five little brothers of mine—who gave up trying to get a living, exceedingly early in that universal struggle—I am indebted for a belief I religiously entertained that they had all been born on their backs with their hands in their trousers-pockets, and had never taken them out in this state of existence. (23–24)

Rather than incidental wit, think of these lines as an allegory of the Young Man from the Provinces in relation to his Family. They actualize the notion that the provinces are, as the metaphor has it, "dead." Here death *is* the provinces. Like the gentle humor around Joe's dialect, these lines are a verbal enactment of a social distance that Pip would want to, or have to, put between himself and his family even if that family had been alive. They signal how much further he has gotten in his own struggle for existence. As Moretti suggests, voice is indeed a specifically novelistic mark of social mobility. And the content of this form is distance, a useful or necessary brutality toward the domestic. Like Wemmick's attitude toward the household pig, Pip's imagination of his dead brothers shows a certain comic indifference to the sufferings of those beings closest to him in domestic space, an indifference that is also a source of charm and power.[19]

The pleasure one gets from language like this might be seen as earned by an individual performance, one author's accomplishment. But if it reminds us of Dickens as performer and "self-made man," it also ought to remind us

---

[19] Another example is the cold-blooded humor about the long-delayed death of Mr. Wopsle's great aunt: "Mr Wopsle's great-aunt conquered a confirmed habit of living into which she had fallen, and Biddy became a part of our establishment" (*Great Expectations,* 128).

of the wider context in which that self-making took place. If his voice is a mark of merit, it is also the expression of a distance that is not personal—of impersonality, one might say, as social fact, as a form of *social* merit. This is to suggest that this charming callousness, a nondomestic marker of upward mobility, can be located on the social landscape.

For example, it has a great deal to do with Jaggers. Jaggers is defined by the crime he works on and with; like Pip, he gets his money from it. If Pip is so often thrown together with this sinister guardian, it is clearly because Jaggers symbolizes some of the truth of what Pip is aiming for. The one case of dramatized self-making in the novel, Jaggers is someone whom we see *earning* a position by his efforts—not coincidentally, efforts in the use of language. And what is distinctive about his use of language is the way it abstracts from the legal responsibility of particular persons. " '[I]t's not personal,' " Wemmick explains, " 'it's professional: only professional' " (192). Characteristically, Jaggers "puts a case"; he treats situations as if the individuals concerned weren't known, or weren't present. This self-making by means of impersonality, standing in as agent for invisible principles, embodies a denial of self-interest that is also of course its own special, indirect form of self-interest. Professional neutrality is also professional profit.

The idea that Dickens and the Victorians might actually have found something to like in Jaggers's professional impersonality can perhaps be backed up with a rapid reference to George Eliot. The only exception Moretti makes, in discussing an "English *Bildungsroman*" that "leaves us, so to speak, with an empty stomach," is Eliot's novel of vocation, and this is because, he says, the novel of vocation aims at "the synthesis of individual expression and collective benefit" (Way of the World, 214). Strangely enough, this "collective benefit" seems to coincide with a certain impersonality. As the word suggests, vocation belongs to the history of an emergent nineteenth-century professionalism. Moretti observes for example that *Daniel Deronda* "turns the sociological vector of the 'family romance' toward the lower classes" (215). Instead of discovering higher origins, Deronda finds roots that tie him to those who are poor and suffering. This might be described as reverse snobbery. But reverse snobbery is a principle of some importance. It is also to be found for example in the Pip/Magwitch bond and in professionalism generally.

In *Daniel Deronda*, the discovery of lower rather than higher origins has been anticipated by a whole professional erotics. "Persons attracted him in proportion to the possibility of his defending them, rescuing them, telling upon their lives with some sort of redeeming influence." Eliot does not hide the self-interest lurking in Deronda's "passion for people who are pelted."[20] His outpouring of libido in the direction of those requiring assistance is not only a personal eccentricity. Only those who are unfortunate enough to need

---

[20] George Eliot, *Daniel Deronda*, ed. Barbara Hardy (Harmondsworth, U.K.: Penguin, 1967), 369, 785. Hereafter *DD*.

your help can define your work, or your life, as intended for "collective benefit." In other words, the logic of Deronda's emotions is the logic of the benefactor, a benefactor who can be confused with a private philanthropist only because he anticipates the social forms of a professionalism that has not yet been put firmly in place.

Although Deronda seems intended as a hero of unblemished character, this logic of the benefactor is by no means identical with moral virtue, or at least with moral virtue of a domestic or preprofessional sort. Deronda's professionally seductive eyes, impersonally personal, "*seemed* to express a special interest in every one on whom he fixed them" (*DD,* 377). His eyes offer help only in the name of an externally imposed authority, "as if one's standard was somehow wrong" (376). Even the fatal abstractness of his character might be seen, allegorically, as the human sacrifice professional expertise exacts from unprofessional experience.[21] Thus it does not leave the narrative of social mobility undisturbed.

If this paradigm can be extended back to Dickens, it would suggest that the spatial enclosure of domesticity does not after all define the narrative closure or center of the upward mobility story—even the ideal closure that the protagonist fails to attain. In spite of appearances, Dickens would not be opting for the walling off of domestic space, site of true, private feeling and moral sensibility, from the inhumanity of the social system outside. The problem of space would not be described as maintaining proper enclosure, segregation, separation of spheres, as the ideology of domesticity suggests. (Nor could Dickens's accomplishment be seen, as it sometimes has been, as a simple deconstructing of this binary.) Space in Dickens would be animated, rather, by a problematic of circulation.

The novel's inns and pubs are nightmarish enough to have come out of an anti-urban, pro-domestic tract.[22] But what is it exactly that is so nightmarish about these nondomestic spaces? Describing the public house on the river where they spend their last night, before the ill-fated escape attempt, Dickens writes: "We found the air as carefully excluded from [the bedrooms], as if air were fatal to life" (*Great Expectations,* 401). Of the room with the bridal cake in Miss Havisham's house, Dickens writes: "From that room, too, the

---

[21] The last four paragraphs draw on my essay "Death and Vocation: Narrativizing Narrative Theory," *PMLA* 107, no. 1 (1992): 38–50.

[22] When Pip obeys the resonant directive "Don't Go Home" (in small caps), he goes instead to a hotel in Covent Garden (chap. 45), where he spends a sleepless night in a room with "an inhospitable smell." He is tortured by the sentence "Don't Go Home" in all its variations, by the fact that he isn't at home and will not have one. The difference between hotel and home is at the forefront. His thoughts are of the room's many other tenants, real or hypothetical, including a suicide: "It was a sort of vault on the ground floor at the back, with a despotic monster of a four-post bedstead in it, straddling over the whole place, putting one of his arbitrary legs into the fireplace and another into the doorway, and squeezing the wretched little washing-stand in quite a Divinely Righteous manner." The monarchical is not for him; this is neither his home nor his castle.

daylight was completely excluded, and it had an airless smell that was oppressive" (94). The problem with the public space is not too free and promiscuous a circulation, as one might have imagined. It is the same as Miss Havisham's problem of complete enclosure, exacerbated domesticity: lack of circulation.[23]

Jaggers of course has no domestic life. His domestic arrangements in Soho are described as follows: "he seemed to bring the office home with him... and to wheel it out of an evening and fall to work" (204). From an ethical/domestic viewpoint, his home is "bare, gloomy, and little used" (203). On the other hand, we are also told, strangely, that Jaggers "never lets a door or window be fastened at night" (198). For Jaggers, despite or because of his entanglement in the prison system, one might say that walling off is no solution to the problems of social relationship. For one is always part of a larger system of circulation that makes a mockery of any effort to enclose. And there is a sense in which the rest of the novel agrees with him.

The circulation of air in *Great Expectations* bears a striking analogy to the circulation of money. Enclosure of space would seem to correspond to possession of money. But the model of upward mobility seems to have less to do with possession than with circulation. The "collective benefit" supplied by the benefactor's role in *Great Expectations* involves not so much the archaism of patronage as the anticipation of an as yet unrealized, impersonal agency. Moretti notes how dry and legalistic Pip's time in London is, ending as it does "with the legal confiscation of Pip's assets" (*Way of the World,* 208). Counterintuitive as it may seem, I think this has to be turned around. As they say, follow the money. It doesn't just disappear into the coffers of the Crown, though symbolically that is not a totally inappropriate destination for it. Pip's only significant actions in the novel involve his talking Miss Havisham into a redistribution of funds on behalf of the more deserving Mr Pocket, and his giving a portion of Magwitch's money to Herbert Pocket. Unintentionally, he thus makes possible his own future as a clerk and eventually a partner in the same enterprise. Pip has learned from Magwitch, it would seem, the role of benefactor. The difference, of course, is that he is a benefactor without money. He is a benefactor without money of his own, a benefactor with other people's money. This is not merely his apprenticeship for the role of clerk that he will eventually adopt (the social position of subordinated skill, skill without ownership). If he resembles Wemmick in

---

[23] Orlick's room in the porter's lodge at Miss Havisham's house, when he works there, is described as follows: "In its small proportions, it was not unlike the kind of place usually assigned to a gate-porter in Paris. Certain keys were hanging on the wall, to which he now added the gate key; and his patchwork-covered bed was in a little division or recess. The whole had a slovenly confined and sleepy look, like a cage for a human dormouse" (*Great Expectations,* 223). Orlick, figure for Pip without the expectations, ironically is the one who brings the dreaded French fad of apartment-house living to London, which had refused it so adamantly that the terms "comfort" and "at home" were used in English by French writers resisting Paris's trend toward multifamily dwellings.

this regard, he also resembles Jaggers. For Jaggers's function in the plot has been, like Pip's own when he uses Magwitch's money to arrange for Herbert's partnership, to stop anyone from following the money trail back to its source. This is what the law does, and it is what Pip does. Pip's good deeds are deeds of *non*transparency; they obscure the source of funds. And in doing so, they turn bad money to good causes. In short, Pip acts not like someone who has finally seen the light of domestic morality, but like a money-launderer. Or let's say rather like a fundraiser for a Non-Governmental Organization, a person of good conscience and good causes whose raw materials include the funds accumulated by the Ford or the Rockefeller Foundation.

This is perhaps how the property-is-theft idea works its way most successfully into the upward mobility narrative. If property comes from Magwitch, then the acquisition of property cannot be what upward mobility is about. Hence there is a certain selflessness about the hero. But this selflessness expresses itself in a peculiar form: by valuing a more equitable *circulation* of property over the personal *possession* of property. And this selflessness is not total; it allows for a certain indirect self-interest. Like Jaggers's actions on Magwitch's behalf, Pip providing for Herbert unintentionally allows Herbert later to provide for Pip. Some selflessness is bartered for some (unacknowledged) self-interest, which shapes the actual, sober, undramatized upward mobility that follows the collapse of the great expectations.

This administrative or professional impersonality is the closest we have come to solving the problem dramatized by Wemmick's domesticity: the "good" person who does "bad" things—bad at work, good at home. For the impersonality of statistics is necessary to the state. Even at their best, the professions and the state engage in a mode of rescue that depends on being able to treat people as if they were not there. I am suggesting, very schematically, that Pip finds his oblique, impersonal self-interest in the sort of function that will come to be supplied by the institutional machinery of civil society and of the state—that he will receive his long-delayed inheritance, if you like, as his share in the impersonality of the Crown, which does inherit the money that Pip can't inherit.

This sort of point has been made before, but usually in a rather cynical mode. It is by way of critique for example that D. A. Miller speaks of Dickens's support, in *Bleak House,* for "the expanded development of the Victorian state bureaucracy."[24] It is in the same Foucaultian, anti-institutional spirit that Tony Bennett speaks, in a recent essay on the spread of museums in the nineteenth century, of how "the development of new capillary systems for the distribution of culture would help cultivate a capacity for voluntary self-regulation in the general population."[25] And it is with pronounced cynicism that Mary Poovey, writing about domesticity in Chadwick's 1842 *Sanitary*

---

[24] D. A. Miller, *The Novel and the Police* (Berkeley: University of California Press, 1988), 64.
[25] Tony Bennett, "The Multiplication of Culture's Utility," *Critical Inquiry* 21, no. 4 (1995): 865.

Report, notes that Chadwick's version of domestic reform did nothing to harm his own professional ambitions. "The twin effects of every component of Chadwick's sanitary plan were, on the one hand, to limit the ability of working-class men to organize themselves into collective political or economic associations and, on the other, to empower the kind of professionalized bureaucrat that Chadwick himself represented."[26]

But the empowering of professionalized bureaucrats is not, after all, a self-evident evil. The insinuation of the state into domestic privacy is not a zero-sum game in which every gain for a bureaucrat's career was a loss for a woman and/or for the working class. As Carolyn Steedman has argued, to see the working-class as a cozily united collectivity beset by the external threats of professional experts and state officials has always been a gendered choice that ignored the actually and potentially positive meaning of state and professional intervention for working-class women.[27] Indeed, this is not so different from a point that Mary Poovey herself makes, in an earlier book, about Florence Nightingale.[28] "In mobilizing the Victorian domestic narrative to reform the poor, Florence Nightingale activated the altruistic language that women's maternal nature underwrote" so as to turn paid nursing into "a quasi-religious calling" (196–97). This was a means of aggressively seizing power and authority from medical doctors, but it was also a strategy that made public space for women's nondomestic expertise and careers. It is in this sense that a narrative of upward mobility could be held to involve, at least to some degree, reaffirming loyalty to one's origins rather than forsaking them.

This is the mode of middle-class membership that one sees in *Great Expectations.* The novel's version of the upward mobility story is thus not Pip's linear ascent, nor the ethical blockage of that ascent. Rather, it is founded on Pip's circling back to try to rescue Magwitch *a second time*—on the idea of an orphan acting like the democratic state at its best, self-consciously recognizing himself in and tending to another orphan, generalizing the individualized uplift of the upward mobility story into a rescue of all by all. Its endpoint, becoming a benefactor without money, is thus not an enclosed domesticity but a space of better circulation. The position Pip is moving toward, though of course not actually filling within the novel, is that of an administrative reformer, public or semi-public servant of a social welfare state—not of course the actual state that was ready to execute Magwitch if he didn't die first, but the reformed, as yet unrealized state that would take over Pip's own role of rescuing Magwitch and all those like him. If it involves

---

[26] Mary Poovey, *Making a Social Body: British Cultural Formation, 1830–1860* (Chicago: University of Chicago Press, 1995), 130.

[27] Carolyn Steedman, *Landscape for a Good Woman: A Story of Two Lives* (London: Virago, 1986).

[28] Mary Poovey, *Uneven Developments: The Ideological Work of Gender in Mid-Victorian England* (Chicago: University of Chicago Press, 1988).

integration to the status quo, this ending also involves the anticipation of something very different.

Beyond its attention to *Great Expectations,* this argument has tried to point toward a salvage of the upward mobility story in general, a story there are many reasons not to love. It has done so on the grounds that, though the genre seems to favor the individual at the expense of the social, it is actually about democracy, as Girard said about mediation in general, and about making democracy real to imperfect, desiring individuals. Seen from the perspective of the mediator rather than that of the protagonist, a narrative that seems directed against the welfare state reveals itself to be, to unequal degrees and in different ways, part of a complex pedagogy whereby desire is taught to adjust to the emergent conditions of the welfare state, to recognize forms of socially mediated "merit" and act on behalf of new forms of "welfare" that correspond to neither the best nor the worst of which contemporary conditions are capable. This is not the place to make the full political case for the welfare state that my argument has presumed. Let me only say that in following out this transhistorical thread I have not been committing the Hegelian sin of teleology. For I have chosen not an ideal endpoint but a mere stopgap (though stopgaps do have a tendency to last), and I have chosen it at a moment when the impulse to extend it further has clearly been blocked and even its provisional usefulness has been everywhere questioned and undermined. If the imperfections of this temporary resting place were not already obvious, more might well be said about the growing contradiction between national-popular defense of the welfare state and offensiveness of the imperialist world system, on which both the welfare state and the upward mobility story seem to depend. Still, it is hard to imagine that anything less messy than this engagement with the present, a present that includes the chilly power of an impersonal state apparatus as well as the annoyingly personal proximities of mentorship and face-to-face patronage, can help us avoid patronizing the past.

9. Tracking the Sentimental Eye

JUDITH STODDART

Asking whether we can ever see as the Victorians saw sounds less like a contemporary hermeneutic exercise than a revival of arch-Victorian hermeneutics. It recalls Ruskin's exhortation on principles of right reading, his insistence that interpreting authors from the past requires "putting ourselves always in the author's place, annihilating our own personality, and seeking to enter into his."[1] Making an Arnoldian attempt to see our historical object as in itself it really was might now seem a dead letter, except, of course, as this spirit of hermeneutics past continues to haunt postmodern critical practice. Whatever our constrained and constructed acts of interpretation might yield (and this is a matter still very much under debate), we know that they do *not* yield Arnoldian certainty. Arnold and a whole Victorian ethics of criticism evoked by his name stand as our defining other. Like early modernist British writers, we defensively mark out our practice as anything but, God forbid, bloody Victorian.

The fact that we still cast our hermeneutical quandaries in terms that would have sounded remarkably familiar to the Victorians should alert us to the indefensibility of some of our cherished critical borders. Most of us will accept the statement that we cannot step beyond our horizon of expectations. But in some recent historicist criticism, the horizon has so contracted that we are left with increasingly miniaturized prospects. Eschewing the universalizing big picture, some critics have produced accounts committed to a historical particularism in which contemporaneity is a self-justifying interpretive procedure. In the manner of the amateur Victorian anthropologist, literary history of this type displaces description with collation. Miscellaneous

---

[1] John Ruskin, *The Works of John Ruskin*, ed. E. T. Cook and Alexander Wedderburn, 39 vols. (London: Allen, 1903–1912), 18:75.

assemblages of *objets trouvés* are invested with meaning by virtue not of their function within an originary context, but of the virtuosity of the researcher who has unearthed them. Some scholars who have criticized the arbitrary periodization of literary history have then reproduced the period on a small scale, investing a year with the internal coherence once attributed to centuries. Such a turn is curiously reminiscent of the nineteenth-century worship of history, summed up by Ranke in his 1854 assertion that "every epoch is immediate to God, and that its value consists, not in what follows it, but in its own existence, its own proper self."[2] After the death of the author, *chronos* has filled the intentional void.

The notion of horizon of expectations, as it originated in Hans Robert Jauss at least, was intended in part to critique this overvaluation of synchrony over diachrony.[3] For Jauss, the historicity of literature was a complex intersection of the two. Writing against a critical tradition concerned to vindicate national identity, Jauss seemed to recognize that periodization—whether of a century or of a single year—involves a similar policing of arbitrarily defined borders. And like nationalist narratives, historicist accounts can too often deflect our resemblances to the archaeologized other. Both the claim to see as the Victorians saw and the claim that we cannot possibly see as the Victorians saw, embedded as we are in our own interpretive frameworks, perpetuate this sense of a historical divide.[4] These two approaches to cultural study are more similar than their proponents suggest. Both estrange the past, even if only to acknowledge the ultimate obscurity of the object of critical desire. And neither position acknowledges to what extent it is implicated in the very culture it claims to study.

Arnoldian clairvoyance was only one hermeneutic imperative in a period obsessed with the limits of interpretation. Carlyle's sprawling historical narratives, or Froude's insistence in "The Science of History" that poetry is in many ways "truer than history" when dealing with the unscientific "accident

---

[2] Leopold Von Ranke, "Über die Epochen der neuren Geschichte," reprinted in part in *The Secret of World History*, ed. and trans. Roger Wines (New York: Fordham University Press, 1981), 159.

[3] See Hans Robert Jauss, "Literary History as a Challenge to Literary Theory," in *Toward an Aesthetic of Reception*, trans. Timothy Bahti (Minneapolis: University of Minnesota Press, 1982).

[4] In Catherine Gallagher's and Stephen Greenblatt's recent defense of new historicism, these two positions are combined in a way that reveals how much is at stake in defending the boundary between past and present. If the past were not other, there would be no critical story, for the tale the new historicist tells is precisely the tale of the gap, of the "something that the authors we study would not have had sufficient distance upon themselves and their own era to grasp" (*Practicing New Historicism* [University of Chicago Press, 2000], 8). For some interesting attempts to imagine a critical position that does not begin from this clearly demarcated difference, see A. Leigh DeNeef, "Of Dialogues and Historicisms," *SAQ* 86 (fall 1987): 497–517; and Marguerite Waller, "Historicism Historicized: Translating Petrarch and Derrida," in *Historical Criticism and the Challenge of Theory*, ed. Janet Levarie Smarr (Urbana: University of Illinois Press, 1993), 183–211.

of facts," introduce turns familiar to current readers.[5] When teaching *Sartor Resartus,* I can always predict that at least one critically alert student will ask to what extent poststructuralists were inspired by Carlyle. This is not just, I think, a case of reading through modern interpretive lenses. It represents a kind of anagnorisis. In the nineteenth century, the idea of history exploded under the pressure of the fossil record. At the same time, new technologies of representation—engravings, cheap print, photography—and new scientific theories about modes of perception challenged assumptions about how individuals see and know the world around them. The questions we are posing here about the limits of critical understanding, and the ways we are posing them, were worked out in part in response to this perceptual revolution. Science and technology may have altered some of our points of reference, but the sun has not altogether set on a Victorian horizon of expectations.

Instead of endlessly reinventing familiar critical postures while defending our difference from these relics of an imperial past, we might more productively recognize the complexity of our own positions in the interplay of diachrony and synchrony. As Victorian geologists realized, sifting the sediments of culture can be a bewildering task. Lyell, in his influential *Principles of Geology* (1833), noted that even formations that seemed strikingly "dissimilar in organization and...character" might turn out to be "of synchronous origin."[6] To what extent do we, in the manner of Graham Swift's protagonist in *Waterland,* dredge the same ground as our Victorian forebears, unaware of the insistent presence of the past in our critical stories? The potential theoretical impasse occurs not when we ask whether we can accurately take the measure of Victorian cultural formations. It may come rather at the moment when we have to consider whether we are still measuring them, and ourselves, with instruments assembled in the period.

The issue around which I will try this question may seem at first the *least* promising place to start. Victorian sentimentalism would appear to be a clear case in which cultural formations have experienced a significant shift. Few modern readers express any sympathy with or taste for nineteenth-century sentimental texts. One need only invoke that familiar chestnut of Victorian sentimentalism, Dickens's *The Old Curiosity Shop,* to produce the predictable critical squirming. On the one hand modern readers see Victorian sentimental art as firmly rooted in a time and place, so constrained by its circumstances that discussions of it must be prefaced by a critical apologia. On the other hand, in their descriptions of sentimentalism, critics often lapse into a kind of dehistoricized reader response in which the author's or readers' emotions can be directly accessed and transcribed.[7] What makes sentimen-

[5] James Anthony Froude, "The Science of History" (1864), reprinted in *Short Studies in Great Subjects,* 3 vols. (London: Longmans, Green, 1901), 1:34, 33.

[6] Charles Lyell, *Principles of Geology,* 3 vols. (London: Murray, 1830), 3:42.

[7] For representative responses of these positions, see Fred Kaplan, *Sacred Tears: Sentimentality in Victorian Literature* (Princeton, N.J.: Princeton University Press, 1987); Murray Roston, *Victorian Contexts: Literature and the Visual Arts* (New York: New York

talism interesting in terms of the hermeneutic quandaries I have outlined is that it consistently evokes this divided response. It is portrayed as at the same time irretrievably distant from modern sympathy and too transparent, too easily decoded to count as high art. There is something about sentimentality that prompts a bifurcated approach to history, an inability to settle into a stable theoretical groove.

The reason for such critical schizophrenia is that Victorian sentimentalism falls under the heading of what might be called, following my arguments above, a protracted horizon of expectations. One horizon of expectations does not displace another in a strict diachronic progression. The fact that we still dismiss sentimental art as naïve and untheoretically spontaneous suggests a continuity with the assumptions of that art, a continuity we seldom recognize. One might put this contention in somewhat crude psychological terms and say that the arch-modern distaste for sentimentality is defensive, a symptomatically insistent rejection of something all too close for comfort. But a more productive approach would be to suggest that the very terms we use to describe sentimentality provide a revealing trace of our synchronicity with certain Victorian formations.

In nearly every critical account, sentimentality is said to record experience in the register of the body; it is the discourse of the heart as opposed to reason, of passion instead of disinterest, of intuition or instinct against social convention. But the body, as we have learned from a number of disciplines, is an active site of social construction. To brand sentimentalism as an unmediated, emotional transcription of experience should set off alarms for readers to whom nature has become as suspect a term as culture. That emotions are inflected by cultural norms is a commonplace in treatments of mental health or sexuality, but not in treatments of sentimentality. Sentimental art is too emotional, too naive, too spontaneous—in short, it is not sufficiently "cultured" to count *as* culture. For some critics positioning sentimentality in this way has made it possible to argue for its importance as oppositional discourse, as a protest against the cultural hegemony of the elite. Such a move still glosses over the significance of the binary at work in such statements. The natural is pitted, in that lasting Rousseauan construction of human nature, against the cultured. But what is more cultured, more charged with ideological and aesthetic import, than what seems most natural?

In his explorations of the notion of taste, Pierre Bourdieu has argued that while "good taste" would seem to describe a natural ability or instinct, it is in fact the product of a highly structured set of competencies. What makes it so powerful as a cultural marker is that those competencies have become largely invisible; this, he claims, is the "paradox which defines the 'realization' of

University Press, 1996); Howard Fulweiler, *Here a Captive Heart Busted: Studies in the Sentimental Journey of Modern Literature* (New York: Fordham University Press, 1993); George H. Ford, *Dickens and His Readers* (Princeton, N.J.: Princeton University Press, 1955).

culture as *becoming natural.*"[8] The logic Bourdieu applies to taste here also applies to what we have so often seen as a *lack* of taste in sentimental art. There is nothing transparently innocent or naïve about the sentimental attitude. Innocence, naïvete, "natural" feeling are structured responses meaningful only in relation to other possible perspectives. Extending Bourdieu's argument, we can say that culture is particularly smoothed over in the case of a perspective defined as most natural, least critical, the response that "goes without saying." Sentimentalism may not be the popular, instinctive response it is usually considered to be, but rather a highly cultivated one.

My point here is not to rehearse a familiar story about art, hegemony, and class dominance. What I want to emphasize is that Victorian sentimentalism, which some critics have characterized as a lack of proper perspective, can be seen as a means of marking out and solidifying a quite particular way of seeing. The relationship between reason and emotion was by no means a clear-cut binary early in the nineteenth century. Artists of the period were not dealing with an accepted division between the heart and the head; they were trying as much to *produce* as to reflect that division in their work. Recent biological and physiological research had complicated enlightenment theories of human nature. For Victorian artists it was not a matter of claiming allegiance to one camp over another; the independent existence of either camp would have to be figured decisively before sides could be taken. The negotiations over this split are particularly evident in discussions of the arts in the late 1830s and 1840s. These decades were marked by what might be called a representational crisis in which political and aesthetic modes of representation were firmly linked in public debates. It was in response to this crisis that the characteristics of the sentimental as we have come to recognize it—a natural, emotional response, a reflex of universal human nature instead of a particular form of cultural competence—seem to emerge.

For the purposes of my argument here, I will confine my discussion to the role certain Victorian sentimental genre paintings might have played in defining this competence. This is in part because it is so tempting to make a static image emblematic of a fixed way of seeing. Unlike the elusive flux of history, a picture seems to stand still. Or so some Victorian artists and critics would have had their audiences believe. In accounts of exhibitions in the early 1840s, one can trace a definite anxiety about whether a painting can freeze a perspective, or whether it merely becomes an extension of particularized acts of viewing. The sentimental eye, I argue, can be characterized by its attempts to stabilize this oscillating perspective.[9] And while we cannot see through this eye, we can track some of its movements. In the process we can

---

[8] Pierre Bourdieu, *The Field of Cultural Production,* ed. Randal Johnson (New York: Columbia University Press, 1993), 234; emphasis in original.

[9] I am adapting Michael Baxandall's phrase for perceptual orientation in *Painting and Experience in Fifteenth-Century Italy,* 2d ed. (Oxford: Oxford University Press, 1988), chap. 2, "The Period Eye."

recognize resonances between Victorian anxieties about the position of the spectator and our own such anxieties, resonances that align the theoretical concerns of this collection more closely with the sentimental perspective than we might be inclined to suppose.

In public discussions of the crisis of representation in the 1830s and 1840s, the fine arts assumed center stage. Painting in particular—which through public exhibitions and reproductions could reach even a nonreading audience—seemed the most promising means of centering the attention of a restless populace. In the 1830s ad hoc parliamentary committees on the arts devised schemes for turning out more deliberate and more uniform consumers of visual culture. Concerned by the apparent superiority of French design (attributed to France's strong system of public museums), Parliament devoted funds to building new premises for national collections, as well as to establishing a national system of arts education. The 1838 opening of the new National Gallery building in Trafalgar Square, and the relocation and expansion of the British Museum between 1823 and 1847, dramatically increased the visibility of and access to collections of masterworks: between 1823 and 1843, the British Museum alone saw a rise in annual attendance from around ninety thousand to more than half a million. Members of Parliament crowed as their efforts seemed to pay off at Prince Albert's 1843 exhibition of cartoons submitted for the decoration of the rebuilt Palace of Westminster, which drew an estimated twenty to thirty thousand visitors a day, visitors who represented a wide range of social classes.[10]

But in accounts of the event—and in writings about the arts in the years that followed—there is a dramatic change in the way the relation between art and this growing public is portrayed. For many observers the most impressive display at the 1843 exhibition was not on the walls but in the corridors: critics looked at the public looking. To a certain extent this reflects the curiosity of the fashionable critic, for whom the exhibition might represent a version of cross-cultural encounter. But when the painter Charles Eastlake recorded his observations of spectators at the exhibition, he registered something more than a pleasurable *frisson* from an afternoon of polite slumming. Despite opening his pronouncement that such an occasion proved the desirability of making the arts available to a wider audience, his description betrays an alarm that the British public about whom government committees had speculated had now taken on an all too tangible presence. Eastlake begins and ends his short diary entry with the impression of unavoidable physical contact as one is jostled and "carried in with the throng" that endlessly moves through the halls "in droves." Whether writing of the

[10] Attendance figures are drawn from Bernard Denvir, ed., *The Early Nineteenth Century: Art, Design and Society, 1789–1852* (London: Longman, 1884), 19, 69. Denvir has suggested that the numbers at the Westminster exhibition were probably much lower. Because I am concerned here with contemporary perceptions of the crowds at the event, I have used the figures cited in most Victorian accounts.

diffusion of objects through the crowd or of the reputation of the arts among this new audience, he casts his reflections in terms of an inevitable pressing of flesh.[11] The moving, grasping spectators (he obsessively focuses on their hands in his account) have little in common with the ideal, abstract, orderly observer Eastlake had conjured in his 1835 essay, "How to Observe." Critics in the 1840s no longer had to imagine ideal encounters with art; they could now witness specific audiences engaging with paintings at a given event and location. As a result, they started to consider not how pictures might influence their viewers, in the manner of the government committees of the previous decade, but how concrete acts of viewing might impinge on a work of art. Like a number of written accounts of the exhibition, Eastlake's records the arrival on the arts scene both of the embodied viewer—individual spectators with distinctive customs of dress, taste, and habits—and of the audience perceived as an animate body, one whose contact with the artwork is driven by its own logic and desires.

Descriptions of the crowds at public exhibitions, echoing the rhetoric of contemporary political debates about chartism, frequently figured viewers as a national audience, a homogeneous body with an easily summarized set of reactions. These efforts to normalize a particular way of viewing are of a piece with other attempts in the 1840s to, in Mary Poovey's phrase, make a social body. And yet such a consolidation was difficult to sustain when talking about aesthetic experience. If government reports in the decade typically "obliterate[d] specific...individuals" in the interest of carving out a new, abstract domain of the social,[12] artists and art critics were working within a domain bounded by already recognized epistemological assumptions, assumptions that had recently foregrounded the probable incommensurability of individual with general understanding. When Eastlake, for example, describes the crush of the constantly moving crowd at the Westminster exhibition, he falls back on language familiar not only in political descriptions of crowds, but also in early nineteenth-century theories of visual perception, which imagined "a restless, active body whose anxious *motilité* (i.e., willed effort against felt resistance) was a precondition of subjectivity."[13] The individuals teeming through exhibitions were not easily subsumed under government statistics; these were not bodies grouped together for observation and classification, but active observers engaged in analyses of their own. The very movement of the visitors through the galleries and exhibitions of the next decade becomes, in the descriptions of contemporaries, a reminder of emerging theories of subjectivity that locate taste, perception, and aesthetic

[11] Charles Eastlake, *Contributions to the Literature of the Fine Arts* (1870); cited in Denvir, *The Early Nineteenth Century*, 68–69.
[12] Mary Poovey, *Making a Social Body: British Cultural Formation, 1830–1864* (Chicago: University of Chicago Press, 1995), 37.
[13] Jonathan Crary, *Techniques of the Observer: On Vision and Modernity in the Nineteenth Century* (Cambridge, Mass.: MIT Press, 1990), 72.

value within specific bodies. As Eastlake's account emphasizes, assemblies of individual viewers could not be effectively policed, not because they were inherently unruly, but because they brought a new power to the exhibition space. Painting did not appear to transfix the attention of a wandering audience. Instead, the art world was itself set in turmoil by the perception that it was under" the surveillance of countless eyes.

Anxiety about the effect of these restless, embodied viewers afflicts contemporary accounts of the fine arts. Regulating the explosion of literacy, one critic argued, was relatively easy; processing words depended on logic and a sense of rhythm, which could be contained by practice in the strict forms of "metres and verse-making." But how could one regulate visual stimulus? The proliferation of visual culture meant that the popular "eye is left unguarded, unprotected, to shift for itself, or to yield to the fascinations the first panderer of evil chooses to offer." Artists, forgetting their mission to "improve" their audience, would strive merely to entrance these "corrupted...eyes," thereby perpetuating "the pestilence of false taste." A culture of newly aroused spectators was particularly susceptible to "the seductions of intemperance and vice," another critic warned; an artist should regard himself not as a "higher-class decorator" adorning private sites of leisure, but as a "priest, ministering" to the hungry eyes of the crowds visiting public galleries.[14]

Behind such metaphors of corruption and seduction lies, in part at least, an eighteenth-century philosophical and political tradition emphasizing what Poovey calls "specular morality." Suspicions about the physical eye also pervaded certain strands of religious thinking: Augustine's warnings about the effects of a *concupiscentia oculorum,* which might divert our minds from inner, spiritual vision, persisted particularly in evangelical discourse.[15] Not only had distinctions between material and ideal vision come under attack in recent physiological research; the emphasis on an embodied spectator implied a new intimacy in the exchange between art and its audience. Even as spectatorship became more visible in the new public spaces devoted to it, it was being imagined as a fundamentally private activity, contained in and constrained by individual bodies. Moreover, if the act of seeing was in essence a bodily function, dependent on the makeup of physical organs and not on spiritual or ideal patterns or types, then the fascination of the eye might be, not a condition to be avoided or corrected, but simply an apt characterization of the way looking works.

Such preoccupations can be too quickly assimilated to a rigid, moralistic aesthetic theory of the kind conventionally associated with the Victorians. Yet the sexualized metaphors these critics use betray an anxiety about

[14] [Eagles], "De Burton on Pictures," *Blackwood's* 58 (1845): 415, 417, 426; "The Prospects of British Art," *British Quarterly Review* 2 (1845): 466, 478.
[15] Poovey, *Making a Social Body,* 34; on Augustine, see Martin Jay, *Downcast Eyes: The Denigration of Vision in Twentieth-Century French Thought* (Berkeley: University of California Press, 1993), 13.

whether aesthetic experience really can perform *any* moral function at all. The same metaphors were exploited by those who celebrated the proliferation of visual culture in the period and who welcomed theories that emphasized art as primarily a sensual pleasure. In the world of public galleries artworks were no longer, like the kept mistresses of the upper classes, hidden away in country houses for occasional aristocratic pleasures; what had once been merely "one of the many playthings wherewith the wealthy idler might fence off some half-hour of care," an 1845 *British Quarterly* reviewer remarked, was "now for the first time becoming a thing for the people." As a result of the "democratic and diffusive art of engraving," reported *Jerrold's Shilling Magazine,* painting had broken from its subservience to aristocratic taste: "she" no longer "lends her pallet" to stroke the vanity of the wealthy. Circulating widely in the public eye, "getting among [the] people," she now sought "rewards from administering to the enjoyments of the multitude," and "her charms are prized accordingly." The punning play on "pallet," which would be at home in the writing of the aesthetes several decades later, depends for its effect on the ambiguities surrounding the field of fine art by the 1840s. Was art the province of isolated genius, or was it merely one medium through which talent could service "the ruling desires of the times"?[16] Was exposure to painting an ennobling experience capable of lifting up the multitudes to heights of culture, or a seductive pleasure of the senses whose power was determined by the capacities of the beholder? What exactly was the relationship between the viewer and the art object? If some biologists and aesthetic theorists were suggesting that physical makeup determined what and how individuals saw, others pushed physiological speculation in a slightly different direction. In studies that would be seminal for the field of psychology later in the century, Johannes Müller argued in the 1830s that the observer was in essence a passive receptor "susceptible to external procedures of manipulation and stimulation."[17] In this view, the eyes of the audience really could be "corrupted" by the "fascinations" of paintings.

These uncertainties come through in reviews of paintings in the period. One image in particular seems to have been caught in the crossfire and used as a means of staking out representative critical positions. No reviewer of the 1844 Royal Academy Exhibition considered Richard Redgrave's *The Sempstress* (fig. 9.1) the best canvas of the show; it certainly does not seem to have been a picture that drew enormous crowds. And yet not only did it generate a heated exchange among critics; it became one of the most famil-

[16] [Eagles], "Prospects of British Art," 466–67; "The Place of the Fine Arts in the Natural System of Society," *Douglas Jerrold's Shilling Magazine* 6 (1847): 80; David Wilkie, *Remarks on Painting,* cited in E.D.H. Johnson, *Paintings of the British Social Scene* (London: Weidenfeld and Nicolson, 1988), 142.

[17] Crary's summary of Müller's conclusions, *Techniques of The Observer,* 92. As Crary notes (90), Charles Eastlake cites Müller's studies in his 1840 translation of Goethe's *Theory of Colours.*

Figure 9.1. Richard Redgrave, *The Sempstress*. Courtesy of the Victoria and Albert Museum.

iar iconic images of the period, one that was reinterpreted by major artists through the end of the century.[18] At first glance it is hard to see why this particular painting, one of many Redgrave produced in what Susan Casteras has called a "chain of tear-jerker catastrophes," should have proved so suggestive. The composition, as I will discuss in a moment, is awkward, and in both form and technique it marks a departure from Redgrave's other paintings of modern life. Why would this work, in the words of T. J. Edelstein, "establish Redgrave as the single most innovative and important practitioner of social iconography"?[19]

[18] For surveys of the sempstress paintings influenced by Redgrave, see T. J. Edelstein, "They Sang 'The Song of the Shirt': The Visual Iconology of the Seamstress," *Victorian Studies* 23 (1980): 183–210; Christina Walkley, *The Ghost in the Looking Glass: The Victorian Seamstress* (London: Owen, 1981).

[19] Susan Casteras, " 'Social Wrongs': The Painted Sermons of Richard Redgrave," in *Richard Redgrave*, ed. Susan Casteras and Ronald Parkinson (New Haven, Conn.: Yale University Press, 1988), 21; Edelstein, "They Sang 'The Song of the Shirt,' " 185.

For Edelstein, as for a number of modern commentators on *The Sempstress,* the answer lies in the way Redgrave turns a political problem—the plight of urban sempstresses—into a sweetly pathetic image, eliciting the viewer's sympathy without stirring him or her into action. Most recent accounts have been committed to reading this image as loosely documentary. As a result it is judged as overly sentimentalized, an inaccurate, somewhat naïve, superficially emotional response to contemporary life.[20] But in the case of Redgrave we are dealing with more than, in Lionel Lambourne's somewhat apologetic terms, "a sensitive man's reaction to dilemmas which confronted the alert social conscience of the period." Redgrave was not merely interested in exposing social issues in a way that would pacify the "guardians of high art."[21] Elected an associate of the Royal Academy in 1840 and a full member in 1851, later master and curriculum planner of the Government Schools of Design, curator of what would become the fine arts collection of the Victoria and Albert Museum, Surveyor of Crown Pictures, overseer of the British Fine Art Section at the 1855 Paris International Exhibition, author of the influential *Manual of Design* and of the first distinctively nationalist account of British painting (still in print as *A Century of British Painters*), Redgrave was one of the most visible guardians of high art throughout Victoria's reign. At the time that he painted *The Sempstress,* he was already deeply involved in the social life and politics of the Royal Academy; his letter written two years later to Lord John Russell on the teaching of design shows that he had closely followed debates about art education in the 1830s and 1840s.[22] In his numerous writings on the practice, history, and teaching of the arts, he touches on the kind of aesthetic controversies I have sketched out here.

The Sempstress thus is mischaracterized as a generous, if not quite honest, effort at social documentary by a struggling humanitarian artist; it is the creation of a highly trained and politically alert painter. And that, I suggest, is precisely why the painting appears to have touched off such strong reactions. Through its technique, composition, and imagery, the painting reflects and

[20] Helene Roberts, for example, judges the "effect" of the painting by a modern journalistic standard; like Redgrave's other pictures, she complains, it falls short of being a real expose, for if Redgrave "asked for greater compassion and kindness for his heroines…it is doubtful whether his paintings would evoke great feelings of guilt in the observer." "Marriage, Redundancy or Sin: The Painter's View of Women in the First Twenty-Five Years of Victoria's Reign," in *Suffer and Be Still: Women in the Victorian Age* (Bloomington: Indiana University Press, 1972), 57. Not only does such a reading set up a simplified binary between realism and sentimentalism, without ever defining either term; it neglects the fact that what we are seeing is a specific mode of representation. Certainly Redgrave himself had a more complex understanding of the process of viewing an artwork; see, e.g., his discussion of the relation between beholders and canvases in F. M. Redgrave, *Richard Redgrave, Memoir* (London: Cassell, 1891), 367–70.

[21] Lionel Lambourne, "Richard Redgrave Today," in *Richard Redgrave,* ed. Casteras and Parkinson, 97; Roberts, "Marriage, Redundancy or Sin," 56.

[22] Details of his life at the Academy are found in his diary entries in *Redgrave, Memoir;* the letter to Lord John Russell is reprinted as an appendix to that volume. In his lectures in the 1850s on art education, he elaborates a practical aesthetic that envisions a relation between viewer and artwork in line with the one I suggest in my reading of *The Sempstress.*

Figure 9.2. Richard Redgrave, *The Poor Teacher*. Courtesy of the Shipley Art Gallery, Tyne and Wear Museums.

figures in new ways the aesthetic ambiguities of the 1840s. It can be read as a representation both of a specific subject in the contemporary scene, and of competing notions of the viewer's relationship to painting, the ends of aesthetic experience, and the relationship of the painterly gaze to the claims of everyday life. As contemporary reviewers worked to classify Redgrave's picture, several worried over the way it seemed to invite intimacy between the spectator and the image. At issue was not, as in recent accounts, its objectivity or accuracy in presenting a scene from modern life. Instead critics used Redgrave's image as an occasion to explain the rules of proper engagement between art and its audience. Where their explanations begin to falter, sentimentality emerges as the term that will help to illuminate what might otherwise appear to be murky ground.

At the time that Redgrave painted *The Sempstress,* he was already known for his series of canvases depicting females in distress. The most recent was *The Poor Teacher* (fig. 9.2), first exhibited at the Royal Academy in 1843. Chosen by Exhibition organizers to be hung "on the line" in the great room of the Academy—a placement indicating significant approval—this picture received almost universal praise from critics. In keeping with the nationalist spirit of the summer of 1843, several critics made it exemplary of a certain strain of distinctively "British" painting. Thackeray, writing for the *Pictorial Times,* took the image to be representative of the best contemporary English school of painters, who "paint from *the heart*" what is "natural" and accords with "gentle sentiment," not "from the old heroic, absurd, incomprehensible, unattainable rules." The elegant polish of Redgrave's picture extended to his choice of subject; while her circumstances might be changed, this was clearly, one reviewer remarked, a child "of parents who have moved in a superior circle of society." Demure in her black gown, dainty feet peeking out from under her skirt, the figure is not far from the conventions of genteel portraiture. Her face accords perfectly with what T.S.R. Boase has described as a generic type in the 1830s: from "the pages of the *Keepsake* annuals" to academic paintings, one can find such "an oval face, with a high forehead, small mouth and large, vacant eyes" used to represent the "ideal of feminine beauty" and "ladylike docility." The black dress, with no evident signs of draping on the lower body, gives relief only to those "ladylike" elements of the figure: her face and her long white hands. The technical finish and highlighting of the picture seem perfectly to exemplify Roberts's claim that early Victorian painters "renounce the tactile surface qualities of womanly beauty" in an effort to "stimulate the viewer's sentiments rather than their senses."[23]

It is something of a surprise after the overwhelmingly positive reception of *The Poor Teacher* to chart the vehemently split reaction to Redgrave's *The Sempstress* in 1844. Thackeray, who had admired Redgrave's painting the previous year, now under his guise as the roving Titmarsh of *Fraser's* condemned *The Sempstress* as a work "inspired by that milk-and-water of human kindness, the flavour of which is so insipid to the roast-beef intellect." Redgrave had taken a perfectly acceptable subject from Thomas Hood's poem, "The Song of the Shirt," stripped it of its "manliness," and reduced it to an illustration of "small sentiment." The proof of this feminization was that the work was "extremely popular—gazed at with vast interest by most spectators." The *Athenaeum* reviewer agreed, charging that the picture was of a sort "cherished by the namby-pamby taste of the fine ladies": it was "too sentimental" in its evocation of an "elegant sorrow," and, as in the case of another of Redgrave's paintings at the exhibition, "call[ed] loudly for vigour and correction." In previous years, the *Athenaeum* chided, Redgrave had demonstrated a "genius capable of truer and better things."[24]

---

[23] W. M. Thackeray, "Letters on the Fine Arts, No. 3" (1843), reprinted in *Stray Papers,* ed. Lewis Melville (New York: Kraus Reprints, 1971), 214; Royal Academy supplement, *Art Union* 5 (1843): 174; T.S.R. Boase, *Oxford History of Art: English Art 1800–1870* (Oxford: Clarendon, 1959), 217; Roberts, "Marriage, Redundancy or Sin," 46.

[24] Thackeray, "May Gambols," reprinted in *The Works of W. M. Thackeray,* 26 vols. (London: Smith, Elder, 1886), 25:199, 198; "Royal Academy," *Athenaeum* 864 (18 May 1844): 459; *Times,* 8 May 1844, 7.

Yet elsewhere in their reviews of the Exhibition both critics use sentimentality as a term of approbation, a desirable characteristic in a work of art. Neither describes how one recognizes the inherent qualities of good as opposed to bad sentimental art; those categories are identifiable neither by subject matter nor by a recognizable set of conventions. What the critics do describe is the difference in the viewer's behavior in front of various canvases. When the audience is stimulated to exhibit "vast interest," the aesthetic rules have been violated. The reviewers who dislike *The Sempstress* have remarkably consistent lines on the proper position of the spectator in relation to an artwork, on the universal principles of aesthetic judgment, and on the intellectual nature of taste. Where Redgrave is taken to task, it is not for a lack of skill or faulty composition; it is for the way his painting seems to provoke a too eager response from the viewer. And that relationship, which is characterized as an overly feminized sentimentality, recalls the sensual descriptions of aesthetic experience we have already encountered. In other words, what Thackeray would later call "hysterical sentimentalism" becomes a way of talking about, labeling, and ultimately rejecting a range of troubling contemporary ideas about perception and visual culture.[25]

Before I expand on that point, I would like to look in more detail at the painting to see what it is that these critics seem to register. Casteras deftly sums up most modern readings of the image: "the single-figure format and symbolism of suffering...make this figure a modern martyr looking to heaven for salvation from her fatigue, desolation, and abuse."[26] But there are a number of significant features of this painting that are either only briefly mentioned in most accounts or neglected altogether, features that potentially complicate pat interpretations. As Redgrave records in his diary, he was particularly concerned with the coloring and technique of this painting; indeed, it is one of the few times he commented at all about the process of his work. "I painted it on an entirely new principle," he notes, and he goes on at length to describe the elaborate technique of preparing the ground and the mixing of the colors.[27] He experimented with an egg yolk tempera, a medium described in Cennino's *The Craftsman's Handbook* (late fourteenth century); it was well suited to a painting with an emphasis on shadow and a limited tonal range. Because of the way that egg tempera dries, it must be built up in thin layers; the result is a characteristic hatched or stippled brushwork. As Redgrave has used that brushwork in *The Sempstress,* it gives a very rough appearance of texture to both the background wall and the figure's clothing: one contemporary critic noted this almost tactile quality, remarking on the

---

[25] Thackeray's phrase for Redgrave's work in "Picture Gossip," *Fraser's* (1845), reprinted in *Works* 25:226.

[26] Casteras, *Images of Victorian Womanhood in English Art* (Rutherford, N.J.: Fairleigh Dickinson University Press, 1987), 112. Edelstein gives a guided tour of iconography of the objects in the room that seem to support such a reading ("They Sang 'The Song of the Shirt,'" 202).

[27] Redgrave, *Richard Redgrave,* 44–45.

Figure 9.3. Richard Redgrave, Sketch for *The Sempstress*. Courtesy of the Forbes Magazine Collection, New York. © All rights reserved.

coarse merino fabric of the dress.[28] In contrast to the smooth black skirt of the figure in *The Poor Teacher*—which blocks the light illuminating her face and hand and is flattened against the viewing plane of the picture in a way that denies the possible curve of any nether limb—this red skirt is textured, shaped, and colored so that we can hardly miss the leg closest to us. Although the sempstress is positioned in a way that faintly echoes the pose of the teacher—both facing sideways from the viewer, hands draped on a table and lap, a foot peeking out of the skirt—she is awkwardly seated so that her leg is placed in the center of the painting (it does not line up comfortably with the rest of her body), and the light of the candle is pushed to its limit to highlight this fact. The other spots of high illumination are not, as in *The Poor Teacher,* the high forehead and the delicate hands, but the breasts, the forward shoulder, the neck, and the lower cheek. The play of light invites the

[28] *Times,* 8 May 1844, 7.

eye to travel between these bright spots, and by contrast to the general darkness of the picture, to come to rest on the figure's neck.

It is clear from Redgrave's original sketch of the painting that this presentation is somewhat different from the more straightforward illustration of Hood's verses he had originally planned (fig. 9.3). In the sketch the brightest illumination falls where one might have anticipated it would be: on the white shirt. The figure is seated behind the table, the legs are hidden by the table and the shirt, and her pose is much more natural, less contorted. The full face is exposed by the light and is much more clearly defined. Her face occupies the apex of a central triangle in the picture, articulated with the back of the chair and emphasized here by the compositional grid. This arrangement is used in several of Redgrave's narrative pictures of women in distress; the women function as the upright moral center of the group.[29] The pitcher exists only as a crude sketch, and the bed is in proper perspective behind the figure: the table occupies the space in front of it, as does the chair (a small bit of the bed is visible behind it). Not only does the illumination change in the finished picture; with the movement of the table and the added line of the extended leg, the triangular arrangement changes to shift our eye back to the clock and the draperies of the bed. The use of red on the bedcovers by the woman's feet brings the bed forward and makes her chair appear to be sitting almost on top of the head of it.

So what would be the point of dwelling on the body of this red-clad sempstress, and of foreshortening the perspective so that she is, so to speak, pushed onto her bed? The sempstress was a familiar figure in public discourse, perhaps the most familiar example of exploited contemporary labor at the time. But she was not merely an image of pathos. As R. D. Grainger's Report for the Children's Employment Commission of 1843 and Mayhew's series of 1849 articles on needlewomen documented, the connection between this kind of work and prostitution was a common one.[30] This was particularly true for shirtmakers, who worked not in the shops but on their own, taking in piecework. Redgrave's choice of red reinforces the doubtful morality of this figure; although a number of recent critics have suggested she is a virtuous orphan fallen on hard times, she is not, like the poor teacher, dressed in mourning. In contrast to the smooth, cold surfaces of *The Poor Teacher*, *The Sempstress* brings us back to the "tactile surface qualities" Roberts finds absent in early Victorian portrayals of women. Redgrave uses all the resources at his command—choice of a recognizable figure, color, composition, light, allusion—to play up the sensual aspect of the act of viewing. The picture does

[29] This is most striking in *The Outcast* (1851), where a female figure of doubtful morality is made the narrative and moral focus of the picture.

[30] See *The Unknown Mayhew*, ed. E. P. Thompson and Eileen Yeo (London: Merlin, 1971) 141; for an account of Grainger's report, see Helen Rogers, " 'The Good Are Not Always Powerful, nor the Powerful Always Good': The Politics of Women's Needlework in Mid-Victorian London," *Victorian Studies* 40 (1997): 589–97.

not seek to "stimulate the viewers' sentiments rather than their senses"; it dramatizes the link between emotion and physical sensation.[31]

The result is a painting that brings us back to those metaphors of seduction I outlined earlier. One might say that if the central figure of this canvas portrays the drama of spiritual insight—nearly blind, looking to the heavens for an illumination that the altered lighting of the painting does not necessarily promise—the process of looking at the painting enacts the drama of the desiring eye. The texture and composition emphasize looking with the senses: sight in the body focused on the body. Martin Jay remarks that "it would be premature to speak of an explicit awareness of the desiring, sexualized body as a source of visual experience" in nineteenth-century art, despite the fact that "physiological stimulation" was now "acknowledged as a determinant of sight."[32] And yet this early Victorian painting seems very aware of the complicity of the viewer in enjoying its "aesthetic" gaze at the fallen woman; even the lines Redgrave has chosen from Hood's poem call our attention to the spectator's involvement in prolonging the figure's distress: "Oh! men with sisters dear,/Oh! men with mothers and wives,/It is not linen you're wearing out,/But human creatures' lives."

Although, not surprisingly, no Victorian critic directly comments on this aspect of the painting, the most enthusiastic review of the painting does bring us directly to one of those physical highlights I have mentioned. The painting does not appeal to the intellect, the *Art Union* critic says approvingly: instead we are invited to react to this image from the "heart." As he develops his reading, however, he evidently is not working this head/heart split in the way we might expect. What he describes is two different modes of relation between the viewer and the female figure of the painting. The wrong way of depicting this subject, he proposes, would be to make the figure directly confront the viewer and speak out on her own behalf. Fortunately, Redgrave has not presented us with such "a low-born drudge" who seeks "to proclaim her patient endurance to the vulgar world." Rather, we "read" her body for signs of her "suffering": it is evident "only in the sunken cheek" and "feverish eye."[33] The sentimentality of the painting inheres in two things here. The first is the fact that we have what Michael Fried calls the convention of the "absorptive" subject in nineteenth-century painting: that is, the representation of a figure who seems unaware of the presence of the spectator.[34] For the *Art Union* critic, a figure who *was* aware of the presence of the specta-

---

[31] Roberts, "Marriage, Redundancy or Sin," 46.

[32] Jay, *Downcast Eyes,* 152.

[33] Royal Academy supplement, *Art Union* 6 (1844): 158.

[34] See especially Fried's essay "The Generation of 1863," in *Manet's Modernism, or, The Face of Painting in the 1860s* (Chicago: University of Chicago Press, 1996), where he cites French reviews of absorptive subjects: "It was the sitter's apparent obliviousness to being beheld," Fried argues, that prompted critics to repeatedly use the terms "intimacy," "penetrating," and "delicious," and "that gave rise to the pleasurable experience" these terms record (219).

tor would, paradoxically, have put us at a greater distance from the painting; she would have forestalled our inclination to "read" her body, the process that is the second defining element of a painting that appeals to the "heart." What this critic codes as feeling, in other words, is a sense of physical contact, the immediacy of the exchange between the artwork and the embodied viewer, as well as the passivity of the figure that allows this exchange to take place. It is no surprise to find that at the beginning of his account of the exhibition he champions a version of aesthetic experience rooted in the desire of physically insistent spectators.

The reviewers who most disliked Redgrave's painting dismiss out of hand any suggestion that the spectator might play a role in defining aesthetic value. The *Athenaeum* critic uses *The Sempstress,* which he finds "too sentimental," as an occasion to post a "warning" against the view that art appeals to "the power of feeling and association, which varies with every individual." There must be an aesthetic "criterion...higher and more fixed" than mere feeling, he argues, or the position of art in society will be "reduced very low." Art, Thackeray chimes in at the opening of his 1844 review, instead of responding to public desire, should "inspir[e] delicate sympathies." Unlike Redgrave's picture, whose "unfortunate object makes...coarse demands upon" the spectator, Thackeray commends subjects that are "unobtrusive" in their "sentiment." His description of the ideal, inoffensive painting remarkably resembles Victorian descriptions of the proper wife, a woman who does not stir up the "hysterical sentimentality" of the doubtful figure in Redgrave's work: "It is a comfort," Thackeray explains, "to have such a companion...in a study to look up at when your eyes are tired with work, and to refresh you with its gentle quiet good-fellowship."[35]

Judging by the language of his critics, Redgrave's painting enacts a version of aesthetic experience that touched raw nerves. It played into the growing anxiety in the art world about the effect of the embodied spectator. As it became increasingly difficult to sort out the role of feeling, intellect, and sensation in aesthetic response, critics felt compelled for political and social reasons to insist on their difference. In the reception of *The Sempstress,* unstable categories begin to solidify along particular aesthetic and ideological divides. Those who welcomed new ideas about the spectator's participation in aesthetic experience applauded the painting's evocation of "feeling." For those who rejected aesthetic sensationalism, Redgrave's painting raised red flags. Significantly, it was in the interest of both sides to gloss over the very consciously academic side of the painting. Redgrave's picture contains recognizable allusions to Caravaggio and to Dutch genre painting; the prominent red pitcher and the neat row of pots and pans recall Flemish paintings by, for example, Teniers. The presentation does not pose as direct documentary;

[35] "Royal Academy," *Athenaeum* (1844): 461; Thackeray, *Works,* 25:196, 227.

rather, it foregrounds conventional painterly devices. And although the absorption of the figure produces, at one level, the effect of the viewer's happening on an actual scene, prompting some viewers to react as if this were not an aesthetic representation—"Who can help exclaiming," another painter wrote to Redgrave, "Poor soul! God help her"[36]—Redgrave uses the narrative details of the background to emphasize that this is a constructed image. The details themselves—the candle, the breaking light of dawn—rely on iconic conventions for their meaning. As Redgrave's use of the lines from Hood indicate, this image is already at one remove from "reality": it is an illustration of the poem, a genre, as Martin Meisel has demonstrated, with conventions of its own.[37] The painting is not, then, just a populist rendition of its subject; it is a very educated, self-consciously academic assemblage.

The separation between a sentimental, popular art and an elite, intellectual art that is beginning to take shape in the reviews of *The Sempstress* cannot easily be supported by the painting itself. But in the battle over two kinds of aesthetic response, it seems increasingly important for all sides that what comes to be known as the sentimental be labeled as essentially "nonaesthetic." In Thackeray's review of the 1845 Academy Exhibition, for example, Redgrave's sentimentality is not associated with a particular version of aesthetic experience: it is completely beyond the aesthetic pale. "Is there not something *naive* and simple in this downright way of exciting compassion," he injects, noting that Redgrave's paintings are not real "art," but merely decorative objects worthy to be offered as "Art-Union prizes." When Redgrave himself later wrote about *The Sempstress,* his description was not so different from Thackeray's. Looking back on his early career in an autobiographical essay for the *Art Journal,* Redgrave remarked that his "best efforts" in art had been humanitarian pictures "aimed at calling attention to the trials and struggles of the poor and the oppressed." If in a work like *The Sempstress* "this has been done feebly," he continues, "it has at least been done from the heart."[38] This account sounds quite different from the diary entry in which he approached the picture in purely technical terms. What Redgrave leaves out in his later accounts is that this art "from the heart" is hardly a feeble effort to represent the condition of the lowly, but a skilled use of academic codes and conventions with their own significance in a charged conversation about the ends and means of representation in art.

[36] Redgrave, *Richard Redgrave,* 45. Fried remarks a similar turn in French reviews of the 1860s: "absorption never failed to work its magic...suspending or eliding the distinction between representation and sitter, or at any rate inciting commentators to lose their rhetorical grip on the distinction in their enthusiastic accounts of the picture before them" (*Manet's Modernism,* 200).

[37] Meisel, *Realizations: Narrative, Pictorial, and Theatrical Arts in Nineteenth-Century England* (Princeton, N.J.: Princeton University Press, 1983), chap. 2.

[38] Thackeray, *Works,* 25:225; Redgrave, "Autobiography of Richard Redgrave," *Art Journal* 12 (1850): 49.

In his description of his painting, Redgrave collapses the distance between the painter's relation to his subject and the viewer's response. But elsewhere Redgrave reveals this seeming proximity between two ways of seeing as a carefully staged effect. In an 1868 lecture on painting, Redgrave explores how what we might call the sentimental effect is produced. It depends on the illusion that what the viewer sees on the canvas is a transcription of an actual moment of vision, one that can be made equivalent to the viewer's own moment of encounter in front of the canvas. Of course, Redgrave explains, the image on the canvas is not, as is the embodied viewer, constrained by temporality in this way. The painterly perspective can thus be differentiated from the eye of the camera, a mechanical apparatus that reproduces the limitations of situated moments of vision. If perception located in bodies was notoriously shifting, unstable, then a painting represented the possibility of a perspective decorporealized, taken out of the flux of the moment and frozen in a time that was neither synchronic nor diachronic, but an abstracted mixture of the two. For it is the privilege of the canvas, he argues, to "collate, as it were...incidents in themselves successive," and to display them "as if they were occurring at the same instant."[39] What the viewer sees is a scene as it never happened, an assemblage whose smooth surface conceals the process of collation. In this artistic space, time not only stands still: the painting creates a time outside of real time, yet composed of traces of particular moments in the compositional process. The genius of sentimental art, in Redgrave's account, is that it makes the viewer's response to this artificial construction seem natural. In stimulating the viewer's sensations, it makes him or her forget the mediation of the artist and experience the image as if it exists only in the moment of its reception.

Redgrave's sentimental canvas resembles in some important respects our postmodern efforts of synthetic representation. Like the work of Redgrave's painter, the critic's construction is always an assemblage, a collection of moments into a synchrony that never was. This does not mean either that such moments never existed, nor that they are irretrievably other. Current debates about literary history are so concerned about the difference between critical proximity and distance that they often lose sight of what Redgrave's account reveals: that either position can be seen as a kind of optical illusion. The apparent distance between ourselves and the Victorians is in part the product of the arbitrary critical frame: freeze time, and there follows logically a before and after. Our desire to contain sentimental art within that frame, to dismiss it as part of a naive past, seems to restage the gesture by which Redgrave's reviewers anxiously dismissed his painting. By using such works to stand for what lies beyond the pale, we ensure that some illusions about critical difference will be sustained.

---

[39] "The Treatment of Subject in Painting," reprinted in *Richard Redgrave, Memoir,* 372.

P A R T   I V

VICTORIAN MEANINGS

10. *Knowing and Telling in Dickens's Retrospects*

Rosemarie Bodenheimer

R etrospective narrative is built on an oscillating arrow of time. It se- lects its past and suffuses it with the language and consciousness of the present. All the while it declares the pastness of that past, through a rhetorical assumption of difference: what was unconscious is now articu- lated; what was innocent is now knowing; what was hidden is now exposed. Critical readings of autobiographical narrative add yet another layer of tem- poral complexity, because the critic is also in the position of retrospective narration, pitting a contemporary knowledge or interpretive system against the narrational knowledges of the text under scrutiny. Both inside and out- side the original text, then, someone is claiming to know more about a past than that past knows about itself. Yet, if we abandon the notion that retro- spective narrative "moves forward" toward keener knowledge and articula- tion, if we accept the oscillating arrow as a present created by the simultane- ity of retrospect and prospect, then the question of where knowledge resides and who has power to claim it is released from a teleological hermeneutics and opened for further scrutiny.

Of the canonical Victorian novelists Charles Dickens has always been the easiest to condescend to in the matter of knowledge. Because Dickens's kind of knowledge is wrapped up in metaphor, very rarely abstracted and never theorized, he "presents" (as one might say of a patient) as material custom- made for psychoanalytic, class, and gender analysis. For both nineteenth- and twentieth-century critics "what Dickens knew" has remained as elusive and tantalizing as does the consciousness of Henry James's Maisie to the adults who construct her according to their own purposes. Although I do not claim to know what Dickens knew, I am convinced that his narratives do tell, in one way or another, much of what our recent criticism claims to discover in them. They dramatize, for example, the constructedness of bourgeois subjectivity; they are founded on a deep awareness of the instability of class identification and of identity as a process of fissure and projection. By revisiting Dickens's retrospective narratives during the autobiographical years 1848–1850, I hope to suggest that these narratives are always engaged in a double process of telling what they know about what they seem to silence.

Retrospective activity is not only the mode but the vexed subject of Dickens's early first-person experiments: the so-called autobiographical fragment he offered to his friend John Forster in 1848, and the novel *David Copperfield*, begun early in 1849.[1] These two writings have of course been considered together many times before, particularly in psychobiographical terms. Dickens's account of his father's imprisonment for debt and his own childhood employment at Warren's Blacking warehouse has long held the place of honor in the early portions of biographical accounts and interpretations, where it has played out in many different fashions its role as an explanatory, originary, traumatic, or screen memory.[2] Without rehearsing the variety of psychosocial stories that have been told about Warren's Blacking, I would like to reconsider the fragment as a particular set of retrospective practices carried out by the thirty-six-year-old Dickens at a moment when the long-suppressed secret of his childhood declassing had come to light in another person's memory. *David Copperfield*, which has often been seen by biographers and critics as a fictional resolution or transcendence of Dickens's confrontation with his childhood shame and pain, will be read here as a narrative canny about its own retrospective strategies, one that consistently punctures its tone of genteel reminiscence with images of the narrator's fragmented and uneasy class identifications.[3] Between the two comes the 1848

---

[1] The dating of the fragment is controversial; many scholars suggest earlier dates for the writing. I have accepted Burgis's recent account as authoritative. Nina Burgess, Introduction, in *David Copperfield* (Oxford: Clarendon, 1981). See Collins for a raising of doubts and questions that do not arise in Burgis's narrative. Philip Collins, "Dickens's Autobiographical Fragment and *David Copperfield*," *Cahiers Victoriens et Edouardiens* 20 (1984): 87–96. Neither the original fragment nor the manuscript of Forster's *Life* has survived.

[2] Major interpretations of the fragment may be found in Edmund Wilson, "Dickens: The Two Scrooges," in *The Wound and the Bow* (New York: Oxford University Press, 1947), 1–104; Jack Lindsay, *Charles Dickens: A Biographical and Critical Study* (London: Andrew Dakers, 1950); Albert D. Hutter, "Reconstructive Autobiography: The Experience at Warren's Blacking," *Dickens Studies Annual* 6 (1977): 1–14; Steven Marcus, "Who Is Fagin?" in *Dickens from Pickwick to Dombey* (New York: Simon and Schuster, 1965), 358–78; and Robert Newsom, "The Hero's Shame," *Dickens Studies Annual* 11 (1983): 1–24.

[3] For Edgar Johnson, who is completely sympathetic with the abandoned child in the fragment, Dickens achieved in *David Copperfield* "some inner catharsis, some coming to terms with himself." Edgar Johnson, *Charles Dickens: His Tragedy and Triumph*, 2 vols. (New York: Simon and Schuster, 1952), 2:752. For Robert Patten, the novel was "a way of resolving tensions, of creating a child that would incorporate the old one but convert defeat into victory." Robert L. Patten, "Autobiography into Autobiography: The Evolution of David Copperfield," in *Approaches to Victorian Autobiography*, ed. George Landow (Athens: Ohio University Press, 1979), 282. Alexander Welsh gave a slight jolt to this line of thinking by claiming that both fragment and novel were written from an assured and stable sense of identity that succeeded the period of uncertainty in the pre-*Dombey* years. For him the fragment is a prideful myth of

Christmas story *The Haunted Man,* in which Dickens figured some of the anxieties raised by the writing of the memoir.

My wish is to restore to Dickens's narratives some of the hermeneutical power that, as late twentieth-century readers, we assume for ourselves. It is not uncommon for us to read Victorian stories backward from their endings, as though those endings gather up and discharge the tensions that have been articulated along the way. Although we are perfectly aware that the marketplace shows its face nowhere more clearly than in the ending of a popular novel, we are nonetheless ready to assume a certain ideological flatness based on the overt terms of the plot, in order to articulate contradictions apparently unaccounted for by an "innocent" Victorian text. Vis-à-vis David Copperfield, we want to play the exposing role of Uriah Heep. The essence of my position is simply this: although our languages of interpretation will light him up differently from Victorian ones, Uriah Heep is already on the case.

I

During the 1840s Dickens's imagination began to move tentatively toward confrontations with painful parts of his past that had, until then, emerged only in the coded forms of his fiction. He spent much of that turbulent decade away from England: in America, in Italy, in Switzerland, in Paris. Always on the move, he was restless and slower to produce than he had been during the years of his rapid ascent to fame.[4] In her introduction to the Clarendon *Copperfield,* Nina Burgis has collected and ordered the written indications that Dickens was thinking about his past and about the possibility of autobiography throughout the 1840s. He was also writing down certain hints and memories in letters to Forster, who was officially requested to serve as his biographer in a letter of April 22, 1848.[5] As Forster tells it in *The Life of Charles Dickens,* the blacking warehouse memory might never have been revealed to him had not Forster relayed to Dickens a recollection of Charles Wentworth Dilke's: Dilke remembered having met the child Dickens when he was working in a warehouse near the Strand.[6] If Forster's connection is accurate, it suggests that Dickens was moved to break his silence about the shock of declassing he had experienced as a twelve-year-old

middle age, which allowed Dickens to take pleasure in the difficulties he had triumphantly overcome. Alexander Welsh, *From Copyright to Copperfield* (Cambridge, Mass.: Harvard University Press, 1987), 108, 156–172.

[4] Welsh has described this as a period of Ericksonian moratorium, during which Dickens confronted the challenges to his identity posed by his disturbing reception in America and emerged a greater writer with a fuller capacity for self-representation.

[5] *The Letters of Charles Dickens,* ed. Walter Dexter, vol. 2 (London: Nonesuch Press, 1937–1938), 82–84.

[6] John Forster, *The Life of Charles Dickens,* ed. J.W.T. Ley (London: Cecil Palmer, 1928), 23.

once he knew that he had been observed to be keeping the secret.[7] This scenario—being seen to be silent about shaming experience or knowledge—becomes an important feature of Dickens's retrospective writing. It is one of the many ways Dickens told his obsessional story about the intimate linkage of gentility and underclass or criminal life.[8]

Forster's presentation of the autobiographical fragment in chapter 2 of the *Life* makes confident analysis difficult, because we cannot be certain whether the fragment was written as a continuous narrative, whether some memories were conveyed orally, whether certain sections were quoted only from the proof sheets of *David Copperfield,* or whether Forster himself reshaped, deleted, or even rewrote portions of the quoted text.[9] As they are given, however, the fragment's paragraphs alternate between passages of detailed recollection and passages that bear passionate witness to the overwhelming feelings of despair, shame, humiliation, and abandonment dramatized without emotional distance by the adult narrator. Although they are set pieces of rhetorically controlled emotion and indictment, these sections claim several times that the extremity of the child's suffering "cannot be written"; that "no words can express the secret agony of my soul" (Forster, *Life of Dickens,* 26). A preserve of secrecy and silence, then, is invoked at the very moment of melodramatic confession: whatever the experience was, it was unspeakably worse than *this.* The narrator, on the other hand, positions himself on a witness stand as one who knows, and tells, nothing but the truth. "No advice, no counsel, no encouragement, no consolation, no support, from anyone that I can call to mind, so help me God." And after a series of sentences beginning "I know I do not exaggerate...I know...I know...I know...I know...I know...," he comes to the climax: "I know that, but for the mercy of God, I might easily have been, for any care that was taken of me, a little robber or a little vagabond" (27, 28). The child's own knowledge and feeling is concealed and overwhelmed by the spectacle of the narrator as outraged adult.

---

[7] Forster was apparently told, and believed, that the episode occurred when Dickens was ten. He dates the conversation about Dilke to March or April 1847. There were other factors that may well have precipitated the actual writing of the fragment in the fall of 1848, most importantly the death of Dickens's sister Fanny Dickens Burnett, who had attended the Royal Academy of Music on scholarship while Dickens worked abjectly at Warren's. Presumably they would have shared a secret sibling version of the family story which Dickens reshaped according to his own lights in the fragment.

[8] Sylvia Manning has profitably suggested that the blacking warehouse incident may have been a confirmation, rather than a traumatic source, of Dickens's class fear and guilt. She notes the ongoing social pretension of the Dickens family in the face of skeletons in the family closet, which included grandparents in domestic service and a grandfather who was a "fugitive embezzler." Sylvia Manning, "Masking and Self-Revelation: Dickens's Three Autobiographies," *Dickens Studies Newsletter* 7 (1976): 72.

[9] For Forster's habit of rewriting and "improving," see Madeline House and Graham Story, eds., Preface to *The Letters of Charles Dickens,* vol. 1, Pilgrim Edition (Oxford: Clarendon, 1965), xi–xix.

The narrator describes his twelve-year-old self as a "solitary and self-dependent child (Forster, *Life of Dickens,* 34), but the fragment constructs solitude primarily as a state of being looked at.[10] As David Copperfield was to observe, the child is "More solitary than Robinson Crusoe, who had nobody to look at him and see that he was solitary."[11] Dickens stages several scenes of three-way specular encounter in which he calls attention to his present self looking at the child while it is observed by (past) others. Eating-houses in particular are theaters for the display of the child-as-spectacle; they reproduce the scenario in which his shame is displayed in the act of being seen to keep the secret of his plight. When the child goes into "the best dining-room at Johnson's alamode beef house," the narrator comments: "What the waiter thought of such a strange little apparition, coming in all alone, I don't know; but I can see him now, staring at me as I ate my dinner, and bringing up the other waiter to look" (Forster, *Life of Dickens,* 26–27). In a repetition of the scene, the child goes into a pub and demands a glass of "your very best—the VERY best—ale," and the landlord calls his wife, who "joined him in surveying me. Here we stand, all three, before me now, in my study in Devonshire-terrace." In this scene the staring adults ask questions, and the child lies about his name, age, living situation, and occupation, "that I might commit nobody" (32). When the working-class protector Bob Fagin attempts to escort the child home after an illness, the child is too ashamed to acknowledge that he is going to his family in the Marshalsea, so he shakes hands on the steps of a house near Southwark Bridge. "As a finishing piece of reality in case of his looking back, I knocked at the door, I recollect, and asked, when the woman opened it, if that was Mr. Robert Fagin's house" (30).

What Dickens makes of his childhood is a complex image in which the narrator watches the child who is seen to be silent about his condition, as well as the watchers to whom the child is an object of curiosity or pity. In her study of Dickensian narration, Audrey Jaffe describes a clear split and an inequality of power between invisible narrators, who maintain their subjectivity because they hold the power of the unseen watcher, and characters, whose visibility turns them into objects, or victims, in someone else's story. In first-person narratives, "the subject of narrative can imaginatively avoid becoming a character in someone else's narrative simply by making others into characters in his or her own story."[12] This description gets close

---

[10] There is enough evidence of continuing family contact in the fragment itself to suggest the exaggeration of these protestations. For a fine defense of the fragment's validity of feeling, however, see Robert Newsom's account of Dickens's shame as a major disorientation and threat to identity, which can involve a sense of self-abandonment as well as a heightened sense of being looked at, by others and by the self. Robert Newsom, "The Hero's Shame," *Dickens Studies Annual* 11 (1983): 1–24.

[11] Charles Dickens, *David Copperfield,* ed. George H. Ford (Boston: Riverside, 1958), 63. All further references cited in the text as *DC.*

[12] Audrey Jaffe, *Vanishing Points: Dickens, Narrative, and the Subject of Omniscience* (Berkeley: University of California Press, 1991), 115.

to the dynamic of the autobiographical fragment, in which the narrator dramatizes the child's pathos in terms of his visibility to others, and flaunts his own power to turn such moments into managed theatrical performances.

Yet the narrator and the child are not quite so readily distinguished. The secret-keeping past self also serves as a mirror or double to the confessional narrator. They fuse, for example, in an odd sentence describing the occasion when the child complains to his father about being lodged at a distance from his family, and is provided with a new room near the Marshalsea, where the rest of the family then lived: "It was the first remonstrance I had ever made about my lot, and perhaps it opened up a little more than I had intended." The child is provided with a solitary back-attic which he experiences as a "Paradise, " perhaps because he has a window prospect from which he can see without being seen (Forster, *Life of Dickens,* 29). But the loudly "remonstrating" autobiographer seems to fear the loss of interpretive control that comes with his own first confession, partly because the episode suggests a level of parental attention that is vehemently denied elsewhere in the text. Moreover, the child's pathos and innocence is belied by his craftiness and secrecy; just as he is falsely represented as two years younger than his age at the time, he is far more knowing than the reader is allowed to know. The narrator is not ashamed of the child's shame; in fact he is proud of the child's silences and concealments. The two figures exist, then, in a present specular relation that dramatizes an uneasy interchangeability among the positions of knowledge, concealment, and self-exposure.[13]

This relation between the silent, crafty child and the outraged narrator represents Dickens's first response to the threat contained in Dilke's (and then Forster's) knowledge of his brief stint as a working-class child. Like all Victorian writers, Dickens would have been well aware of the power that could be wielded by biographers revealing secrets after an author's death. By entrusting his designated biographer with the autobiographical fragments, he could forestall posthumous family scandal by telling the story himself, while continuing to live and write without giving away his fertile secret. The fragment would eventually provide the retrospective knowledge through which his writing would be interpreted (as it has, to an extent Dickens could hardly have imagined). And the narrator's cry of outrage and accusation would overwhelm the figure of the canny child horrified by his descent into working-class drudgery, a figure that might otherwise lie open to posthumous unmasking and accusation.

---

[13] Although Jaffe argues for a definite inequality of power between narrators and characters, her incidental comments and questions often support my own sense that identity in Dickens depends upon the interchangeability of subject and object, so that, as Jaffe puts it in her discussion of *Bleak House,* "subject and object exist, suspended, only as reflections of one another." Jaffe, *Vanishing Points,* 136.

II

Writing the memories for Forster certainly "opened up a little more than [Dickens] had intended." In the fictions he invented during the same period, Dickens interrogated, reformulated, and refragmented the first semisecret acknowledgment of his past. *The Haunted Man,* a strange Christmas book written in October and November 1848, was composed nearly at the same time as the memoir. Although it is not a first-person narrative, it worries the lures and threats of autobiography under the cover of a sentimental plot about the sacredness of memory.

This fable is generated from a dialogue between a man haunted by his past, the renowned chemist Redlaw, and a Spectre or Phantom who is an exact physical replica of Redlaw. In this dialogue of mirror-figures, the Phantom tells Redlaw the story of his own past; his is the voice of autobiographical narration.[14] Both characters use the first person, as though they were in competition for their shared identity. "I am he, neglected in my youth and miserably poor, who strove and suffered," the Phantom begins, and Redlaw returns, "I *am* that man." The story told by the Phantom is full of loss, pain, accusation, and resentment; it is as though Dickens had personified the narrative voice of the fragment in a ghostly character. Redlaw hears it, claims it, and resists it; he is haunted by his own story, but he won't tell it himself. Splitting suffering from telling, the doubled figures restage the memoir's specular relation between child and adult as an adult conflict about confronting and accusing the past.

Then the Phantom turns into a Faustian tempter: he offers Redlaw the opportunity to be rid of his haunting memories. The "ghost's bargain" comes with the condition that Redlaw's mere presence will destroy the power of memory, and therefore of sympathy, in the people he encounters. The workings of this curse and its eventual cure form the moral business of a familiar Christmas hearth story that insists that keeping memories alive and green is the key to love and domestic harmony. But what does the strange bargain mean? The same voice that tells the resentful tale aloud promises freedom from it, as autobiography might promise exorcism. The condition of this freedom is a sort of publication: a mysterious diffusion that blights the moral capacities of those it touches. Redlaw does not know exactly how his blighting power works; like publication, or like infection, it spreads beyond his control or knowledge (*HM*, 305). *The Haunted Man* might then be read as an allegory of autobiographical anxiety: what uncontrollable damage might result from "giving away" ineradicable memories? What would happen to Dickens's relationship with his audiences if he revealed his class-tainted past and his personal anger and shame?

---

[14] Charles Dickens, "The Haunted Man," in *The Christmas Books*, ed. Michael Slater, vol. 2 (London: Penguin, 1971), 264–68. Further references cited in the text as *HM*.

Redlaw's acceptance of the ghost's bargain immediately precipitates the appearance of a monstrous child, a second double-figure who follows Redlaw as his shadow. This beast-like wild child is immune to all fellow feeling, and cares only about accumulating food and money. He is a recognizably guilty version of the child in the autobiographical fragment, obsessed with counting shillings and meals, "who might easily have been, for any care that was taken of me, a little robber or a little vagabond." Like a photographic negative, this figure suggests a reversal of the fragment's portrait of the "little gentleman." The wild child's only sign of humanity lies in his frantic desire to be near the redemptive woman of the fable; his obsessive attraction to the maternal hearth also reverses the maternal betrayal articulated in the fragment's pathos-ridden portrait of the innocent child who must forage for himself.

In the writing of *The Haunted Man* Dickens managed to figure his anxiety about the general dangers of autobiographical telling, as well as to expose some other sides of the story he told in the memoir. In an 1856 letter to Wilkie Collins, Dickens wrote, after having made some autobiographical confession, "This is the first time I ever set down these particulars, and, glancing them over, I feel like a wild beast in a caravan describing himself in his keeper's absence."[15] Reinstating the keeper, the Christmas tale contains the autobiographical impulse within a highly moralized cage of plot, strips the precociously knowing child of his pathos and innocence, replaces accusatory recollection with pastoral memory, and pays its dues to maternal love. *David Copperfield*, Dickens's "favourite child" (*DC*, 3), elaborates brilliantly, through its multiply specular techniques, on the two sides of the retrospective act that come into view when the autobiographical fragment and *The Haunted Man* are juxtaposed. The novel is less a resolution than a medium in which the specular exchanges within and between the two earlier texts could be multiplied and played out, as in a liquid suspension.

III

David Copperfield has recently become a favorite text through which to think about the cultural construction of Victorian subjectivity. I take it as a current consensus that the novel celebrates its hero's gradual achievement, through the bourgeois virtues of hard work and self-discipline, of a middle-class identity guaranteed by the rocklike security of his marriage to a paragon of the domestic sphere. This virtuous stability is rendered innocent by the

---

[15] *Letters of Charles Dickens*, 2:777–78. I am indebted to Jean Ferguson Carr for pointing to this metaphor. Carr goes on to use it in a different way, casting Forster as the designated "keeper" of Dickens's autobiographical secrets. Jean Ferguson Carr, "Dickens and Autobiography: A Wild Beast and His Keeper," *ELH* 52 (1985): 447–69.

novel's system of displacement: the othering and casting out of several figures on whom are projected the ugly undersides of ambition, illicit sexual desire, class shame, and class contempt that David represses in himself. The creation of a "sanitized" protagonist is often assumed to demonstrate the novel's construction of, or at least its impossible desire for, a unified middle-class subject.[16]

Although this outline has some plausibility if the book is read backward from its ending, few of the novel's pages are devoted to thinking about what David ends up with, and many are precisely about how such endings do not occur. The novel is full of domestic spaces, all variants of one another, most of them based on absence, all in one way or another violated or threatened. David's so-called progress is more like a perpetual re-cycling: he cannot journey to a new place or announce a clear break with a painful past without being immediately confronted by a figure who revives that past or a situation that bears an uncanny resemblance to one he has left behind. The past is always present, both in the plot and in the proleptic retrospection, in which what purports to be memory acts simultaneously as prediction. The fantasy of middle-class security founded on a rock is compelling only to the extent that it illuminates the disturbing fragility of class identity that haunts the novel. Once immersed in the narrative texture, we are always on uncertain ground.

The question of how to read that uncertainty is fundamentally connected with the problems of knowledge in the novel. What is the relative status of innocence and knowledge? And who knows what about whom? Answers to these questions depend on the way retrospective narrative is imagined. The entity we can't help but call "David" is a series of positions, dispersed first among other characters, and second among narrating perspectives. Although the narrative frequently creates a gap between narrator-David and character-David by calling attention to the act of retrospection, or by dramatizing an experienced voice commenting with affectionate detachment on a younger self, there are also many passages in which it is impossible to disentangle the knowledges of the split "I."[17]

---

[16] D.A. Miller's entrancing essay "Secret Subjects, Open Secrets" (chap. 6) is a wonderful meditation on the way that being seen to keep a secret creates an (illusory) guarantee of subjectivity in a determining social system. D.A. Miller, *The Novel and the Police* (Berkeley: University of California Press, 1988). For the most thorough rendition of the case for the domestic "solution," see Mary Poovey, *Uneven Developments: The Ideological Work of Gender in Mid-Victorian England* (Chicago: University of Chicago Press, 1988), chap. 4. See also Elizabeth Langland, *Nobody's Angels: Middle-Class Women and Domestic Ideology in Victorian Culture* (Ithaca: Cornell University Press, 1995), 82–88; and the work on class subtexts by John O. Jordan, "The Social Sub-Text of David Copperfield," *Dickens Studies Annual* 14 (1985): 61–92; and Chris R. Vanden Bossche, "Cookery, not Rookery: Family and Class in *David Copperfield*," *Dickens Studies Annual* 15 (1986): 87–109.

[17] Audrey Jaffe's study offers just one example of how difficult it is to work within a simple narrator-character duality. Her discussion of *David Copperfield* turns on the difference between invisible narrator and objectified character but finds itself nonetheless appealing to a unified

To argue that the novel is a system of repressions depends upon separating the innocence of the character from the knowingness of the retrospective narrator. One must argue that someone—but who?—is keeping "David"— whoever that is—innocent; that is, someone is refusing to name the fact that "David" acts and feels just like Uriah Heep in some ways, just like James Steerforth in some ways, just like Mr. Dick in other ways, just like Rosa Dartle in yet others. Not admitting his resemblance to others, "David" is then rendered untainted by the sexual and class desires and vengeances that run rampant in his friends and acquaintances. By refusing to blame those who betray him he becomes himself blameless. He is, the argument goes, never made to accept responsibility for knowing the contradictions of his culture that are played out by virtually every other character. Mary Poovey formulates the problem ingeniously: she sees the duplicity of the class system replicated in the duplicity of the narrative device: "the splitting of the protagonist into an innocent hero, who does not know such deceitfulness because he is too young and good, and a worldly narrator, who knows but will not tell."[18] Audrey Jaffe finds that the narrator's identification with his younger self renders him "unwilling and unable to articulate the implications of what he sees."[19] Such distinctions make it possible to demonstrate the novel's willful construction of an innocent middle-class subject in the face, so to speak, of all the evidence against it.

The nature of retrospective narrative, which produces an already knowing, already guilty innocence, makes it difficult to sustain the kind of separation on which this argument depends. The problem Dickens faced in *David Copperfield* was how to tell a loving story about aspiration fueled by shame, guilt, and resentment that won't go away. By dispersing "David" among multiply specular possibilities, and by orchestrating his implication with the arrogance of middle-class power and wiles of unscrupulous ambition, the novel manages both to display the components of the problem and to provide perspectives on the pastoral voice with which it charms and soothes its middle-class readers.

Most of the characters in *Copperfield,* like the figures in the autobiographical fragment and *The Haunted Man,* have painful, humiliating pasts from which they try in vain to dissociate themselves. Each one reanimates anxieties about telling, suppressing, or exposing secrets. Rosa Dartle's scar writes her past on her body, and she makes the writing visible by inflaming it with barely suppressed rage. Betsey Trotwood obsessively purges her tiny lawn of donkeys but cannot keep her exiled husband from making periodic returns. Mr. Dick transforms his awful memories into the metaphor of King Charles's head, but the metaphor relieves him only for the length of a kite-

---

"David," and sometimes to "Dickens" or even "a more controlling narrator." Jaffe, *Vanishing Points,* 112–28.

[18] Poovey, *Uneven Developments,* 121.

[19] Jaffe, *Vanishing Points,* 125.

fly. Uriah Heep's experience of lower-middle-class humiliation becomes a desire to use his knowledge to dominate and humiliate the middle class in return. Mr. Micawber erases his past failures by living in an ever hopeful present that condemns him to a life of cyclical repetition. Agnes Wickfield—for even she has a story—lives silently and consciously amid the humiliation of her father's alchoholism and the Heeps' predatory invasion of her domestic space. Through the proliferation of instances, the question of how to compose a retrospect—a narrative relation between past and present—becomes a central concern. Keeping David's narrative tonality in the state of knowing-but-not-drawing-conclusions, Dickens situates it amid a whole set of other relations between knowledge and power, expression and silence. And David's narrative may well be Dickens's personification of a knowledge that struggles quite openly both to display itself and to compose itself in a "mannerly" or genteel way.

I take as my first examples the moments that often hook our twentieth-century imaginations by calling attention to themselves as repressions. When David's mother dies—after ruining his young life through her remarriage—he claims that he remembered her from then on "as the young mother of my earliest impressions." "The idea of her as she had been of late had vanished from me," he says; and "In her death she winged her way back to her calm untroubled youth, and cancelled all the rest." The dead baby on her breast "was myself, as I had once been, hushed for ever on her bosom" (*DC*, 109). Like Clara Copperfield, James Steerforth is not to be condemned for his sexual betrayal; he, too, is covered with a prebetrayal memory, "lying easily, with his head upon his arm, as I had often seen him lie at school" (337, 607). It is difficult to see how such moments constitute repressions when they are so forthcoming about being repressions. In Dickens's characteristic way, everything gets into the sentences, one way or another. David knows he has been betrayed; there is plenty to "cancel." His desire to fix the betrayer in an idyllic "time before" is presented as an act of the imagination that desires to dwell upon innocence and wishes to "hush forever" the indictments it is capable of making.

Moreover, the moments this imagination chooses as its innocent beginnings were never innocent to begin with. The so-called Edenic unity with the mother is narrated in chapter 2 as an already fallen state of separation and knowledge. This present-tense garden dream, where "the fruit clusters on the trees, riper and richer than fruit has ever been since, in any other garden," is but "a preserve of butterflies"; it is full of emptiness—empty pigeon-house, empty dog-house—figuring the empty place of the father. The "I" stands by, already guilty and pretending; while his mother gathers fruit, he's "bolting furtive gooseberries and trying to look unmoved." The fragile pastoral is instantly wiped away by a great wind, to be replaced by an Oedipal drama in which the son is already knowing, already on to his mother's vanity: "nobody knows better than I do that she likes to look so well, and is proud of being so pretty" (*DC*, 20). Like so many other memories conjured up in the present tense, this one is proleptic: it already knows what's going to happen and tells us so. The "pre-knowingness" of the narrative is spelled out again in David's first dialogue: he asks about second marriages and then, lo and behold, his mother brings Murdstone home. If we return to the passage in which David first watches Steerforth sleeping at school, it becomes clear that this image of the sleeper, also surrounded by premonitory warnings of a "veiled future," functions as a desire for unconsciousness even in the original scene. There has been nothing innocent about Steerforth's extraction of protection money or David's acquiescence to Steerforth's "great power" on that first evening of their acquaintance (75). Such passages present a David who chooses to be silent about matters both he and the reader clearly understand.

This narrative, then, does not so much indulge in repression as represent its activities. What David fails to say is never a surprise; we have known it all along. Moreover, everything he fears to be or to say is done or spoken for him, by some other character who replicates some situation of his own. The problem this novel ultimately raises is not that it represses or displaces knowledge about middle-class instability, culpability, or fear of sexual and underclass contamination, for such knowledge is everywhere on its surface.[20] As I understand it, *David Copperfield* is concerned about what to do with that knowledge, and it is here that it engages questions that separate it from those we have lately been inclined to pose.

IV

Retrospective stories regularly produce a dispersal and multiplication of subjectivity among various characters: how is it possible to define an "I" without reflecting or refracting it through others? Throughout his writing Dickens revels in doubles, partners, and parodies. "The other one," as Jonas Chuzzlewit puts it, is always present to his imagination. In fact, it is virtually impossible to be alone in Dickens: in their most solitary moments, his characters produce in the narrative an answering gaze. Even in descriptions of deserted landscapes, a head will, likely as not, pop unexpectedly into the scene.

In *David Copperfield* the multiplication of character is particularly rich in implication. The famous opening sentence, "Whether I shall turn out to be the hero of my life, or whether that station will be held by anybody else, these pages must show," proclaims a narrative of uncertain identity and antici-

---

[20] As D. A. Miller puts it, "the social function of secrecy isomorphic with its novelistic function is not to conceal knowledge, so much as to conceal the knowledge of the knowledge." Miller, *Novel and the Police*, 206. While Miller offers a contrast between the subjectivity of David and the boxes that enclose other characters, I would see "David" as a series of splits personified by those other characters.

pates a potential interchangeability between the "I" and an indefinite number of "anybody elses" (*DC*, 9). These interchangeabilities do not stop at boundaries of gender: characters marked as female participate in the mirroring and elaboration of the "I." David is not so much separated from as filled with other characters, each of whom plays out a variant of his shaky class and gender positions.

Dickens announces the interchangeability of subjectivities through dream states, through David's "fascinations" with others, and through the many appearances of characters' heads in windows.[21] The window—a kind of two-way mirror—appears frequently in Dickens (and ubiquitously in *David Copperfield*) to evoke an unstable field of specular and interchangeable identity. The narrator of the autobiographical fragment recalls with special intensity a particular coffee-shop with a glass-plate painted with the sign COFFEE-ROOM "addressed towards the street." From inside it had to be "read...backward on the wrong side MOOR EEFFOC" (Forster, *Life of Dickens*, 28). Just as the ordinary name can be simultaneously read from an "inside" point of view that turns it into an exotic insult, window scenes create reciprocal gazes that double characters "backward on the wrong side."

The window metaphor is multiplied and diffused throughout the text of *David Copperfield*. When David bites Murdstone and is confined to his room for five days, the passage describing both his culpability and his shame rewrites the autobiographical fragment with a conviction that is lacking in chapter 11, where Dickens simply transcribes parts of the memoir into the text of the novel.[22] David watches the other boys playing outside "from a distance within the room, being ashamed to show myself at the window lest they should know I was a prisoner" (*DC*, 53). The passage resonates with the language of the memoir: "The length of those five days I can convey no idea of to any one. They occupy the place of years in my remembrance.... all this appears to have gone round and round for years instead of days, it is so vividly and strongly stamped on my remembrance." When David is sent

---

[21] Windows in Dickens are often discussed in relation to the moment in the autobiographical fragment when the child, working in the window of Warren's Blacking, is observed in his dexterity by little crowds of passersby. One day after the father is released from prison but while the child is still working Dickens sees his father approach the window and wonders "how he could bear it" (Forster, *Life of Dickens*, 34). This scene has been singled out as especially traumatic and has been linked to the scene in *Oliver Twist* when Fagin and Monks peer through the window at the newly "middle class" Oliver, as well as to Pip's fear, in *Great Expectations*, of being watched through the forge window by a scornful Estella. See Marcus, "Who Is Fagin?" 370–375; Newsom, "Hero's Shame," 16; and Peter Ackroyd, *Dickens* (New York: HarperCollins, 1991), 94. I would emphasize the typicality of this specular encounter in the fragment as a whole. As in other passages, the narration shifts from the child-as-spectacle to the point of view of the one who looks at him—in this case the specular figure of the father, lately observed by the son in his own imprisonment.

[22] The transcription of the memoir into the Murdstone and Grinby episode is unconvincing, because the excessive emotion does not quite fit with the situation described in the novel. This does not seem to be a common opinion; for praise of Dickens's seamless incorporation of fragment into novel, see especially Collins, "Dickens's Autobiographical Fragment," 93–95.

away to school and condemned to wear a placard reading "Take care of him. He bites," he suffers in a hell of imagined gazes directed at his back by servants and tradesmen, until he begins to believe that he may be identical with his label, "a kind of wild boy who did bite" (68). Being read "backward on the wrong side" by servants and tradespeople replicates the scenarios of the memoir in a way that includes both the victimized spectacle-child of the fragment and its wild child double-figure in *The Haunted Man*. David has, after all, bitten back. These doubts about his identity are underlined by the next image in the text: the old door on which his schoolmates have carved, securely and indelibly, their own middle-class names.

Windows appear regularly to announce the presence of characters whose reciprocal gazes destabilize innocent or pastoral versions of the self. As he begins the second chapter, the narrator dramatizes the act of becoming a spectator to his own earliest memories, conjuring "out of the cloud" present-tense images of the house and garden. It is not long before this sentence appears: "There is one cock who gets upon a post to crow, and seems to take particular notice of me as I look at him through the kitchen window, who makes me shiver, he is so fierce" (*DC*, 18–19). The watcher is instantly transformed into the watched by a figure whose ostentatious and angry crowing punctures the sweetly sad tone of pastoral memory. Betsey Trotwood provides a "proof of her identity" by first appearing with her nose against the window, terrifying the timid mother she will later replace (11). When David arrives at Betsey's house he reciprocates by looking into the parlor window. Finding there an "unbroken stillness" he looks to the window above, at the disconcerting countenance of Mr. Dick, an avatar of his autobiographical endeavor (152). This double is later redoubled, when David revisits Blunderstone Rookery in solitary pilgrimage, and sees the face of "a poor lunatic gentleman" watching at the window from which he had formerly gazed at the tombstone of his dead father (249). Uriah Heep, another of David's important avatars, appears first as "a cadaverous face" in "a small window on the first floor" of the Wickfield house (173).

In chapter 7 the narrator recurs to the habit of staging himself as spectator to his present-tense memories, this time to characterize his days at Creakle's school. David's perverse fascination with the schoolmaster's cruel power is rendered in a remarkable window scene:

> Here I am in the playground, with my eye still fascinated by him, though I can't see him. The window at a little distance from which I know he is having his dinner, stands for him, and I eye that instead. If he shows his face near it, mine assumes an imploring and submissive expression. (*DC*, 76)

This passage, like the others, places David and Creakle in a relation of specular exchange. Brilliantly entangling the "I" with what the "eye" is drawn to, it suggests that David is deeply implicated in the worship of power, that like Uriah Heep he is privy to the hypocrisy of humility that fraudulently maintains an appearance of acquiescence to class or power difference. The implicit connection of identity with the window "which stands for him" provides one of those extraordinary moments in which Dickens's narrative tells what it's up to in a fleeting phrase.

V

David's multiple engagements with other characters who play out his own identity splits are staged most intensely in those scenes where he plays the role of silenced witness or spectator. I will concentrate on two prominent examples: the firing of Mr. Mell (chapter 7), and Rosa Dartle's attack on the seduced and abandoned Emily (chapter 50). These moments have a strange power, a concentration of erotic energy that is never absorbed or explained out of existence by the plot structure. Eve Sedgwick has described comparable encounters as they appear in Dickens's late novels, where erotic rivalry creates male homosocial bonds whose fantasy energies are "mapped along the axes of social and political power; so that the revelation of intrapsychic structures is inextricable from the revelation of the mechanism of class domination."[23] This extraordinarily suggestive formulation can help to illuminate *David Copperfield,* though I would add that Dickens also incorporates sexually (or metaphorically) fallen female figures into the structure of male fantasies about class power and humiliation.

In the schoolmaster, Mr. Mell, David encounters a grown-up version of the child in the autobiographical fragment: a shamed, anxious, and yet loving child of an indigent, institutionalized parent, who pretends to be no one's child in order to maintain his status in the eyes of his employer. When Mell brings the boy David to visit an old woman in an almshouse, the writing conjures up the liminal state between sleeping and waking that so often in Dickens announces the blurring of boundaries between characters. Both the recollecting narrator and the sleepy child are said to experience this condition, in which "she fades in her turn, and he fades, and all fades, and there is no flute, no Master, no Salem House, no David Copperfield, no anything but heavy sleep" (*DC,* 65–66). In that nonstate, David sees, without naming his knowledge, that the old woman is Mr. Mell's mother.

The revelation of this "low" connection, confided in a secret and undramatized conversation between David and his upper-class protector Steerforth, leads to the firing of Mr. Mell in a scene that stages his public humiliation before a class of manically energetic jeering boys: "laughing boys, singing boys, talking boys, dancing boys, howling boys; boys shuffled with their feet,

---

[23] Eve Kosofsky Sedgwick, *Between Men: English Literature and Male Homosocial Desire* (New York: Columbia University Press, 1985), 162.

boys whirled about him, grinning, making faces, mimicking him behind his back and before his eyes; mimicking his poverty, his boots, his coat, his mother, everything about him that they should have had consideration for" (*DC,* 80). Mell stands in for David/Dickens, receiving exactly the treatment that David had feared from his schoolmates when he arrived at the school wearing on his back the placard that precipitates identity splits within, and the kind of humilation staged in the memoir in the repeated scenes showing the child as the object of speculation for others.

Hovering on the brink of violence, the firing scene is overloaded with currents and cross-currents of feeling that eroticize the relation between David's admiration of Steerforth's class power and his identification with its victim. Mell, David, and Steerforth are all parts of the conflict between knowing and telling: the son who hushes up his parent's circumstances, the telling child who betrays the secret, the arrogant public exposer who displays the secret, and the declassed adult whose hand on the child's head protects and forgives him for his betrayal. It is given to Mell to stutter out in uncanny repetitions the autobiographical work that this episode performs: "I have not forgotten myself, I—I have remembered myself, sir" (*DC,* 81–82).

Perhaps the most disconcerting scene in *David Copperfield* occurs when David, hidden behind a door, spies on Rosa Dartle's ferocious attack on the fallen Emily (chapter 50). Rosa appears as another uncanny figure who undoes David's innocent and polite responses to Steerforth. Her scar is to David's eye an autobiographical writing on the body, a metaphor for the undisguisable power of represssed resentment. When he retires to sleep he finds her portrait "looking eagerly at me," and he returns the gaze: "The painter hadn't made the scar, but *I* made it, and there it was, coming and going" (*DC,* 232). As with Creakle and the window that "stands for him," the specular relation is an internal one, independent of the other's presence.

In Rosa's scene with Emily the identifications run several ways at once, casting David simultaneously in the roles of seducer, punisher, punished, and betrayed woman. The confrontation between the two women who share a history of loving Steerforth despite his seduction and betrayal presents a case of excessive rage against one who mirrors back or stands for the self. Rosa vehemently denies that she and Emily have anything in common, although she has been drawn to Emily exactly because she wants to gaze upon, reject, and threaten to expose an image of herself. The extremity of Rosa's rage—the moment when she strikes at Emily—is sparked when Emily portrays herself as the innocent, loving, and trusting victim of Steerforth's deceit. Rosa wants to discredit this "pretty mask" (*DC,* 552) as she wants to attack David's own assumption of innocence and betrayal in the matter of Steerforth. She wants, in other words, to destroy the sentimental way David has told Emily's story—and his own—as the story of an innocent victim, by replacing it with one in which Emily is a conniving, class-contaminating seductress.

David represents himself as frozen and mesmerized by the scene, periodically erupting in spurts of nearly ludicrous emotion. "How long was I to bear this? How long could I bear it?" (552). There is little to prevent him from rushing in to end the confrontation except the need to witness the drama of his subject positions. The fallen woman who stole Steerforth away must be adequately punished, with Rosa acting as David's surrogate. David must himself be adequately punished for being, like Emily, sexually and socially attracted to Steerforth's status as a promise of conferred gentility and power. Finally, David and Steerforth's mixed desire and contempt for working-class Emily must be expressed aloud by Rosa. As in the firing of Mr. Mell, David is cast as a silent witness to his own multiple and contradictory identifications, while violent, excessive emotions mark the drama in ways that are not diminished or recaptured by the plot.

By novel's end David is in a state of depressed self-punishment, as if he mutely understands that the deaths of Dora, Steerforth, and Ham, the fall of Emily, and even the exposure and imprisonment of Uriah Heep are parts of an emotional history for which he is responsible. His punishment takes the form of denying himself Agnes. As he has so often done before, he desires to erase his history, imagining a time when "I might possibly hope to cancel the mistaken past, and to be so blessed as to marry her," only to conclude, "She might have been, but that was past!" (*DC*, 624–25). Agnes's answer, the novel's sentimental climax, repudiates the myth of new beginnings and cancelled pasts that has lured David on through the entire course of the narrative: she says, "I have loved you all my life!" (658). Like Ham Peggotty and like Rosa Dartle, Agnes has been repeatedly rejected and hurt by the lover with whom she grew up as with a sibling. Her refusal to elaborate on what she endures from her loyalties in the face of repeated betrayals—not to mention her father's alcoholism, blackmail, forgery, and extortion—marks her, of course, with the sign of all-sacrificial Victorian womanhood. It also marks her with the sign of knowledge. She knows the worst; she always has; but she loves. When David marries Agnes he marries, so to speak, a forgiven version of his own history.[24]

VI

David's "achievement" of Agnes is the symbolic end of a process in which David himself is repeatedly seen to be silent, while the drama of what he knows is compulsively staged in the theater of his consciousness. The effect,

[24] Kerry McSweeney comes to a related conclusion, that Agnes "is the epitome and embodiment of David's past" who reconciles both good and painful memories (111). McSweeney's essay also follows the path from fragment to novel, with a very different emphasis on the Wordsworthian "inner" identity created through the continuity of memory in the novel. Kerry McSweeney, "*David Copperfield* and the Music of Memory," *Dickens Studies Annual* 23 (1994): 93–119.

finally, is not that "David" remains innocent but that his way of talking remains polite. Politeness is the narrative guarantee of a gentility that is otherwise in doubt, shamefully implicated with seduction and criminality. But even politeness is endangered.

David's most obvious double-figure is Uriah Heep, who derives power from his knowledge of the contradictions, silences, and verbal pieties that sustain middle-class life.[25] Like Rosa Dartle, but more intimately, Heep undermines the polite poses of David's writing. His ever-watchful eyes, "so unsheltered and unshaded, that I remember wondering how he went to sleep" (*DC*, 173), are mesmerizing. As they appear in David's returned gaze, these eyes can see around the barrier of writing:

> Though his face was toward me, I thought, for some time, that he could not see me; but looking that way more attentively, it made me uncomfortable to observe that, every now and then, his sleepless eyes would come below the writing, like two red suns, and stealthily stare at me for I dare say a whole minute at a time, during which his pen went, or pretended to go, as cleverly as ever. (175)

Throughout the novel Uriah's lashless eyes can read "below the writing," discerning there the hidden skeletons of David's class shame and desire.

In chapter 25 David unwillingly invites Uriah into his rooms, his bed, his nightcap, and his nightmares—all because he adheres to the rules of politeness. Uriah's power over David arises from his manipulations of those social rules that regulate what may and may not be spoken aloud. He remembers every polite lie David has told him in the past, and he pretends to treat each as if it were literally and sincerely meant. He repeatedly adjures David to remember, to recollect, not to forget, in a parody of David's pious nostalgia: "It's like the blowing of old breezes or the ringing of old bellses to hear *you* say Uriah" (*DC*, 294). Brilliantly entrapping David in a position that allows him to say or do nothing without violating his own linguistic pieties, Uriah humiliates him by turning the language of polite middle-class self-representation into a weapon.

When he entraps David into silent collusion about his own designs to destroy Wickfield and marry Agnes (a design that displays David's unarticulated desire), Uriah displays the manipulative underside of self-silencing in a scene which emphasizes the deep intimacy of the two figures. He engenders in David a dream state which includes murderous, sexualized rage: "I believe I had a delirious idea of seizing the red-hot poker out of the fire and running

---

[25] Uriah Heep gets the last word in other critical narratives than mine; see Poovey, *Uneven Developments*, 116–23; and Jaffe, *Vanishing Points*, 126. Poovey calls him "the novel's conscience" (120); Jaffe suggests that he "plays 'I' to David's 'you,'" creating "a contest about knowledge." In my view, Uriah is not the novel's single figure of exposure but only the most acute personification of Dickens's self-consciousness about his narrative procedures.

him through with it" (*DC,* 295), yet "I was attracted to him in very repulsion" (297). The violence comes to its climax only after Uriah has publicly exposed David's secret suspicion of Annie Strong's infidelity (chapter 42). As the doubled figures stand together "front to front," David strikes his face. Uriah "caught the hand in his, and we stood in that connexion, looking at each other. We stood so, a long time; long enough for me to see the white marks of my fingers die out of the deep red of his cheek, and leave it a deeper red" (474–75). David's violence forges the most intimate physical link between the figures, and allows Uriah both to turn David into a violent wild child and to display David's own strategies for muffling knowledge by "turning the other cheek" and forgiving him. "He knew me better than I knew myself," David acknowledges (476). What Uriah knows—what Dickens knew—is not only that gentility colludes with manipulative power, but that the novel's appealing tone of nostalgia and forgiveness is a strategy of upward mobility, potentially corrupt and readily exposable.

David Copperfield oscillates between its fascinated desire for Uriah Heep, who sees and exposes David's silences, and its official desire for Agnes Wickfield, who knows and holds her tongue. These two intimates know the same things, one in the mode of resentment, the other in the mode of protection and forgiveness. The plot may, as plots do, reward one and punish the other, but David remains poised between them, hovering always in the disquieting arena of specular exchange.

The quality I want finally to evoke might best be captured in an anecdote Forster tells about Dickens's boyhood. Within a short time after his release from Warren's Blacking, when he was a student at Wellington House Academy, Dickens would (according to a schoolmate's report) take to the streets pretending to be a poor boy, and he would beg charity from old ladies. "On these adventures, when the old ladies were quite staggered by the impudence of the demand, Dickens would explode with laughter and take to his heels" (Forster, Life of Dickens, 44). If this story is true, it suggests Dickens's compulsion to play out situations in which he knows he is not what he looks like or what he claims to be. The narrative of the blacking warehouse episode says "I am (not) a working-class orphan"; the schoolboy's prank, "I am (not) a middle-class child." Like characters in several of Dickens's other novels, *David Copperfield* repeatedly proclaims "I am (not) a gentleman"—and runs.

11. *Inside the Shark's Mouth*

William Lovett's Struggle for Political Language

MARGERY SABIN

Eagerness to rewrite social and literary history from below often seems
to outstrip skills for reading newly featured texts. Under the guise of
sympathizing with oppressed social groups of the past, many current
critical methods and assumptions paradoxically end by muffling voices in
ways that surprisingly resemble their earlier fate. My example here is William
Lovett, early Chartist leader and author of the autobiography *Life and
Struggles of William Lovett in His Pursuit of Bread, Knowledge, and
Freedom.*[1] In her 1985 annotated bibliography of British working-class autobiographies, Nan Hackett, for example, at once promotes Lovett's book
as the most "representative" Victorian example of the genre and denies it
any qualities that might reward literary attention: "No puns, wordplay,
metaphors, or nuances of language lightened or brightened the plodding narrative of his life.... He revealed no emotion, and aside from a few anecdotes
about village superstitions, the reader can find little that is amusing."[2]
Lovett's most recent biographer, Joel Wiener, similarly complains that
Lovett's story lacks "colour," "texture," or "genuine passion," with the result that it offers "little explanation of his passion for justice."[3]

A version of this essay first appeared in *Raritan: A Quarterly Review* (18, no. 2 [Fall 1998]).

[1] William Lovett, *Life and Struggles of William Lovett in His Pursuit of Bread, Knowledge,
and Freedom,* 2 vols., ed. R. Tawney (London: G. Bell and Sons, 1920). Tawney's edition is the
most available text in American libraries, and is the edition cited by page number in the body
of my text.

[2] Nan Hackett, *British Working-Class Autobiographies: An Annotated Bibliography* (New
York: AMS Press, 1985), 124.

[3] Joel Wiener, *William Lovett* (Manchester, U.K.: Manchester University Press, 1989), 6.

This disparagement by recent scholars acquires poignancy in the light of Lovett's explicit wish to communicate effectively with readers of a later age. *Life and Struggles,* published in 1876 at the end of Lovett's life, is dedicated first to "the working classes of a future day" so that they "may know something of the early struggles of some of those who contended for the political rights they may then be enjoying," then to a wider audience of future "historians and writers," so they not be left with only the "garbled tales" and "caricature" of the official record. It is a posthumous irony that some progressive literary scholars and historians are disinterring the texts of British working-class struggle, only to reinstate the caricature that it was Lovett's life's work to displace.

Although Lovett was honored in the early years of the British Labour Party and again in the decade or so of expanding social history that followed E. P. Thompson's 1966 *Making of the English Working Class,*[4] a tone of disappointment, even animosity, has more recently accompanied radical debunking of the "respectable" working class that Lovett has been taken to epitomize.[5] Suggesting perhaps a longstanding ambivalence, or even a familial quarrel, within the Anglo-American Left, one of Lovett's harshest critics is Dorothy Thompson, whose influential book, *The Chartists: Popular Politics in the Industrial Revolution,* relegates Lovett and his London followers to the backwater of pre-industrial radicalism. Whereas her husband, E. P. Thompson, remarks "admirable and moving" features of *Life and Struggles,* Dorothy Thompson limits her comments on Lovett to a few scolding asides

---

[4] Scholarly works influenced by the spirit and substance of *The Making of the English Working Class* (New York: Vintage, 1966) include anthologies and editions, as well as critical studies. See especially John Burnett, *Annals of Labour: Autobiographies of British Working Class People, 1820–1920* (Bloomington: Indiana University Press, 1974), published in England under the title *Useful Toil* (Harmondsworth: Penguin, 1974); John Burnett, *Destiny Obscure: Autobiographies of Childhood, Education, and Family from the 1820s to the 1920s* (Harmondsworth: Penguin, 1984); David Vincent, ed., *Testaments of Radicalism: Memoirs of Working Class Politicians: 1790–1885* (London: Europa, 1977); Brian Harrison and Patricia Hollis, eds., *Robert Lowery: Radical and Chartist* (London: Europa, 1979); John Burnett, David Vincent, and David Mayall, eds., *The Autobiography of the Working Class: An Annotated, Critical Bibliography,* 3 vols. (New York: New York University Press, 1984). The best critical study is David Vincent's *Bread, Knowledge, and Freedom: A Study of Nineteenth-Century Working Class Autobiography* (London: Methuen, 1981).

Influential admirers of Lovett in the Liberal-Labour tradition have included: R. G. Gammage, *History of the Chartist Movement: 1837–1854* (Newcastle-on-Tyne: Browne and Browne, 1894); Julius West, *History of the Chartist Movement* (London: Constable, 1920); Max Beer, *A History of British Socialism,* 2 vols. (London: G. Bell and Sons, 1919–1920); R. H. Tawney, Introduction to his edition of *Life and Struggles of William Lovett,* 2 vols. (London: G. Bell and Sons, 1920); G.D.H. Cole, *Chartist Portraits* (London: Macmillan, 1941); Mark Hovell, *The Chartist Movement,* ed. and completed by T. F. Tout (Manchester, U.K.: Manchester University Press, 1970).

[5] James Epstein discusses Lovett's reputation in relation to the historiography of working-class radicalism in the introduction to *The Lion of Freedom: Feargus O'Connor and the Chartist Movement: 1832–1842* (London: Croom Helm, 1982), 1–6.

for his "enormous insensitivity to the concerns of the great body of the working class."[6]

Criticism of Lovett's class position becomes especially provocative when joined to the irrefutable historical point that at a time of limited literacy, virtually any working-class author is atypical, as remarked by John Burnett in the preface to his anthology of autobiographical fragments, *Annals of Labour*: "The autobiographer or diarist was engaging in an activity which set him apart from the majority of his fellow men."[7] David Vincent, the best explicator of Victorian working-class autobiography, notably counters this kind of objection by his embrace of variety within the working classes. He argues, moreover, that there is "little evidence that in embracing the art-form of the autobiography [the writers] were distancing themselves from the aspirations of their class."[8] Yet somewhat contradictorily, Vincent also observes that Lovett and many others of the autobiographers were engaged in "an intellectual and often geographical journey away from the structure of beliefs and practices of the communities in which they had grown up."[9] Vincent does not fully confront the difficult question of how it is possible to represent (in language or politics) the "aspirations" of a group while simultaneously moving out of its "structure of beliefs and practices."

In this essay I delve further into this tension between individual and collective aspirations, not so much to resolve it as to show its centrality to Lovett's own self-consciousness in both his writing and his political career. I call my method "literary" because it interprets Lovett's concerns through close attention to the details and designs of his writing and to the thematic preoccupation with language in his autobiography.[10] This kind of attention slows down adjudication of "texture" and "genuine passion" in written language, partly by taking into account rhetorical conventions and historical shifts in taste. When heard in dialogue with other Victorian voices, even

---

[6] E. P. Thompson, *The Making of the English Working Class*, 741; Dorothy Thompson, *The Chartists: Popular Politics in the Industrial Revolution* (New York: Pantheon, 1984), 296.

[7] Burnett, *Annals of Labour*, 11–12; Nan Hackett similarly remarks that "writing an autobiography is not a typical act for a member of any class, let alone of a class whose members were generally illiterate" (*British Working Class Autobiographies*, 14).

[8] Vincent, *Bread, Knowledge, and Freedom*, 198.

[9] Ibid., 168–69.

[10] Gareth Stedman Jones has called for renewed attention to "the place of language and form" in Chartist political writing, arguing against "the prevalent social-historical approach to Chartism, whose starting-point is some conception of class or occupational consciousness." See "Rethinking Chartism," in *Languages of Class: Studies in English Working Class History: 1832–1982* (Cambridge: Cambridge University Press, 1983), 19–22, 94–95. An earlier version of this essay appears as "The Language of Chartism," in *The Chartist Experience*, ed. James Epstein and Dorothy Thompson (London: Macmillan, 1982). James Epstein follows Jones's recommendation to study Chartist political language, but he defends the "class perspective" criticized by Jones. See "The Constitutional Idiom: Radical Reasoning, Rhetoric and Action in Early Nineteenth-Century England," *Journal of Social History* 23, no. 3 (1990): 553–74. A later version of this essay forms the first chapter of Epstein's *Radical Expression: Political Language, Ritual, and Symbol in England, 1790–1850* (New York: Oxford University Press, 1994). Neither Jones nor Epstein discusses the language of autobiographical narrative.

Lovett's stylistic limitations may be traced to conscious struggles against stereotypes of working-class expressivity. I begin with Lovett's striking image of entrapment as a child inside a dead shark's mouth. It is his most traumatic childhood memory in *Life and Struggles,* and it sets a pattern that recurs in other of his adventures. The incident comes at the end of a long paragraph recounting the child's early rebellion against his widowed mother's rigid "Methodist Connexion" in their fishing village in Cornwall. That regimen included no books but the Bible and Watts's Hymns, and chapel attendance "three times of a Sunday" (*Life and Struggles,* 8). As a child, Lovett avoided chapel for the Cornwall beach, where he could play with boys outlawed by his mother as "ignorant, idle and vicious" and could make "colours" for drawing, from stones dug out of the rocks. The shark episode concludes Lovett's narrative of childhood, as if it marked the end and chief lesson he would set against the restrictive curriculum of the Bible and Watts's hymns:

> It happened that a very large basking shark was found floating on the ocean, by some of the fishermen of the town, and towed on shore. It was of course a favorable opportunity for an assemblage of boys; and while the fishermen were busy in cutting it open, and taking out the great quantity of liver and oil found in it, the boys were busy in their way of extracting amusement out of it. The mouth of the fish having been propped open by means of handspikes, some boys—myself among the number—had got into its mouth cutting away a black, stiff bristly fringe, that lined a part of it, and which bore a comb-like appearance. While we were thus busily employed, other mischievous fellows were busy in kicking the bottom of the handspikes on one side, which brought the jaws plop together and laid us sprawling at the bottom. Our cries soon brought assistance, and the mouth of the fish was opened, but the plight we were in from the oil and slime into which we were tumbled, can be better imagined than described. (*Life and Struggles,* 10)

Lovett as a boy prefers looking into things directly rather than submitting to sermons about their assigned place in the divine scheme. His language for the shark's mouth, with its "black, stiff bristly fringe" of "comb-like appearance," transfers to the boy's observation the exactitude of the later teacher of natural science who would master enough Latin to write a working-class textbook of human anatomy (in plain English and with drawings) for his educational campaign against "superstition."

Lovett's frustrations, however, also seem foreshadowed here, in the terse differentiation between some boys and others: between the curious explorers of the shark's mouth and the mischievous tricksters who kick out the handspikes. Some of his mother's strictures stuck: while not all boys are ignorant and vicious, some are, and they are the ones who send you sprawling to the bottom of the slime. The division corresponds to Lovett's view of what happened to him later, in Chartism, where what he saw as reckless rabble-rousers overtook his nonviolent protest movement, landing Lovett, along with hundreds of other Chartist leaders, in the slime of prison—another and worse trauma from which his health and faith in Chartist activism never recovered. Lovett's critics, now and in his lifetime, might see this impulse to separate the benign from the mischievous among his peers as the incipient "elitism" that proved fatal to Lovett as a popular leader. Why blame his plight on other boys rather than on the shark—especially if you take that moribund but still dangerous creature as a trope for the early nineteenth-century British state?

I may already be false to Lovett as a writer, however, in reading so much into his anecdote. He does not play with tropes the way George Orwell, for example, plays with Jonah and the whale in his famous essay about politics and writing, "Inside the Whale."[11] Lovett's biblical training shows in the narrative spareness of his style, but without exegetical expansiveness. A sense of constraint in language—sometimes willed, sometimes inadvertent—separates Lovett's plain style from the fluency of an Orwell as well as from the verbal extravagance of the great Victorian novelists. Dickens could have animated the shark scene with more amusing language for its excitement, its horror, and its metaphoric possibilities. Apart from the exact phrasing for the shark's mouth, Lovett puts all the expressive burden on a few falsely elevated phrases ("an assemblage of boys," "extracting amusement"), which deaden the feeling of boyhood, even though the narrative content is compelling. Lovett's writing gains colloquial vitality when he gets to naming the bad things, as when the kicking out of the handspikes "brought the jaws plop together." But there is an awkward instability of diction in this writing that muffles the emotion, rather in the way that the boys' cries from inside the shark were hard to hear.

For me, the very disjunction between narrative vividness and verbal constraint acquires its own dramatic force in Lovett's writing in relation both to the traps he escaped and to those in which he got caught. To be trapped in wordless cries seems to me one of Lovett's biggest fears, both for himself and for his whole class. Lovett's sometimes awkward style puts one in touch with the difficulty of writing plain yet supple and expressive English, especially for a man of his class in the nineteenth century. Possession of the language was a form of property and power systematically denied to people like himself, so that its acquisition had to involve a strenuous personal struggle. The ultimate value of what might be thought of as this verbal enfranchisement remains controversial, as is the value of the franchise to vote that was the first demand of the Chartist Petition and Bill that Lovett himself drafted in 1837, as Secretary of the London Working Men's Association.

The struggle for adequate language in Lovett's personal narrative is inseparable from his pursuit of just political and social language in his public

---

[11] George Orwell, "Inside the Whale," in *A Collection of Essays* (New York: Harcourt Brace Jovanovich, 1946), 210–13.

career. His political writing follows the dictum of his older contemporary, William Cobbett: "Tyranny has no enemy so formidable as the pen."[12] Although sounding like a masthead of the radical press to which Cobbett contributed so much, this sentence actually appears in Cobbett's introduction to *A Grammar of the English Language,* designed for the use of "young persons in general," but more especially for unschooled youth: "soldiers, sailors, apprentices, and ploughboys." Lovett as a young man came to know Cobbett in radical London circles of the 1820s, but Cobbett's *Grammar* of 1818 came into circulation a bit too late to help him. He describes how he relied on an old copy of Lindley Murray, lent him by a kind old schoolmaster in his first London lodging house when he arrived penniless from Cornwall in 1821.

Lindley Murray's grammar, already in its sixteenth edition by 1797, drily presented the rules of English syntax in terminology adapted from Latin, followed by moralizing sentences for "syntactical parsing": for example, "Vice degrades us. *Vice* is a common substantive, of the neuter gender, the third person, in the singular number, and the nominative case."[13] If the parsing could not be mastered, something of the moralism might stick, especially since the same few lessons in submission recur in many syntactic variations: "What feelings are more uneasy and painful than the workings of sour and angry passions?" or "To correct the spirit of discontent, let us consider how little we deserve, and how much we enjoy."[14]

Cobbett had memorized another such eighteenth-century grammar, by John Lowth, a feat whose glory and pain motivate his idea of grammar as potentially radical power.[15] In the ingratiating form of familiar letters to a son, Cobbett invokes struggles in the cause of freedom as the inducement to mastery of grammar. Plain but grammatical English, he explains, teaches not submissiveness but effective defiance: "it enables us not only to express our meaning fully and clearly, but so to express it as to enable us to defy the ingenuity of man to give to our words any other meaning than that which we ourselves intend them to express."[16]

---

[12] William Cobbett, *A Grammar of the English Language* (New York: n.p.; printed for the author by Clayton and Kingsland, 1818), 9.

[13] *Abridgement of Murray's English Grammar...designed for the Younger Classes of Learners,* ed. Israel Alger ("Alger's Murray") (Boston: Lincoln and Edmands, 1824), 111.

[14] Ibid., 108.

[15] Cobbett's account of his self-directed study of English grammar appeared in *Advice to Young Men* (1829), and is reprinted in the composite of Cobbett's autobiographical writing, *The Progress of a Plough-Boy to a Seat in Parliament,* ed. William Reitzel (London: Faber and Faber, 1933), 22–23. Olivia Smith examines the radicalism of Cobbett's *Grammar* in relation to eighteenth-century conventions and models, as exemplified by Lowth and Lindley Murray, in *The Politics of Language, 1791–1819* (Oxford: Clarendon, 1984), 239–49. The political implications of Cobbett's *Grammar* were earlier discussed in G.D.H. Cole, *The Life of William Cobbett* (New York: Harcourt Brace, 1924), 270–71; a more critical assessment of the *Grammar's* political implications appears in John W. Osborne, *William Cobbett: His Thought and His Times* (New Brunswick, N.J.: Rutgers University Press, 1966), 233–35.

[16] Cobbett, *Grammar,* 14.

Lovett shapes his emergence from the restrictive norms of his Cornwall childhood around his discovery of language as a way of asserting and controlling meanings. Later, he would be frustrated and eventually defeated by a political uncontrollability of interpretation not envisaged in Cobbett's radical dictum. But his youthful moment of vocation appears as an intoxicating sequence of promising revelations. The experiences belong to the early 1820s in London, when Lovett was drifting into working men's discussion groups in the evenings, while by day still struggling to earn bread as an unapprenticed carpenter. At his first such meeting, what riveted his attention was not so much the topic or substance of the speech as the sheer fact of public speech as a phenomenon, for "it was the first time that I had ever heard impromptu speaking out of the pulpit—my notions then being that such speaking was a kind of inspiration from god" (*Life and Struggles,* 35). The possibility of language as a form of human inspiration and secular inquiry had never struck him before, "and from what I heard on that eve, I felt for the first time in my life how very ignorant I was and how very deficient in being able to give a reason for the opinions and the hopes I entertained."

The anecdotes that follow within the same long paragraph extend this image of language as a miraculous human capability. At one of the meetings of the Mechanics' Institute, the still new institution of public lectures to promote "useful knowledge" among the people, the well-known Dr. Birkbeck displayed the phenomenon of "*several dumb boys*" who had been taught to speak, a "miracle" that he explained by showing how they were taught "by the eye instead of the ear":

> first by noticing the action of the mouth and outward movements of the larynx...and trying to imitate the sounds, and then proceeding to words and sentences. They had in this way made such proficiency that they could readily answer any question asked of them; indeed, one of them repeated a portion of Gray's Elegy, and that very distinctly, the only defect being in the modulation of the voice, as they could not be brought to distinguish the various tones of it. (*Life and Struggles,* 36)

Lovett's choice to recount this incident is fascinating because his own written language, even in this anecdote, may itself seem defective in tone. He does not, for example, manipulate his syntax and diction to bring out the irony of a "dumb" boy tonelessly reciting from Gray's Elegy, a poem of somewhat patronizing pity for the "mute, inglorious" dead. Lovett's own expressiveness in writing relies less on differentiated tones than on his extraordinarily suggestive patterns of association. The paragraph that begins with the "sheer fact" of public speech moves through the "miracle" of "dumb" recitation to culminate in the magic of original expression that an "author" might dare:

I remember that on leaving the lecture-room on that occasion I got into conversation with Sir Richard Phillips, the author, and walked with him round and round St. Paul's churchyard, Newgate Street, and the old Bailey for several hours, it being a bright moonlight night, while he explained to me many of his scientific theories, among others one which he entertained in opposition to Sir Isaac Newton's theory of gravitation, Sir Richard illustrating his theory by diagrams made with a piece of chalk on the walls and window shutters. (*Life and Struggles,* 37)

On this night of moonlight magic, here is a man who goes thrillingly beyond toneless mimicry to demonstrate the "miracle" of opposing the greatest scientific authority of the age. Instead of dutifully reciting, Phillips freely inscribes his own originality in chalk on church and prison walls. We cannot know whether Lovett, writing his autobiography, somehow recalls Blake's "London," with its bloodier inscriptions. Phillips might well have made the connection, for Lovett's new acquaintance was an entrepreneurial bookseller and popular writer who had spent eighteen months in prison in 1793 for selling Paine's *Rights of Man*.[17] Lovett commemorates a moment of the early 1820s when an old Jacobin author's graphic opposition to scientific law might seem a dreamlike image of Lovett's own nascent impulses to protest equally authoritative laws of social gravitation.

Virtually every episode in Lovett's account of his apprenticeship for adult life reinforces his growing sense of power to use language as a challenge to authority or established rule. Political self-assertions parallel the personal ones. There was his defiant opposition when, as shopkeeper for an Owenite cooperative bazaar, he was entrapped into alleged violation of the pamphlet tax. Together with the experienced radical publisher Henry Hetherington, he succeeded through written appeal in getting the authorities to back down. Lovett credits radical journalists like Hetherington with teaching him how to channel protest through the niceties of political and legal language. He shows himself soon going beyond apprenticeship in his independent challenges, as when he led a committee to protest the "anti-democratic" behavior of the leader of the Co-operative Movement, Robert Owen himself. At issue was Owen's tampering with a committee invitation to Members of Parliament. Lovett recalls Owen highhandedly brushing off complaints "with the greatest composure," insisting: "we must consent to be ruled by despots till we had acquired sufficient knowledge to govern ourselves" (*Life and Struggles,* 51). In a preview of his later reaction to what he perceived as similarly despotic leadership in Chartism, Lovett and his colleagues were "flabbergasted"; eventually Lovett quit the Owenite cooperative movement and

---

[17] Phillips's "rooted idea that the theory of gravitation had no foundation" was deemed worthy of inclusion in the entry about him in the *Dictionary of National Biography,* ed. Sir Leslie Stephen and Sir Sidney Lee (Oxford: Oxford University Press, 1917–), 15:1096.

pursued his different idea of leadership in one and another of the working men's associations that would eventually become the London nucleus of Chartism.

Mainstream Victorian writers, even those most sympathetic to the working-class plight, pay little heed to the struggle for verbal enfranchisement so important to Lovett's Chartism. Thomas Carlyle, Charles Dickens, Elizabeth Gaskell, even Friedrich Engels, all deny the working classes ability to function effectively in plain English, and they base their sympathetic appreciation, as well as their disdain, on the very fact of this verbal exclusion. Cobbett's vision of a self-taught English grammar met overwhelming counterinsistence that inarticulate cries essentially defined working-class language.

Gaskell, for example, in the preface to her Chartist novel *Mary Barton,* writes of her anxiety "to give some utterance to the agony which, from time to time, convulses this dumb people."[18] Gaskell echoes Carlyle's urgent call a decade earlier, in his pamphlet *Chartism,* for some "clear interpretation of the thought which at heart torments these wild inarticulate souls, struggling there, with inarticulate uproar, like dumb creatures in pain, unable to speak what it is in them."[19] And writing to Gaskell in praise of her book, Carlyle in 1848 is still harping on dumbness, praising Gaskell for her contribution toward developing a huge subject, "which has lain dumb too long."[20]

Carlyle was probably the first to substitute his own interpretive voice for the "dumb" poor in Chartism. Carlyle dismisses the political language of the movement as the "clattering of ballot-boxes." Like strikes, demonstrations, and riots, the political demands are only symptoms, "boils on the surface" of a deeper social disease: "How inexpressibly useful were true insight into it; a genuine understanding by the upper classes of society of what it is that the under classes intrinsically mean." By the end of *Chartism,* Carlyle entirely discards the stated political goals of the People's Charter and National Petition (with one and a half million signatures). Those documents, drafted by Lovett, plainly and clearly laid out six points to achieve political self-representation for the laboring classes, starting with universal male suffrage. Carlyle differed from the Whig and Tory politicians who overwhelmingly rejected the Chartist Bill and Petition mainly in his conviction that the "living essence" of Chartism could not be put down by mere parliamentary dismissal. Carlyle's interpretation nevertheless validated Parliament's deaf ear by asserting that the "toiling classes" do not *essentially* want the vote. Nor do they even want economic ameliorations, he adds, "for there are so many things which cash will not pay."[21]

---

[18] Elizabeth Gaskell, *Mary Barton* (London: Penguin, 1970), 38.
[19] *Thomas Carlyle: Selected Writings,* ed. Alan Shelstone (London: Penguin, 1971), 155.
[20] Letter from Thomas Carlyle to ECG, 8 November 1848, John Rylands, MS 730/14. Cited by Jenny Uglow, *Elizabeth Gaskell: A Habit of Stories* (New York: Farrar, Straus, Giroux, 1993), 217.
[21] Carlyle, *Selected Writings,* 199.

Since Carlyle's readership had no intention of giving up any of their own economic or political power, the idea that the working classes were not really asking for either must have been reassuring. Carlyle ventriloquizes in his own voice what he hears as the single prayer of the people at the heart of their uproar: "Give me a leader; a true leader . . . that he may guide me on the true way, that I may be loyal to him, that I may swear fealty to him and follow him, and feel that it is well with me!"[22]

Gaskell's *Mary Barton* follows Carlyle in representing her Chartist hero, John Barton, as not only indifferent to Chartist political language, but entirely oblivious to it. Although a regular at meetings, a reader of the Chartist press, and even a delegate from Manchester to carry the great Petition to London, Barton hasn't the slightest idea of what the Petition says. As Gaskell ventriloquizes his expectation, Barton is heading to London with a childlike notion that after they tell Parliament of the working men's misery, "they'll surely do somewhat wiser for us than we can guess at now."[23] Although there were deep quarrels within Chartism about what "ulterior measures" to plan (or threaten) in response to Parliament's expected rebuff, the necessity of political self-representation was the shared and widely publicized conviction of all Chartists.[24] Neither "moral force" nor "physical force" Chartism settled for the naïve dependency on Parliament that Gaskell attributes to Barton.

Disappointment in London begins Barton's descent into the murder of the mill owner's son, a crime that reduces him to total silence until his deathbed repentance. Gaskell exhorts compassion for this tragedy because Barton's rage follows from the unwillingness of the ruling classes to hear the cries of the suffering poor. Barton's victim, Henry Carson, had been caught drawing caricatures of the workers' delegation that had come to protest wage cuts in the mill. But Gaskell herself presents a caricature of Chartism. To give what she sympathetically calls "the rough, untutored words" of the Chartist delegation no content other than a cry for help from their betters is to deny the core of Chartist politics. In relation to Lovett, the caricature denies two decades of strenuous self-education in language that could take control of meaning and, in Cobbett's phrase, "defy the ingenuity of man" to distort it.

Engels represents another version of determination to limit working-class language to cries of pain and rage. Engels dedicated his 1845 *Condition of the Working Class in England* to Carlyle, from whom he learned the same certainty as Gaskell about the inarticulateness of working-class misery. But where Carlyle interpreted brute rage to signify diseased yearning for obedience, Engels takes the same wild noise to differentiate workers from brutes:

[22] Ibid., 191.
[23] Gaskell, *Mary Barton*, 141.
[24] Underlying agreement among Chartists about the need for political self-representation by the working classes is emphasized by Jones, "Rethinking Chartism," 97–110; and by Epstein, *Lion of Freedom*, 101–7, 138–39, and "Constitutional Idiom," 553–58.

"This rage, this passion, is rather the proof that the workers feel the inhumanity of their position, that they refuse to be degraded to the level of brutes."[25] Engels proceeds from rage as "proof" of proletarian humanity to the inverse proposition that the absence of rage signifies withdrawal from the proletariat, and even from humanity:

> This may be seen in the case of those who do not share this wrath; they either bow humbly before the fate that overtakes them, live a respectable life as well as they can, do not concern themselves as to the cause of public affairs, help the bourgeoisie to forge the chains of the workers yet more securely, and stand upon the plane of intellectual nullity that prevailed before the industrial period began; or they are tossed about by fate, lose their moral hold upon themselves...live from day to day, drink and fall into licentiousness; and in both cases they are brutes.

According to Engels, the working man "can save his manhood only through hatred and rebellion."[26]

Life and Struggles presents Lovett moving from Cornwall to London in pursuit of a very different idea of working-class manhood. Not that he didn't admire instances of rebellious energy in the village. Lovett begins his book with a tribute to nonverbal action against authority in Cornwall, which by the way introduces the book's preoccupation with the resources of the deaf and dumb. Lovett's first anecdote features a deaf woman, "Honour Hitchens" (*Life and Struggles*, 3), who saved her father from one of the press-gangs that tyrannized the Cornwall coast during the Napoleonic wars. The young men of the town protected themselves as best they could by hiding in the country, where soldiers on horseback with cutlasses often hunted them down. Lovett memorializes a more heroic female self-defense:

> On one of those exciting occasions, it so happened that an old man and his daughter were out at one end of the town beside a small stream cleansing fish.... Being thus engaged when the press-gang landed, and she being deaf, one of the gang had been and seized her father, and was bearing him off before she was aware of it. On raising her head, and seeing her father borne off a prisoner, she snatched up one of the dog-fishes she was opening, and running up to the man she asked him what he was going to do with her daddy. Pointing to the man-of-war at a distance, he told her he was going to take him aboard that big ship. The words had scarcely passed his lips before she fetched him a blow across his face with the rough dog-fish, that made him relinquish his hold. Then seizing her father with one hand, and resolutely defending him with the dog-fish in the

---

[25] Friedrich Engels, *The Condition of the Working Class in England*, ed. Victor Kernan (London: Penguin, 1987), 144.
[26] Ibid., 223.

other, she kept her opponent at bay till other women and boys came to her assistance. Thus was Honour Hitchens, by her courage, enabled to bear off her daddy in triumph amid the cheers and rejoicings of half the women and boys of the neighborhood.

It is the women of the village who get Lovett's praise for physical courage and quick-wittedness; men figure little in the opening Cornwall chapter. While honoring the women, however, the gender distinction seems connected to a certain detachment of Lovett's aspirations from the female examples.[27] Their limitations appear again in the form of another, more talkative female subversive, "aunt Tammy," a woman whose "nimble and abusive tongue" had given her a reputation as a "white witch." Lovett tells the story of how aunt Tammy succeeded in disrupting court proceedings in a case against her daughter for stealing apples. Aunt Tammy's talent for "abusive drolleries" enabled her to turn the entire proceeding into a farce. Calling each magistrate by name, she elaborately forced each of them to accept a piece of her own apple-cake "amid much fun and laughter." But the fun did not in the end get her daughter released. Aunt Tammy managed to embarrass the magistrates, but she was still required to pay a fine for the daughter's offense. In a sense, aunt Tammy did not tamely submit, in that before leaving she promised with mock amiability to visit each magistrate at home to collect for the fine she had no money to pay: " 'I shall first call on Parson Rogers, and I know I shall get something from him, and I believe, after that, none of you will be shabby enough to send me away empty-handed' " (*Life and Struggles,* 20).

Aunt Tammy's performance, the limit of subversive speech in Lovett's village, gives a little space for the kind of theatrical mimicry and hijinks that Dickens was such a genius for celebrating as a sign of the vitality of popular culture. While revering Dickens for his "inimitable" style, his "kindly and graphic pictures" of humble life (*Life and Struggles,* 424), Lovett values mimicry less than did Dickens. Aunt Tammy's mimicry is self-degrading in that it involves exaggerating her servility; she embarrasses the court only by reducing herself to a caricature of a beggar. After this story, Lovett's narrative turns immediately to his departure for London and more manly opportunities.

Lovett's pursuit of direct, articulate challenge to structures of law and government has recently been denigrated in terms with surprising echoes of mainstream Victorian writing, now under the auspices of post-Marxist political sociology. In a 1986 essay whose title recalls Carlyle, "Class without Words:

---

[27] Gender identifications within Chartist discourse give added polemical charge to Lovett's association of articulate rational speech with manliness. The contrary insinuation that only physical force is manly was frequently suggested by the more confrontational Chartists and is endorsed by Feargus O'Connor's 1839 remark that "Moral force and physical force were man and wife. Moral force was the wife, and knew when to call in her husband to her aid." Cited by Epstein, *Lion of Freedom,* 124, from the short-lived London newspaper *Charter,* 24 March 1839.

Symbolic Communication in the Chartist Movement," Paul Pickering belittles rational discourse in working-class politics in favor of symbolic personal theater.[28] The platform oratory that rallied and sustained Chartism as a mass movement was a "social action" rather than a communication in language, Pickering argues, especially since band music, laughter, cheering, and the sheer size of outdoor meetings often made speeches inaudible.[29] The most effective Chartist orators understood how to manipulate the images, gestures, and iconography of popular politics so as to stir up group solidarity behind their own selves as leaders.

Pickering does not regret or criticize this power of theatrical self-promotion, but rather admires the star performer of Chartism: Feargus O'Connor, the charismatic Irish gentleman-agitator who figures as Lovett's mischievous nemesis both in *Life and Struggles* and in early Chartist historiography. Revisionary praise of O'Connor does not credit him with better thoughts or language than Lovett, only with incomparably greater theatrical skill. Even contemporary admirers of O'Connor remarked on the emptiness of his "harangues" when transposed to print: without "the infectious vehemence of his spirited manner," observed one follower, what was left was "bombast, broken metaphor and inflated language."[30]

O'Connor's most effective piece of theater without words, according to Pickering, was the "triumphal procession" he staged in 1841 to celebrate his release from a year's imprisonment in York Castle. O'Connor's own Chartist newspaper, *The Northern Star,* reported the thrilling spectacle: O'Connor in a full suit of fustian, "made out of one piece which had been manufactured expressly for the occasion," carried through the cheering streets in an "elaborate triumphal car...of pink and green velvet...formed in the shape of a conch-shell and drawn by six white stallions."[31] The newspaper also reprinted O'Connor's superfluous explanation of his costume: "I have appeared, Brother Chartists and working men, amongst you in fustian, the emblem of your order, in order to convince you, at a single glance, that what I was when I left you, the same I do return to you." Through the suit of fustian, Pickering says, O'Connor "symbolically" renounced his gentlemanly status, for "into the cloth was woven the shared experiences and identity of working-class life."[32]

The artifice of O'Connor's show did not apparently detract from its political impressiveness, nor did the incongruous combination of fustian and

[28] Paul Pickering, "Class without Words: Symbolic Communication in the Chartist Movement," *Past and Present* 112 (1986): 144–62. Pickering draws on John Brewer's *Party Ideology and Popular Politics at the Accession of George III* (Cambridge: Cambridge University Press, 1981) for his analysis of "symbols" as "a belief-system 'made concrete,'" 158 n. 62.

[29] Pickering, "Class without Words," 151–53.

[30] William O'Neill Daunt, cited by Pickering, "Class without Words," 152, from citation by Epstein, *Lion of Freedom,* 10–11.

[31] *Northern Star,* 4 September 1841, 6. Cited by Pickering, "Class without Words," 157.

[32] Pickering, "Class without Words," 159–60.

velvet, or the discrepancy between emblematically "shared" experience and the reality of O'Connor's privileges in prison, where he had enjoyed private quarters, special food, visitors, and other amenities accorded him as a land-holding, university-educated barrister who was a former M.P. from Ireland. Pickering doesn't comment on these incongruities. The important point to him is that O'Connor's critics, headed by Lovett, were wrong to despise what Lovett called "foolish displays and gaudy trappings." Lovett's "mistake," Pickering remarks, "was greatly to underestimate the deep significance of personal theatre."[33]

Life and Struggles shows Lovett, however, to have been entirely aware of personal theatricality as a form of power—for him, a degrading and dangerous power in working-class politics. Lovett despised O'Connor's personal performances, not because he underrated their effectiveness, but on the contrary because he feared the new despotism foreshadowed in O'Connor's very success in turning himself into a symbol: "You are the great I AM of politics, the great personification of Radicalism" (*Life and Struggles*, 166), Lovett had already written sardonically in a public letter against O'Connor in 1837. To Lovett, O'Connor fit all too well into ruling-class Victorian opinion of working-class yearning for leadership from above. Lovett, by contrast, wanted to stage demonstrations that would strengthen democratic working-class self-reliance and public respect for the terms of its expression. His failure was not a "mistake," in the sense of an unintentional or correctable error, but a judgment of what kind of theater would promote the democracy he sought.

Current critical admiration of O'Connor's charisma accords more closely with the Carlylean admiration for heroes than with Lovett's revulsion toward any form of idolatry. Lovett's account of early London Chartism insists on the need for independence from self-professed leaders of the people: "the masses, in their political organization, were taught to look up to "*'great men'* (or to men *professing greatness*) rather than to great principles" (94). Although Lovett fully expected the Chartist Petition to be rejected by Parliament at this time, commitment to the Charter's principles of "right and justice" remained more important to him than immediate success because it was the necessary "school of self-instruction" in the language and spirit of democracy: "the spirit of plain men seeking their political and social rights" (127), as he asserted in his bold 1837 address to the new Queen Victoria (reprinted in *Life and Struggles*). The fact that Lovett and his associates were prohibited from presenting their address to the Queen in person unless they could appear at a levee in court dress provoked a further bluntly worded protest that shows Lovett's plain style to be itself a symbolic as well as practical commitment: "we have neither the means nor the inclination to indulge in such absurdities as dress-swords, coats and wigs."

[33] Ibid., 160 n. 69.

In *Life and Struggles,* the episode that represents Lovett at the high but already vulnerable point of his own symbolic theater occurred in March 1832, a few months before the Reform Bill and still seven years before the Chartist Petition. It had been a winter of cholera bad enough to arouse public dread about "contagion" emanating from the urban slums where the disease was most miserably intense. In response to public alarm, Lovett recounts, the royal chaplain prevailed upon the government to ordain a general fast "for beseeching God to remove the cholera from among us" (*Life and Struggles,* 80). This bit of official theater provoked Lovett, along with colleagues from the National Union of Working Classes, to plan a counter-event to protest what they saw as the "hypocrisy" of holding the "Almighty" responsible for diseases spread by "iniquitous" social neglect. On the day of the fast, they planned to stage a *feast,* to underscore the nature of true "Christian feeling"; by subscription, the National Union would provide a *good dinner:* "those who could afford it to provide for those who could not," and the feast's symbolic meaning as protest would be publicized by a "peaceable and orderly walk before dinner" through London's major thoroughfares. In addition to the 20,000 members of the National Union, an estimated 100,000 additional working-class "walkers" showed up to march.

The mixture of spectacle and language, boldness and subtlety in this theater of civil disobedience points to both the weakness and the strength of Lovett's style. The strength shows in the sheer size and directness of protest against the marshalling of piety in support of official indifference to suffering. The weakness was that Lovett could not, in the event, control performance of his script. Although technically protected by constitutional right, the unarmed march was from the start interpreted as a public threat; police were sent to the scene "armed with staves and drawn cutlasses." By acting on this interpretation, the authorities further showed their power to disrupt and change the script by their own theatrical interventions. The police forced detours at various points of the planned itinerary, and on Tottenham Court Road, blocked the progress of the procession altogether. Worst of all to Lovett, he could not retain control of every individual marcher. In particular, one William Benbow (well known later in Chartism for his confrontational spirit) "lost all patience," forced his way into the barricade, and provided the police with cause to use their weapons freely on the unarmed crowd.[34] Lovett in the end was recast in the role of dangerous agitator, thrown into jail with Benbow and another leader of the march, all three equally charged as "disaffected and ill-disposed persons, who with force and

---

[34] See E. P. Thompson, *The Making of the English Working Class,* 820; William Benbow's reputation for violence is remarked by Iowerth Prothero, "William Benbow and the Concept of the 'General Strike,'" *Past and Present* 63 (1974): 147. Prothero discusses Benbow's commitment to the strategy of provoking authorities to violence in order to begin a physical revolution in which, Benbow believed, the vast majority of the nation would quickly participate and triumph (132–171).

arms had made a great riot, tumult and disturbance" (82–83). Lovett was himself compelled to fast rather than feast after all: the rest of his day was spent in a prison cell, next to "a pailful of filth, left by the last occupants." Finally at night a friend managed to pass "a few crumbs of biscuit" through the wire grating over the prison door. The total experience of the day prefigures the breakdown into violence of the Birmingham Bull Ring meeting of 1839, when Lovett's protest against police provocation led to his year-long sentence under even worse prison conditions.

In *Life and Struggles,* Lovett reaffirms his commitment to nonviolent symbolic action, while sadly acknowledging that he was unable to make it effective on the public stage of the 1830s. The verbal play of fast/feast may be more communicative on the written page of *Life and Struggles* than it was on the street, where the police needed only one irrepressible participant to change the public symbolism of the whole event; instead of the planned reproach to official hypocrisy, it became one in a sequence of signs that social protest by the lower orders was controllable only by police force.

Yet O'Connor's opposite theatrical style in the end achieved little. Even those who admire the organizational effectiveness of O'Connor's charisma acknowledge its political futility: the dynamic of protest, provocation (whether by police or participants), violence, then speedy and brutal suppression recurred in a declining cycle throughout the decade of Chartism, until all the principal leaders were imprisoned, deported, disaffected, or (as in the case of O'Connor himself) consigned to an asylum for the insane. The social and political reforms of the 1850s, 1860s, and 1870s occurred in a variety of ways, all carefully dissociated by the authorities from Chartist auspices. From a literary point of view, O'Connor's platform style has proved even more ephemeral, for his glamor fades in print. Far from generating new respect for working-class aspiration, revival of O'Connor's reputation accompanies increased cynicism about the importance of language in politics and elsewhere.

Even the most sympathetic reader of Lovett's *Life and Struggles,* however, has to concede that he ruined his book by burying the disappointments of his life after 1842 under heaps of reprinted Petitions and Addresses, as if the book were a last chance to win a hearing for his public pronouncements. While the consistency of this over-copious record contributes to the portrait of Lovett's steadfastness, it is the personal narrative that gives *Life and Struggles* its vital identity. The deep-dyed integrity of his mental life works as a kind of artless art, thematically linking verbal details, so that even his seemingly eccentric narrative choices become charged with emotional and symbolic suggestiveness.

Thus the single incident chosen by Lovett to represent the aftermath of his traumatic year of imprisonment at once represents and defends the principles that cost him leadership of the Chartist movement. In implicit contrast to the triumphal show following O'Connor's prison release, Lovett reports that he was too broken in health by imprisonment (without privileges) to attend the public celebrations planned by his London friends. He headed instead directly to Cornwall to recuperate with family. Riding to his brother's house in Cornwall on the top of an omnibus (minus velvet conch or white stallions), Lovett got into conversation with a man who shared his interest in mineralogy:

> A little time before I got down I gave him my address in exchange for his own; but when he saw my name, he said "What! William Lovett, the Chartist?" "Yes," I replied, "the same individual." "Why," said he, scrutinizing me very earnestly, "*you don't look like one*"; evidently believing that a Chartist was something monstrous. "Well," I said, "as you gave me an invitation to call on you without knowing me, now you do know that I am a Chartist, your invitation had best be cancelled." "Not so," he replied good-humouredly; "we met on scientific grounds, and I do not trouble myself about politics, and if you call I shall be glad to see you." I did so in a short time, when he showed me his collection, and I purchased a few specimens of him. He proved to be a Superintendant of the Wesleyan Ministers of that district, and, I doubt not, a very estimable man, for all his notions about Chartism. (*Life and Struggles*, 249)

"Chartist" is a label Lovett remained determined to claim to the end of his life. But he was equally intent to cultivate an appearance quite opposite to O'Connor's emblematic costuming. Lovett is proud that he looks ordinary. He doesn't look like a Chartist. What should a Chartist look like? Should he be wearing and also speaking fustian? The formal diction in the dialogue sounds perhaps a bit dressed up for the Cornwall road, but it quite exactly asserts the important point that his name designates him as a Chartist and also as an "individual," with all the claims to dignity that standard Victorian English gave to that word. The idea of a notorious Chartist who looks and speaks like a respectable, ordinary individual elicits earnest scrutiny from the stranger because the combination goes against contemporary stereotype. The amiable Methodist Superintendant could accept such a peculiar specimen for a "scientific relationship," and Lovett, for all his dislike of the Methodist chapel, could allow for the "estimable" quality of the Superintendant as a man. But Lovett seeks no more than a limited exchange with this man because a significant part of Lovett's identity remained bound to collective political goals the Methodist Superintendant did not share.

If the whole arena of working-class politics came to resemble a shark's mouth, Lovett still chose to stay in it rather than to pursue any of the available Victorian middle-class rewards of individualism through science, moneymaking, or art. Nor did he "bow humbly" before fate or "fall into licentiousness," according to Engels's restricted alternatives to working-class rage. Chartist and individual, however, came to be identified with separate and opposed ideologies in the Victorian period. Lovett alternately got locked into one side or the other of a polarity that still endures.

From one point of view, Lovett's resistance to fustian undoubtedly limited both his political and his literary accomplishment, for his plain style could neither rally the masses nor convert (or amuse) a middle-class public. His ideal, however, does survive as the key (if also the repeatedly frustrated) value in Anglo-American liberal democracy—as articulated, for example, in Orwell's "Politics and the English Language."[35] While current sociological and literary theory helps to explain Lovett's failures and limitations, reading him in his own terms has the equally bracing effect of putting radical academic preference for fustian, or even inarticulate cries, in historical perspective. My reading of Lovett does not strive to reinstate Enlightenment belief in a grammar that would "defy the ingenuity" of misinterpretation. Lovett's *Life and Struggles* itself requires even more interpretive ingenuity than many books to draw out the implications of its spare words. Yet Lovett was enough of a writer to enact in print his struggle for a language he saw as essential to democratic justice. Recognition of that struggle seems both possible and important to attain through an activity of reading that resembles sympathetic listening to a particular person's voice. Without that attentiveness, interpretation runs the risk of reinstating Carlylean arrogance, whereby only the superior interpreter can articulate the meanings of "dumb creatures in pain, unable to speak what it is in them." The undifferentiated category of a working class without words imprisons the working-class writer in a dumbness projected from the interpreter's own reluctance to hear.

[35] Orwell, "Politics and the English Language," in *A Collection of Essays*, 156–71.

12. *Knowing a Life*

Edith Simcox—Sat est vixisse?

GILLIAN BEER

As scholars we expect to know our subjects inside out—and that produces some psychological as well as epistemological problems. I am an intimate of Edith Simcox, who died in 1901 at the age of fifty-six. I know Edith Simcox from the inside out, through reading her books (published under her own name), her many articles for the *Academy* and other journals (the earlier of which are published under the name H. Lawrenny), and, most compellingly, her secret journal, where she rarely names herself or the person she longs for and which she kept under lock and key during her lifetime.[1] I know her through her writing, and writing makes life. It can take us across time into the felt detail of another individual's moods and needs to a degree that painting never can and music does not try to.

Writing can also mislead us about how much of a person we know. I share Edith Simcox's secret life but not her public activity. I do not know much about what she looked like as herself: generically, she was small, dark, be-

"Knowing a Life: Edith Simcox—Sat est vixisse?" Copyright © 1995, 2001 by Gillian Beer.
[1] Among her essays and monographs are "Autobiographies," *North British Review* o.s., 51 (1870): 383–414; "Autobiography of a Shirt Maker," MS, Bodley Library, Oxford, now published as *A Monument to the Memory of George Eliot,* ed. Constance M. Fulmer and Margaret E. Barfield (New York: Garland, 1998); *Natural Law: An Essay in Ethics* (London: Trübner, 1877); "George Eliot," *Nineteenth Century* 9 (1881): 778–801; "Eight Years of Co-operative Shirtmaking," *Nineteenth Century* 15 (1884): 1037–54; *Episodes in the Lives of Men, Women, and Lovers* (London: Trübner, 1882); *Primitive Civilizations or Outlines of the History of Ownership in Archaic Communities* (London: Swan Sonnenschein, 1894). She was a founding and frequent contributor to the *Academy,* first as H. Lawrenny and then under her own name from the time of her "George Eliot" essay on. She wrote for the *Fortnightly Review,* the *North British Review, Frazers,* and other journals; see for example, "The Organization of Unremunerative Industry," November 1878, and "The Industrial Employment of Women," February 1879, in *Frazers Magazine.*

spectacled, female. She probably smelled quite strong, with her prodigious walks through London and her heavy clothing. I would not know her if I met her in the street—unless, perhaps, she were wearing those late-Victorian clothes. That signals one problem of historical interpretation: I have assimilated her recorded inner life *inside my mind* without being able to evoke with anything like the same companionship her social being, shared physical conditions, the surface of the roads she walked, the cut of the shirts produced in her shirt-makers' cooperative, the apparatus of cross-class relationships, the dynamics of the committee rooms of school boards and socialists, almost all men. Moreover, of course, my knowledge of her is not mutual: she does not know me. My activity of knowing her must, it seems, be one of identification rather than of acquaintance: it has no social preliminaries, no exchange.

I know her *inside* out. To that degree I have entered a private space that is both intense and blinded. While Simcox was writing her often excruciating journal, detailing the inexorable passion she felt for George Eliot, and during Eliot's lifetime often writing in obsessional despair, she was also busy composing a major work on ethics, *Natural Law;* organizing women workers in a cooperative; translating from German for the language theorist and philosopher Max Müller; reviewing works in several European languages for the *Academy;* writing the Constitution for the Second Socialist International; working on the London School Board, and living at home with her mother, whom she barely mentions until after George Eliot is dead. The diary form, especially a secret diary, has a way of occupying all available psychic space and discounting the outside world. So does reading. There is a special doubled confidence and allure (as well as a certain treachery) in entering the mind of a person with a secret. Simcox's secret, her passion, is now well known, but it is revived in all its enfolded intensity in the activity of reading. Secrecy and reading go together and reinforce a privileged (perhaps fictive) intimacy with past individuals. Indeed, I must acknowledge that having first read the "Autobiography of a Shirtmaker" in the Bodley Library at Oxford fifteen years ago in all its minute purple-inked handwriting, and having returned at intervals to it since, I felt the qualm of disappointment, as well as pleasure, when it was finally published in 1998, edited by Constance M. Fulmer and Margaret E. Barfield under the unfortunately limiting title *A Monument to the Memory of George Eliot.*[2]

The title is nevertheless one that Simcox herself would undoubtedly have approved, for her own understanding of her achievement placed it always in relation to her love for George Eliot. This makes Simcox, in her struggle to find a language adequate at once for passion and activism, sometimes obscure as well as resentful. And yet the blast of her lucid self-recognition more

---

[2] *A Monument to the Memory of George Eliot: Edith J. Simcox's "Autobiography of a Shirtmaker"* (New York: Garland, 1998).

often confronts difficulties, with a radicalism that allows her to disturb the social categories of later Victorian England. Her powers of analysis and reflection, moreover, make space for a different kind of dialogue: one in which the critic of today can bring into play current writing. The categories of class, sexuality, poverty, with which Simcox herself was in dispute remain in contention.

A further irony emerges: Edith Simcox is not now known for her public challenges but only because of her secret description of her love for a famous person, Marian Lewes: George Eliot. Simcox's life extends its presence beyond death first because of that writing and experience. Without the "Shirtmaker" Simcox's career would probably have vanished utterly. It will have had its strong effects but unknown to us now, dispersed into the afterlives of deeds as most deeds are. Musing on her twin desires—for engrossing personal love and for active betterment of the lives of those in poverty—Edith Simcox herself reflects, on Christmas Day 1879, on the necessary insufficiency of fulfillment:

> I recognize the double difficulty still. If life had brought me, not her love but better chances of work outside, I might have learnt to forget the first dread just when its safeguard grew needed. [The dread is of "the hardening, narrowing tendency of life in action which outstrips the pace of possible personal feeling."] If life had brought me—what I knew it never would—the absorbing rapture of an answered, answering love, I know I should have fallen prey, like others, have lived on my happiness while it lasted and let life end with its death. Had one had this choice of good gifts, strange as she would think it, my bent would always have been to choose the first limitation—I would rather do than feel, rather act on others' feelings than be myself the outlet, the channel, by which human passion passes from feeling into nothingness. But fortune has given me neither gift in dangerous completeness, and between the two there emerges for me a vision of the ideal among the real possibilities of arduous life.[3]

The long passage of reflection closes: "since she could not have it so, what might have been pleasure is released as energy—I want Trübner's Catalogue on Egypt and Assyria." That "want" is from Simcox's third source of life: not only private passion, or contemporary activism, but systematic enquiry, into justice, into regularities (natural law), into conditions of life in ancient cultures, particularly as they bore on women's property. Property for Simcox bears its full sense: that which is proper to a person as well as possessions, what belongs to women's identities. This allows her to train her attention on her own society, because that society for her is never absolute.

---

[3] Simcox, *Shirtmaker*, 107, 25 December 1879.

In her last major work, *Primitive Civilisations or Outlines of the History of Ownership in Archaic Communities* (1894), Edith Simcox de-universalizes the family: the monogamous Victorian norm becomes the experimental, with no guarantee of success:

> There is no one of the leading traits of modern family life which can be put forward as so pre-eminently and absolutely natural as to be universal. Polygamy flourished along with rarer experiments in monogamy, and has been practised by women as well as men.... Our notion of what is natural in family relationships is compounded of all those features of family life which, upon calm retrospect, appear to our present taste as useful and agreeable, wholesome and pleasant.... The ideal of the present day has never been exactly realised in the past. (*Primitive Civilisations*, 9)

Her pithy satire on our tendency to read out from "our present taste" and invent a history of the world backwards is typical of the challenges she mounts. It is a tonic reminder to be wary of reading back into her life "the ideal of the present day." Yet, like any other scholar, Simcox knows that her enquiry into the past must bear on the present day—and is generated by the present day's concerns. So she gives us ways of thinking about the family as a structure not only of kin but of desire, both through her commentary and through her life. Simcox's challenges issue also from her own experience of living across social classes and across gender and of taking part in the precarious metafamily produced by the love both she and John Cross felt for George Eliot in the 1870s. The parental dyad of George Eliot and G. H. Lewes is augmented by these emulous sibling rivals, twenty years younger than the Leweses and both desperate for George Eliot's attention and love. Simcox writes acidly on one occasion[4]: "I had hardly begun to despair of reaching more interesting topics when the fatal Johnny came in, he had missed his train yesterday & had a book to return by way of pretext."[5]

And she repeats rather too often for comfort the awkward joke that George Eliot and G. H. Lewes began that she mustn't poison Johnny's shirt (an allusion both to the shirt of Nessus and to the shirt-making cooperative with which Simcox was involved); it is a joke that gives a particular glint to the

---

[4] See Norma Vince on the "Autobiography of a Shirt Maker," *Women: A Cultural Review* 6 (1995). Some of the material in my present essay first appeared in the same issue of *Women* as Vince's article under the title "Passion, Politics, Philosophy: The Work of Edith Simcox," and I am grateful to the editors for permission to incorporate it here. For a more detailed account of Simcox's life see K. A. McKenzie, *Edith Simcox and George Eliot* (Oxford: Oxford University Press, 1961). Though McKenzie's book was written in a period of very different assumptions from those of the present, his research into Simcox's later life is still invaluable.

[5] Simcox, *Shirtmaker*, 19, 7 January 1878.

title she added to her journal—"Autobiography of a Shirtmaker."[6] With the helpless insight of the rival she dreaded and foresaw what to everyone else seemed improbable: the marriage of George Eliot to John Cross. And after that marriage she means to end her journal as she records: "An absence of nine months, which she could have abridged by a cheap word, makes it impossible to ignore one's fate—to live a long way off."[7] But in the event she continues the journal, past the death of George Eliot not long after that entry, and almost to the end of her own life more than twenty years later.

In their introduction to *Feminist Interpretations and Political Theory*, Mary Lyndon Shanley and Carole Pateman emphasize that

> the tradition of Western political thought rests on a conception of the "political" that is constructed through an exclusion of women and all that is represented by femininity and women's bodies. Sexual difference and sexuality are usually treated as marginal to or outside of the subject matter of political theory, but the different attributes, capacities and characteristics ascribed to men and women by political theorists are central to the way in which each has defined the "political." Manhood and politics go hand in hand, and everything that stands in contrast to and opposed to political life and the political virtues has been represented by women, their capacities and the tasks seen as natural to their sex, especially motherhood. Many political theorists have seen women as having a vital part to play in social life—but not as citizens and political actors. Rather, women have been designated as the upholders of the private foundation of the political world of men; or, as Saxonhouse argues of Aristotle, femininity symbolizes the private ties, restraint and stability that support the polis.[8]

A number of these comments bear with peculiar aptness upon the problematics of Edith Simcox's experience (21 August 1844–15 September 1901) and upon her resistance to the codes, the exclusions, and the hierarchies im-

---

[6] "I said I knew I should poison his shirts some day, & she hoped I wouldn't, he saved them a great deal of trouble about money affairs, besides being the best of sons and brothers I said of course that was just why, I was jealous." 3 January 1878. I am grateful to the Bodley Library for permission to quote from the holograph journal. Cf. Simcox, *Shirtmaker*, 21.

In exchanging letters, George Eliot and John Cross habitually called each other "Aunt" and "Nephew" until their marriage. Reading letters from George Eliot to John Cross, Simcox had cause to be jealous. For example, 29 April 1878:

> It is a precious thought to me that you care for that part of me which will live when the "Auntship" is gone—"non omnis moriar" is a keen hope with me. Yet I like to be loved in this faulty frail (yet venerable) flesh.
>
> My Master [i.e., G. H. Lewes] insists that I shall go and walk with him. So I have had only three minutes to scribble in.
>
> Always your affectionate
>
> Aunt

[7] Simcox, *Shirtmaker*, 133. 19 November 1880.

[8] Mary Shanley and Carole Pateman, *Feminist Interpretations and Political Theory* (Cambridge: Polity Press, 1991), 3.

plicit in the organization of knowledge and society as she experienced it. In *Primitive Civilisations,*[9] Simcox made the same discrimination in the introduction as do Shanley and Pateman. Discussing ancient Egypt, China, and Babylonia she comments that

> The term gynaecocratic has been applied to some of these communities, on the ground of their sharing the widespread archaic conception of family relationships, in which the mother is regarded as the natural head and namesake of the household; but it is scarcely appropriate, since the higher status and greater social influence enjoyed by women in these States did not result in their taking any greater share in the actual government, though it may have tended to minimise the action of the State in matters related to the family. (*Primitive Civilisations,* I, 9)

The question of the mother and maternal roles became for Simcox one means of bringing into question—indeed, into jeopardy—many of the systems (gender, social class, classificatory) within whose confines she was also bound to work.

In *The Ear of the Other, Otobiography, Transference, Translation* Derrida in the course of discussing Nietzsche's autobiographical writing argues that in the patriarchical order there is "no woman or trace of woman...save the mother...the faceless figure of a *figurant.* She gives rise to all the figures by losing herself in the background of the scene like an anonymous persona."[10] Derrida figures the ear (*oto*biography) as feminine ("it is to her—this ear—that I myself feign to address" [33]), and he presents maternal language as that resonance or "maternal syntax" from out of which controlled language is selected. As Marianne Hirsch puts it: "Psychoanalytic theories of creativity tend to identify the place of the mother as the very absence which lies at the point of linguistic origin."[11] Simcox brings to the fore—and into question—the identification of the mother with the obliterated and unconscious. She reintroduces the idea of the mother as the highest outcome of language. Not content with one birth mother (who is indeed a shadowy figure until her late writing), she claims a second, writerly and eroticized mother in George Eliot.[12] George Eliot, after a time, came to resist that claim: "she said she did not like for me to call her 'Mother.'"

[9] Edith Simcox, *Primitive Civilizations* (London: Macmillan, 1894); its two volumes run to more than a thousand pages.

[10] Jacques Derrida, *The Ear of the Other, Otobiography, Transference, Translation: Texts and Discussions with Jacques Derrida,* ed. Christie V. McDonald, trans. Peggy Kamuf (New York: Schocken Books, 1985), 38.

[11] Marianne Hirsch, *The Mother-Daughter Plot: Narrative, Psychoanalysis, Feminism* (Bloomington: Indiana University Press, 1989), 52.

[12] Simcox, *Shirtmaker,* 18, 6 January 1878: "I have forced myself into the acceptance of truths repugnant to my inmost nature the effort of submission took all my strength & I have none left to live with afterwards. Last night again if my Mother [i.e., George Eliot] were a hus-

She went on, she knew it was her fault, she had begun, she was apt to be rash and commit herself in one mood to what was irksome to her in another—not with her own mother, but her associations otherwise with the name were as of a task and it was a fact that her feeling for me was *not* at all a mother's—any other name she did not mind.[13]

In *My Literary Life* (1899) Lynn Linton speaks of her own early affection for the "frank, genial, natural, and brimful of happiness" young Marian Evans just after "her flight with George Lewes. When they returned home, I called upon them by their joint request" (*Literary Life*, 96). She emphasizes this early sympathy in order to give point to her next remarks. The price of George Eliot's achieved fame, claims Linton, is that "she was a made woman—not in the French sense—but made by self-manipulation, as one makes a statue or a vase. I have never known any one who seemed to me so purely artificial as George Eliot" (98). "Her self-created Self...the benign Sibyl...so consciously 'George Eliot'...the goddess on her pedestal."[14]

For Edith Simcox that "self-created" (or, as it might now be called, "self-fashioned") quality had particular value. It allowed her to cross between the "natural" figure of the mother and the "made" figure of the artist and to find (with many pains) a discourse for her sexuality and for her politics. At the least, she was able to find a way of moving across classes and systems without ever taking them for granted. On an occasion when George Eliot came to visit her Simcox threw her arms around her, persuaded her to take off her "spotted net veil," and settled into an argument about "the dangerousness of making 'right' into a metaphysical abstraction, severed from the intuitions which might constitute its nature, and said that I felt myself that that might be a snare."

> She was rather slow to believe that it could be a snare to me to take anything for granted.[15]

A droll voice momentarily sounds through: Marian Lewes teasing her younger friend for her indefatigable skepticism, perhaps respecting it too.

Simcox was a political actor, par excellence, one beset by the roles her gendered body was required to play—one who repudiated all those representations of femininity as passive, or marginal, or powerful in the home only. In her essay on Schopenhauer she remarked on his insistence "that children inherit their moral character from their father, their intellectual qualities from

---

band and a lover how tragical it would seem I lay in bed strangled with the sobs I could not stop and feared to have overheard."

[13] Simcox, *Shirtmaker*, 110, 26 December 1879.

[14] Lynn Linton, *My Literary Life* (London: Constable, 1899), 96, 98.

[15] Simcox, *Shirtmaker*, 26, 13 February 1878.

their mother" while wryly noting the male hyperbole: "for the gifts of the mother, he held, were much intensified in transmission to the nobler sex."[16]

It is not enough simply to seek Simcox as an individual if we are to have a hope of understanding her and, through her, the disturbances in the systems she inhabited. For anyone pursuing an understanding of Simcox's life in its time a passage in the journal comes as both a helpful and a limiting observation: "the solemnity of the political necessity. One *cannot* be right alone."[17] Simcox shares linguistically with her contemporaries the pressures between individualism, energy, and unconsciousness harbored in that specifically Victorian activity of creating new ideas by adding the prefix *auto* to words previously unreflexive, un-self-examining. The term "autobiography," which she appropriates for her diary, is itself a nineteenth-century coinage, credited to Southey by the OED, desiderated by Carlyle ("What would we give for such an Autobiography of Shakespeare" [1828]), and transferred to the natural world by Charles Lyell in the description of geology as "the autobiography of the earth." It is part of a great efflorescence of words to describe self-reference, self-generation, and self-regulation. This cluster of lexical items is particular to the nineteenth century, and especially to the Victorian period. Terms such as autochthony (aboriginal occupation); autocriticism (literary criticism of one's own work); autograph, in the sense of signing one's name for a collection; even autolaryngoscopy (examination of one's own larynx); and a multitude of nonce-words and scientific terms are all members of the group of coinages. So, more fundamentally, are the terms *autonomous* and *automatic*. (*Autonomy* was in use much earlier, but not *autonomous,* with its self-referential adjectival quality.)

Latent in all these terms is the paradoxical double emphasis on self-examination and on the unexaminable: the conflict is expressed in the idea, so important both to the technology and the psychology of the time, of the *automatic,* the reflex. Autotype, for example, noted by the *Oxford English Dictionary* as occurring first in the 1850s and 1860s, signifies both "a type of the thing itself" (as Kingsley argues utterance must be of the soul) and "a process of photographic printing." Machines and bodily reflexes are both automatic: systems so closely self-satisfying that they can be entered from without only at the price of interruption and perhaps damage. Put another way, such systems could be seen as communalities so sustaining that they are put at risk by the insistences of conscious individualism.

The tussle between writing as a representative within a group or as a particular being is crucial to the Victorian psychodrama, and particularly so for women writing their lives. The tussle between the demand that women erase themselves and the demand that they sustain integrity and thereby presence

[16] Edith Simcox, "Arthur Schopenhauer," *Contemporary Review* 21 (1873): 443.
[17] Simcox, *Shirtmaker,* 137, 27 December 1880.

muddies the terms "self" and "other." Indeed, Sherry Turkle's pithy exposition of Lacan's views fits particularly well the social as well as the psychic position of many Victorian women: "The ego never exists as a coherent entity. From the beginning, it is a composite of false and distorted introjections, so that I and other are inextricably confused in the language of the self. When you look inside there are mirrors and snapshots. But there is no I."[18] Simcox, determinedly single, endlessly analytical and self-questioning, composed an "I," but it was one that could never be satisfied in solitude. Rather, it was a tool—sometimes scalpel, sometimes crowbar—for procuring communal change. It was also an instrument of self-laceration.

Her own life included erotic secrecy as well as active politics, and her writing spanned the whole range of possible audiences and possible authorial positions between arcane and public: from the impossible single reader of her private journal, through philosophical treatises, apothegmic essays, a *roman à clef,* the translation of philosophical and scientific texts, the recounting and analyzing her experience in the cooperative workshop to persuade middle-class readers to sympathize with workers' experience, and later acting as simultaneous translator between French, German, and English colleagues in the international socialist movement.[19]

Simcox was driven to an extreme of secrecy in finding a discourse for her own erotic experience in her locked journal "Autobiography of a Shirtmaker," while during the same period she was writing a work of philosophy, *Natural Law,* that was published in Trübner's series and praised in many professional journals. Just after the publication of that work she set up with Mary Hamilton a cooperative of women shirt-makers and worked within that for eight years. Political theory and political practice coexisted but did not sit quite straight side by side in her life. So through the 1870s and into the 1880s she is working on her philosophical treatise, helping to set up one of the first trade unions for women, establishing a shirt-maker's cooperative, and discovering a language to articulate the needs of her own sexuality and desire. These diverse activities fold upon one another, without full accord. As she commented in her essay on "Autobiographies": "The internal and external lives of individuals do not run in parallel lines, nor advance at an equal pace; and the attempt to make their crises synchronize only distorts the real succession of events and opinions."[20] That early essay, written before she met George Eliot, is concerned with authenticity and consciousness (particularly self-consciousness) as an ethical tool. "Mere intellect is as little capable of dramatic self-consciousness as mere animalism," she argues (399). She pinpoints, too, by a curious insight, the repetitiousness of ideas and intellectual endeavor when isolated from activity: "Less originality is displayed in think-

[18] *London Review of Books* 11, no. 1 (1989): 3.
[19] See McKenzie, *Edith Simcox and George Eliot,* 44.
[20] *North British Review* (January 1870): 410.

ing everybody's thoughts than in living everybody's life" (413). Each life is more various, more "original," than the ideas held in common and esteemed within a community. She shifts the hierarchy, refusing to value intellectual activity above living, pointing to a staleness of rehearsal in the mind that does not match the inventiveness of individual life as, irreplaceably and unforeseeable, it composes itself. The zest of this position is, of course, her own intense intellectuality.

The classificatory divide between action and thought perturbs her. Inner and outer are not, to her mind, to be read as identical with private and public.

> The tendency to distinguish between action and thought as alternative fields of energy leaves the former contentedly monotonous, mechanical, and unfruitful, and causes the latter, properly a method or instrument, to be mistaken for an end in itself—the chart, that is, for the voyage, the compass for the desired land. (413)

Perhaps as an outcome (and certainly alongside) her need to test the bounds of the discourses for erotic relations, she became preternaturally aware of all kinds of stereotypes and quizzical about all systems. While George Eliot lives in the body as Mrs. Lewes, the love engrosses Simcox intellectually, emotionally, and physically; yet it does not prevent her doing the bills, walking across Hyde Park in the dark, translating German philosophy, working in the shop, and writing highly crafted and challenging essays. The love she feels can find no public language in which to make itself, as this passage written five years into the relationship powerfully declares:

> Now I am divided between passionate longing, unhealthy dreams, impatience, resignation, the counting of endless days, heart-aching love, and patient gratefulness—to say nothing of Heroditus and Fraser. Oh when, when, when! I am hungry! Oh how the howl that is in my mind there are no words to spell, but it echoes wolfishly.[21]

Reading—writing—howling—the language of unappeased desire here reaches back to a semiotics of a kind that Woolf and Kristeva have each described.

The only discourses available to Simcox for describing her love are those that necessitate adopting languages of inequality, either the child-parent dyad or the distance of worship. In a letter written, and perhaps sent,[22] after

---

[21] Simcox, *Shirtmaker*, 45, 30 October, 1878.
[22] Simcox frequently records in the journal the writing of letters to George Eliot that she does not send. This letter is folded into the journal and must therefore be a copy or draft if the letter was sent.

Lewes's death Simcox acknowledges the irremediable inequality of feeling between her and George Eliot:

> Do you see Darling that I can only love you three lawful ways, idolatrously as Fraters the Virgin Mary, in romance wise as Petrarch, Laura, or with a child's fondness for the mother one leans on notwithstanding the irreverence of one's longing to pet or take care of her... friendship is a precious thing indeed but between friends I think if there is love at all it must be equal, and whichever way we take it, our relation is between unequals.

The bleakness here is also forthright. Even in the letter quoted she sees her love of George Eliot as *unlawful*, not unnatural: laws can be changed.[23] Were we to read only Simcox's secret diary we might sympathize with it as the nightmare of individualism, as well as of conflicted gender roles. The journal gives extraordinarily powerful access to "conscious unsatisfied craving," the endless retrospection of the ungratified lover, twisting and turning slight signs and clues in the search for a surplus of meaning. The reader at a distance across time is always *de trop* and can find ease only through identification, or as was the case in earlier commentary, embarrassment and medicalization.[24]

Simcox knew in her bones, her genitals, and her head the agony of being powerless, and she transferred that knowledge into her empathy with others quite differently oppressed and impoverished. She managed to make this ghastly sexual sorrow of unrequited feeling politically effective. She did so through activism, where she recognizes that the mothering role is equivocal in its effects: "Idleness is the mother of misery and megrims, but not all women can go to Girton or make books," she wrote about her shirt-making cooperative.[25]

Her writing on the condition of women and on the possibilities of social change are equally autobiographical writing; here, instead of a present locked

---

[23] Bonnie Zimmerman tentatively suggests that Simcox "seems to have perceived her love as not quite natural." See "'The Dark Eye Beaming': Female Friendship in George Eliot's Fiction," in *Lesbian Texts and Contexts: Radical Revisions*, ed. Karla Jay and Joanne Glasgow (London: Only Women, 1992), 141. But that begs questions of what is "natural" not likely to have passed by the author of *Natural Law* and *Episodes in the Life of Men, Women, and Lovers;* not quite *lawful*, rather, as she says in this letter outside the historically bounded systems of authority and agreement. Such systems can be changed.

[24] Gordon Haight writes: "The Victorians' conception of love between those of the same sex cannot be fairly understood by an age steeped in Freud. Where they saw only beautiful friendship, the modern reader suspects perversion." Haight, "Introduction," in K. A. McKenzie, *Edith Simcox and George Eliot* (Oxford: Oxford University Press, 1961), xv. McKenzie himself, despite his sympathetic account of her life, concludes by writing: "One could perhaps conclude from what we know of her temperament and behavior that physically she belonged to the type which psychiatrists call leptosomatic, and that she tended towards schizophrenia" (135).

[25] Simcox, "Eight Years of Cooperative Shirtmaking," *Nineteenth Century* (June 1884): 1039.

into an endlessly uninterpretable past, the present of the writing gives buoy-
ant access to precisely imagined social change. "Our dream was of a strictly
self-supporting clothes-factory, where women should do all the work, and
divide the profits among them." Simcox's self-knowledge has given her an
acute awareness of how ill systems fit their self-description:

> For the moment the religious and charitable world is interested in the denizens
> of the slums; but will that world bear to be told that the slums are peopled by
> those whom they themselves help to send there? What about the shilling bibles
> and sixpenny or penny testaments which it is supposed to be a good work to
> disseminate? The women who fold and sew these books must live in the slums,
> with the rest of the vast army whose life amongst us is a slow death upon star-
> vation wages. Ladies who "work among the poor" think it right to save their
> money for charity, and buy cheap costumes, made far off by the same sister-
> hood; and who can tell the ladies that their so-called charity is a theft, and they
> themselves parties to more oppression than the district visiting of a lifetime can
> atone?[26]

Simcox discovers in her cooperative both the unideal difficulties of cooperation and the degree to which people are knotted together:

> It is hard for the rich and idle to understand that the jealousies and covetous-
> ness of the poor all turn upon the race for work, not the race for wages, and
> that the call for self-denial and forethought lies not in accepting work, but in
> daring to refuse it, to risk present personal privation rather than become a party
> to enforcing more unfavourable conditions on all the workers in the trade.
> (1044)

Another kind of fit between the figure of George Eliot and Simcox's longed-
for world of action is disclosed when the women are searching for premises
for the cooperative, a word that, as Simcox remarks, "stinks in the nostrils
of every shopkeeper."

> As idle amateurs, we could get a good house in a quiet street for 80 l., together
> with all the deferential civility due to highly "desirable tenants." As working
> shirtmakers, after refreshing our radicalism with a glimpse of "th'oppressor's
> scorn, the proud man's contumely," we were fortunate in securing half a house
> for 90 l., under a landlord whose exceptional amenity explained itself afterwards
> when we learned that he was an admirer of George Eliot's works. (1040–41)

[26] Ibid., 1054.

Irony and appreciation mingle in this wry account of liberal behavior (part of the half-life, after-life, of George Eliot) for which Simcox is properly grateful and about which she is properly mordant. The "sacred name of competition," she asserts, with its accomplices in the "underpayment of honest industry," "is itself the most fertile mother of all those three": drink, vice, and improvidence.

Simcox works sometimes awkwardly across class, as across gender and family, but the crisp and unillusioned affection she feels for her company of women, and the admiration for their craft, carries her past condescension into fellow-knowledge: "to form any conception of the bitterness, the fanatical zeal, and disinterested fury of conviction with which a cutter and fitter can debate the set of a shirt-front, one must go back to the history of the early Church and its minuter and abstruser heresies" (1042).

In the end, what depressed her in *Daniel Deronda*—the "faithful transcript of the coexistence of unreconciled tendencies"[27] together with the recognition that there is no private life that is not largely determined by a wider public life—are what she internalizes from George Eliot's writing. But she increasingly diverges from the social determinism implicit in Eliot's tempered dictum; Simcox puts her energies into practical change and into a major study of the past control of property. In Natural Law she defines existence as the "power of producing and undergoing modification...it is only by changes in ourselves that we discern the existence of change, or changing things, beyond ourselves" (*Natural Law*, 3). Her emphasis in this work is equally on the interactive and the conflicted. In her writing what reads at first as abstraction still refuses to resolve conflict: "to call Nature names implies a reference to more than one experience, however real, intimate, and infelicitous: the appropriate name will characterise the universal experience, which is mixed" (351).[28]

"Real, intimate, and infelicitous" experience generated wider questioning for Simcox. She did intellectual work with the strains and puzzlement that she had to live with in her relationship with George Eliot and more generally in her understanding of her own sexuality. She refused to accept social taxonomies: that was also part of her learnt skill as a philosopher. She did political work with the crossing of class boundaries: she put all categories under stress. Is authority "natural"?—that is the fundamental question in *Natural Law*. Can images drawn from the family serve as organizing principles for the wider community? With her erotic daughterly self-representation the family becomes a swooningly dangerous set of relations rather than a rigid set of social roles. Yet it also seems to me that one cannot know

---

[27] Simcox, *Shirtmaker*, 102, 29 October 1879.

[28] In "A Troubled Friendship," *George Eliot Review* (1999), I argue that George Eliot's silence about *Natural Law* has the effect of blocking Simcox's path as a philosopher and that, for George Eliot, Simcox represented a younger self and rival who had more successfully traveled the path of philosophy that Eliot had left when she moved into fiction.

enough about Simcox by staying inside her, or solely by investigating, as I do in this paragraph, the personal incentives that permeate her philosophical work.

One might set alongside that will to interpretation-from-within the comments of the philosopher Peter Simon in *Parts: A Study in Ontology*:

> The individual events befalling a certain person are strung together and called his or her *life*. While there are certainly causal connections among such events, causal relations lead into and out of the person's life, and it is not clear that all events in a life are indirectly causally connected. The unifying relation is simply that of *genidentity*, involving the same continuant, and is applicable not just to persons, but to all continuants.[29]

Simcox held on to the phrase "sat est vixisse" for comfort to her craving in her relationship with George Eliot: "It is enough to have lived." It forms the title of the last of her *Episodes in the Lives of Men, Women and Lovers*, that strange amalgam of stories, musings, and philosophical yearnings—that making sense of thought—which is the amateur's best understanding of philosophical enterprise. The essay is prefaced with a quotation from the Talmud: "The day is short and the work is great. It is not incumbent upon thee to complete the work, but thou must not therefore cease from it." The first sentence is a young boy questioning the narrator: "I say, Philo! how is it that most people's lives somehow don't seem to come to much?" (271). The narrator broods for five pages before giving an answer:

> I said: "Is it reasonable to ask of life that it should always be 'coming' to something different from the living moment that is? The moments that interest us most in life and attach us to it most do not hang together like the parts of a syllogism; our living interest is in the elements, not in the whole they form at last; and perhaps that is why those who have not yet lived through those thrilling moments are least ready to accept the moments as themselves the crown of life."[30]

Simcox gives through her narrator an answer to the idea that her life, like most people's, didn't come to much. Simon reinforces her skepticism about the syllogistic demands placed on life experience: "It is not clear that all events in a life are indirectly causally related." Through reading her writing we can glimpse also that *genidentity*, that assemblage of works and days spent in unhistoric acts just beyond any possible knowledge we can reach. Not so much through writing, but through "pleasure become energy" in her

---

[29] Peter Simon, *Parts: A Study in Ontology* (New Haven, Conn.: Yale University Press, 1987), 351.
[30] Simcox, *Episodes in the Lives of Men, Women, and Lovers*, 276–77.

own and others' independent activism a hundred years ago, it has come about "that things are not so ill with you and me as they might have been." Quite how, and to what extent, is not to be known. Irresistibly, the last diffusive paragraph of *Middlemarch* comes to mind. But there survives also the privy knowledge, gained only *through* her writing, of a particular life still thrilling, capable of springing anew off the page.

Notes on Contributors

Suzy Anger is assistant professor of English at the University of Maryland, Baltimore County. She has published essays on nineteenth-century British literature and is currently completing a book on Victorian hermeneutics.

Gillian Beer is the King Edward VII Professor of English Literature at the University of Cambridge and President of Clare Hall College there. Among her books are *Darwin's Plots* (second edition, 2000), *George Eliot* (1986), and *Open Fields: Science in Cultural Encounter* (1996). She has published essays on Vernon Lee, May Kendall and Constance Naden, and Edith Simcox. She has a particular interest in the relations between science and other forms of creativity, especially literature.

Rosemarie Bodenheimer is professor of English at Boston College. She is the author of *The Politics of Story in Victorian Social Fiction* and *The Real Life of Mary Ann Evans: George Eliot: Her Letters and Fiction.* She is currently working on Dickens and autobiography.

Christopher Herbert is professor of English at Northwestern University. His most recent book, *Victorian Relativity: Radical Thought and Scientific Discovery,* is forthcoming from the University of Chicago Press. His previous published work includes two other books, *Culture and Anomie: Ethnographic Imagination in the Nineteenth Century* (1991) and *Trollope and Comic Pleasure* (1987), and numerous essays in the field of Victorian studies.

Gerhard Joseph, a professor of English at Lehman College and the Graduate School of the City University of New York, has written two books on Tennyson and a number of essays on other nineteenth-century subjects.

George Levine is Kenneth Burke Professor of English, and director of the Center for the Critical Analysis of Contemporary Culture, at Rutgers University. He is author of several books, including *The Realistic Imagination*

(1981) and *Darwin and the Novelists* (1988). He has recently completed a book on objectivity and narrative and has edited *The Cambridge Companion to George Eliot.*

JONATHAN LOESBERG is professor and Chair of the Department of Literature at American University. He has written two books, *Fictions of Consciousness: Mill, Newman and the Reading of Victorian Prose* (1986) and *Aestheticism and Deconstruction: Pater, Derrida and de Man* (1991), as well as articles on nineteenth-century literature and literary theory. He is currently working on a book on aesthetics and literary theory.

MARY POOVEY is professor of English and founding director of the Institute for the History of the Production of Knowledge at New York University. She has published widely on eighteenth- and nineteenth-century British literature and history, feminist theory, and the history of medicine. Her latest book, *A History of the Modern Fact: Problems of Knowledge in the Sciences of Wealth and Society* (1998), was awarded the 1999–2000 Louis Gottschalk Prize.

BRUCE ROBBINS teaches English and comparative literature at Rutgers University. He is the author of *Feeling Global: Internationalism in Distress* (1999), *The Servant's Hand: English Fiction from Below* (1986), and *Secular Vocations: Intellectuals, Professionalism, Culture* (1993). He has edited *Intellectuals: Aesthetics, Politics, Academics* (1990) and *The Phantom Public Sphere* (1993) and co-edited *Cosmopolitics: Thinking and Feeling beyond the Nation* (1998).

MARGERY SABIN is Lorraine Chiu Wang Professor of English at Wellesley College. Her publications include *English Romanticism and the French Tradition* (1976), *The Dialect of the Tribe: Speech and Community in Modern Fiction* (1987), and numerous articles and book reviews about Victorian, modern, and postcolonial subjects and about the relationship between literary reading and cultural studies. Her book *Dissenters, Mavericks, and Hybrids: Writing in English about India, 1765–2000* will appear in 2002.

JUDITH STODDART is associate professor of English at Michigan State University, where she teaches Victorian literature and cultural theory. She is the author of *Ruskin's Culture Wars: Fors Clavigera and the Crisis of Late Victorian Liberalism* (1998). She is currently working on a study of Victorian ideas of perception and their impact on theories of representation in narrative painting, photography, and novels.

HERBERT F. TUCKER is the author of *Browning's Beginnings* (1980) and *Tennyson and the Doom of Romanticism* (1988). He has edited *Critical Essays on Alfred Lord Tennyson* (1993) and the Blackwell *Companion to Victorian Literature and Culture* (1999), and co-edited *Under Criticism* (with David Sofield, 1998) and *Victorian Literature 1830–1900* (with Dorothy Mermin, 2001). Currently writing *The Proof of Epic in Britain 1790–1910,* he is professor of English at the University of Virginia, where he also serves as associate editor of *New Literary History*.

CAROLYN WILLIAMS teaches in the Department of English at Rutgers University, where she is also associate director of the Center for the Critical Analysis of Contemporary Culture. Her book on Pater, *Transfigured World: Walter Pater's Aesthetic Historicism* (1989), was published by Cornell University Press. She is currently absorbed in two studies, one on Victorian melodrama and another on the comic operas of Gilbert and Sullivan.

Index